ENIS TILDEN LYNCH

NALS AND POLITICIANS
ER CLEVELAND
S" TWEED
IN VAN BUREN
WILD SEVENTIES

THE WILD S

THE
WILD
SEVENTIES

DENIS TILDEN LYNCH

D. APPLETON-CENTURY COMPANY
Incorporated
NEW YORK   LONDON
1941

To an old friend

HENRY C. JOHNSTON, M.D.

A gentleman of Virginia, and a slave of the suffering

CONTENTS

vii

Contents

Contents

Contents

Contents

Contents

ILLUSTRATIONS

Drawings by Abbey, Bellew, Homer, Keppler,
Nast, Rogers and others

xiii

Illustrations

THE WILD SEVENTIES

1

THE PEOPLE CELEBRATE—

A GANG RAISES KIDD'S FLAG

THE GAS-LIGHTS OF THE METROPOLIS WERE ABLAZE, AND the mild weather of this New Year's Eve was agreeable to all save the unchanging small boy, who grumbled because he had had no opportunity to try his new sled or skates, for there was neither ice nor snow, nor prospect of any. But older boys were not concerned with the weather. They had planned an evening of sight-seeing which would end, for thousands of them, when they gathered with their elders at the head of Wall Street to listen to "the glorious chimes of Trinity" usher in 1870 and a decade unparalleled' in times of peace for unrest and violence. Musketry rattled and cannon roared as insurrection, spurred on by revolution-clamoring Communists, terrorized the North; while newly freed slaves, goaded by mercenary carpet-baggers, battled with their former masters for supremacy in the South. The worst enemies of the Republic, the spoilsman and the demagogue, rising to new heights, became supreme over our party form of government. They introduced the legislative purge to our shores, and to avert rout at the polls, attempted to shatter the third-term tradition, and failing, stole the office of President of the United States—a fitting crown to their theft of several governorships and numerous minor elective posts. It was a period of depression, with hunger in the hovel, hardship in the mansion, and bankruptcy in public morality.

The debased public morals were evident to the older boys as they visited the Bowery, a sight of sights on New Year's Eve. Crooked gamblers presided at little folding tables on the curb and entertained the unwary with the shell game and three-card monte. Music and snatches of ribald song issued from vile dens, denominated concert saloons, where generous patrons of petting females in pink tights passed out quietly from the knock-out drops put in their drink by accommodating waiters. Music, but of another sort, came from orderly beer-gardens, first introduced to these shores by German immigrants in the fifties. A third type of drinking place, the dram shop, provided suitable music with the din of drunken brawls.

One who saw these sights that night prefaced his experiences on the Bowery and its cross-streets thus:

"The money kings and the palaces of Broadway are worth visiting, but to get an idea of the people who rule this metropolis, one must go down among the tenements and the drinking saloons of the whiskey wards." This was a legalistic truth; but as the *Tribune* reporter knew, these poor, worthy and dissolute alike, were the helpless pawns of the city's real rulers. He noted that every square mile contained more inhabitants than Chicago, Cincinnati, or St. Louis, and that the crowds were so dense on Grand Street and the Bowery "that one found difficulty in walking a block." Then he continued:

The concert saloons were brilliantly lighted, and the girls were dressed in holiday attire, hoping thereby to entice many curious countrymen into their music dens. The 3,000 bar-rooms did a wonderful business, and a constant stream of ghastly forms shuffled through the doorways. Now and then, in the midst of the tumult, one could not help pausing to watch the thinly clad girls as they emerged from the gin shops with a long black bottle of gin, and disappear in the crowd. . . . Every conceivable

kind of merchandise was offered for sale on the sidewalks. . . .
The gutters were occupied by dealers in old clothes. . . . Near a
corner sat an old woman grating horse-radish. . . . An endless
procession of young ladies poured into the Bowery, sweeping
up and down the broad pavements. On either side the horse-cars
were full to overflowing. . . . The beer-gardens are among the
most noteworthy of all the Bowery institutions. The arched roofs
were covered with frescoes, and at either side there is a raised
platform for the benefit of those who wish to drink apart from
the common herd. . . .

These things were not for the youngsters. They preferred
the street stalls where the wooden jumping-jacks, the tin
horses, and kindred creations seemed more than toys beneath the flickering glare of the massive pancake-like kerosene lamps, resplendent in their new coats of brilliant circus
blue. Equally alluring were wooden Indians on castered
pedestals outside the tobacco shops. The warrior braves and
squaws of twenty and thirty years earlier were now com-
panioned by kilted Scots, sailors, baseball players, actors,
and other sculptures—all realistically polychromed in lus-
trous enamel—that baffled the juvenile minds. They recognized the smiling Chinese with his long queue, the monocled
Dundreary, and the leering Punchinello; but other creations
of the wood-carver, such as the Grand Mogul and some of
the actors, puzzled the boys. Some of them knew that the
redskin with the classic Caucasian features was Edwin For-
rest in the title rôle of John A. Stone's tragedy, *Metamora,
or, The Last of the Wampanoags*. To small boy and grown-
up alike, they were all wooden Indians.

Then there were the things called Bowery statues, which
were not peculiar to this street. The Bowery statues walked
and talked like men. They were the robots of vice—over-
dressed, evil-looking fellows who chewed big cigars and
lived on the wages of street-walkers.

Many came to the Bowery from the fashionable sections above Eighth Street, and from staid, respectable old blocks of red brick private dwellings in the whiskey wards, for their New Year's calling-cards. These were written by un-employed bookkeepers who imitated the three-card monte and shell-game operators by setting up little tables on the sidewalk, borrowing the light of a store or dram-shop win-dow as they wrote on hot-pressed rag paper, in faultlessly shaded Spencerian script, "A Happy New Year," or some similar greeting, with the patron's name in the lower left-hand corner. Printed cards were then coming into vogue and being sent by post, but the old Dutch custom of New Year calling was stubbornly trying to hold on, and this ceremony required the personal note.

Suddenly church chimes, ships' sirens, bells, horns, and every type of firearm deafeningly proclaimed that it was Saturday, January 1, 1870.

The celebration was over. The streets became deserted as the horse-cars, stage-coaches, and ferry-boats ceased to be crowded to capacity, and tired cabmen, after carting home their last "respectable" drunks, drove to their stables, and quiet settled upon the city.

The same mild weather prevailed on New Year's Day. The younger women of well-to-do families wore Paisleys and lace-thread shawls to church, while their elders draped heavy woolen shawls over their shoulders. Astrakhan and other fur coats were common among the very old. The finest astrakhan fetched $25, while shawls of lace cost five times that sum, and good woolen shawls could be had for as little as $2.50.

By midafternoon, when a light rain began to fall, the New Year calling was at its height. Every one kept open house, save the extremely poor and the newly arrived im-migrants unacquainted with Knickerbocker traditions. In most homes of the prosperous, two punch-bowls, always filled to the brim, adorned the mahogany console in the hall, flanked with dishes of raisins and figs, and cookies made from a recipe that antedated Peter Minuit and Wouter van Twiller; and the sideboard in the dining-room gleamed with decanters of brandy and other strong drink. Some houses, where teetotalism prevailed, had but one punch-bowl containing nothing stronger than an unfermented fruit juice.

These customs were not the only reminders of Knickerbocker days, for some of the city's suburbs were still as strongly under Dutch sway as they were before the first English occupation.

One of these places was Sleepy Hollow, the picturesque Westchester village immortalized by the author of lovable Rip Van Winkle. Here, on this New Year's Day, a jealousy-crazed farmer welcomed the man he suspected with a load of buckshot and then let his own wife have the second barrel. The avowed double-slayer, his wife, and the officials in this tragedy, were old Knickerbockers. The judge was a Paulding, the coroner a Van Tassell, and the prosecuting officer was of the line of Joannes Dyckman, commissary and vice-director of Fort Orange, now Albany, and the first presiding magistrate of the court established there in 1652 by Peter Stuyvesant. The putative paramour alone bore a name alien to old Dutch records.

Down in the metropolis some of the lads, after having made too many New Year calls at private homes and public houses, quarreled in Livingston's saloon, Third Avenue and Seventy-sixth Street. The row ended when pistols were discharged and two men fell. Fortunately, in each case, the bullet only plowed through the scalp, barely grazing the skull.

And while the city generally was making merry, officials of the city and county of New York met at the city hall to discharge their duties as required by law. The Board of

Supervisors reëlected State Senator William M. Tweed president; a *Times* reporter quoted Tweed, upon taking the chair, as saying that the supervisors "would watch carefully over the financial interests of the county, and reduce the rate of taxation until this city became the most lightly taxed of any large city in the Union."

"Hon. William M. Tweed.—(From a Photograph by Brady.)" So reads the caption on this portrait of The Boss which appeared in *Harper's Weekly,* January 21, 1871. Newspapers and periodicals were still deferential to him, and none even suggested corruption, save the *Tribune.* But then, Greeley was an irresponsible journalist.

These were fair words, and a splendid New Year's resolution. But the *Tribune* was skeptical of Tweed and the other city rulers, for it said:

"The freebooters who are to rob the taxearners and tax-payers of New York organized yesterday what they face-tiously call the city government. Over the city hall floated the municipal coat of arms, its white ground and black figures strongly suggesting the death's-head and cross-bones of Captain Kidd."

This was unjust to the memory of Captain Kidd.

Despite the *Tribune's* railing, it was a happy New Year's Day in the main. Even the prisoners in the Tombs, a three-minute walk north of city hall, enjoyed holiday fare. The prisoners in the six cells above the Centre Street entrance, just over the quarters of the warden and the prison office, were having a royal time. Their windows looked out directly on the street. The taxpayers derived a revenue from these prisoners, for these de luxe cells were rented at $10 a week. And these prisoners, for a bribe to the keeper, were permitted to buy small quantities of wine or beer. The very poor among the city's prisoners were housed on the Franklin Street side, in what had once been a police station. It was now one big room, and here were confined the drunk and disorderly, the tramps and the vagrants. Their sentences were never for longer than ten days. The newspapers usually called it the strong room of the Tombs, but sometimes they designated it by its underworld name—Bummers' Hall.

One of its inmates this New Year's Day was John Lord, "a man of advanced years." He had been committed as a vagrant the day before. There was little else a judge could do for a starving old man. But John Lord was also ill. His sober cell-mates tried to make him comfortable. But it was too late. The Tombs physician said: "He died from the effects of exposure and utter poverty."

A journalist suggested that an old man should not be cast into prison merely because he was hungry, homeless, and ailing. He was probably down on the local judges, like most of his colleagues. There were a few decent men on the bench, but the rest were no better than Bowery statues.

2

THE TEMPLE OF JUSTICE

BECOMES A BROTHEL

W E HAVE JUDGES WHO MAKE UP FOR THEIR DEFICIENCY in learning by an abundance of bawdy jests and filthy oaths," said the *Times*. "We have others who are the bosom friends of pimps and thieves, and take care to be on the bench whenever any of their chums are in trouble."

The judges who were not pals of thieves and pimps were, with rare exceptions, silent on the defilement of the halls of justice. Corruption also possessed the Police Department, although its superintendent, John A. Kennedy, was an honest man. The same was true of the prosecutor's office.

One of the few honest men on the bench was Police Justice Joseph Dowling. He was deficient in learning, but he made up for it with an abundance of aggressive integrity. It did not gain him promotion; but he was able to shave without being ashamed of the face in the mirror. On the fourth day of the new year, in disposing of a case involving a female pickpocket, Justice Dowling said:

"The police are in league with the thieves. The police of the Fifteenth Precinct cover these women in their pocketpicking. I also know they receive a commission on every trick they get through. This accounts for the audacity of the thieves and the increasing number of the victims."

Dowling knew the ways of thieves and prostitutes—and of the police as well—as no other man on the bench. He had

little money, and resided at 47 Franklin Street, near the
Tombs. He was born near-by, in the whiskiest ward of the
town, the Bloody Old Sixth—the Five Points. This neighbor-

Cardozo was notorious as a bosom friend of pimps and thieves.
The caption under this safe-cracking scene reads: "... run to Judge
Cardozo; he will accept this bail, you as my bondsman." *Harper's
Weekly,* January 27, 1872.

hood had always been his home. Consequently, he grew up
among thieves and fallen women. He was one of many similar products of these haunts of poverty and crime, each one

demonstrating the old truth that there are neither bad herbs nor bad men, only bad cultivators. His parents gave him a healthy body and an uncompromising conscience. Because of this, it might be said that he came of a well-to-do family. But in material things, these Dowlings were among the poorest of the poor. Although devout, there were occasions when Dowling's father did not say grace at mealtime, for there were times when there was no food in the house. At six, young Dowling began selling papers, and he walked the streets of his home ward unmolested after every other Five Points lad learned he could best any one his size. It was a case of hit or be hit. Dowling preferred to do the hitting. At fifteen, being of man's stature, he found work in Tommy Hadden's sailors' boarding-house at 374 Water Street. He ran errands, swept floors, showed seafaring men to their rooms, and in time was promoted to bartender. For like all sailors' boarding-houses, an important adjunct of Tommy Hadden's was the grog shop. Women of the street stood at the bar, or sat at tables, escorted or unescorted, and had their drinks in Tommy Hadden's boarding-house. There was a restaurant at the back of the bar. But there was no dance hall then, for Tommy had not as yet fallen upon evil ways. The absence of a dance hall was unusual. The food was good, rooms were rented to men only, and robbery was taboo. These were also rare qualities, for, when Dowling worked for Hadden—in fact, all through the seventies and for two decades later—the average sailors' boarding-house was little better than a den of thieves and harlots. This, too, was true of most saloons on the water-front. In 1870, seventeen thousand sailors were robbed—about the usual quota—on the lower end of Manhattan Island, and hundreds were beaten in the process. Foreign consuls and shipping masters of all nations vainly protested against these hold-ups.

Young Dowling knew life in the raw. Whenever a street-walker asked him for a drink on tick, he would give her a glass on the house. He obtained their confidence and, if one showed a desire to reform, he learned her church affiliation. Then he would visit a cleric of her denomination. A dozen or more girls were either restored to their families or placed in honest labor through Bartender Dowling's instrumentality. All this was done by a mere youth, for Dowling quit Hadden's boarding-house before he was twenty-one. After driving a truck for a time, Dowling was appointed to the police force and earned a reputation as a detective. But it was his shoulder-hitting ability that won him newspaper fame. With bare fists he routed gangs of rowdies on the Bowery and stout ruffians on the water-front. There was no civil service then. Appointments were for four years. These cost money, if one lacked political influence. Having no money, Dowling made himself useful at the polls. Matthew Brennan, who was successively police justice, comptroller, police commissioner, and sheriff, took Dowling under his wing. He had Dowling advanced from patrolman to roundsman, then to sergeant, and finally to captain. It was Dowling's boast that he arrested but one unfortunate woman. She had robbed a drunk of his wallet and watch.

When Brennan had him appointed to the bench, Dowling walked on clouds. His only knowledge of law had been acquired in his contacts with courts and criminals. On the bench, he remained the cop he had always been, tough and honest. Brennan remained Dowling's champion as long as he could. When Dowling began assailing the police, Brennan, for his own political well-being, ceased to defend him. And Brennan held his tongue when a ripper bill, masked as a reform measure and aimed at Dowling and three other honest police justices, was introduced in the legislature of

1870. But the decent journals denounced the measure, and the bill died in committee.

Another of Dowling's mold was Police Justice Thomas A. Ledwith. He was also poor. Some of his kin were laborers; one had a saloon on Third Avenue. All were honest. Ledwith resided at 69 Essex Street, in another whiskey ward. When fifteen street-walkers were arraigned before him in Jefferson Market Court on a raw February morning, Ledwith said to the police officer:

Captain Byrnes, allow me to say that while unscrupulous politicians may make it their business to have poor women arrested for blackmailing purposes, I will not be an accomplice to any such scheme. Break up the panel houses and gambling hells which abound in your precinct, and then look for these poor creatures. There are a number of panel houses of the worst kind in your precinct—this is of my own knowledge. I dismiss these women.

In his comments from the bench on the fourth day of the new year, Dowling did not exaggerate the frequency of hold-ups due to the police protection of thieves. These offenses were so common that a newspaper report of one on January 7, 1870, bore the cynical caption: "Another Street Attack."

All these things were galling to Police Superintendent Kennedy who knew he could clean up the town if given a chance. He would begin by closing the vile dens where criminals foregathered. He had no mad notion that the police could abolish prostitution. But he did know that the worst of the dens could be closed, and permanently, if he received only a little leeway. He knew also he could end the alliance between his department and the underworld. He became so zealous in his pleadings that he was not only promised a free hand, but remedial legislation. Whereupon, on the day of "another street attack," Kennedy penned the following order:

OFFICE OF THE SUPERINTENDENT
Metropolitan Police
No. 300 Mulberry Street.

Jan. 7, 1870
General Order No. 597

To CAPTAINS OF POLICE:

You will, during the ensuing week, make a thorough and complete census of houses of prostitution and assignation, carefully distinguishing each class, and giving the locality by street and number; and also the number of prostitutes living in each of such houses.

You will also, in addition, ascertain the locality of each concert saloon of low repute and the number of females who frequent them, either as performers or attendants.

You will also indicate each of the houses above referred to having the reputation of panel cribs.

You will also, in each of the above specified cases, ascertain the full names of the proprietors; and in cases where fictitious names are used, you will record both real and assumed names.

You will make a full report of the above to this office on Tuesday, 25th instant, setting forth each item of inquiry in an intelligent manner.

JOHN A. KENNEDY
Superintendent of Police

A word or so to make Kennedy's order understandable to all: A concert saloon was a synonym for concert den, a drinking place where anything from a tin-pan piano to a small orchestra provided music of varying degree. Drink and food were served by youthful waitresses in scanty dress—hence the name, pretty-waitress saloons. The hired singers and dancers in these places were distinguishable by their scantier attire. The waitresses wore aprons over their pink tights. Waitresses and performers sat at the tables with patrons, and drank and danced with them. There were a few concert saloons where no drinks were served; there, sheer lewdness alone was offered.

Concert dens abounded in the Five Points, on Broadway, between Canal and Fourth Streets, on Sixth Avenue from Amity Street (now West Third) northward for a mile; there were scores on the cross-streets between Broadway and the Bowery, from Canal Street to Fourth Street. The streets immediately to the west of Broadway—Mercer, Green and Wooster—boasted nearly as many concert saloons as they did outright brothels; these concert dens were as vile as anything in the Five Points or along the water-front. Thieves, pimps, and roughs frequented all. There were no professional killers, because murder was still an art, not an industry. The rough, invaluable on Election Day, used his fists, brass knuckles, or a sand-bag. If he miscalculated and struck too hard, he usually paid for his poor judgment on the gallows in the courtyard of the Tombs.

Panel cribs, as used in Kennedy's general order, were the panel houses which Ledwith advised Byrnes to close, instead of arresting street-walkers. These places are houses of prostitution or assignation, or low hotels, where bedroom doors are equipped with silently opening panels to enable a prostitute's accomplice to reach into the pockets of her unsuspecting companion's garments as they hang, seemingly safe, over a chair near the trick door.

The town read Kennedy's general order with astonished gratification. The people were prepared for the decennial census of the Federal Government, but not for this. They knew that this order, so far as Kennedy was concerned, was not an ingenious blackmailing scheme on a stupendous scale. Ever since the concert saloons invaded Broadway two years before, they had been periodically raided. At first the mer-

chants and hotel keepers of the city's principal street regarded the police activity as an answer to their demands
that Broadway be restored to its former respectability. They
soon learned that the raids were inspired, as a newspaper
phrased it, by the "necessity for a little ready money for
political or other purposes, or when a Ring magistrate desired
to take a trip to Europe or needed to replenish his purse."

Similar raids, and for like motives, were made on
gambling dens. But Kennedy's General Order No. 597 was
aimed only at the breeding spots of crime and disease. He
knew that every gaming place paid tribute to politicians and
to some of his own subordinates, and that several police
officials were owned outright by them. Men who would take
money from gambling would not necessarily touch the wages
of shame. It was a rare politician who touched this graft.
This was a perquisite of corrupt judges and dishonest police.
So Kennedy had deliberately avoided any reference to faro
banks, lotteries, or other games of chance. No one could,
openly at least, defend the dens of vice, of which the concert
saloons were the worst. They flaunted their wares with
brazen defiance. Robberies and scenes of violence were common in these places. Some of them abounded in panel cribs
on the upper floors. Those on Broadway bore fanciful names
such as the Boulevard, Dew Drop Inn, Assembly, Oriental,
Canterbury; the vilest of all was the Matinee Garden at the
southwest corner of Broadway and Amity Street. Only in
their deceptive names and lavish furnishings did they differ
from the lowest of their type. The Oriental was at 626 Broadway, the Canterbury at 632, and the Assembly at 634-636.
One freezing January night, shortly before nine o'clock,
these three places were raided simultaneously, and the proprietors, three bartenders, and sixty-five women were
arrested: "The girls were made to cover their nakedness with
shawls and cloaks and were taken in twos and threes to the

Spring Street police station where they set up a blasphemous din on getting into their cells." All were later freed. The police lacked evidence!

Just around the corner from police headquarters, on Houston Street, was a dingy, two-storied frame dwelling, once painted white. This building was the first to attract the attention of a nocturnal passer-by, for a lantern swung above the main entrance. This lantern was of generous proportions, and its red and green panes of glass sheltered a kerosene lamp. This was Harry Hill's concert saloon. The door beneath the lantern opened from the street into the bar and restaurant. A narrow entrance on the right led to the dance hall overhead. At the street end of the long room stood a bar, and at the other, a low stage. On the right was the orchestra, a piano, violin, and bass viol; on the left was a large Punch-and-Judy box. It was Harry Hill's boast that his place was respectable. Hill had no women in his employ. No concert saloon was more widely known. While the patrons rested after a dance, a Punch-and-Judy show entertained them. The puppets would have delighted a child; their lines would have brought blushes to the cheeks of a drunken longshoreman. Only youthful prostitutes, well-gowned at that, could enter Harry Hill's. Women were admitted free; men paid a dollar. Noted prize-fighters and gamblers mingled here with the élite of the criminal world. But Harry Hill banned pimps, for he prided himself on his respectability. If a high official was showing the sights to some friends, he could always rely on Harry's aid. For Harry would take them to the dance hall, stop whatever was going on, and announce: "We will now have a Virginia reel, and in this number, the girls will take them off." As the preparations were hastened, even the most guileless youth no longer had any doubt of the type of woman he was entertaining, for as the dance began, he was carrying some of her garments on his arm. No roughs patronized Harry Hill's. They used the resorts of the water-front and the Five Points where the lewdness was coarse, and where the risqué songs had only a piano or concertina accompaniment.

The scarlet census was completed within the alloted time. But its only service was to reveal new dens of infamy to corrupt judges and politicians. This was about the last time the politicians hoodwinked Kennedy, for he resigned his office in the spring. No one in authority urged him to remain. He would have been cast out unceremoniously long before but for fear of popular wrath.

There were Ring judges who did not take, directly at least, any tribute from the low concert saloons and other dens of vice. But the press suspected, and lawyers knew, that they had their own brothel—once the temple of Justice. Their chambers were panel cribs. The keeper was Albert Cardozo, aptly called the Machiavelli of the Bench. He was the special tool of Tweed's financial props, Jay Gould and James Fisk, Jr., railroad looters extraordinary. Cardozo was venal in a big way. He corruptly ordered payment of $400,000 from the funds of a bank in the hands of one of his pet receivers. He opened the cell doors for criminals after their conviction—if they had the price. The magnitude of his illegal jail deliveries was then unknown, but it was whispered he had made a sizable fortune in this way alone, and his ways were many. Like his confederates, Justices John H. McCunn and George G. Barnard, Cardozo peddled writs and other court orders to the highest bidders. Cardozo and Barnard were the richest of the Ring judges. Barnard had been on the bench thirteen years, starting as recorder in 1857, and had never let an opportunity slip. Any one with the necessary wherewithal, golden or political, could see him on judicial matters at any hour of the day or night. Cardozo lacked Barnard's soldierly carriage, foppish dress, and judicial background, but he had a daring the others lacked. He won unenviable distinction by introducing the lettre de cachet to America. His Bastille was the Tombs. Two of his prisoners were

"The Clown in the Judicial Ring." Below the caption appeared the following from the *Tribune:* "The court room of Judge Barnard has been a place of amusement.... Every day his indecent sarcasms and vulgar jests keep his court room crowded with laughing spectators...." *Harper's Weekly,* April 13, 1872.

penniless women, Mary Pearsall, keeper of a house of prostitution, and Johanna O'Connor, both of whom he kept incommunicado for seventeen days. Their case stands out in

sad contrast to the convicts he liberated from the penitentiary at so much per head. What rich man or powerful politician these two lowly women had offended no one who knew
would tell. To a lawyer who intervened in behalf of the
women, Cardozo said: "Do not touch this case; if you do,
you will displease me; if you take this case, you need never
expect any favor from me while I am on the bench."

Unlike Justices Dowling and Ledwith, whose blather about
corruption made them the laughing-stock of the Ring, the
unholy three did not live in the whiskey wards. McCunn
lived simply in an unpretentious home at 208 West Twenty-
first Street. But the modest domicile was deceptive, for
McCunn could not say offhand how many houses, all tenanted, he owned—his guess was more than twenty. Cardozo
and Barnard resided in showy mansions in the most fashionable stretch of town. Both were just off Fifth Avenue, Barnard at 23 West Twenty-first Street and Cardozo at 12 West
Forty-seventh Street.

The bar knew that Cardozo and his fellows were guilty of
"mal and corrupt conduct in office" and of "high crimes and
misdemeanors." Lawyers talked of need for action, and at
last, after continuous prodding from newspapers not controlled by the Ring, a little start was made as the winter of
1869-70 was drawing to a close. A newspaper of February 2,
in describing the organization of the bar association, said
the lawyers declared "that they ought to have more control
over admissions to the bar" and demanded a repeal of the
laws which have made "access to the bar as easy as to the
theater." Did you wish to be a lawyer? All you required was
the price, $500 and up. Sometimes a politician's word would
do it. Most grafting politicians were made lawyers in this
way. Tweed was one.

A month later the lawyers held another meeting. One of
them, Samuel J. Tilden, said: "The public knows only too

well how disastrously the bench has been degraded by two or three judges. If the bar is to be merely an institution that seeks to win cases, and to win them by back-door access to the judiciary, then it is not only degraded, but it is corrupt."

People wondered at this timid outburst. To them, Tilden was the state boss, being chairman of the Democratic State Committee. The governor was a Democrat and both branches of the state legislature were Democratic. The people reasonably thought that a mere nod from Tilden would have ended the corruption. But the Ring judges laughed at the restrained attack upon them. They knew Tilden held the state chairmanship by Tweed's grace. Tweed was boss of city and state. He had grown to dislike and distrust Tilden because he was ambitious. In private conferences of party leaders, Tweed frequently rounded on Tilden like a trooper, and sometimes abused him in public. The judges were wondering what the Boss would say when the pair met after Tilden's attack on the judges. They did not have long to wait.

3

A PERFECT CITY MACHINE—ITS LOOT

TWEED AND TILDEN MET IN ALBANY ON APRIL 4, 1870, THE day before the Ring's charter for the metropolis was signed by the governor. The charter, effective immediately, launched the Ring on an orgy of looting unparalleled in the city's long, graft-ridden history. One month after the charter was in effect, Tweed, with the mayor of the city and its comptroller, authorized the payment of $6,312,500 for work and supplies for the new court-house. More than $5,500,000 of this sum was fraudulent, and was divided among the Ring members. This was but a small part of their loot.

Tweed, broke at the outbreak of the Civil War, was estimated to be worth $12,000,000 before 1870 was well under way. He, however, modestly denied ever having more than $2,000,000 to $3,000,000. This is understatement. He was the third largest owner of real estate in New York in 1871. His loot from the Supervisors' Ring in 1868 exceeded three-quarters of a million dollars, and he had many profitable years on the Board of Supervisors. His power and opportunities had increased since then, and whatever charge may be lodged against him, he stands guiltless of being a piker.

The meeting between Tilden and Tweed was in the old brownstone state capitol. As chairman of the senate committee on cities, Tweed was presiding over the final hearing on the charter, which bristled with jokers, as those innocent-appearing clauses are known in legislative jargon. A novice in bill-drafting would have detected them in a single

22

reading. Tilden was not a novice. He had served in the state assembly twenty-four years earlier. He was also active in the state constitutional convention of that year, 1846. He had been a lieutenant of Martin Van Buren. In 1855 he ran unsuccessfully for attorney-general. His entire adult life had been devoted to two subjects: law and politics. He was there to oppose the charter. But he was silent on its many jokers.

Tweed was not concerned over Tilden's opposition to the charter or anything else, for he had on the desk before him a petition approving the measure signed by men higher in public esteem than Tilden. The signers included the leading merchants and bankers of the metropolis, and its outstanding philanthropist, the venerable Peter Cooper, president of the Citizens' Association, the first civic group organized to fight municipal corruption.

Tilden knew every joker in the charter and what each one spelled in potential loot. He could have torn it apart. But his opposition was cautious, apologetic. His conduct in public life was guided by Tweed's political credo. Thus the Boss expressed it, under oath, when he felt death was imminent: "A politician in coming forward takes things as they are."

Tilden's thin voice irritated Tweed, although the tone was humble and the words apologetic. Tweed listened—and marveled. What was that? Was Tilden denying that he aided Tweed's enemies? Tweed knew that was false. He knew Tilden was secretly fomenting a revolt against him in Tammany. But the galling part of it was that Tweed could not tell him so now. Tweed despised hypocrites, as he once informed Tilden in a brimstone speech. But he could not use such language at a public hearing.

"And let me say here," continued Tilden meekly, "that if I know my own heart, I have no feeling of unkindness to any human being. To yourself, Mr. Chairman—"

Tweed interrupted Tilden. Tweed was violently angry.

Oaths clamored for escape. But he swallowed them and exclaimed: "I am sick of the discussion of this question!"

Tilden humbly completed his thought: "To yourself, Mr. Chairman, or to anybody else, I am unconscious of ever

Peter Cooper

From a photograph by Rockwood. *Harper's Weekly*, February 21, 1874.

having done an unkind act or entertained an unkind feeling."

Tweed did not care what Tilden said, false or true. It did not matter. He needed no one's help now. His charter was safe. Everything had been fixed. He had won the indorsement of the hoodwinked Peter Cooper and other eminent citizens of the town. That took hard work and real money. But he required a mask of respectability for his charter. That was imperative. He knew the charter would pass the senate the next day with about the same division that prevailed in the assembly the week before. He had paid enough to ensure its passage. He modestly testified later it cost him $600,000. Tilden said Tweed paid more than a million to get the charter through the two houses. Tweed may have erred, for a few hundred thousand meant little to him then. Fisk and Gould, and some individuals holding city contracts, supplied whatever Tweed used. A few legislative votes came exceptionally high. Tweed paid five Republican senators from the rural districts $40,000 each to support the charter. Other senatorial votes—the price is higher in the senate than in the assembly—cost $5,000 each. Some took only $1,000. But $1,000 went a long way in 1870. Tweed swore he bribed every member of the senate save two. One was a thief he had cast out, Henry W. Genêt, the unworthy grandson of Citizen Edmond Charles Genêt. He was the only senator Tweed did not attempt to bribe. The other was Senator Francis S. Thayer, of Troy. Thayer was poor; he spurned a fortune.

The charter passed the senate the following day with Thayer and Genêt alone voting against it. Tweed did not have to bribe the governor, John T. Hoffman, to sign the grant. Tweed had elevated Hoffman from the mayoralty of the metropolis in 1868 to the governorship by stealing an election. To ensure the success of this theft, Tweed had used Tilden's name without his knowledge, but without protest from him when the fact became known. Besides, Hoffman would be up for reëlection in the fall. Also, Hoffman was ambitious to be President, and he could rely on Tweed's help, for, with Hoffman in the White House, Tweed would show the nation how amateurish were the plunderers who were then disgracing the administration of the gullible Grant. Moreover, Tweed had Hoffman completely cowed. Once, when Hoffman threatened to balk, Tweed brought him under control with the announcement he would nominate himself for governor at the end of Hoffman's term.

Every one understood Tweed's anger with Tilden over the charter. The only organized opposition to it came from Tweed's opponents in Tammany Hall. Tweed, who had ears everywhere, knew that Tilden had advised the leaders of the revolting bloc. These were: Senator Genêt who was soon to escape from jail after his arrest for stealing from the city; Sheriff James O'Brien, who parted with Tweed when the Boss refused to approve his extortionate bills amounting to $350,000; Edmund Jones, head of a printing company, whose bills against the municipality Tweed had also refused to approve, for a like reason, and John Morrissey, member of the House of Representatives.

Morrissey was one of the most picturesque and popular politicians in the city, and was the only opponent Tweed feared at the polls. He was a professional gambler—openly so. He had a past. As a lad of eighteen, he had been indicted for assault with intent to kill. This was at Troy, in December, 1849. Four months later he was indicted for burglary, assault and battery, for which he spent sixty days in the Albany penitentiary. Seven years after he was arrested in New York City and held in the murder of Bill Poole, also spelled Pool. He had defeated Poole in a brutal prize-ring bout on the North River dock at the foot of Amos Street, now West Tenth Street, and while there was always ill feeling between the two, Morrissey had no hand in the death of Poole or any other man. Poole was slain in a bar-room brawl by a drunken ex-cop. Morrissey was nowhere near at the time. There were several other arrests of Morrissey, all in the metropolis. On October 26, 1856, he was one of twenty-seven indicted for "instigating a prize-fight."

A Nast cartoon of John Morrissey in *Harper's Weekly*

Morrissey was born ahead of his time. With his popularity and political influence he would probably have been drafted for governor had he been born half a century later. In his youth, he would fight—always with fists—on the slightest provocation. In 1857 he had two good-sized rows, one with William P. Conway, who accused him of assault with intent to kill—it had a familiar ring to Morrissey now. In the following month, on June 19, he mauled two policemen, Thomas H. Bulmer and F. H. Daget, somewhat severely, and two indictments were found, each charging murderous assault. His weapons were his fists. His last arrest, on October 27, 1865, was for ordinary assault and battery. Morrissey was growing soft. At this time he was a man of wealth and held the controlling interest in the Saratoga race-track. He owned two gambling houses, one in the metropolis and one at New York's famed spa. In the fifties he was twice arrested for gambling. Morrissey's juvenile offenses, his prize-fighting, his brawls and his gambling, were known to the entire town. His political enemies arranged for their publication on several occasions, thereby increasing his popularity.

Morrissey organized and commanded Tweed's army of repeaters, recruiting the best from Philadelphia, New York's chief stand-by all through the years for ballot-box stuffers. Tweed had rewarded him handsomely and helped to make him well off. In 1870 Morrissey was worth half a million dollars or more. He was now a Tammany ward leader. Every journalist in the city knew him as a straight-shooter, and even an opposition paper always gave him ample space to reply to an attack—a rare thing, for all newspapers were proudly partizan.

Morrissey and Tweed quarreled in 1870, but neither ever explained why. The three thieves who joined Morrissey in leading the opposition to Tweed were not exactly the sort to be acclaimed reformers by Tilden or any one else. Eight days before the Tweed charter passed the senate, these four and their followers forced Tweed to convoke a meeting of the Tammany General Committee, the source of all political power in the organization. A majority of the committee signed the petition requesting the meeting, and Tweed had no choice but to comply. The move surprised him. He knew if he had time he could buy off most of them. One of his avowed rules of conduct was: "We used money wherever we could."

So Tweed turned to a stalwart Republican and devoted friend, Police Commissioner Henry Smith. As Grand Sachem of the Society of Tammany, Tweed was the custodian of the building known as Tammany Hall, and speaking as Grand Sachem, he told Smith he feared a riot in the Hall if the meeting was held. Tweed also told Smith the riot would unquestionably spread next door to Bryant's Minstrel Hall and create a panic in the theater, possibly with dreadful loss of life.

Commissioner Smith had sworn to uphold the law and to protect the people from riot and bloodshed. He could not be false to his oath. So when Morrissey, O'Brien, Jones, Genêt, and their fellow-reformers reached Tammany Hall, they found half of the city's police, swinging night-sticks, on duty on Fourteenth Street. They were massed at both entrances of Tammany Hall and had garrisoned the Hall itself. They also held Bryant's Minstrel Hall. Law and order—and Tweed—were triumphant.

And when the leaders of the Young Democracy, the name adopted by the reformers, began to count noses the next day, they found fewer than the night before. Tweed's purse had played blackbird with many of them.

Tweed was eight years older than Morrissey and had celebrated his forty-seventh birthday on April 3, two days before the senate passed his charter. There was one splendid thing about the charter. It was called a home-rule grant.

The honest part of the press hinted at what might be expected from the charter. But why didn't the Citizens' Association, organized to fight everything corrupt in municipal life, oppose it? It had lawyers among its directors, and it is fair to assume that some of them had read the charter. It had a paid expert on municipal government, one Nathaniel Sands. But it failed dismally in this crisis, as similar bodies have since done. Tweed bought and paid for the praise of his charter by the Citizens' Association. Tweed blazed the trail. He demonstrated that it is necessary to buy only two or three key men among a group of reformers to hoodwink the lot. It is seldom that many members of such an organization will devote their time to civic problems; the work is generally left to one or two of their number. Tweed bought Sands, who convinced Cooper—to quote Tilden—that "the Ring had become conservative—were not ambitious for more wealth—were on the side of the taxpayers."

Tilden tried to swing his old friend against the charter, but Cooper listened politely to him and then replied he was certain Tweed had turned over a new leaf. Cooper thought so much of Tweed's conversion that he permitted Sands to accept a place from Tweed on the Tax Commission at $15,000 a year. In addition, the reformers paid Sands $10,000 a year as secretary.

Cooper had become suspicious of Tilden's political motives. Like every one else, he knew Tilden as a political partner of Tweed; he had seen his name as Democratic State Chairman signed to a letter mailed to Democratic leaders in every upstate city and town a week before the election of 1868 asking each one to telegraph his estimate of the vote the moment the polls closed. And the telegrams were to be addressed to William M. Tweed, Tammany Hall. Tweed required this information to determine how many votes he must steal in the city to elect his man Hoffman governor. A canvass made by the Democrats themselves upstate forecast Hoffman's defeat by a decisive majority. So the trick had to be turned in the metropolis—after the votes had been cast. And with the information thus obtained, Tweed stole the election by counting Hoffman in.

"As long as I count the votes, what are you going to do about it?" is the poser the artist attributes to Tweed as he stands beside a ballot box. *Harper's Weekly,* October 7, 1871.

Horace Greeley, the following year, accused Tilden of being "at least a passive accomplice in the giant frauds of last November." Then Greeley threw these irremovable barbs:

Your name was used, without public protest on your part, in circulars sowed broadcast over the state, whereof the manifest intent was to "make assurance doubly sure" that the frauds here perpetrated should not be overborne by the honest vote of the rural districts. And you, not merely by silence, but by positive assumption, have covered these frauds with the mantle of your respectability. On the principle that the receiver is as bad as the thief, you are as deeply implicated in them as though your name were Tweed, O'Brien, or Oakey Hall.

The O'Brien of Greeley's letter was Sheriff O'Brien; Oakey Hall, the Elegant Oakey, was A. Oakey Hall, Tweed's crooked mayor who owed his first full term in the city hall to another of Tweed's election thefts. Hall was New York's first wise-cracking mayor; he turned to the stage after his lurid career in the city hall. He was also a playwright. It was the Elegant Oakey who, with Tweed and Comptroller Richard B. Connolly, stole more than $5,500,000 from the city on May 5 when they approved padded bills aggregating $6,312,500, a power conferred on the trio by the Tweed charter. A little earlier, on the Saturday following the signing of the charter, Hall issued a signed statement describing the men he had appointed to office under the Tweed charter, laying emphasis on the non-partizan character of some of these appointments—which were mandatory under the charter. Hall was available to reporters at the city hall almost any time, on anything. But frequently he put his views on paper and signed them as mayor. These statements, which would have been gladly published as news, at least in substance, by the important papers, were paid for by the city as advertising at the rate of one dollar a line although they appeared in the news columns. These outright bribes went to the venal press of the town, which included a majority of the eighty-seven daily and weekly papers published in the metropolis. Tweed paid a flat retainer of $1,000 a month to some evening newspapers. The *Evening Post,* owned and edited by William Cullen Bryant, topped the rest with a monthly bribe of $5,000. In eighteen months, Tweed was to pay $2,703,308.48 of the city's moneys to corrupt newspapers in the guise of advertising. Some newspapers were also bribed through padded printing bills. The Tweed Ring proper— there were earlier rings of which Tweed was a part or the head—lasted thirty months from its inception on January 1, 1869.

This dollar-a-line statement of Mayor Hall illuminates some of the many-faceted methods of Tweed:

> Every citizen ought to feel that the policeman, the fireman, with the health physicians, who protects him in his life or property, should be freed from party bias and have no political duty to discharge, indeed, that he should be controlled by no other considerations than those of fidelity.... In accordance with the preceding view, there are four Democrats and one Republican in the Department of Docks. The Department of Charities and Correction, as well as the Fire Department, will stand three Democrats to two Republicans. The Health Department will be composed of five Democratic members and three Republicans. The Police Department is equally divided in politics....

Why should a Democratic administration in a city that was overwhelmingly Democratic give these high-salaried commissionerships, with the power and influence therein inherent, to Republicans? Well, the Tweed Ring, or any other corrupt political combination anywhere could not exist for any considerable time without the acquiescence of a considerable part of the leaders of the minority party. There is but one way to create this highly necessary acquiescence, and that is through systematic bribery. The bribery can be direct, through the personal corruption of leaders of the minority party, or indirect, through the appointment of these leaders or their supporters to office. Tweed used both. And the more Republicans he could put on the city pay-roll, the less he would have to pay out of his own pocket. No one knew, not even Tweed himself, how many Republicans he had led to the public crib or placed on his personal pay-roll to stifle Republican criticism. These men were called Tammany Republicans and dominated their party in New York City.

Hall made one appointment this second Saturday in April that was preëminently partizan. This was the appointment of Tweed as head of the Department of Public Works. This new post was the most important place at the mayor's disposal, for the new charter, in creating a board of audit with unlimited power to pass on all claims against the municipality, past and present, stipulated that it was to consist of the mayor, the comptroller, and the commissioner of public works. The charter also provided that Tweed's term of office in the Board of Audit was to be for four years, three years beyond Hall's current term of office. Another joker substantially prohibited Tweed's removal during these four years, for the charter decreed he could only be removed on charges preferred by the mayor and heard by all six judges of the Court of Common Pleas. The absence of a single judge—and more than half were Tweed's judges—would prevent his removal.

All the appointments made under the new charter were for terms of four to eight years. In this way the Tweed Ring would be protected from exposure for some time to come, barring an unforeseen and unanticipated accident. These departmental heads, all beholden to the Ring, and its beneficiaries, would have in their keeping the books that could put Tweed and his Ring and themselves in jail. The section creating the Board of Audit originated with the Elegant Oakey; but the charter as a whole was the work of Peter Barr Sweeny, nicknamed Peter Bismarck and Peter Brains, a cunning lawyer, and inordinately avaricious.

Sweeny, Hall, Comptroller Connolly (alias Slippery Dick), and Tweed constituted the most notorious of our rings. Tweed had known other rings, but it remained for the Tweed Ring to take over the reformers and the temple of Justice, leaving only a niche for the blindfolded goddess. Every bench below the Court of Appeals was largely in its control. The Ring was growing. If it had but held to its original purpose to swindle the city out of one of every three dollars paid out, it might have gone on for years. The loot was to be divided five ways, an equal share to each of the Ring members, and the remaining fifth to be halved between a bribery fund and the Ring's agents, A. E. Woodward, a clerk in the Board of Supervisors for many years, and James Watson, the county auditor. But immediately after the charter became law the Ring decided to take at least half of all moneys paid out of the city treasury, and more if it was deemed safe. On this basis they allocated to themselves more than $5,500,000 of the $6,312,500 they authorized to be paid out of the city treasury on May 5. Here the Ring's share was nearly 90 per cent of the padded bills they had approved. Shortly thereafter Connolly protested he was not getting enough, and Tweed raised the basic minimum of the Ring's cut to two-thirds of all moneys paid out. This basic minimum was shortly increased to 85 per cent. And to show Connolly that he had not forgotten to think in big ways, Tweed suggested they give to Sweeny and the Elegant Oakey only half of their just share of the loot, and divide the difference between themselves. This was eminently satisfactory to Slippery Dick.

Now they were cheating one another and the thieving became an orgy. When bills did not come in fast enough from the city's creditors, Tweed had checks drawn to the order of individuals, firms, hospitals, and other charitable institutions that existed only in the fancy of the Ring.

If an intimate had asked Tweed, in the spring of 1870, if there was any possibility of smashing the Ring, the Boss would have laughed heartily. For he was satisfied that he had anticipated everything and overlooked nothing. He had bought the press, or a substantial section of it. He had effectively bribed the only other considerable opposition in the city—the Republican party. And he owned the clearinghouse of the reformers—the Citizens' Association. He had checked the revolt against him in Tammany, again with bribery. He had the poor of the city with him—their price a basket of food, a bundle of clothes, a ton of coal, and, sometimes, a little cash. He did all these things with the money of the taxpayers and the taxearners, rich and poor, minor and adult, citizen and alien.

Tweed did not use bribery alone. To have done so would have made him the target of every extortionist with even a suspicion of what was going on. So he visited reprisals upon his outstanding enemies.

There were many honest journalists in the town, owners of newspapers and members of their staffs. One of the most brilliant of these was Charles Nordhoff, managing editor of Bryant's *Post*. He was daring as well. His writings offended the Ring. Tweed was paying Nordhoff's paper $5,000 monthly. So he asked for Nordhoff's dismissal. Exit Nordhoff.

Then there was another ring of which Tweed was chief. He had been a member of it for some fifteen years, and its head during most of this time. This was the Supervisors' Ring which, as we have seen, netted Tweed $750,000 in one year. All the supervisors, save John Fox and James Hayes, were friends of Tweed.

These two had joined Morrissey, Genêt, O'Brien, and the rest in the revolt of the reformers in Tammany. So Tweed abolished the Board of Supervisors, and Hayes and Fox, like Nordhoff, found themselves suddenly on the street. Tweed found jobs in various city departments for the other members of the now extinct Board of Supervisors. Before the board was actually abolished, the Republican journals joined the Tweed organs in praising the Boss for this excellent move. Of course, no one suspected, outside of the Ring, why Tweed wiped out the board. The *Times* then thought nothing too good for Tweed, and said of him:

> Senator Tweed is in a fair way to distinguish himself as a reformer. Having gone so far as the champion of ... the charter, he seems to have no idea of turning back ... he has put the people of Manhattan Island under great obligation. His last proposition, to abolish the Board of Supervisors and transfer their functions to the mayor, recorder and new board of aldermen, is the crowning act of all.
>
> It strikes a blow at one of the most corrupt departments of government, and one which is as useless as the fifth wheel to a coach. We trust that Senator Tweed will manifest the same energy in the advocacy of this last reform which marked his action in regard to the charter.

The *Times* shared the Republican morning field with the *Tribune*. The writer of this editorial twaddle had no illusions regarding Tweed; it is a fair assumption that he wrote it under orders from James B. Taylor, one of the three directors of the *Times* in 1870. Taylor was partner of Tweed in the New York Printing Company, one of the business concerns used by Tweed in looting the city.

This editorial was typical of the pæan of praise chorused by servile newspapers in honor of Tweed. While he was occasionally criticized by journals that now praised him, there was but one consistent critic among the notable publications of the town. This was *Harper's Weekly*, where Thomas Nast's uncensored cartoons tore away at Tweed and his crooked colleagues. The Boss did not mind the printed word so much, for the poor, his last line of defense, were mainly illiterate. But they could understand a brilliantly executed pictorial attack.

4

A WALL STREET RING

USES GOLD AND PERFUMED WOMEN

WITH THE DESTRUCTION OF THE SUPERVISORS' RING, TWEED held membership in another ring beside the one that bore his name. This was the Erie Ring, headed by James Fisk, Jr. Fisk was the drollest of our public plunderers and a stranger to shame. He was humorously brazen about his thieving. There were a few train robberies in 1870. In one near San Francisco, the bandits escaped with $3,100. In commenting on this robbery, the *Times* said it was nothing for San Francisco to get excited about—James Fisk had stolen a whole railroad.

Fisk was insanely boastful of having stolen the Erie Railroad. Jason Gould, or Jay, had a hand in it, and together they directed the wholesale bribery of the necessary agencies of government to achieve their end. But Fisk's audacious planning was the major factor. When Fisk read that James Fisk—not James Fisk, Jr.—had stolen a whole railroad, his twinkling eyes saw in the omitted "Jr." another opportunity to give the public a laugh—he was always trying to give them laughs, and generally succeeded. So he wrote to the paper pretending that it had erroneously referred to his father who, the boss of the Erie Ring assured the *Times*, never had any interest in railroads, and requested the journal to correct the "unintentional mistake." Of course it was Fisk, Jr., not

his father, who stole the Erie Railroad; and the wise-cracking
thief wanted the world to know it.

Yet Fisk—let us call him that from now on—bridled at the
slightest reflection on his father. When the Springfield *Republican* slurred the elder Fisk, the son brought suit for libel.
Then he waited until Samuel Bowles, the offending editor,
arrived in New York. Fisk had no intention of pressing the
libel action. Next to Greeley, Bowles was the most distinguished Republican journalist in the East. When Fisk heard
that Bowles was in town, he obtained a warrant from Judge
McCunn. Bowles was seized in the lobby of the Fifth Avenue Hotel and thrown into a cell in Ludlow Street jail, where
he was kept overnight.

Fisk was essentially a showman. A native of Burlington,
Vermont, he had been a waiter in a tavern and a barker in a
circus. As a boy he peddled dry-goods and notions with his
father through the villages of his native state. After his circus
experience he transformed his father's canvas-covered wagon
into a garishly decorated vehicle drawn by gaily caparisoned
horses. Soon he had several of these general stores on wheels,
and the jangling bells of the horses, as they snapped into
action on approaching a farmhouse or hamlet, told the Green
Mountain folk that Fisk was on the way. He had arrived in
the metropolis in 1863, only seven years before, but now
few were more widely known.

Fisk maintained a harem as an adjunct to his Wall Street
adventures. His pet harlot was Josephine Mansfield, who
played hostess to the Ring judges in her brothel-home at 359
West Twenty-third Street, just down the block from Fisk's
Grand Opera-House on the northwest corner of Twenty-
third Street and Eighth Avenue. Fisk invited all his valued
acquaintances to Josie's, from Gould and Tweed down. And
Josie always had other fair ones to help her entertain. Fisk
relied on Josie's devotion to him, although she was but one

of his mistresses. It was common talk among the well-informed that he had several; popular fancy numbered them by the dozen. General William S. Hillyer, who had been on Grant's staff during the Tennessee and Vicksburg campaigns, accused Fisk in the fall of 1870 of having seven con-

Samuel Bowles
After a photograph by Sarony. *Harper's Weekly*, February 2, 1878.

cubines. One of Fisk's hired judges imprisoned a man of greater distinction for saying less. All that saved Hillyer from a cell of Fisk's choosing was fear of violence, for Hillyer always went armed. How much Fisk squandered on his hired women is not known, save in the case of Josie. Here the

court records disclose that her brownstone home cost Erie
Railroad stockholders $40,000. His cash gifts to her exceeded
$1,000 a month. This was more than double the annual wage
of his underpaid trainmen. From the Erie he looted $820,000
to buy the Grand Opera-House. Adjoining the opera-house,
on the Twenty-third Street side, was Fisk's home, which
Josie seldom visited.

Fisk spent princely sums on the opera-house annually.
Here again not even a dependable guess is available. On its
stage sang opera troupes from Italy, England, and Germany,
before he made it the acknowledged home in America of
French opéra bouffe. His principals and his musicians were
generously paid. He had a succession of noted impresarios.
When the serious-minded ballet dancers and chorus-girls
they had brought from Europe inquired plaintively what
Fisk thought they were, some of these men made graceful
exits after finding other places of employment for the girls.
But a sufficient number always remained for Fisk's purposes.

The town talked. This made Fisk more audacious. When
the warm spring days of 1870 arrived he was again at the
reins, driving a six-in-hand dray, laden with his scented
ones, through Central Park and the city's principal streets.
One spring day when the metropolis was gay with bud and
sprouting leaf and songsters from the South, a metropolitan
journalist sent this despatch from the state capital:

> The stolen money in the hands of the Erie directors which has
> corrupted two legislatures, is not likely to fail with the third. . . .
> With Tweed as one of the directors enthroned in the Senate,
> and since the triumph in the charter war, omnipotent in both
> houses, and with an executive who is its mere tool, and with a
> corruption fund large enough to purchase any and all of the
> committees of the legislature, the Erie corporation can defy pub-
> lic opinion and snap its fingers at the simpletons whom it has
> robbed.

This Albany despatch of April 13 was an oft-repeated story now. The members of the legislature, with a few refreshing exceptions, had been hopelessly corrupt or shamelessly craven for at least three years. When the Erie looters were buying the legislature two years earlier, an agent of Erie, representing not Fisk the pander, but Drew the pious churchman, and founder of the theological seminary bearing his name, who then controlled Erie, offered $500 to E. Mc-Kinney Glenn of Wayne County. Glenn was a first-year man, new to the ways of legislative halls. As the session progressed, and he learned the extent of the bribery, he demanded an investigation. It was also Tweed's first year in the legislature—he was on the senate side. His speaker of the assembly, Walter Hitchman, appointed a committee which reported that a thorough examination of the Erie's books demonstrated that the road had never spent a penny to influence any legislature, corruptly or otherwise.

Glenn smiled grimly while the report was being read. He had anticipated a little whitewashing, but not all this. His three months in the legislature had taught him to expect callousness. When the clerk finished reading the whitewashing, Glenn announced his resignation, and the people of Wayne County's Second Assembly District were without representation from April 11 to December 31, 1868. But they rewarded their courageous assemblyman by returning him to his same old seat.

The legislature of 1870 did not know Glenn. A second year of the polluted capitol was as much as he could endure. Hitchman was there, again on the speaker's rostrum, and the 1870 legislative session closed on April 26 with the customary maudlin speeches of swaying lawmakers protesting undying affection for each other as the contents of desks were thrown around the chamber—all in good fun. Sometimes a member was knocked senseless by a flying missile.

The lads went home after the two houses were adjourned sine die, richer than when they came.

There were other rings in the legislature besides Tweed's. Next in political importance to the Tweed Ring was the gang ruling Brooklyn, the nation's third most populous city, proudly denominated the City of Churches in school-books. The Brooklyn Ring was nominally Democratic. When the 1870 legislative session closed, the Ring no longer feared journalistic critics at home, for all had been silenced. As the New Year dawned the Ring bought a Republican daily and threatened to make it the Democratic party's organ if the Ring's remaining newspaper foe, the Brooklyn *Eagle*, Democratic in politics, did not sell its property. The *Eagle* sold. In discussing this civic tragedy, the *Tribune* said: "The *Eagle* has gone into the hands of the Democratic ring and will henceforth seek to shield from exposure and punishment the rascalities which have brought so many of the lesser lights of the Brooklyn democracy to the doors of state prison." Said the *Times*, five days later:

The Democratic ring of Kings County has had for years the absolute control of the political machinery which governs Brooklyn. . . . The real governors of Brooklyn are its contractors. Any bill they want is put through the legislature, and they paid $80,000 for one bill last winter. When the Brooklyn *Eagle* fought the ring, the ring purchased the Brooklyn *Union* and threatened Mr. Van Anden, the proprietor of the *Eagle*, with an opposition Democratic paper. Mr. Van Anden did not feel called upon to risk so great a property in such a contest, and offered to sell the *Eagle* to the ring for $300,000. The offer was accepted, and thus the ring captured and silenced the Democratic organ.

There was a sneak-thief note in the Brooklyn Ring. It even stole outright from the city's poor, and in their name. Its appropriation for the poor of Brooklyn in 1870 was more than four times the amount appropriated in 1861 when nearly 3 per cent of the population, including some 7,786 wives and children of soldiers at the front, were on the relief rolls. In 1861, $131,078 was allocated to the poor of Brooklyn; in 1870, this sum was increased to $550,000. How much of this went into the pockets of politicians could not be estimated, but the constantly rising ratio in the moneys for institutional and outdoor relief madly outran the increase in population.

5

CORRUPTION'S LAST LINE OF DEFENSE

THE FIRST SATURDAY IN JUNE, 1870, BROUGHT OUT THE FIRST big crowd of the season to Central Park to see the school-boys playing baseball near the Sixth Avenue entrance. A reporter mingled with the throngs that viewed the sport from the surrounding heights. Keep-off-the-grass signs had not been invented. "The turnout of carriages of all descriptions, from the six-in-hand dray to the tiny barouche drawn by goats, was very large." The cheering sections comprised groups of lusty-lunged school-boys "to the number of 1,000 or more." And on the rocky heights, "a large number of ladies and gentlemen sat for hours watching the games." Some came on foot, others by stage and horse-car, and quite a few in their own carriages. There was considerable discussion in the cheering sections about "the singular railroad on stilts" which was still being tested. Less than three weeks before, a trial passenger train, consisting of two cars loaded with pig-iron, and twelve officials and employees of the West Side Elevated Railroad, crashed to the street when the supporting pillars gave way. All that saved the engine from following them was the long chain used in towing the train. What would happen if there were several trains using the road at one time? No honest man would have anything to do with such a railroad and only a corrupt legislature would permit any such thing. And the brazenness of the road's officials! They said no one was killed! Who would believe that? And there was chatter about the forthcoming visit of an Indian delegation, headed by Red Cloud, Chief of the Sioux Nation.

Every now and then, women spectators applied musk-scented handkerchiefs to their nostrils as offensive odors were wafted from the rocky eminence to the west. This was the largest rag-picker colony in the metropolis, and extended from Sixty-fifth to Seventieth streets, and from our present Central Park West to Columbus Avenue. Many called it the "village of slab shanties on the rocks." Few cross-streets north of Fifty-ninth Street, especially on the West Side, were cut through at this time; in their stead were peaceful lanes and old farm roads. In midafternoon the baseball nines had a real rival in the concert, which began promptly at three o'clock, when some four thousand assembled on the Mall, under the awnings around the musicians' stand, on the lawn, and in the arbor near the Casino. Until six o'clock chimed, "a constant stream of vehicles" passed the music lovers, and then up the Eastern Drive through the Park, to Harlem Lane, returning by the same route, "many of them stopping at the St. Vincent Hotel on the way back." It was the best day the boatmen on the big lake had that year, every row-boat being in constant use.

Ten days later the Sioux arrived. Among Red Cloud's followers was Red Dog, one of the last of the great orators of this fighting race. When these two chiefs and eighteen of their braves strode upon the platform of Cooper Union, they were welcomed by Peter Cooper, head of the institution he had founded for the education of workers in the sciences and the arts. It was a hot and stuffy June day, but the auditorium was filled to capacity, for it was not every day one could see Red Cloud wearing a high-crowned stovepipe hat such as Lincoln had worn when he spoke from the same platform. Many would have preferred to have seen Red Cloud wearing eagle feathers and beaded jacket instead of his paleface costume, but the braves looked picturesque enough. Their incongruous garb was forgotten when their top-hatted chief rose to speak. His words called for an interpreter, but not his emotions. Nor was an interpreter needed to tell the rapt audience when Red Cloud mentioned the Great Spirit, for his hands were uplifted, his eyes gazed heavenward, and in his voice was reverence unmistakable.

The Indians asked that the whites send just men to them as Indian agents, and that the Indians be no longer deceived, plundered, and betrayed. The whole race was being punished for the crimes committed by frontier Indians "who had been corrupted and demoralized by the white man's whiskey." Then Red Cloud added appealingly: "You have children. So have we. We want to rear our children well and ask you to help us in doing so."

Now it was Red Dog's turn. He was no longer young; his waistline was a few inches more than he liked. But the voice, the gestures, and the words were youth eternal and "would have satisfied Demosthenes himself"—to borrow a phrase from one at the press table. Seeing that the interpreter was alert, Red Dog gathered his blanket around him and said:

I have but a few words to say to you, my friends. When the Great Spirit raised us, he raised us with good men for counselors, and he raised you with good men for counselors. But yours are all the time getting bad while ours remain good. These are my young men. I am their chief. Look among them and see if you can find any among them who are rich. They are poor because they are all honest. Whenever I call my young men together in council, they listen to what I say.

When the Great Father first sent out men to our people, I was poor and thin. Now I am large and stout and fat. It is because so many liars have been sent out there—and I have been stuffed full with their lies.

I know all of you are men of sense and men of respect, and

I therefore ask you confidently that when men are sent out to our country, they shall be righteous men and just men, and will not do us harm.

I don't want any more men sent out there who are so poor that they think only of filling their pockets. We want those who will help to protect us on our reservations, and save us from those who are viciously disposed toward us.

Close to Cooper on the platform sat Nathaniel Sands, his Republican-reformer guide. Sands could have told him that Red Dog's moralizing was worthy of savages and simpletons alone.

Yet Red Dog's speech, with equal pertinency and with little change, could have been addressed by any white man in the audience to the Tammany braves and their Republican and reformer allies in the metropolis, or to the Grant administration in Washington—and with like effect.

After the Sioux warriors had returned to their own helpless people, a Tammany brave's new gambling house at Saratoga became the center of popular interest. It was called John Morrissey's club-house, and the *Times* described it as "the chief point of attraction to all new-comers." There was no gambling until noon, and for two hours each morning Morrissey admitted sight-seers; at any hour, non-gambling friends of the politician could enjoy themselves in the whist parlor at an innocent game of this forerunner of bridge. Each room boasted an ample sideboard, generously provided with all kinds of wine. All drinks were free, and no patron or visitor had to call a second time for a glass of sherry or a magnum of champagne, for there were thirty colored servants in constant attendance. Sumptuous beyond the dreams of the average gambler were the furnishings, on which Morrissey had spent $100,000. Carpets of rich pile covered the floors. Curtains of lace, silk, and damask, in soft greens and reds, draped massive windows. Huge French mirrors adorned the tapestried walls. All the furniture had been fashioned from fine-grained walnut by masters of cabinetry under Morrissey's direction. He knew the wood then in vogue, but to the consternation of the artisans, he insisted that his monogram be carved deeply on each piece wherever

The ancient device of exchanging doles for votes was satirized by Nast in *Harper's Weekly*, January 14, 1871, with the above portrayal of the Boss and Sweeny as characters in a Christmas pantomime. Says Tweed to Sweeny: "Let's blind them with this, and then take some more."

possible, and then had each "J. M." picked out in gold leaf. Another of Morrissey's orders was to adorn every piece of furniture with a tiger's head. Morrissey might fight Tweed, but he was loyal to Tammany. A tiger's head of massive gold, with eyes of flawless rubies, hung from Morrissey's heavy gold watch-chain.

This tiger charm was the emblem of the exclusive Americus Club which had its humble beginning in 1857 among some young workers in the old Seventh Ward when its boundaries were the East River, Catherine Street, East Broadway, and Division Street. This was Tweed's old bailiwick, and Americus, or Big Six, was the name of the neighborhood volunteer fire-engine company. Tweed had given the name Americus, in honor of the navigator, to the company of volunteer red shirts which gave him his start in politics; also its emblem, the Bengal tiger's head. He had no hand in launching the Americus Club. Its original initiation fee consisted of nothing more than a reputation for good fellowship and a willingness to share the expense of hiring a small sailboat occasionally for a week-end on the beach at Greenwich, Connecticut, where the fishing and swimming were both dependable. Tweed was well off when he joined the club in 1866. He made the initiation fee $1,000 and encouraged the wearing of such charms as we have seen on Morrissey. These cost $2,000. All the upper crust of Tweed's followers were members of the Americus Club in 1870, Democrats and Republicans alike. Nast was now employing the tiger in his anti-Ring cartoons as the symbol of Tammany Hall. His first use of the tiger was toward the end of 1869, but Tweed had made it the Tammany emblem in the summer of 1868 prior to the Democratic State Convention which nominated Hoffman for governor. All Tammany delegates to this convention wore badges adorned with tiger's heads as distinguishing marks.

Games of chance for stakes as high as those wagered at Morrissey's Saratoga club-house were common at the Americus Club. Morrissey no longer visited the Americus Club lest his presence lead some to conclude he had capitulated to Tweed. But neither Morrissey's absence, nor his forthright opposition, gave Tweed considerable concern. He was confident of his strength. Morrissey and his associates might alienate some, and Tilden and his kind others; but Tweed staked his all on the city's ignorant voters whose poverty was well-nigh incredible. It was so extreme that when journalists described it they either quoted health-department officials or policemen, or named the officials who accompanied them on their rounds of the Five Points and other slum sections of the city.

These slum dwellers were Tweed's Old Guard.

6

THE ARISTOCRACY OF THE LOWLY

THE FEDERAL CENSUS OF 1870 PUT THE POPULATION OF NEW York City at 942,292. Of this number, 419,094 were born abroad, chiefly in Ireland and Germany, with the Irish predominating. The alien element represented a little more than 44 per cent of the total number of inhabitants. This ratio did not hold at the ballot-box, where the naturalized voters were outnumbered three to one. But voters of Irish and German descent, together with naturalized Germans and Irish, constituted about half of the electors.

At least 55 per cent of the population, or 518,260, lived in the slums and were divided among themselves on questions of race and creed. They brought these hatreds from Europe, and other hatreds were engendered here by the political parties of proscription, the Anti-Masonic and the Native American. The latter, called the Know Nothing party, because its oathbound members when asked about it responded that they knew nothing, was too good a thing for the politicians to let die, and it has thriven all through the years under one name or another, changing its hates and its methods to suit the prevailing mob spirit, whether spontaneous or engendered. Know Nothings, also styled the Dark Lantern party, proscribed all foreign-born, regardless of faith, and all Roman Catholics, regardless of nativity.

On these hatreds born of race and creed and political chicane Tweed placed his greatest reliance. Here again, he was blazing the trail for other machine leaders the country over. The newspapers he controlled might fail him, the reform element represented by the Citizens' Association which he had bribed might see the light, and even some of the Democratic and Republican leaders on whom he depended for a trick or two on Election Day might desert him. But still there remained the ignorant poor who hated each other because they worshiped differently, or came from different countries, or from different parts of the same nation.

"This population," said Boss Tweed, "is too hopelessly split up into races and factions to govern it under universal suffrage, except by the bribery of patronage, or corruption."

No one familiar with New York, or any other large city, before or since Tweed's day, can honestly challenge the tragic truth of Tweed's cynical dictum. Tweed, however, did not go far enough. The decay in our body politic was not due directly to the purchasable illiterate vote created by manhood suffrage, or to factionalism born of racial or religious bigotry, but to the gradual withdrawal of good men, albeit short-sighted, from the political field before the advancing hordes of the enfranchised prolétaires. Some one had to lead, and the knave and demagogue took over. To particularize, let us consider Tweed's own state. The New York state constitutional convention of 1821 lifted the property qualification from suffrage, thus paving the way for ballot-box stuffing, assaults on voters at the polls, wholesale stealing of votes, and like brazen offenses against the franchise. Hitherto, the only systematic violation, or rather evasion, of the election law had been in New York City where men clubbed together to evade the property qualification. Through nominal ownership of a house and lot, they became electors, or to borrow an old-world phrase, fagot voters.

Only one election theft marred this era of honest voting. This was in 1792, when John Jay, chief justice of the United

States Supreme Court, was robbed of the governorship after defeating George Clinton for reëlection by a majority of nearly four hundred votes. Under color of law, the Clintonian majority in the Board of Canvassers rejected the ballots from Clinton, Tioga, and Otsego counties, where Jay had decisive and unchallenged majorities, thereby showing a fictive majority of 108 for Clinton; to prevent a recount, they burned the rejected ballots. A threat of civil war prevented any other violation of the ballot-box in the early days. The first repeating occurred in 1827, in Tweed's native city. One group of hired repeaters, consisting of five mere youths, the eldest nineteen, and a carter, drove to six polling places, where all six voted—which is one way of making thirty-six votes out of one. This was the beginning of the general debauchery of the franchise.

The first legislative corruption was committed in 1803 by applicants for a charter for the New York State Bank, in Albany, who let some legislators subscribe for shares below par with the assurance that the stock would go above par with the granting of the charter. Two years later, coarser methods were used by sponsors of the Merchants' Bank of New York City who obtained a charter by outright bribery. Their agent in the upper house, Ebenezer Purdy, resigned from the senate to avoid expulsion for bribery. There was no act under which he could be prosecuted, for the framers of our first laws did not imagine mercenaries would be elected to office in the Republic which was born of sacrifice and devotion. Thereafter, it was a rare bank charter or other valuable grant that emerged from the legislature without a price being paid. The orgy of graft was getting a good start.

Nor were venal judges a product of manhood suffrage. In the constitutional convention of 1821, Peter R. Livingston posed "whether it is not the case that when a man of any

political standing has had a suit depending at a circuit court,
he has not consulted with his counsel to know what judge
was to preside at the circuit; and whether he has not been
frequently told that a political judge was to preside, and it
would not do to let the cause come on." The judges of the
pre-manhood suffrage days were not elected—all were appointed. But corrupt jurists existed long before our Republic,
and were part of the glory that was Greece and the grandeur
that was Rome. Four centuries before the Christian era,
Aristophanes stung them with his waggish wasps as he
lashed out at other unworthy public servants of his day, who
differed from those of the decade with which we are concerned only in method and degree. Tweed, too, had his
demagogic spouters, and he had no doubt of carrying the
impending election as he had carried others—with voters
drawn from the major half of the metropolitan population.

This major half eked out a hand-to-mouth existence. These
crust-hunters—it would be mockery to call them bread-
winners—were the unskilled workers and the unfortunate
who form the permanent population of urban limbos; temporarily sharing their lot were master craftsmen and skilled
laborers cast by hard times into the town's hovels. Fully one-
third, perhaps one-half, of all mechanics in New York City
were unemployed. This condition was general in all large
towns throughout the country.

The panic of 1873 was in the making.

The healthiest crust-hunters lived in shanties clustered on
the sparsely settled rocky sections and other poor land north
of Fifty-ninth Street, and along the water-front. The upper
part of the western side of Manhattan Island was a series of
shanty hamlets broken by a few country-seats, some small
farms, and the old villages of Bloomingdale and Manhattanville. In 1870 the city had another attack of growing pains,
called the uptown movement, and many shanty villages were

to vanish by the end of the decade. Seven shanties, clustered together, were demolished on a Sunday, while their late occupants watched helplessly. But no great harm was done, as the owners of the land, who were preparing to build an apartment-house on the site, had repeatedly warned the squatters to move, and they decided to hold out till the last minute. These seven shanties were "at Tenth Avenue and Seventy-ninth Street, overlooking the Hudson." In one of them lived John Bhernes, his wife, and their five children. But John Bhernes was not poor. He was a landlord, and had built six other shanties on the same parcel of land, and his six tenants paid him rent. This is the only record of a shanty landlord we have encountered. That it was at least a rare occurrence is indicated by the neighborhood name for these shanties—Bhernesville.

Many shanty dwellers raised vegetables, and, because every penny counted, most of them did not buy milk but kept goats on the land they held through tolerance of its owners. Those who considered their neighbors staked the goats. But so many goats roamed at large, and foraged in gardens, that the Board of Aldermen on April 2, 1874, passed the following ordinance:

"No goat shall be at large in any part of the streets, avenues, lanes, alleys, piers, wharves, or public places in the City of New York under penalty of $3 for every such goat which shall be found at large, to be paid by the owner or person having charge, care, or keeping thereof."

Alderman John J. Morris, a West-Side grocer, in sponsoring the ordinance, told his colleagues that "a goat can destroy $500 worth of shrubbery in an afternoon." Alderman George Koch, a merry German furniture merchant, won a laugh when he said: "I move that it be referred to the committee on reform."

After having their little fun, the aldermen unanimously

adopted the ordinance which was patterned on one relating to swine and cattle. But cattle received special privileges denied to swine and goats. Cows, by special act, were permitted at any hour of the day or night on Forty-second Street, from river to river.

There were shanties on some of the main thoroughfares. There were several on Broadway, from its junction with Sixth Avenue at Thirty-third Street, northward to what is now Columbus Circle. This stretch of Broadway was lined chiefly with frame dwellings, two-story brick houses, stables, a factory, liquor shops, and notion stores. These Broadway shanties were ordered vacated on May 1, 1873, when the old thoroughfare was widened.

The largest of the shanty colonies was the rag-pickers' "village of slab shanties on the rocks" which we met earlier. These city shanties were the crudest form of permanent habitation. A sturdy boy could build one. He required only a hammer and saw, a few nails, some old boxes or discarded wood of any sort, scraps of tin for the flat roof, and a length or two of stovepipe for a chimney. They seldom exceeded eight feet in height, and varied in size from a spacious rambling affair sheltering a large family comfortably to a bachelor's home with but room enough for a cot or shake-down, a chair or two, or boxes that served as seats.

Some shanties were the homes of carefree workers, unskilled laborers exclusively, who preferred to put the money it would take to rent a furnished room into cheap whiskey. Self-respecting shanty dwellers avoided the abodes of these improvident ones. Other single men, of industrious habits, merely down on their luck, also built shanties.

There was a group of bachelor-laborer shanties "on the rocks at Fourth Avenue and Seventy-eighth Street." In one of the shanties lived Philip Olwell, and near-by, in another hut, James Orr kept bachelor hall. They were good friends and two-fisted drinkers. One night Olwell invited Orr to his shack for a drink. Olwell had but one chair, and it lacked a back. But there was a cot, which served as a seat for the host. The only other furnishings were a kerosene lantern and a small stove. Behind the stove, the kindling was piled. Alongside, resting against the wall, was a hatchet.

As the night wore on Olwell and Orr became shouting drunk. Even shanty dwellers require quiet to sleep, and neighbors "on the rocks" looked for a policeman. The officer found the cot wrecked, the chair in pieces, the stove overturned, the hatchet bloodstained, Olwell swaying and spluttering unintelligibly, and Orr lifeless on the floor.

The great part of the hard drinking among the poor was done by single men and women. This was especially true in the tenements. But among the rag-pickers, drinking was practically unknown. These were too occupied with their labor, which called for long hours of tramping through the city's streets. And they were all church-goers.

These rag-pickers, mostly German and Irish, constituted the aristocracy of the lowly. There were more than three thousand engaged in this humble work. The majority were men with families. Widows also managed to keep their families together with no equipment other than a bag and a long-handled poker to fathom the mysteries of garbage-cans and ash-barrels and the nondescript piles in the gutters. A few spinsters supported themselves by rag-picking. Six young women rag-pickers shared two rooms—the entire top floor—of a vile Baxter Street tenement. They had their choice between rag-picking and prostitution, for there was no work to be had—factories were idle and servant-girls were a drug on the market. Any stray piece of paper, for paper then was made of rag, was thrust into bags with odds and ends of tattered garments and other rags, bottles and broken glass, scraps of metal, bones, fat, cinders, lumps of coal, bits of wood, discarded shoes. Some of these shoes provided covering for the rag-picker and his family; others were sold to cobblers in the slums who repaired them to sell to those unable to buy new ones. Shoes too far gone for wear went into the woodpile, for old leather gives a steady heat.

Many blocks in Manhattan, south of Houston Street, were locally known as Bone Alley or Rag-pickers' Row. The most northern Rag-pickers' Row—as distinguished from a shanty settlement—was on West Thirty-eighth Street, between Eleventh Avenue and the Hudson; Twelfth Avenue at this point was then part of the river. This Rag-pickers' Row had once been charming wooden cottages. Rags were hung out to dry on what remained of the once tidy picket-fences. Sometimes rag-pickers would congregate in shacks in the rear of a tenement or stable. These were the Bone Alleys. The last Bone Alley on Manhattan Island was on the south side of East Thirteenth Street, between Avenues B and C. It gave up the ghost at the turn of the century.

Down in the slums in the older part of the city were numerous old houses of substantial brick and stone where dwelt families whose names are part of our national heritage. Shortly after the close of the Civil War, rag-pickers took possession of many of these old dwellings, which were all of simple Colonial design. One rag shop had been the home of President Monroe. It stood on the northwest corner of Prince and Lafayette streets, and an Italian junkman occupied the Monroe home throughout the administration of Calvin Coolidge.

But in the seventies it was a rare Italian who lived north of Canal Street, the northern boundary of the Five Points and three streets south of the Monroe house. The first sizable Italian settlement was on Baxter Street. In 1870 none had invaded the street just to the east, Mulberry, which was to become the heart of the first real Italian colony in the United

States. Behind a squalid tenement at 85 Mulberry stood another of weather-worn clapboards, rickety and seemingly
ready to fall.

A tenement in Mulberry Street, New York
Harper's Weekly, September 13, 1873.

From this rear tenement, twice daily, Patrick Connor,
stoop-shouldered and cheery, fared forth on his humble
rounds of street and alley, wharf and anywhere else likely

to produce a trifle for the capacious burlap bag that reached almost to the end of his ragged coat-tails. After his work was done, a wild flower adorned his lapel. No small boy ever sneaked after Paddy Connor and tugged his coat-tails or the bag slung over his shoulder. Those who knew him respected him and greeted him warmly, and the mischief-minded who did not, gave him a wide berth, for two mongrel dogs, his inseparable companions, trotted at his heels. It was said that Connor had been a schoolmaster in his younger days. This may have had no other basis than his gentle voice, kindly ways, and ready wit. Connor never spoke of his past. He was called eccentric. That was probably because he defined rag-pickers as followers of a noble calling because "they rescued the things others would destroy." Or maybe it was because he delighted to talk of his little family.

"The dogs feed themselves, so I don't have to worry about them," said Connor to an inquiring stranger on the street. "But it's the mouths at home that give me no end of worry."

A journalist invited to Connor's home was received by the old man in his Sunday best and then was introduced to the family.

"I have eight mouths just now to fill besides my own, for you must remember the dogs feed themselves," said Connor.

These dependents were two squirrels, four canaries, a parrot, and a cat.

"The cat protects the others from the rats," Connor explained.

The cat, parrot, canaries, squirrels, dogs, and Connor all lived in one room. This was their home. It was all Connor could afford.

The slum-dwelling rag-pickers, like Paddy Connor, made two rounds daily, one starting at dawn, another in the late forenoon. They stowed iron and bones in the cellar; but the more valuable stock, such as rags, bottles, brass, copper, and lead were kept under beds and chairs, in cupboards and corners, in any bit of available space. In summer, fireplaces were pressed into service, especially for the fat, which was always kept in a covered metal container to save it from the rats. The soap-fat man called daily with his cart; but the rags and junk, a phrase embracing everything but fat, were lugged weekly to the nearest junkman.

These humble toilers who, in their working hours, resembled animated scarecrows, enjoyed the respect of the community. They were a devout lot whose major material objective was to give their children the chance denied them, or the chance they had lost. In a day when the unskilled worker from foreign shores could neither read nor write, and sent his children out to toil at an early age as a matter of course, these rag-pickers were exceptions, as shown in this newspaper excerpt: "The children invariably go to school. Many of the parents can read and write. All go to church. Some of them are Catholic and some are Protestant, the latter mostly Germans."

If a little of the virtues of these rag-pickers could have been shared with their rulers, there would have been less concern and fewer protests among thoughtful New Yorkers as the campaign of 1870 approached.

7

THE DREGS AT THE TOP

THE ONLY PROTESTS IN THE CAMPAIGN OF 1870 CAME FROM Republicans, not against Tammany, but their own leaders, who took orders from the Tweed Ring. Under the caption, "The Dregs at the Top," a *Times* editorial spoke of "the excess of corrupt and incompetent leadership with which the Republican party in this city is afflicted," of "the unprincipled traders in politics who make a merchandise of the party they impudently pretend to manage, and render all its interests subordinate to their aggrandizement." The Republican state chairman was Alonzo B. Cornell, son of the founder of Cornell University, later governor of New York and an honest one. The Democratic state chairman was Tilden, who said of Cornell: ". . . he was running errands for some branch of the Ring, and serving around the legislative halls for what are daintily termed counsel fees." Tilden shouted the charge when the all-powerful Ring was no more. Cornell might have truthfully replied that Tilden was the Ring's state chairman and did not dare raise his voice against it until it was toppling.

The corrupt bipartizan alliance was denounced by Republican journals throughout the North, and some of them proposed that the New York State Republican organization be severed from the rest of the party. They argued that the corruption in New York City, for which the Democratic machine was directly responsible, could not have endured if the Republican organization had not tolerated it. At this time, Tweed owned outright fifty-nine Republican leaders in New York City. They were his hired men. Some held public office by his grace; others he paid out of pocket.

By way of appeasing their critical partizans outside the state and silencing the attacks within, the machine permitted the election of the honest, outspoken General John Cochrane as head of the regular Republican organization in the city. Cochrane was the choice of Greeley and other decent Republicans who commanded a majority in the organization. Cochrane and his fellow Greeleyites anticipated a row and were prepared to fight it out with the plug-ugly opposition, the Tammany Republicans. But Tweed passed the word that Cochrane's election was to go through without a hitch, and to avert a possible riot on the night of the balloting, Tweed had one hundred policemen garrisoned ostentatiously in the United States Internal Revenue Office, adjoining the Republican headquarters at Broadway and Twenty-second Street. For there was no telling what some of the lads might do if a handful of them got fighting drunk. Cochrane, who had commanded a brigade in the Army of the Potomac, had a few shoulder-hitters of his own on tap, and police or no police, the meeting would not be taken over by the minority without a desperate rough-and-tumble.

The election of Cochrane was a real concession. He had alienated the Republican leaders throughout the nation by denouncing them as "a medley of trading, scurvy politicians" at the Cleveland convention of Independent Republicans which nominated him for Vice-President on the ticket headed by John C. Frémont. Both later withdrew in favor of Lincoln. In the six years that had since elapsed, Cochrane frequently repeated his opinion, with variations. His unswerving devotion to Greeley made Cochrane objectionable to both the Democratic and Republican machines, which felt the editor's barbs from time to time. Greeley and Cochrane were alike dangerous: they were reformers who let windmills alone.

But the Republican machine leaders were not dependent on the regular organization in New York City, for they had

General John Cochrane
Leslie's Weekly, November 16, 1872.

the powerful faction, headed by Thomas Murphy and called the Twenty-third Street organization because of its address. Murphy's group, flourishing since the Civil War, supported Roscoe Conkling, the state's senior Senator, in his struggle for party control with Reuben E. Fenton, junior United States Senator and former governor. Murphy was a wealthy

hat manufacturer—he was later to be beggared by politics—
and contributed generously from his own purse toward
maintaining his organization. Greeley and his adherents
championed Fenton.

Some weeks after the machine had extended the olive-
branch, the fight for party control broke out anew when
Grant sent to the Senate the nomination of Murphy as collector of the Port of New York. The subsequent explanation
of Senator William M. Stewart of Nevada, that Murphy had
made himself so serviceable to Grant in showing him the
roads around Long Branch that the appointment came as a
reward, is at least naïve. The appointment was a direct blow
at Fenton, and so designed. Fenton and Murphy were enemies. Murphy's organization had opposed Fenton's reëlection as governor in 1866, adopting resolutions in favor of
Tweed's man, Hoffman. Murphy nearly did the trick, for
Hoffman lost by only 13,789, in a total vote of 718,841.
Murphy was a state senator at the time, elected on a straight
Republican ticket.

Murphy's appointment roused a storm of protest in the
nation's press. The *Commercial Advertiser* alone defended
it in New York. The *Times* characterized this journal as
"chiefly remarkable for its corrupt politics and atrocious
grammar," and said that "the President has taken a step
which his enemies will exult over and his friends deplore."
The *Tribune* observed that Murphy did not "honestly belong
to any wing of the Republican party," and its managing editor, Whitelaw Reid, wrote to John Bigelow: "There is an
utter surrender of the civil service to the coarsest use by the
coarsest men. Mr. Grinnell goes out of the Custom-House
to make room for Mr. Murphy."

Fenton held up Murphy's appointment until Conkling,
prompted by Senator Stewart, an adviser of Grant, insisted
on a vote on July 11. Two of Murphy's special pleaders were

Chester A. Arthur, later President of the United States, and Charles J. Folger, also a Republican, who had been elected an associate judge of the Court of Appeals on May 17, 1870, under the new judiciary article of the New York Constitution. It was an unusual election in New York City, for in addition to the customary stealing, a wholesale fraud was perpetrated on the eleven hundred Negro voters of the metropolis. As each of the eleven hundred presented himself at the polls, he was told he had already voted! Several score of the Negroes foolishly protested. They were promptly thrown into jail for attempted repeating and kept there till the polls closed. What had happened was that five hundred white repeaters had voted as Negroes the moment the polls opened. They did not even bother to use burnt cork.

When Conkling pressed for a vote on the Murphy appointment, Fenton knew his leadership was at stake. Fenton had made no secret of his presidential ambition, which did not enhance his popularity with Grant, and it was patent to all that Conkling had been selected by the administration to destroy Fenton.

In striving to block the appointment, Fenton assailed Murphy, Arthur, and Folger. He charged Folger with owing his elevation to the Court of Appeals to Murphy's corrupt influence with Tammany. He said Murphy "was able to borrow, of Tammany's 50,000 fraudulent votes, 4,000 for Folger in the Sixth, Eighth, and Twenty-first wards." Next he produced a certified copy of a deed disclosing Murphy as a partner in a real-estate flyer with three members of the Tweed Ring, Sweeny, Connolly, and Tweed himself. As for Arthur, Fenton pointed out that he had defended Murphy when the hat manufacturer was accused of corruption in war contracts, and he was now counsel to the New York City Tax Commission through Murphy's influence with Tammany.

When Fenton finished, Conkling was recognized. Fenton

had struck hard blows, but all were fair. Conkling was intoxicated by his rôle as the administration spokesman. To this may be attributed, in all charity, the peroration of his reply—the most wanton personal attack Congress had known. Fenton had lived in Chautauqua since his birth. He first practised law but turned merchant while still young. He enjoyed the esteem of his neighbors, who successively elected him to local office and to the lower house of Congress. He was serving his eighth year as a Representative when chosen governor. As Conkling was ready to strike foully at his colleague, he walked down the aisle to Fenton's desk and declaimed: "It is true that Murphy is a mechanic, a hatter by trade; that he worked at his trade in Albany supporting an aged father and mother and crippled brother."

Fenton had not accused Murphy of neglecting his parents or a crippled brother. What he did say was summed up by the Civil Service Commission more than a year later when it reported that no port collector was more destitute of fit qualifications for the office than Murphy. Conkling paused dramatically after praising Murphy as a son and brother. Then he drew a red-taped document from an inside pocket, thrust it accusingly at Fenton and exclaimed: "And while thus engaged, another visited Albany and played a very different rôle, the particulars of which I will not relate except at the special request of my colleague."

When this treacherous blow was struck, Fenton buried his face in his hands as if to shut out the long-forgotten tragedy Conkling conjured up—his arrest as a young man on suspicion of having stolen $12,000 intrusted to him for deposit in an Albany bank. Fenton had lost the money. Conkling had the record of the case, which showed that Fenton had been acquitted of the charge. As a lawyer, Conkling knew he could not have referred to Fenton's misfortune so basely, without penalty, save on a legislative floor.

A vote was taken after Conkling finished. Many senators declined to vote; only three voted against confirmation. But Greeley, Reid, and other New York Republicans continued their fight against the unfit Murphy and forced him out at the end of eighteen months.

8

PICKPOCKETS AND THIEVES RULE
ONE CONVENTION, BRIBERS ANOTHER

THE SPECTACLE OF A PRESIDENT USING HIS INFLUENCE ON behalf of a faction at a party convention outside of his own state, and a not overscrupulous faction at that, was presented when the New York Republicans met in Saratoga toward the end of the summer of 1870 to choose a state ticket. Conkling was there, armed with a personal letter from Grant urging him to attend as a delegate. Accompanied by Murphy, Conkling called on delegates and told them support for Fenton was opposition to Grant, backing up his declaration with Grant's epistolary bludgeon. To Federal office-holders Grant's letter meant: "Vote with Conkling or lose your job." Fenton men without office were offered soft berths and easy money to desert their leader. To the knowing ones, the letter spelled more than an interest in the struggle for party control in New York: it was Grant's declaration of war on all who stood in the way of his renomination at the end of the term.

The first test of strength was on the election of temporary chairman. George William Curtis, editor of *Harper's Weekly* and Conkling's choice, won, and Conkling proceeded to make himself the party boss in the state. Conkling did not displace Fenton without a welter of double-crossing. His lieutenants had assured Greeley that Conkling favored him for governor. Greeley coveted the nomination and was the

popular choice. Conkling also promised Curtis to nominate
him for governor. Curtis had many personal followers in the
convention. But Conkling himself favored neither Curtis nor
Greeley. He was for the Grant administration's candidate,
General Stewart L. Woodford, of Brooklyn, lieutenant-
governor under Fenton in his second term. Woodford was
nominated on the third ballot.

The first ballot showed Woodford with a slight lead. The
vote stood: Woodford, 153; Greeley, 143; Curtis, 104½. The
contest then narrowed itself down to Greeley and Woodford. Curtis was eliminated before he started because he was
uncontrollable, as was Greeley. Both were beyond the dictation of any party boss; Greeley, if elected governor, would
be a formidable contender for the presidency.

On the second ballot Greeley lost four votes and Curtis
seventeen. A few minutes later, Fenton's leadership vanished
when the third ballot showed Woodford nominated with
more than sixty votes in excess of the required majority. The
tally stood: Woodford, 258; Greeley, 105½; Curtis, 20.

The most surprised man was Woodford, who had offered
to retire in favor of his friend, Greeley. The Fenton delegates voted solidly for Greeley. Fenton's first choice was
Marshall O. Roberts, one of the country's richest men, a
merchant prince, owner of railroads and steamships. Roberts
had anticipated that Conkling, with the patronage of the
Grant administration at his disposal, would control the convention, and wrote the *Tribune* that he would not accept the
nomination. Fenton then cast his lot with Greeley. If Conkling's aides had been sincere when they promised Greeley
the support of their chief, Greeley would have been named
for governor on the first ballot, for Fenton was loyal throughout. Likewise, if Conkling had not been false to Curtis, he
would have been nominated. Two years later, Greeley

charged "that some of our delegates were bought out of our hands." The Conkling faction were the purchasers.

Within a fortnight after the Republicans named their ticket, the Democrats met in Rochester. It was a convention to delight Maître François Villon. Its political side was truthfully summed up by a metropolitan journalist who telegraphed his paper on September 21: "Tammany is supreme and the delegates assembled to register its decrees. Mr. Tweed nodded and they obeyed."

Tweed's program was carried through without a hitch, Governor Hoffman again heading the ticket. Two years more and Tweed envisioned him as a candidate for President.

Tilden presided over this convention, by grace of Tweed. Tilden was a patient, quiet enemy. His secret allies, the Young Democracy, were accused by Tammany with being host to the largest, boldest, and rowdiest gang of pickpockets and all-around thieves that ever attended a convention. These light-fingered gentry provided the only diversion in what was otherwise a cut-and-dried affair. The Young Democracy countered that the thieves had been brought to Rochester by Tammany. They plied their trade openly and brazenly. One victim was Mayor John Lutes, of Rochester. Another was Tilden. His watch was snatched as he was leaving the hall after the convention adjourned. Of course, he did not get it back. These thieves were no respecters of persons.

When the New York City delegates talked of remaining in Rochester overnight, the police urged them to leave before sundown, saying they were numerically unable to protect either the delegates or the people of Rochester from the thieves. The police were prepared for an ordinary invasion of criminals, but not for a regiment of well-armed desperadoes. The proprietor of the Osburn House, where many of the delegates—and thieves—lodged, complained that his hotel and his guests had been robbed and pillaged to the amount of fifteen thousand dollars, which the Democratic State Committee repaid.

The Democratic managers heeded the plea, and ordered all delegates to return home at once. The downstate delegates and their guests left on two Erie trains. The thieves went with them and boldly helped themselves to the delegates' liquor. This was merely a start. The well-armed crooks were in complete control of the train. As men and women alighted at way-stations, the thieves held them up and, at pistol point, took watches, pins, chains, charms, rings, necklaces, and bracelets. Women with silk lace shawls, worth one hundred dollars and more, lost these with their trinkets. Ticket-agents along the line telegraphed to Jersey City, the southern terminus of the road. As the trains approached Jersey City the crooks held up many delegates, rifling their pockets and stealing their jewelry.

Two squads of police met the trains. They took thirty-five prisoners, most of whom had pistols and revolvers. A score or so had bracelets, necklaces, or other pieces of feminine jewelry. One prisoner truthfully described himself as Alexander Frear, Tweed's spokesman in the state assembly, and Commissioner of Charities and Correction in the metropolis. Frear was tossed into a cell as unceremoniously as the rest.

Frear spent several hours in jail before friends obtained his release. He was distressed at the newspaper reports of his arrest which implied that he was a thief, and denied he had been arrested. The press nailed this untruth by publishing the text of the court order releasing him. Of the remaining thirty-four, twenty-nine were discharged the following morning.

Tilden lost more than his watch at the convention; he lost considerable esteem. Republican journals pilloried him for presiding over the gathering. Said the *Times*:

We know that Tilden is an honest man himself—but was an honest man ever before associated with such scamps? When an old lawyer of his standing gets up at a political convention and warns us against the Prussian military system and the French Cæsarism, and says nothing of Tammany Hall—is shocked by King Wilhelm and Bismarck, and isn't at all troubled by Tweed, or Sweeny, or O'Brien, or Barnard, or Hoffman—it is evident that honest men must find some other way of political salvation than the Democracy can offer us.

This was sound advice. But where could honest men turn? Not to the Republican party, for its state convention was as silent as Tilden and the Democratic convention on the subject of the Ring. Had any one tried to write an anti-Tweed plank into the Republican platform, he would have been outvoted. Or if he shamed the delegates, including those on the Tweed pay-roll, into adopting a plank, it would have resembled the pitiful straddle of the Republicans on the Franco-German War. This plank—the Democrats had one not unlike it—follows:

"Resolved, that the Republicans of the United States of America send congratulations to the United States of Germany, and heartily join with our German brethren in rejoicing at the righteous victories of the fatherland, and fondly trust that the brave people who have given a republic to France may soon establish free institutions in their own country."

9

JOHN JACOB ASTOR AIDS THE LOOTERS

AFTER THE ROCHESTER AND SARATOGA CONVENTIONS, THE politicians set up their thimblerig stand in the metropolis. Mayor Hall, as had been expected, was renominated by the Democrats; the Republican bosses, mostly Tweed men, did the unexpected by fusing with independent Democrats and naming an honest Democrat we have met earlier, Judge Ledwith. With this sop to decency, the Republican sham was complete. In Cochrane, they had a man of spotless reputation for leader, and his counterpart in their mayoralty nominee. But the medley of trading, scurvy politicians, to repeat Cochrane's phrase, were using a traditional device—putting up an honest man to knock him down.

The decent element now had an aggressive ally in the *Times,* which was hammering at the Tweed Ring in a devastating crescendo. Taylor, one of the three directors of the journal, and Tweed's partner, had died, and the fight against the Ring had been on since September 20, the eve of the Democratic State Convention. On that day Tweed was invited to write a treatise on the art of growing rich in as many years as can be counted on the fingers of one hand. As the *Times* put it:

You begin with nothing and in five or six years you can boast of your ten million. How is it done? We wish Mr. Tweed or Mr. Sweeny or some of their friends would tell us. The general public say there is foul play somewhere. They are under the impression that monstrous abuses of their funds, corrupt bargains with railroad sharpers, outrageous plots to swindle the general community, account for the vast fortunes heaped up by men who spring up like mushrooms.

The next day Louis John Jennings, an Englishman, author of these editorials, became more personal and spoke of Tweed's fortune as "acquired with the rapidity which exceeded the wildest story in the Arabian Nights. . . . The time will come when his biography will be pronounced more incredible than the life and adventures of Munchausen." A little later Jennings referred to corrupt Republican leaders without naming them. A few days elapsed and he named four, including Nathaniel Sands, the brains of the reform group.

Here was a note that Nast omitted from his cartoons—nonpartizanship. These cartoons were one-sided, being anti-Tammany and pro-Republican, and their efficacy was further weakened by the artist's wanton attacks on the Roman Catholic Church. Nast, himself German-born, also blundered in ridiculing the city's two largest groups, the Irish and the Germans. All this made it simple for the Ring's whisper squads to tell voters in the slums that the opposition to Tweed originated in racial and religious prejudices, and was a recrudescence of Know Nothingism. Of course, they said nothing of the past of Tweed's mayoralty candidate, for the Elegant Oakey had been a Know Nothing when it was profitable to be a dark-lantern boy, as he had been a Republican when it paid him to be one. The whisper squads told only what would aid their cause. They reminded Catholics that Nast was employed by the Harpers, and that Fletcher Harper, one of the firm, had been elected mayor on the Native American ticket in 1844 when his supporters paraded with "No Popery" banners. To the Protestant immigrants the whisper squads emphasized the Know Nothing proscription

of the foreign-born, irrespective of faith, in public office.
And wherever it would tell, the whisper squads recalled
Tweed's refusal to truckle with the Know Nothings at the

"A procession which it would afford the citizens of New York real
pleasure to see" is Artist Bellew's vision of the arrest of Tweed, Hall,
Connolly, Sweeny, et al. *Harper's Weekly*, September 9, 1871.

outset of his public career although it meant political preferment; and that Tweed, of native Protestant stock, would
have nothing to do with any form of bigotry, no matter what
it might cost him.

These things explained why *Harper's Weekly* was down on Tweed and his friends! But the far-seeing Jennings gave the whisper squads no such talking-point. However, they did not neglect Jennings: he had had to leave England for his lies about people; and as for his employer, George Jones, the publisher of the *Times,* he had broken with Tammany after it refused to let him rob the city with crooked advertising bills.

A few of these whisper squads are generally more effective with the ignorant than many flying squadrons of disciples of Demosthenes. They are an old invention but it was left to Tweed to make them a permanent adjunct of a machine.

Jones and Jennings went on with their battle, a little disheartened to find unselfish citizens of high integrity and noble purpose like Peter Cooper relying on Sands for guidance, and ever rising to his defense. But they were hoping for an awakening and did their little toward bringing it about. Jennings said that if the Citizens' Association is "willing to pay for it, no one will begrudge them the luxury; but ... the course of Mr. Sands's efforts seems to tend exclusively to promote the substantial welfare of the Sands family." Sands at this time—although only the Ring knew it then—had $75,000 of the taxpayers' money in his pocket, ostensibly for the sale of city bonds. Asked by Jennings to resign his office, Sands just sat tight.

The daily poundings of the *Times* were having their effect, and, while a party poll forecast a Democratic triumph in state and city, the Ring leaders campaigned as though their lives depended upon it. Fisk had his employees electioneering for Hoffman along the line of the Erie, and he himself made his début as a spellbinder at the big Tammany rally of the campaign, when fifty thousand Democrats, rich and poor, marched in teeming rain to the old Fourteenth Street Wigwam, carrying torches and Greek fire, and wearing red shirts in tribute to Tweed, who had worn one when he ran with Americus Fire-Engine Company No. 6.

When Tweed called the meeting to order he faced an opposition novel in the North, although common in the South, for Grant had ordered the Eighth Infantry to New York to supplement the troops on Governor's Island to protect the polls on Election Day. He also despatched two war-ships, the *Guerrière* and the *Narragansett,* to New York Harbor. In addition, the National Guard were to support the Federal troops, if called upon by the United States marshal.

Grant's orders gave Tweed his theme. He called upon all Democrats to "frown down all attempts at mob violence, or anything which shall have a tendency to intimidate those who are entitled to vote, and against any endeavor to prevent access to or ingress from the polls on Election Day." This was an order, and Tweed's orders were law. "No act of violence will mar that day," Tweed warned. "We know and feel that although an aggressive hand is upon us, yet we must, by a judicial exercise of law and order, which is our only protection, show that New York is a law-abiding and, as the world knows, a well-governed city."

It was a well-turned speech which merited the deafening applause of blind partizanship; no one applauded more heartily than the distinguished Democrats on the platform, including the Elegant Oakey, Horatio Seymour, and August Belmont, the agent in America of the world banking-house of Rothschild. Wealth had brought Belmont the chairmanship of the Democratic National Committee, and other political honors. Tweed broke through the final waves of applause to nominate Belmont for permanent chairman of the rally. After a roar of "ayes," Belmont took his place at the speaker's stand. He looked a pygmy beside Tweed, who lacked an inch of six feet. In an accent as Teutonic as his original name,

Schoenberg, the banker praised the virtues of the Elegant Oakey, Hoffman, and other Ring candidates.

"Never before have we been called upon to vote for a ticket which commands so strongly our hearty and affectionate approval," he said.

The applause of the evening reached its peak when Belmont introduced one of Tweed's Republican allies, James Fisk, Jr., who lost no time in confessing the errors of his way. Yes, he had been host to President Grant, but he would not gamble with Republicans any longer. He was through with all of them. Up and down the stage he strode, pulling at his trooper's mustache, or posing daintily as he studiously stroked his beardless cheeks and chin while delivering some gem of clownish comedy. Belmont was not behind in the applause when Fisk proclaimed that henceforth, now and forever, he would be a true Democrat. Fisk was saved! Then the Prince of Erie promised that not only would he vote the Democratic ticket from top to bottom, but would pledge his twenty-five thousand employees on the Erie to do likewise.

There was nothing novel in such a promise, save its frankness. Many employers of labor had been doing it for nearly half a century. There were listeners of Fisk who knew that this evil had been foretold by James Kent, the great chancellor, when universal suffrage—women were not people then —was considered in the New York State constitutional convention of 1821. Kent saw in it a menace to liberty, and described New York City's growth as "enough to startle and awaken those who are pursuing the *ignis fatuus* of universal suffrage." Then the author of the *Commentaries* continued:

"In 1773 it had 21,000 souls; 1801 it had 60,000 souls; 1806 it had 76,000 souls; 1820 it has 123,000 souls. It is rapidly swelling into an unwieldy population ... with the burdensome pauperism of an European metropolis." Next he turned prophet as he warned: "In less than a century, that

city, with the operation of universal suffrage, and under skilful direction, will govern this state." He did not anticipate
that his prophecy would be fulfilled in two generations. For
the metropolis had held the state in its grip since 1868 and
was to continue its hold, save for an occasional short spell,
down through the years. Kent foresaw Fisk and his kind
dictating the vote of his employees when he said:

We are destined to become a great manufacturing as well as
commercial state. We have already numerous and prosperous
factories of one kind or another; and one master-capitalist, with
his one hundred apprentices and journeymen and agents and
dependents, will bear down at the polls an equal number of
farmers of small estates in his vicinity, who cannot safely unite
for their common defense. Large manufacturing and mechani-
cal establishments can act in an instant, with the unity and
efficacy of disciplined troops.

After unwittingly bearing testimony to the fulfilment of
the worst of Kent's fears, Fisk assumed his finest circus form,
and urged his new-found partizans to visit him at the opera-
house—"if you don't think it will tamper with your morals."
The entire hall cheered and laughed as he coyly denied
harboring any political ambitions and likened himself to
Greeley, who had been defeated the previous fall when he
ran for state comptroller—one of several defeats at the polls.

"I am something like Horace Greeley," said Fisk, "for if
I am elected at all, I shall be elected to stay at home."

The people were paying a high price for their laughter
that night, as supporters of Judge Ledwith, the anti-Ring
candidate for mayor, reminded them.

At a Ledwith meeting, held shortly after the Tammany
rally, Belmont was denounced along with Fisk. Men were
beginning to act as if they were again in a land of freedom,
with no fear of the tomahawk justice of Cardozo & Co. They

reminded Belmont that as the agent of the House of
Rothschild, with its reputation for probity, and as one permitted to move in respectable social circles, he should not
have presented Fisk to any audience, and that he might have

Nast pictures Justice overturning the corrupt bench of Cardozo & Co.
Harper's Weekly, January 27, 1872.

refrained from praising corrupt candidates. The *Times*
dubbed Fisk and Belmont the Castor and Pollux of Gotham
politics. Fisk's appearance in Tammany Hall enabled General Hillyer to rouse a Ledwith audience to a boisterous
frenzy with:

"Tammany tells us that virtue is played out, and in support of this, they point to James Fisk and his seven concubines."

Ledwith himself recalled the systematic stealing of elections year in and year out, and urged honest men to shoot through the mouth any inspector of elections they saw tampering with their votes. Turning to the rumored thievings of the Ring, he said: "The charge is made that $5,000,000 to $6,000,000 has been stolen." And the charge was repeated by free men and free press alike; all demanded that the city's financial records be opened for public inspection.

As Election Day approached, this demand became a deafening roar. The added charge was made that the city's credit was impaired. So the Ring, with a great fanfare, announced an impartial audit of the city's finances by a committee of six eminent citizens, respected and rich. Three were Republicans, one a Democrat, and two were independents. Four ranked among the wealthiest in the land. The richest, John Jacob Astor, was chairman. He was a Republican, as were Marshall O. Roberts—the recent gubernatorial possibility—and Moses Taylor. Taylor was a merchant prince with his own fleet of ships, plying chiefly between the United States, Cuba, and Central American ports. He was president of the City Bank, owned coal and iron mines, and had large holdings in railroads. A fourth man of millions was Edward Schell, a Democrat, whose chief interest was banking. His brother Augustus was high in Tammany councils, a generous giver to campaign funds, president of the New York Historical Society, and a patron of the arts. The independents, E. D. Brown and George K. Sistare, were also prominent in the financial world.

During the final week of the election, those in the know wondered how incriminating the findings of the Astor audit committee would be. The day before election, the committee

published a report assuring the people they had examined
the vouchers, books, and other documents—all betraying the
widespread thefts of the Ring—and concluding with this
whitewash:

"And we further certify the account books of the department are faithfully kept, that we have personally examined
the securities of the department and sinking fund and found
them correct. We have come to the conclusion and certify
that the financial affairs of the city under the charge of the
Comptroller are administered in a correct and faithful manner."

The untruthful report destroyed whatever chance there
was of ousting the Ring, as only a day remained. The vote
for mayor, on the face of the returns, was: Hall, 71,037;
Ledwith, 46,392. Woodford ran some 12,000 votes behind
Ledwith, while Hall trailed about 15,000 behind Hoffman.
The governor led Woodford in the city by 52,277; the vote
stood: Hoffman, 86,668; Woodford, 34,391. The state-wide
vote was: Hoffman, 399,532; Woodford, 366,436.

The city poll of more than 121,000 in a population of
942,292, including 419,094 foreign born, was fraudulent per
se. The vote, an increase of nearly 20 per cent in two years,
represented 100 voters at the polls out of every 778 men,
women and children, alien and citizens. In the Five Points,
the Bloody Old Sixth, where non-citizens predominated, the
count represented 100 voters in every 389 of the population.
Repeating was the order of the day, and false counting the
order of the night.

Immediately before the election, the *Herald,* a Democratic
paper, said the Ring had at least $1,000,000 to spend on
election bribes and "could buy every man that was in the
market," and cynically predicted that the Ring, "with the al-
mighty dollar, is sure of holding New York."

The most singular feature of the campaign was the utter

silence of the venal judges and other members of the inner circle of the Ring to the charges hurled against them. Hoffman was denounced for reappointing Ingraham, Barnard, and Cardozo to the General Term, or Appellate Division, of the Supreme Court. Besides these three, there were thirty Supreme Court justices in the state. A law forced through the legislature at the behest of the newly formed Association of the Bar of the City of New York, empowered the governor to appoint any of the thirty-three to the General Term. But Hoffman nullified the law by reappointing the Ring judges to this appeals bench.

After the election, Cardozo schemed to stop the attacks on himself and his judicial associates, as well as their masters, and drafted a bill empowering himself and Barnard to punish for contempt any journalist or public speaker who assailed the Ring. These two judges were to define what constituted contempt, and the Ring critic would remain in the Tombs at the pleasure of Barnard and Cardozo. The Ring railroaded it through both houses unanimously. But none of Cardozo's intended victims went to jail.

While working on this bill, Cardozo freed an anti-Ring politician he had imprisoned in the Tombs for forty days on a trumped-up charge of perjury. This was another of the many instances where Cardozo suspended the writ of habeas corpus, although the Constitution provides:

"The privilege of the Writ of Habeas Corpus shall not be suspended, unless when in Cases of Rebellion or Invasion the Public Safety may require it."

But there was a rebellion—against Cardozo and his pals. Their safety required the suspension of the writ of habeas corpus, the proudest and most priceless possession of a free people.

10

HUMOR AMONG THIEVES

M ANY WHO HAD FOUGHT THE RING DESPAIRED OF OVER-
throwing it as they analyzed the election returns. It
was a period of rejoicing for the Ring. Its lieutenants started
a public subscription for a statue to Tweed "in consideration
of his services to the commonwealth of New York." Magistrate Edward J. Shandley was president, and engraved cards
advised subscribers to forward contributions to "Bernard
Smythe, Receiver of Taxes, office, 32 Chambers Street."
When Tweed's articulate foes, led by Jennings, suggested
that statues also be erected to John Jacob Astor and other
members of Tweed's whitewashing committee, along with
brazen effigies of Fisk and Gould, Tweed put a quietus to
the enterprise. Then Shandley said the sponsors of the
Tweed statue would build a charitable institution bearing
Tweed's name, lest future generations forget the fame of
"that statesman, philanthropist, and patriot." One of the
trustees of the Tweed statue fund was Sheriff James O'Brien,
erstwhile leader of the Young Democracy, who had returned
to the Tweed camp in the hope that the Ring would author-
ize payment of his fraudulent bill of $350,000 against the
city.

It was Shandley's task to raise money for Tammany's fund
to provide Christmas dinners and food and coal for the
needy during the winter. Tweed headed the list with
$50,000. In addition, he gave $1,000 to fifteen aldermen for
their own ward relief rolls. Democrats and Republicans fared

alike in Tweed's benefactions. Four days after Christmas, Jennings, in the *Times*, recalled that Tweed was an editor as well as a philanthropist and that city advertising for a single issue of his paper, the *Transcript*, netted him more than $75,000. He added:

"When a man can plunder the people at the rate of $75,000 or $80,000 a day, it does not cost him much of an effort to give a few odd thousand dollars to the poor. Who, in fact, have done so much as Tweed and his cronies to make people poor? . . . Having created their destitution, the Tweed Gang now contemptuously flings a bone to them to stop their mouths. . . . Bought newspapers cry out, 'How generous!' . . ."

Tweed now set out to buy the *Times*. Associated with him in the enterprise were Fisk, Gould, Peter Cooper, and at least one member of the whitewashing committee, Moses Taylor. In denying any intention of selling the *Times*, Jones, its principal owner, said:

Mr. Nathaniel Sands, secretary of the Citizens' Association, has been for some time actively engaged in the effort to purchase or otherwise silence this journal in the interest of his Tammany employers. . . . Rather than prove false to the public in the present crisis, I would, if necessity by any possibility arose, immediately start another journal to denounce these frauds upon the people which are so great a scandal to the city, and I should carry with me . . . the colleagues who have already stood by me through a long and arduous contest.

The snow was on the streets of the city when Jones chilled the ambition of "the unprincipled Republicans" of which Sands was the spear-head. Save for such items as advertising largesse to the *Transcript*, no newspaper had anything definite on which to make the slightest charge against the Ring. Waste of public funds is not a crime. But two men, working

Thomas Nast's concept of Tweed and a common thief in *Harper's Weekly*, January 6, 1872. The cartoonist's caption reads: "Can the law reach him?—The dwarf and the thief."

independently of each other, and for different reasons, were obtaining possession of the closely guarded secrets of the Ring's thievery.

One was Matthew J. O'Rourke, a journalist, who had been appointed county bookkeeper on February 1, 1870. O'Rourke now had the telltale books indicating the extensive looting of the Ring. The other was William Copeland, appointed clerk by Connolly to please O'Brien. Unknown to any one save O'Brien, Copeland was making transcripts of Connolly's records—the records of the comptroller's office which Astor and his fellow whitewashers pretended to examine just before election.

Gossip had it that the Ring was stealing millions through fictitious charges for work on the new court-house in City Hall Park. But no one imagined that mere repairs to plumbing and gas fixtures in the Tweed court-house would yield John H. Keyser $1,149,874.50, or that Keyser's entire bills for plumbing were to fall a few dollars short of $3,000,000. Nor did any one dream that $5,691,144.28 would be paid to the firm of James H. Ingersoll & Co. for furniture for the court-house. Or that Andrew J. Garvey, a plasterer, would receive $138,187 for two days' work, and a total of $2,870,-464.06 for the rest of his labors on the court-house. George S. Miller, a carpenter, received $360,747.61 for one month's work; another, Archibald Hall—no relation of the Elegant Oakey—received $151,480.86. Hall, Miller, and others who received, as shown by the records, a total of more than $12,000,000 for building, decorating, equipping, and furnishing the court-house, actually received only a fraction of this sum—just how much is anybody's guess. A just price for the entire undertaking has been placed as low as $1,250,000. The top figure is $3,000,000. Net result: $9,000,000 to $10,750,000 stolen from the pockets of the people.

The accounts in Connolly's office showed every conceivable kind of a fraud. The Ring, after having voted the dead, found a new use for them. They charged the sum of $51,414.70 for the hire of carriages for mourning aldermen who attended two funerals. Of this sum, $28,379.70 went to Edward Van Ranst and $23,035 to Thomas Conway—or at least the books credited these liverymen with receiving such amounts.

A month after the November election, while Copeland and O'Rourke were quietly working, the Yonkers *Gazette* reported that a bill had been drawn by the Ring's representatives "to gobble up the towns of Yonkers, Morrisania, West Farms, Westchester, East Chester, New Rochelle and Pelham." This measure was the origin of the borough and county of the Bronx, although four years were to elapse before any part of Westchester County was to be incorporated in the metropolis, and many years more before the section was to bear any more distinctive name than the annexed territory, or the annexed towns, or the annexed wards.

"Manhattan Island is becoming too contracted a field for their enterprise," said Jennings, referring to the Ring, in commenting on the proposed annexation. Then he continued:

The fat jobs on which they have thriven for years past will soon be exhausted. There will be no more court-houses to be built, no more streets or avenues to be opened, widened, or extended. The opportunities for combined speculations in real estate with the public money are also diminishing here every day. But in the green pastures of Westchester County, the Ring sees fresh mines of future wealth. . . . Once let these pastures be annexed and become a part of our city, and there will be such an upturning of Westchester soil as the plodding farmers of that region never dreamt of. They will see grand boulevards in place of corduroy roads; broad avenues will open through all their cowyards; they will have macadamized drives and asphaltum walks; magnificent streets will traverse their waste places, laid out at right angles, nicely graded, and paved with Nicholson, Russ, Belgian, or Fiske, as one or another of these pavements shall furnish the most profitable job. . . . As for the aristocratic denizens of Yonkers, we are surprised that they manifest any opposition to this annexation scheme, or think themselves entitled to be consulted on the matter. Their local organ says the subject is one that should be thoroughly ventilated. This only shows what crude notions of government are entertained by people who have not had the benefit of Ring rule. The idea of ventilating any of Tweed and Sweeny's active projects would be regarded as rank mutiny by their subjects here. They may be whitewashed, but not ventilated. It will be time enough for the people of Yonkers to discuss this annexation question after the Ring have got their bill through the legislature. At present it is none of their business. After they are annexed they will be entitled to a representative in our Board of Aldermen, and that ought to satisfy any reasonable ambition.

The Ring was more generous to people of the annexed territory than Jennings surmised, for they planned to give them two aldermen, one to each of the new wards, the Twenty-second and Twenty-third. Two wards meant twice as many jobs as one ward. Jennings misunderstood "the plodding farmers of that region," for these simple souls had several grand jests at the expense of the metropolis before they became part of it on January 1, 1874. One was the issuance of $278,000 in serial bonds for a road through the cowyards and waste places of the new wards. These bonds, issued by the old town of West Farms before its corporate existence ceased, all pay 7 per cent per annum, and will continue to do so until the Year of Our Lord, 2147. The actual interest cost will total $2,468,435—nearly ten times the amount of the principal, which is amortized at the rate of $1,000 annually, save for the years 2122, 2123, and 2147, when the serial maturity will be $500. All that was done in building Central Avenue—now no more—was within the law; for waste of public funds is not a crime. In fact, it is often the road to success and riches.

11

MENDING A MACHINE, A VANISHED

LEGISLATOR, AND SOME TRIVIA

THE ANNEXED TERRITORY WAS LITTLE IN THE RING'S thoughts in 1871. It was a busy year for all of them. An analysis of the slump in the Elegant Oakey's vote the preceding November disclosed that quite a few Irish in the slums had voted for Ledwith in spite of the Know Nothing blather of the whisper squads. So Slippery Dick Connolly, head of a numerically inconsequential group of Irishmen, the St. Patrick's Mutual Alliance, originated a fantastic scheme to reclaim the lost Irish vote. Accordingly, the Ring introduced a bill to make the seventeenth of March a legal holiday. But this was not all, for school trustees of the Seventh Ward—Tweed's old ward—recommended "most earnestly" the teaching of Irish in the public schools. Even the pupils in the six schools for Negro children were to be taught Irish. The trustees held that Irish must be taught if the schools were "to keep pace with the age." A few men of Irish blood, with more regard for sacred things than Slippery Dick, killed the scheme as the New York City Council of Political Reform issued a call for a mass-meeting in Cooper Union on April 6. Men who could not be deluded by Sands and other professional reformers, started the new organization. Among them were Republicans like William M. Evarts, statesman, diplomat, and lawyer of rare talent, and Democrats of the type of William F. Havemeyer, banker and sugar refiner, whose two mayoralty terms more than twenty years before were distinguished by honesty and progress. The meeting discussed "the alarming aspects of public affairs generally," but it accomplished little more than to give people something to talk about.

Almost immediately thereafter, one of Tweed's shoulder-hitters, Jimmy Irving, entered the Capitol liquored up, and engaged in a row with Smith M. Weed, a fellow assemblyman and a crony of Tilden. Irving encountered Weed under the speaker's rostrum and struck him, as the hundred-and-twenty-odd assemblymen watched helplessly. The frail Weed sought escape in the clerk's office. Irving followed, and struck him again, laying his cheek-bone open. As Weed fell, his head struck a door, inflicting another ugly wound. Irving resigned the next day to avoid expulsion. His resignation left the Democrats short of the constitutional majority by one vote.

This vote had to be secured if several sorely needed Ring measures were to pass the lower house, including the tax levy for the metropolis and election law amendments. Led by Greeley, Republican editors demanded that the Republican assemblymen oppose these bills. To avoid a major party scandal, the Republicans caucused, and a majority having decided against the bills, all Republicans were solemnly bound to oppose them. But for this caucus, Tweed could have repeated his feats of other years and bought most of the Republican minority. He needed only one vote, however, and found it with the aid of $100,000, of which $75,000 was paid in cash. The bought legislator was Orange S. Winans, of Dunkirk. As he voted for the first of the Tweed bills, his fellow Republicans shouted "Shame! Traitor! Sold out!" Two days later, Greeley placed the following advertisement on his editorial page:

For Sale or To Let for Business Purposes—a member of assembly. Rent for the season, $100,000, or will be sold cheap for cash. Possession as soon as the tax levy and election bills are passed, the present lessee having no further use for the property. Inquire of William M. Tweed, Albany, or O. S. Winans, on the premises.

This was Monday, April 17. On the following Friday the legislature adjourned sine die. When Winans returned home the people of Dunkirk shunned him. His wife abandoned

"Make Room for the Leper" headed this concept of the bribery of Oscar S. Winans, who subsequently disappeared as if the earth had swallowed him. *Harper's Weekly*, May 6, 1871.

him. He sought solace in drink. No one had a word of pity for him save a clergyman. Winans fled town. He was last seen boarding a west-bound train. He was drunk. Thereafter no one heard from him, and no one knows what became of him. He just vanished.

Another event that spring helped to set the stage for the exposure of the Ring's thievery. This was the wedding on May 31 of Tweed's daughter, Mary Amelia, to a scion of a prominent southern family. A list of the wedding presents was prepared for the press. These gifts cost $700,000. Jay Gould gave silverware costing $250. His partner Fisk, and the wife of Slippery Dick, gave exquisitely wrought silver ice-bowls, worth $500 each. State Senator Thomas J. Creamer's gold and silverware represented $1,000; Judge Barnard's gold, diamond, and pearl necklace was of like value. State Senator Michael Norton outdid Creamer with a $1,500 gold chain and diamond pendant. Hugh Smith, graft collector for the Elegant Oakey, gave an emerald and diamond locket that cost him or the mayor $5,000. Thomas C. Fields, a mere assemblyman, erroneously described as "probably the most corrupt man that ever sat in the legislature," parted with $5,000 for a gold and diamond necklace with earrings to match. The wife of John J. Blair, another Ring assemblyman, gave a cameo, diamond, and pearl set, costing $2,500. There were other diamond sets for $5,000, one from a shrinking violet whose card read: "A sincere friend of W. M. Tweed." Peter Brains Sweeny parted with $1,000 for a diamond and enamel bracelet, and his brother James, who collected the graft for Peter, followed suit, only there was no enamel on his gift. And Genêt signalized his return to the fold with a gift of a $2,000 diamond cross.

There were exactly forty silver services, and scores of gifts of jewelry, fans, clocks, candle-sticks, vases, paintings, and statues. The price of the bride's dress—$5,000—was known to all who read.

It was a grand wedding, and, in keeping with the times, no concealment was made of this fact.

There was a complete lowering of the public tone. A few stout hearts in high place stood up against this wave of degradation which, to quote the conservative Union League, "affected injuriously" bench and bar, trading place and banking house, pulpit and classroom, and "many" political leaders of all parties. The League studiously forgot the press which, with some honorable exceptions, reflected the spirit of the times. The nation was off on a moral holiday, and Tweed was enjoying himself magnificently, yet with comparative restraint. He had only one concubine to Fisk's seven. To avoid gossip, he housed her in the coachman's house at his country estate at Greenwich, Connecticut, and he was so outwardly punctilious in his deportment that the Methodist Society of the town permitted him to decorate their house of worship.

12

ROUT AND RIOT

O N JUNE 1, 1871, THE RING HAD A JOB AT ITS DISPOSAL, O'Rourke having resigned as county bookkeeper the day before. In the few weeks of his work he had indeed served the city, for his transcripts showed thefts in armory accounts of more than $2,500,000 in less than thirty months; $1,377,527.86 was purportedly spent in repairs to armories, of which nearly half a million dollars was charged against work on ten old stables rented as armories by the Ring for $85,000 a year. For a month O'Rourke tried to dispose of these records to several newspapers. About the same time, Copeland quit his job in the comptroller's office with transcripts showing other frauds of the Ring, including the new court-house loot. These he turned over to O'Brien.

The acts of both men had a common inspiration—Tilden. He had worked with Tweed and other Ring members long enough to realize that his political progress depended upon a new set-up, and this involved the Ring's destruction. He was credited with convincing O'Brien that the rout of the Ring would make him boss of New York. While waiting, O'Brien cashed in on his fraudulent claim against the city for $350,000, which Tweed and Slippery Dick bought at full value, each taking half, on O'Brien's representations that he could persuade Tilden to drop his fight. Part of the purchase price was a mortgage for $128,000 on one of Tweed's properties. This deal was made before a notary three months after the *Times* began publication of the evidence of the Ring's frauds on July 8.

A few days before the first instalment appeared, the Ring deputized Slippery Dick to offer $5,000,000 to Jones to suppress the publication of the transcripts—all copies of records which the whitewashing firm of Astor & Co. had assured the voters on the eve of the preceding Election Day were incontrovertible proof of the correct and faithful administration of the city's finances. Slippery Dick had no more luck with Jones than the Ring had with Nast, who spurned $500,000 in return for a long vacation in Europe.

The panic state of the Ring is evidenced by these offers, for another cartoonist, although less able, would have replaced Nast, and it is fair to assume that the resourceful Tilden was not without an extra set of the transcripts. Panic also possessed the tools of the Ring. Garvey the plasterer voiced his fears to the Elegant Oakey, who consoled him with: "Who is there to sue?"

The first instalment of the transcripts appeared on a Saturday as Slippery Dick was counseling the Elegant Oakey to stand pat on his ban on an Orangemen's parade the following Wednesday. What did it mean in votes? Slippery Dick had the figures handy. Of the thousands of Protestant Irish in the city, only 1,500 were Orangemen. Against this mere handful stood 250,000 Catholics. Sure, Slippery Dick could speak for every one of them, and they would all be with the ticket in the fall if the Orangemen didn't march.

Panic and pretense dictated this advice, for that very day Archbishop McCloskey sent a letter to the priests directing his people to "array themselves on the side of order and peace and allow the Orangemen to parade." The letter, with its implied request to the city officials to sanction the parade, was read from every Catholic pulpit the next day. The opening sentence read: "The Archbishop wishes the Catholic people to absent themselves from the Orange procession on next Wednesday, the 12th instant."

Every priest in the city supplemented the Archbishop's command with an admonition of his own.

Jeremiah O'D. Rossa, better known as O'Donovan Rossa
Harper's Weekly, 1871.

O'Donovan Rossa, a Catholic and a Fenian chief who had risked his life for a free Ireland, denounced the opposition to the parade as unworthy of Irishmen and Americans. "Let the Orangemen celebrate," advised Rossa at a meeting of leaders of Irish organizations at Hibernia Hall on Prince Street. He was greeted with cries of "Hold your jaw!" and "Throw him out!" Many of Rossa's opponents were Ring office-holders.

Anti-Ring newspapers championed the Orangemen's right to parade, while disapproving of them as an oath-bound anti-Catholic group. Greeley voiced their sentiments thus: "This journal has no sympathy with the Orangemen.... We have an instinctive dislike to anything claiming to be religion which is mainly a war upon the religion of somebody else."

Hoffman left the capital in a vain effort to see the Elegant Oakey. The governor returned to Albany late Monday, leaving behind his military aide, General James McQuade, to tell the mayor that the parade must be permitted. When McQuade telegraphed Hoffman that the Elegant Oakey would not budge, the governor issued a proclamation assuring military and police escorts to "all bodies of men desiring to assemble and march in peaceable procession" in the metropolis on Orangemen's Day.

Hoffman arrived in town on the day of the parade, and drove immediately to police headquarters, arriving there at 6 A.M. Eight national-guard regiments were at their armories at the same hour. Parade permits had meanwhile been issued, and at nine o'clock about three hundred policemen were patrolling Eighth Avenue and the side streets, from Fisk's opera-house at Twenty-third Street, north to Thirtieth. A strong cordon of police protected Lamartine's Hall, Eighth Avenue and Thirty-ninth Street, the meeting place of several local lodges of Orangemen and the American Protestant Association. One A.P.A. group also planned to march. The A.P.A.'s—successors to the Know Nothings—and the Orangemen began straggling into the hall at noon.

One regiment assigned to escort the Orangemen and A.P.A.'s from their hall to Cooper Union was the Ninth, of which Fisk was Colonel. Almost all the veterans, officers and men resigned in a body when Fisk, without any military training, was forced upon them. Rich bonuses for recruits, prizes to company commanders for filling their ranks, and other examples of Fisk's generosity soon brought the Ninth up to full strength. Many of the recruits had been rejected by other guard units. Fisk established his own camp at Long Branch for the regiment and named it in honor of Jay Gould. He frequently took them in a body to see his opéra bouffe. No New York guardsmen were ever more pampered—or more undisciplined.

At two o'clock about one hundred and sixty Orangemen and A.P.A.'s were in line. At their head rode John Johnston, grand marshal. Next was Twyford's band of twelve pieces. Then came the Gideon Lodge of Orangemen led by John D. Askin, an undertaker. Then came a group of A.P.A.'s, their banner inscribed: "True Sons of Liberty, Lodge 22, A.P.A." Another A.P.A. banner read: "American Freemen, Fall In."

Little more than the Orange and A.P.A. banners were visible from the thronged sidewalks, the lodge members being hemmed in by soldiers and policemen. The Seventh Regiment was at the head of the procession followed by two platoons of police and some forty journalists. Then came the Orangemen and A.P.A.'s, four abreast, their left flank guarded by the Twenty-second Regiment, six files deep, their right by the Eighty-fourth Regiment, in similar formation. These two regiments, in turn, were flanked by policemen in double file. Two platoons of police closed the rear ranks of the A.P.A.'s and Orangemen. Next in line were the Sixth and Ninth regiments, trailed by two empty stages, in lieu of ambulances, and a platoon of policemen.

Several thousand lined the sidewalks waiting to see the parade get under way. Among the spectators were men on mischief bent. All morning long little groups of these men had been milling in and out of saloons on the side streets and along the avenue, quenching their thirst. Their aggregate number was not more than a thousand. Most of them were drunk, or half drunk, as the parade formed. A platoon of policemen could have handled them. But some of the policemen and soldiers had also whiled away the time in the neighborhood saloons. We have this report of Colonel Cheseborough, adjutant of General Shaler, in command of the troops:

"Captain McDonald, Police, reports that the Commandant of A Company, Eighty-fourth Regiment, was intoxicated when he left Police Headquarters."

This drunken officer's command was at the head of the right flank that walled in the Orangemen and A.P.A.'s. Many members of his command were also drunk.

Almost on the stroke of two came the command, "Forward, march!" And above the roll of drums and the tread of marching feet were heard the howitzers rumbling over the cobblestones. Presently a small part of the crowd hissed and hooted. As the parade started, Fisk came running up the avenue, counter to the line of march. He was in his shirtsleeves, hatless, and without a weapon. He reached his command just as it neared Twenty-sixth Street. An officer gave him a sword, and Fisk was again playing soldier.

Fisk had rejoined his command but a few seconds when a yelling mob of forty men came tearing through Twenty-fourth Street. Simultaneously, from the roof of a house on the southeast corner of this street and the avenue, came a shower of bricks, cobblestones, sticks, and other missiles.

The police, under Captain John H. Petty, met the mob on the curb, and in a moment cops and rioters were a writhing mass on the corner.

At this instant the head of the procession had crossed Twenty-third Street, and the first rank of the Orangemen and A.P.A.'s were opposite Eighth Avenue and Twenty-fourth Street. One report is that a shot was fired from a house on the northeast corner of the two thoroughfares. If it was aimed at the celebrants, some one standing beside the assassin tried to wrench the weapon from his hand, for it found its mark four hundred feet to the north, ripping off the head of Private Henry C. Page, of Company K, Ninth Regiment. The dead guardsman had been manager of Fisk's opera-house. Another account said that Page was killed by the accidental discharge of a drunken comrade's musket.

But there is no doubt of what happened after this shot was fired. The men of Company A, Eighty-fourth Regiment, many of whom were intoxicated and whose commandant was described as drunk in Colonel Cheseborough's report, began firing indiscriminately. Many of these soldiers fired into the struggling mass of policemen and rioters at Twenty-fourth Street and Eighth Avenue, not Twenty-fifth Street, as Police Inspector George W. Walling erroneously reported.

Captain Petty threw himself to the sidewalk as the muskets roared. Patrolman John O'Connor fell across him, a musket ball through his side. Others, how many is not known, were also wounded in this fusillade.

When O'Connor fell, panic seized almost the entire line, and save for the Seventh, men in all the regiments were following the example of the drunks in Company A, Eighty-fourth Regiment, and shooting without orders.

The firing was brief. Two soldiers and one policeman were dead, and twenty-six policemen and soldiers wounded. Of the wounded militiamen, at least two died later. Among the rioters and spectators, the lowest estimated number of dead was forty-six, including many women and children; civilians wounded by gunshot, reported by the police, were sixty-one. Stones and other missiles injured thirty-seven others known to the police. There was no way of ascertaining the total number of civilian dead and wounded, for many were carried away by their companions.

Fisk disappeared in the smoke of battle, and there are various accounts of how he did it. All agree that he fled and finally wound up that evening at Long Branch, without a visible scratch. He said he had been struck on the ankle with a piece of lead pipe and assumed a limp for several days. He was a grand actor.

13

THE METROPOLIS IN A LYNCHING MOOD

THE ORANGE RIOT EMPHASIZED NEW YORK'S MISGOVERNMENT as nothing else could have done. Three days after the riot Greeley observed that "the thoughtless will infer that New York is subject to the sway of its worst element, when in truth the very contrary was demonstrated." One did not have to go beyond the teeming thousands of Roman Catholics in the city, and the comparatively few who were at the scene of the riot, for the truth of this. "Authority will always be respected so long as it is respectable," philosophized Greeley. He cited New Jersey, where Theodore F. Randolph was governor. Randolph, like Hoffman, was a Democrat. But unlike Hoffman, Randolph was not a Ring tool, and his authority was respected. "Irish Catholics," continued Greeley, "are a mighty host in Jersey City, Newark, Paterson, New Brunswick, etc., yet the Orangemen were not molested wherever and however they saw fit to honor the triumph of William over James. It would have been just the same here had our rulers been Randolphs." After recalling the prompt and vigorous denunciations of planned violence by "the Roman Catholic Archbishop and clergy," Greeley wrote: "The police and military of our city are largely composed of Roman Catholics, who obeyed the call of duty as cheerfully and thoroughly as any Protestant."

When the riot ceased to be of newspaper interest, Greeley wrote that the Elegant Oakey and Slippery Dick "cannot honorably neglect now to bring a libel suit against the

Times," which had called the mayor and comptroller thieves. "The *Times* says it calls you thieves," continued Greeley, "because it can prove you so in a court of law to which it invites you. You cannot afford to ignore that invitation... without infamy."

There was only one valiant champion of the Ring among the city's leading newspapers now—the venal *World* of Manton Marble. When the *Nation* proposed forming a vigilance committee to hang the Ring members, the *World* protested. Whereupon the *Nation* responded:

Hall, Connolly, Tweed, Barnard, and all that class to which they belong... fear no penalty for their misdeeds except a violent death. They are indifferent to public opinion and have matters so arranged that the prison pen has no terrors for them, and a natural death they calculate upon. But the prospect of a violent death, which would suddenly stop their champagne, knock the satin sofas from under them, shut out the velvet carpets from their view, cause their fast horses to vanish into thin air, and launch them into the cold unknown, would terrify them exceedingly; and such a death, we repeat, a large and growing body of respectable citizens think they ought to die—first and foremost, in order to stop their thieving and rid the community of them, and secondly, to prevent an unwholesome influence on public and private morals of the spectacle of the peaceful close of their career in the enjoyment of their stealings.

The talk of hanging was constant, and some of the Ring regarded it as more than mere persiflage.

On the night of September 4, a non-partizan mass-meeting in Cooper Union decided to prosecute the Ring thieves and sue for the return of the stolen millions. The blunt-tongued Havemeyer, who presided, touched the sore spot, not only in the city, but in the Republic, when he said:

"Official life, no longer honorable, has become a business." Then he added: "Offices are created not so much to reward political favorites as to purchase the aid of corrupt men to stamp out liberty in our midst. The most exorbitant salaries are paid to the most incompetent officials."

Other Havemeyers have since said the same thing, without changing conditions, save for an occasional brief respite.

Other speakers discussed the armory swindles disclosed by O'Rourke and the court-house thefts revealed by Copeland. But no one had dreamed that the total stealings, known and suspected, would exceed many times the $15,000,000 then estimated.

When James Emmott listed some of the known fraudulent payments, and asked, "What are you going to do with these men?" a poorly dressed man in the audience answered, "Hang them!" Emmott was a Republican, and had sat in the Supreme Court. Representative Robert Barnwell Roosevelt, brother of Theodore, whose fourteen-year-old son was to become the glorious "T. R." of a later generation, evoked a wild outburst when he declared: "An aroused and outraged public is not patient; and Judge Ledwith laid down good law when he told his friends that if they saw an election inspector tamper with their ballots they could shoot him on the spot." After the applause ceased, Roosevelt completed his thought thus: "The man who cheats a nation out of its birthright has committed the highest of crimes, and deserves no mercy."

Roosevelt practised law but preferred journalism, in which he attained distinction. He was an ardent fisherman, a pioneer conservationist, and wrote delightfully of cooking as well as of catching fish, both fresh and salt water. He was elected to Congress in 1870 on the Tammany ticket.

Another speaker, Edwards Pierrepont, great-grandson of the Rev. James Pierrepont, a founder of Yale, doubted that the next legislature would be immune to the Ring's tempting bribes, voicing his doubts in a rhetorical question, which he answered in this violent fashion:

"I have pointed out to you the peaceful ways to right these wrongs. But if these ways will not do, and if, emboldened

Robert Barnwell Roosevelt
From a photograph by Sarony. *Harper's Weekly*, September 23, 1871.

by success, yet new men come into the field of fraud to plunder you still more, as they surely will, then I need not tell you the other way. You will hear it in the yells of an infuriated mob, in the fire and rapine and slaughter, in the noise of musketry and of cannon."

It was a strange meeting. A poor unknown suggested hanging the Ring members; a member of the House indorsed the advice to shoot election thieves; and a former judge and Federal prosecutor outdid both with his implied approval of an insurrection.

Cooper Union was not large enough to accommodate all who sought admittance, and an overflow meeting, addressed by General Cochrane and others, was held in the street.

Both meetings came to an end after Joseph H. Choate moved the adoption of resolutions creating a Committee of Seventy to conduct civil and criminal suits, and to hall-mark honest candidates for office irrespective of party. A few days back, Tweed had cut short an interview with: "What are you going to do about it?" And as Choate held the resolutions aloft, he shouted back: "This is what we are going to do about it."

But the talk of violence did not down. The day after the Cooper Union meetings, a group of prominent taxpayers considered organizing a vigilance committee to hang the Ring and its leading tools to lamp-posts. Joseph Hazlen, a lawyer, said this was the only way. Thus he reasoned:

Can you go to the grand jury, which is filled with their tools? Can you go to the district attorney, who is their pliant servant? Can you obtain protection from the police, who are these men's bodyguard? Can you call upon the governor of the state who extols the virtues of Tweed, the purity of Hall, the brains of Sweeny, and the charming simplicity of Connolly? Can you, in fine, appeal to our courts? If so, where? Get an order from some honest judge—Barnard will vacate it. Get another— Cardozo will vacate it. Get a third, and Ingraham will modify it. Appeal, and the General Term will sustain Barnard and Cardozo and Ingraham—who compose the General Term!

Older and wiser counsel was found in George W. Benster, now retired from the bench, who said: "Whatever way, under God, we may be rescued, it must be by law, or we will only add to our disgrace."

This was also the thought of Tilden, whose bachelor home on Gramercy Park was now a nest of praiseworthy conspirators. He had dodged the Cooper Union meeting. But three days later, John Foley, maker of gold pens and a member of the Committee of Seventy, emerged from Tilden's home with a petition seeking to enjoin the Ring from raising or spending one cent of public funds. This was on September 7.

The Ring had no available funds in the city treasury, although they had collected in taxes more than $6,000,000 in excess of budget requirements for the period ending October 31, and had issued—no one knew how many—municipal securities for millions more. The petition was presented to the crooked Barnard, who signed it after an agent of Tilden told him his courageous act would make him governor.

Barnard's injunction had a twofold effect. Tweed described one. Said he: "He put the injunction upon us and, in the straitened condition of our credit, which was extended on every side, it broke us. You see our patronage had become so enormous and so costly that the injunction, which might not have troubled us at any other time, destroyed all our power to raise money from the banks or elsewhere, and left us strapped." The second effect of the injunction, even before it was actually granted, was to drive the Ring quadrumvirate into a panicky state.

Tweed confessed that he thought of killing either Jones or Jennings, or himself. An attempt was made to incite the city laborers, whose pay was held up, to riot. Slippery Dick, literally ill from fear, sought an interview with Tilden the day before Barnard issued his injunction. At a conference in

Tilden's home, Slippery Dick agreed to appoint Andrew H. Green, of the Committee of Seventy, deputy controller, thus turning over the office, with all its secrets, to Tilden's allies. The next day the Elegant Oakey, although powerless to remove a comptroller, announced the removal of Slippery Dick and the appointment of General George B. McClellan in his place. McClellan, his party's candidate for President in 1864, promptly repudiated this frenzied act.

The Ring then planned a legal move to oust Green. It was now the turn of Tilden and his associates to become panicky, for with Green deposed for even half a day, the guards he had thrown round the comptroller's office would be removed, and the office records would vanish. All civil and criminal actions against the Ring must be founded on the records.

Tilden saw two means of escape. The first was to obtain vacating orders as fast as Cardozo or Ingraham issued fraudulent fiats; the second was to obtain a legal opinion from Charles O'Conor, upholding the validity of Green's appointment. Tilden turned to O'Conor, who held no office.

O'Conor was a rare figure who might have been deified in earlier days. He was the son of a brilliant lawyer, journalist, and pamphleteer, Thomas O'Connor—the son restored the ancient spelling—one of the Men of Ninety-eight who fled Ireland with Thomas Addis Emmett, and settled in New York in 1801. O'Conor was an idol of the crowds and revered by legal scholars. Upon his retirement from the bar four years earlier, his admirers presented to the state a Parian bust of him which holds the place of honor in the noble Grecian pile housing the Appellate Division, on Madison Square. The sculpture was not publicly displayed until after O'Conor's death in 1884, according to his wish. At a meeting of the American Association of Law Librarians at the beginning of the second term of the second Roosevelt, Dr. Frederick C. Hicks, Librarian of the Yale Law School, said: "I can never, without mental obeisance, look at the bookcase in the New York Law Institute which contains the hundred volumes of the appeals papers of Charles O'Conor." Tilden obtained O'Conor's opinion, and thereafter no one challenged the validity of Green's appointment. O'Conor could have driven through the slums, where the impoverished Irish dwelt, and raised a mob of many thousands to do his bidding.

14

THE UNIVERSITY PRESIDENT

TURNED WARD POLITICIAN

BOTH PARTIES WERE NOW PREPARING FOR THEIR STATE CON-ventions, the prelude to the Grant-Greeley campaign of the following year. The Democratic call was for October 4, and the Republican for a week earlier. Again there were two Republican delegations from New York City, the Twenty-third Street organization, headed by Murphy, and the regulars who, earlier in the year, had elected Greeley chairman of the local general committee. In accepting the office, Greeley vainly pleaded for harmony that the party might triumph in city and state. "I cannot afford to be identified with a faction if I act at all, and it must be in the interest and with the approval of the entire party," said Greeley. Observing that the committee members had been duly chosen by "the associations of the several assembly districts," he added: "If this is not the Republican general committee, then there is none, and the organization in this city is defunct." He illustrated the party's helplessness locally by saying: "We are in the condition of the sufferer who, to his friend's observation, 'That is a bad cold you have,' responded, 'Bad or good, it is the best I've got.'"

To demonstrate his unselfishness, he proposed a new primary election so both factions might choose a county committee representative of the entire rank and file. This was rejected by the Conkling-Murphy faction chiefly be-

cause Greeley shared the opinion of many foremost Republicans that Grant should not be renominated. While his
strictures on the President were restrained on this occasion,
Greeley dwelt for a moment on the "mistakes" the President
had made in his appointments, saying: "Whatever blame
may justly attach to this [Grant's appointments] fall rightly
on us who took him from the head of the army and made
him our Civil Chief Magistrate, fully aware that he had
never voted the Republican ticket, if indeed, he had voted
at all." Grant had voted once before his nomination—for
Buchanan, a Democrat.

The anti-Greeley Republicans were supported by the
Times and the *Herald,* and ten days before the state convention, a reporter of James Gordon Bennett's journal visited
the regular organization headquarters at Broadway and
Twenty-second Street, just above Jerry Thomas' chop-house—
famous for its whiskey. On this mild evening the *Herald*
man saw, "standing in the hall door, a number of men who
have their mustaches dyed, and in a general tone of face
resemble gamblers or ropers-in." Others looked like bandits.
Who were these bandits and gamblers and ropers-in? "This
is the sidewalk committee of the Republican General Committee. They have upstairs for the head and font of their
offending, nominally, Mr. Horace Greeley." But those upstairs, or in the hall door, were not a patch on the Conkling-
Murphy contingent which boasted the toughest plug-ugly
office-holders in the city. These shoulder-hitters left for the
convention intent on keeping the Fenton-Greeley delegates
in their place.

Despite the solid phalanx of postmasters, revenue col-
lectors, and other Federal office-holders, Fenton hoped to
achieve the almost impossible in politics—a come-back. He
had triumphed in January when his supporters in the as-

sembly controlled the Republican caucus and named James
W. Husted as the minority opponent of Tweed's man Hitchman for speaker. The night before the convention, Fenton
had a majority of the delegates, with about fifteen votes to
spare.

Andrew D. White

From a photograph by Sarony. *Leslie's Weekly*, August 19, 1879.

Before the delegates assembled, Andrew D. White, president of Cornell University, asked Fenton-Greeley men to vote for him as chairman of the convention "on the solemn pledge that he would so act as to promote harmony." As a consequence, White wheedled away—the verb is Greeley's—twenty-one gullible rural delegates, loyal Greeleyites all. Then a few more were weaned from Fenton and Greeley with promises of Federal jobs, and when the convention was called to order by State Chairman Cornell, Conkling had rounded up a slender majority for White—"Conkling's cloak of respectability."

The Fenton-Greeley faction had a foretaste of what had been planned for them when their metropolitan delegates were visited with violence as they attempted to enter the convention hall. At the head of the group were Whitelaw Reid, Moses H. Grinnell, and General Cochrane. James Armstrong, a sergeant-at-arms, barred them. Armstrong was captain of the night watch at the Custom-House, and a member of Murphy's Twenty-third Street organization. When Reid and his companions ignored Armstrong's orders, he struck the nearest man, P. A. Lambrecht, with a heavy mallet, cutting him above the eye. John Biglin, a noted oarsman, grabbed a chair and brought it down on Armstrong's head, stretching him cold. The Greeleyites then entered the hall.

One of the most disreputable sessions of a political gathering began immediately after Cornell opened the convention. Chauncey M. Depew was the Fenton-Greeley choice for temporary chairman, a post that carried with it the appointment of important committees; but Cornell ruled his nomination out of order on the pretext that Depew was not a delegate. In the attendant uproar, Cornell reversed this unfair ruling. Depew now withdrew in the interest of harmony. Other unjust rulings, before the convention got down to a vote, precipitated a tumult which threatened to become a riot. Police

were summoned, and violence was averted. Then the
Conkling steam-roller swung into action and elected White
by a majority of 29.

Chauncey M. Depew
Leslie's Weekly, September 28, 1872.

White was a Conkling man, but no one suspected that the
head of Cornell University, rich beyond temptation, would
do a political boss's dirty work. White was schooled in the
ways of politicians. For a year he was an attaché of the
American legation in St. Petersburg; he served four years in

the New York state senate, and knew every twist and turn of convention politics. His first major task was to appoint the committees. To the important Committee on Contested Seats, he named fourteen men, each with a full vote. On the basis of the vote for chairman, the Fenton-Greeley faction was entitled to a full six and one-half votes. But of the fourteen White named, only two were Fenton-Greeley men. The packed committee brought in a majority report, prepared long in advance, recommending that the Custom-House Gang and the Greeley delegates be seated, each delegate with a half vote, and by way of rubbing salt into the wound, also recommending that the Conkling-Murphy organization be recognized as the regular organization in New York City, thus attempting to outlaw the Greeley general committee. The convention lacked power to pass upon the legitimacy of any city, county, ward, or assembly-district organization, and could not justly stamp any organization as regular. By way of a compromise, Representative Hamilton Ward moved a substitute resolution directing the state committee to consolidate and perfect the two rival organizations in New York City. Of course, the state committee had no such power; but Ward's design spelled harmony and honesty, and was approved by the Fenton-Greeley leaders. As White was about to put the motion—he was premeditatively slow in getting under way, as if waiting for a cue—Conkling arose and exclaimed: "Not yet the question, Mr. President." This was the cue White was expecting. Conkling was not for compromise; he was for crushing Greeley and the Fenton-Greeley organization. In opposing Ward's substitute, Conkling indulged in a bitter speech, saying:

Does any member of the convention who differs with me say that I go too far when I affirm, as the New York *Tribune* has affirmed in repeated instances, of which I have extracts before me, that William M. Tweed and Oakey Hall, and the men who have disgraced us before the civilized world, have tampered with, controlled and debased the Republican organization in the City of New York? I think no member of this convention denies that proposition; if so, let him speak, for him have I offended.

Many delegates chorused: "I deny it!"

Conkling turned these denials into a laugh, but one Greeley delegate, having in mind the unbroken alliance between Conkling's chief lieutenant and the Tweed Ring, shouted: "How about Murphy?"

Conkling ignored the embarrassing question, and the convention laughed at its master's discomfiture. Conkling, in the remainder of his speech, made no secret of his desire to have only Grant delegates from New York City at next year's national convention; to do this, Greeley and his organization must be destroyed. When Conkling finished, Ward's compromise was defeated, and immediately thereafter General Cochrane and the rest of the regular organization from the metropolis bolted and held a rump convention, just to let off steam. Several Brooklyn delegates joined them. All who spoke denounced Conkling and Murphy, and praised Greeley. White came in for a goodly share of the denunciation. Several bolting delegates suggested petitioning him to resign "his high office as president of Cornell University." And said Rufus F. Andrews: "We cannot afford to send our sons to an institution where a corrupt president presides over its destinies."

White made his double crossing all the more reprehensible by saying that he assumed the fourteen men on the Committee on Contested Seats fairly represented both wings of the party, as he had been informed when the names were handed to him. He had to say something then, but he might have omitted this weasel explanation from his autobiography.

The press, except the Conkling organs, excoriated White, and Greeley accused him of being guilty of "an outrage never before perpetrated by a presiding officer of any prominent deliberative body." An ordinary college president might have blundered; but not White, who was a master of practical politics. He did what many penniless ward politicians have refused to do—he deliberately betrayed guileless, trustful men into voting for him.

Conkling offered a sop to the Greeleyites by nominating G. Hilton Scribner for secretary of state. The rest of the ticket was: Nelson K. Hopkins, comptroller; Thomas Raines, state treasurer; Francis C. Barlow, attorney-general; William B. Taylor, canal commissioner; Thomas Kirkpatrick, prison inspector.

15

ABSENT CONTROL OF A CONVENTION

FEW MEN HAVE HAD A LARGER AUDIENCE THAN HAD TILDEN when, as chairman of the Democratic State Committee, he opened the Rochester convention. For nearly three months the civilized world had received, by telegraph and cable, the daily developments in the Tweed Ring investigation; now its attention was fixed on Rochester where Tilden had the stellar rôle in an unparalleled, doom-laden drama of shameless villainy. But it was a part for which he was unfitted by his extreme caution. In the opening scene, when daring and unrestrained denunciation would have wrested control of the convention from the Ring and won the grateful plaudits of a nation, Tilden temporized. He had two days in which to battle the forces of corruption, in and out of his party. Such a struggle would have been Olympian, and he would probably have emerged from it as his party's candidate for President. But he chose to make a short and dignified attack, devoid of personalities. It was hardly an attack, but an arraignment such as is made in a court of law when all the niceties of judicial precedure are observed. This restrained and cautious indictment of the Ring, while it established Tilden as of statesmanlike mold, revealed him as completely devoid of the artifices of a demagogue, which are prerequisites of leadership in a republic where suffrage is almost universal. He sought to make amends the second day, but he was too late. Moreover, he again muted the thunder to a lamblike bleat.

Tilden arrived in Rochester on Monday, accompanied by his old friend, Francis Kernan of Utica, and Kernan's townsman, General McQuade, whom we met on the eve of the Orange riot. Kernan had been defeated for reëlection to Congress in 1864 by Conkling; but he had an influence that passed the confines of the Mohawk Valley.

Tweed arrived the following night with two hundred friends and office-holders, and the entire Tammany delegation. In two hours he displayed a political generalship that in itself gave the lie to Nast's cartoons depicting him as a drunken Falstaff. Before Tweed's arrival, Tilden and his allies were in control, but by midnight, Tweed had reduced the opposition to a negligible minority, and formulated a plan to rout his convention foes. As Tweed finished his labors, a torchlight procession of several hundred, marching eight abreast and led by a band of thirty pieces, halted in front of his hotel and serenaded him.

Tweed was not a delegate, but when the convention was called to order some twelve hours later, the first signs of his strategy were apparent. The seats reserved for the Tammany delegates were vacant. Unaware of what was in store for him, Tilden delivered the key-note speech, assailing Grant and the administration by name, but failing to identify the humblest retainer of the Ring in his cautious references to the corruption in the metropolis—which he blamed in part on the Republicans. Yet two hours before Tilden began speaking, news had reached Rochester of the shameful spectacle of New York City's mayor arraigned on a criminal charge, the first fruits of the prosecution of the Ring. The Elegant Oakey was accused of having authorized payments in an illegal manner. It was not a serious charge. But it was a fair beginning. Tilden began his address with recollections which warmed every heart that did not hate him. He praised

WHOLESALE.

RETAIL.

The four principal figures in the upper half of the cartoon are Tweed and Sweeny, with the spectacled Hall and the smiling Slippery Dick Connolly behind them. *Harper's Weekly*, Sept. 16, 1871.

the two Clintons, Van Buren, Silas Wright, and William L. Marcy, and attacked Grant. He said:

Every Democratic National Convention would, by common consent, reject from its consideration a man who had filled the public offices with his relatives, or who had been enriched by costly presents while exercising thc immense power of the presidency to promote men's interests or gratify men's ambitions. I do not wish to speak harshly of the illustrious soldier who fills the presidential chair. He may not have been conscious of the fatal example he has set. But when the two ideas of personal gain and the bestowal of public office are allowed to become one . . . it is but a step to the sale of the greatest of trusts. Intellect, training, virtue, will soon succumb to wealth.

There was nothing demagogic in Tilden's next utterance, a prophecy since fulfilled, far too often, in these United States. Tilden was rich, so he cannot be accused of class prejudice. Said he:

"Vulgar millionaires will grasp the highest seats of honor and power as they would put a new emblazonment upon their carriages or a gaudy livery upon their servants."

But there was a false note in this utterance, a partizan note. Tilden was chairman of the Democratic State Committee and was addressing a party convention. And taken in connection with what followed, he was attacking the Republican opposition. He might have added, to be eminently fair, that what he was predicting had also occurred in the past, and that years back, August Belmont, chairman of the Democratic National Committee, had been justly accused of having "bought the honor of representing this Republic abroad"—the post of United States chargé d'affaires at The Hague.

Tilden next noted that the ascendancy of his party in New York began after the state constitutional convention in 1821, when "Van Buren, Marcy, Wright, and Flagg ruled." And he added, with truth:

"They were men of absolute personal honor and truth, and in all the counties they attracted to themselves similar men. They wielded party power not only for pure measures but for honest men. If a young man who had served one session in the legislature came back to lobby, he lost his standing with the party leaders. Corruption in the legislative bodies was almost unknown."

After these references to Van Buren and his three great lights of the Albany Regency, our first political machine, he cited an instance of the Regency's rigid party discipline when it forced three Democratic state senators to resign because they held back a railroad bill to gamble in its stocks.

"Take that era of the ascendancy of the Republican party and of the party from which it sprang," he continued. "Your legislative bodies invariably—almost immediately—became purchasable. Twice within that time the great office of Senator of the United States—the seat of Clinton, Van Buren, Wright, and Marcy—has been put up and knocked down to the highest bidder."

Tilden paused as delegates leaned forward in their chairs. To name these two purchasers of Senate seats would eliminate all doubt as to the outcome of the election. For eight years the Empire State talked of the purchase of a Senate seat by Edwin D. Morgan, twice governor of New York, on whom Williams College had conferred the degree of Doctor of Laws for his benefactions. Morgan was temporarily in political oblivion, but not Conkling, whose seat in the Senate had also been purchased, according to common report. It was whispered that friends put up the cash for Conkling's seat.

What proof Tilden had, beyond the rumors and implied charges in the press and at gatherings of politicians, that

Morgan bought his seat in 1863 and that admirers of
Conkling, with $200,000, outbid all others four years later,
does not appear, for he dropped the subject after making
the charge.

Tilden then paid tribute to the honesty of the Germans
and Irish, and in his next breath, said: "The municipal corruption of New York City is the result of irresponsible power
acting in the secrecy of bureaus and commissions. It is the
outgrowth of twenty years of Republican legislation at
Albany, and a partnership of plunder between men of both
parties established during that period."

If Tilden regarded the hearty applause when he finished
as an indication of his hold on the delegates, he was quickly
disillusioned. For after the convention had unanimously
elected Representative Clarkson N. Potter temporary chairman, the delegates cheered loudly when a Brooklyn delegate announced that Tammany had a communication to
offer. Charles G. Cornell presented the document, signed by
himself and his fellow Tammanies, demanding a "rigid and
searching investigation" of the charges in the public press
"involving the official integrity of prominent members of the
Tammany Hall General Committee." Then the signers,
"actuated solely by a desire to promote the harmony of the
party and the success of the regular Democratic candidates,
both state and local, at the coming election," waived the
right to participate in the proceedings of the convention.

When the clerk finished reading, the same Brooklynite
moved the adoption of the following: "Resolved, that in the
call of the roll, New York [County] be omitted in the future
proceedings of this body, and no delegate be deemed as
sitting from that locality."

Tilden saw the trap and rose to protest, for he planned
to seat the anti-Ring Democrats in the section reserved for
Tammany. This had been foreseen by Tweed, who, although

absent, was directing the proceedings of the convention. As Tilden began speaking, the Brooklyn delegate silenced him, and shut off all debate on the resolution, by moving the previous question. And Tweed's convention overwhelmingly sustained the gag motion.

The organization of the convention continued uneventfully until Horatio Seymour's name was mentioned. Whereupon the entire convention cheered the party's 1868 nominee for President as "our next President." Seymour bowed his thanks. He had been approved by Tweed for permanent chairman of the convention. But when word reached Tweed that Seymour had a speech prepared assailing the Ring as unprincipled thieves, he was told to omit this oratory if he desired the honor. About this time Seymour moved the privileges of the floor for his townsman, Kernan. Tweed's Brooklyn spokesman objected to the motion as irregular, solely to humiliate Seymour, for Kernan was later admitted. Seymour, however, took the hint, made a graceful exit by pleading illness, and returned to Utica.

After Seymour retired, Tilden attempted to retrieve his lost position at the second session of the convention, but his words were lost in tumultuous shouts that he was out of order. When quiet was restored, Tilden said calmly:

I was stating what I consider the objection to Tammany Hall, aside from the cloud that now covers that concern, and I am free to avow that I shall not vote for any one of Mr. Tweed's members of the legislature. And if that is to be regarded as the regular ticket, I will resign my place as chairman of the state committee and retire to the bosom of my plundered fellow citizens. When I come to do my duty as an elector, I shall cast my vote for honest men.

This was the birth of Tilden's political leadership. Till now he had been a machine rubber stamp. Tweed was the

machine. The rôle had not been pleasant, and Tilden played
it as others of economic independence, with political ambitions, had played it since the 1840's. Tilden was ambitious,
and to quote Tweed's truism again, "A politician in coming

Francis Kernan

Leslie's Weekly, September 28, 1872.

forward takes things as they are." So Tilden accepted the
Ring until it was safe to reject it. The Ring was now crum-
bling.

But Tilden should have said these things yesterday, and
used names. The only effect of his belated attack was to

divide his party on the eve of a campaign, without increasing the strength of his own faction. For immediately after he had finished, Tweed's ticket was renominated, all save the secretary of state who declined a renomination, and the convention and its work went before the electorate bearing Tweed's label. Tweed publicly derided Tilden, along with Kernan and Seymour, as "three troublesome old fools." And the Boss returned to town measurably happy, for the platform hung the responsibility for the thievings of the Ring on the Republican party. On this score the Democrats solemnly appealed "to the record and to the facts to prove that the deplorable condition of affairs existing in New York was augmented and fastened upon the city by a system of irresponsible government instituted by the Republican party, and continued through many years, under which the growth of extravagance, peculation, and fraud was inevitable." This was only a variation of Tilden's muted outcry against the Ring.

Tilden later estimated that this whitewash cost the state ticket "at least 10,000 or 12,000" Democratic votes in the city. It alienated thousands upstate, thereby overwhelming the Democratic candidates.

16

THE SLUMS ABANDON THE RING

NEXT TO CRUSHING THE RING ITSELF, TILDEN'S MAJOR CONcern was to elect dependable men to the legislature. For as he wrote later, reform of the New York City judiciary "was not only intrinsically the most important to the welfare, safety, and honor" of the community, "but was a measure without which every other reform would prove nugatory." And this reform could only be accomplished in the legislature.

Judiciary reform meant not only remedial legislation but the impeachment of the Ring judges. As this reform might depend on the city vote, Tilden planned to use Aaron Burr's successful device of 1800 when he nominated for the assembly, on the city ticket, George Clinton, Horatio Gates, Brockholst Livingston, Samuel Osgood, and others less famous. Burr went to the assembly as Tilden was to go.

As in 1800, the New York City electorate was roused to fever pitch. Green, Tilden's representative in Slippery Dick's office, kept up the voters' temperature with daily disclosures of the Ring's methods. His lists of pay-roll patriots who did nothing for salaries filched from the taxpayers' pockets, save graft a little more wherever possible, astounded the town. Typical was Gratz Nathan, listed as a clerk at $3,000 a year. Nathan was a lawyer and a nephew of Cardozo. But as the press tersely noted, Nathan "has never, at any time, done duty as a clerk." Tilden and O'Conor were working on other material discovered by Green which was being withheld temporarily from the press. These concerned one of Boss Tweed's bank accounts.

When the Ring packed a grand jury to hear charges against Mayor Hall, Nast made the above twelve cuts of Hall and called them "Portraits of the Mayor's Grand Jury." *Harper's Weekly*, October 21, 1871.

Meanwhile, the Elegant Oakey unwittingly dramatized the desperation of the Ring. As mayor, he and five judges selected the twenty-three members of the grand jury which was to vote on an indictment against him. The foreman of the grand jury, a man of seventy-five and consequently exempt from jury service was William Hall, an uncle of the accused mayor. The Elegant Oakey had another relative among these good men and true, Robert Hall, a cousin. Another grand juror was John W. Guentzer, Tammany leader of the Eighteenth Ward. Others on this packed grand jury were: George W. Butt, the Bayard Street liveryman who remained faithful to Tweed to the end; Charles Guidet, a friend of both Tweed and the Elegant Oakey; George W. Haws, president of an insurance company of which Tweed's son Richard was receiver; Charles Johnson, owner of a stable rented to the city as an armory; Christopher O'Connor, a pool-room keeper and Ring hanger-on. In all, about eighteen of the twenty-three grand jurors were tools of the Ring. As an outraged town looked on, O'Conor had Barnard issue an order dissolving this packed grand jury.

Tweed's arrest in a civil suit, on an affidavit sworn to by Tilden, quickly followed. They had nothing criminal on Tweed as yet. The charge involved the payment of $5,512,-541.57 on fraudulent vouchers. More than $1,000,000 of this sum was traced to Tweed's bank account. Tweed was spared the humiliation of manual arrest, for he was released simultaneously with the service of the warrant as Jay Gould put up $1,000,000 in real estate, and four others together put up another $1,000,000. The bail was $1,000,000, but in New York, when real estate is offered, double the amount of the bond is required.

Tweed's arrest, coming eleven days before election, was the crowning blow of the campaign against the Ring. Such had been the temper of the people for days, that the Ring's Republican allies did not dare make their usual election deals. Tilden succeeded, somewhat, in his plan to have a legislative ticket of unusual appeal. O'Conor declined to stand for the assembly, but reminded Tilden that "a member of the legislature need not reside in the district that elects him," and added: "Kernan would be a grand candidate for the senate against Tweed or Norton." Both Norton and Tweed relied largely on the Irish vote. When Kernan failed them, O'Conor produced O'Donovan Rossa to oppose Tweed. Together they persuaded Erastus C. Benedict, lawyer and educator, poet and philanthropist, to run against Norton. Benedict's *American Admiralty Practise* had been the sole authority for this branch of law for nearly a quarter of a century; his metrical translations of medieval poems were on many a bookshelf. Another distinguished Democrat nominated jointly by the Reform Democrats and Republicans for senator was Daniel F. Tiemann, a member of Tammany Hall, who had been elected mayor in 1857 when a similar fusion temporarily suppressed the infamous Fernando Wood, aptly described by John Bigelow as the most corrupt man that ever sat in the mayor's chair. Tiemann was a man of wealth and owned the city hall for a time, purchasing it for $50,000 when the sheriff auctioned it off to satisfy a judgment, the city treasury having been drained dry in Wood's administration.

Topping all the anti-Ring candidates in prominence was former Governor Seymour, who ran against the notorious Tom Fields, in the Nineteenth Assembly District. Tom, it will be remembered, gave $5,000 in diamonds to Tweed's daughter for a wedding gift. Tilden ran for the assembly in the Eighteenth District.

A few of the anti-Ring nominations can be justified solely on the grounds of political expediency. One of these was O'Brien, who was elected to the senate.

The most colorful figure of the campaign was General Franz Sigel, candidate for register, whose pronounced accent in any one else would have aroused a non-German audience to laughter. But Sigel was different: he was a hero of the Civil War. The Republicans idolized him. The Demo-

crats respected him. Upon Sigel and Rossa devolved the
task of undoing the work of the Ring orators who had beguiled countless poor into believing they had nothing to lose
from taxes because they had nothing to tax. Another Ring
canard was that Sigel's election would mean the removal
from the register's office of every man of Irish birth or
descent. Rossa met this issue. Into the countless Rag-pickers'
Rows and Bone Alleys Rossa and Sigel went with their message. In Tweed's district the bribery of the voters was expected to reach a new high. To offset this, Rossa printed a
circular so pat that Greeley first-paged it in the *Tribune*.
With a few changes, Rossa's appeal would serve in any campaign where corruption is the issue. It was written at white
heat, and read:

Reasons why Irishmen should vote for O'Donovan Rossa and
not for W. M. Tweed.

First, Because O'Donovan Rossa is an honest man and Tweed
is not.

Second, Because Tweed is under arrest for robbery and assist-
ing to rob the citizens of New York of millions of dollars for
which the poor people of this district will have to pay in high
rents and in high prices for provisions, while O'Donovan Rossa
has emulated the deeds of Washington and suffered a long term
of imprisonment in English dungeons.

What has O'Donovan Rossa done that any Irishman should
vote against him? He has not gulled you or made money on you
as Tweed has done.

Tweed has taken lessons from the oppressors of Ireland, and
has introduced a kind of political loaferism in the IVth Senate
District; his friends call it charity; but you know Tweed and his
tools understand the dodge.

Will you voters of the IVth Senate District be bought so cheap
—bought by the money stolen from your own pocket?

Vote against the political loafer, Tweed, and for the patriot,
O'Donovan Rossa!

Every friend of freedom applauded Tipperary for electing O'Donovan Rossa to the English Parliament while he was in an English dungeon. Irishmen in every part of the world now look to the voters of the IVth Senate District of New York to help send the same O'Donovan Rossa to the State Senate, while the Board of Municipal Correction will send Tweed to Sing Sing where he belongs.

On the Saturday preceding election, O'Conor made his first political speech in years, and urged voters of the Nineteenth Assembly District to elect Seymour. His address was patterned on a written appeal he and other prominent Democrats and Republicans of the district had issued a few days earlier in which they pictured Tom Fields as a thief and swindler "who obtained over $470,000 in 1870 presumably to pay volunteer firemen" in the Nineteenth Assembly District. Of this sum Fields "kept for himself more than one-half." O'Conor told of another swindle where Fields obtained $77,000 from the city for damages to a bus line and kept $70,000 for himself and gave $7,000 to the bus company. "These are two of the many raids upon the city treasury by Thomas C. Fields," said O'Conor.

But the Ring waged the fight in its usual way, spending money lavishly and dinning into the ears of its audiences in the poorer sections that the fight on Tweed and his organization was being waged by rich men who alone had anything to fear from high taxes. Greeley saw the danger of this insidious argument. So he did a rare thing, and appeared with a signed article in the *Tribune's* news columns. Greeley wrote not only for that campaign—he wrote for all time, as witness:

It is too generally believed that the rich pay all the taxes upon Houses, Lots, Grounds, etc., in a great city like ours. Hence many poor men give little thought to the constant and rapid growth of Municipal extravagance and prodigality. *They* are not dunned by the tax-collector—no part of the vast amount paid into the city's treasury is wrung directly from their hands. In their view, taxation is the concern of landlords and capitalists, not of journeymen and laborers who own no homes and, of course, pay no taxes.

But they *do* pay: they *must* pay. If a tenement house is valued by the assessors at $50,000, the tax on it at 2 per cent is $1,000 per annum. Who pays it? The landlord immediately; the tenants ultimately. . . .

All of us are subsisted upon the fruits of labor; all taxes are paid therefrom. He who has made millions by office and politics may well give back to poverty a part of it in alms; but he cannot give so much as he has taken and have anything left. If he scatters gold coins among the poor as though they were pebbles, he must have made it by some means inconsistent with old-fashioned honesty and fidelity to public trust. . . .

Every dollar taken from the public treasury, in payment for services not required, in excessive payment for services actually performed, is so much money unjustly wrested from private citizens for the aggrandizement of the wielders of power. It is a discouragement as well as a burden to honest industry which sees its modest earnings swept into the hoard of official profligacy. It lures aspiring youth from the school-room and the work-bench to crowd primary meetings and figure in caucuses in the sanguine hope of finding in politics a means of living without useful productive labor. . . .

The campaigning in most parts of the city ended Election Eve. But in the poorer sections the Committee of Seventy and the Greeley Republicans had lesser Franz Sigels and O'Donovan Rossas appealing to the workers and the unemployed well into the small hours of the morning. They spoke and harangued in saloons and on street corners.

The metropolis was apprehensive as the polls opened. Riots were feared. Four regiments of the National Guard were held in readiness for any untoward trouble. The advantage was with the Ring. It controlled the police, the legal guardians of the polls. The police also appointed the election inspectors, both Republican and Democratic. The police guarded the ballots after they were counted—and anything might happen then.

Save in Tweed's district, there was little mauling of anti-Ring men at the polls. The heaviest vote was cast in the slums. The stay-at-home vote was not so large, and confined, as usual, to the better residential districts. The customary ballot-box stuffing and stealing prevailed, although to a lesser degree.

The astonishing thing was the heavy anti-Ring vote in the slums. Men long strangers to a piece of steak, and some of them with families who prayed more fervently as the winter approached, "Give us this day our daily bread," spurned the Ring bribes. Their votes routed the Ring and ensured the election of the Republican state ticket. Sigel and the anti-Ring judges were swept into office. Sigel had a majority of 28,117. Unfortunately, the unholy three, Cardozo, Barnard, and McCunn, were not up for reëlection.

Rossa and the other anti-Ring candidates for senator were elected in the city's five senatorial districts. But Tweed was fraudulently counted in after a day of unchecked violence. Greeley described the frauds in Tweed's district as enormous, and the intimidation of voters without parallel. "Ballots for O'Donovan Rossa were kept out of the ballot-boxes by sheer ruffianism," he said, "and in many precincts, it was literally unsafe to vote against the Boss."

Before the voting was an hour old, most of the anti-Ring election inspectors had been driven from the polls in Tweed's district. Some who decided to stand their ground were disposed of in various ways. One of these, Michael Costello, asked the police to arrest a repeater. Edward Coppers, the

Tammany inspector, signaled to four thugs who instantly bore Costello to the floor, kicked and pummeled him while four policemen looked on approvingly. The mauling ceased when Costello was unconscious. The policemen revived him and arrested him on the charge of assaulting an officer!

Tilden, Seymour, and fourteen other anti-Ring candidates for the assembly were elected. But Seymour was dishonestly counted out in favor of Tom Fields. Yet with all the election thievery, the Ring had only six of the city's twenty-one assemblymen. The results were similar elsewhere in the state. Democrats, good and bad, were generally defeated and, consequently, the Republicans controlled both houses of the legislature by better than three to one. In the metropolis, the Ring made a little better showing with candidates for assistant alderman, but only two of its nominees for alderman survived the popular wrath.

17

WHY THE MASTER GRAFTERS, SAVE ONE, ESCAPED—WHY A SOLDIER-SCHOLAR SAID, "TO HELL WITH REFORM!"

THE DAY AFTER ELECTION, WHEN THERE WAS NO LONGER any doubt of the rout of the Ring candidates, the nation looked forward to a series of prosecutions commensurate with the magnitude of the crimes of Tweed and his associates. In the metropolis, the demand for swift justice had become almost unanimous overnight. Tweed had been arrested. So had Hall. But this was not enough, and as days and months passed with only one major prosecution, that of Tweed, the press and public shouted for action.

The prime movers in the fight on Tweed—the leaders in his own party—were alarmed by these shouts. Tilden and other party chiefs had been concerned primarily in a struggle for party control. They had crushed the Ring, and they, not Tweed and his satellites, would henceforth control. The chief concern of the lawyers engaged in the struggle was to remove the Ring judges from the bench—not all, for the lower courts remained untouched. To have attempted a general purification of the bench in the metropolis would have alienated too many party wheel-horses and endangered the fruits of victory. A triumphant group in a fight for party supremacy can rely on the loyalty of the average district or ward leader if they do not go too far. And Tilden, a resourceful veteran of many party battles, knew where to stop. But he also knew that a successful politician listens to the crowd.

The crowd was shouting to jail all the Ring members and their thieving beneficiaries. This was a far larger order than Tilden and other party bosses intended to fill. Yet they must make a pretense of compliance. They had no intention of destroying those who now acknowledged their leadership. The crowd did not understand, and saw in the Ring a thing of evil, now no more. But those who stepped into the shoes of Tweed and his lieutenants knew otherwise. Other rings had preceded the Tweed Ring and no one went to jail. Others were to follow in New York and in other large centers of population. The Ring is dead! Long live the Ring! Usually the Ring is only in temporary exile when the people think it is banished forever. The Tweed Ring, itself, did not sell protection to the underworld. This was a perquisite of its satellites. It trafficked in nominations and appointments to office, legislation, judicial decisions, taxes, public contracts, franchises, and other favors of value at the disposal of a political machine in power. The predecessors of the Tweed Ring had been content with modest loot; their avarice was not orgiastic; they were content with stealing ten to fifteen dollars out of every hundred dollars paid on the city's bills. Then, too, the directors of these rings did not control a state machine, nor were any of them opposed by a man acquainted with every move in the game of politics, the possessor of millions and an unquenchable thirst for power—a man ready to spend generously of his riches to achieve his political ambitions. The spoliations of these rings rarely became public until the thieves were out of power, and the statute of limitations—assuming a desire to prosecute—usually operated in behalf of the thieves. One ring returned to power because its head gave the electors a good laugh. This was the Wood

Ring. When Wood's successor in office, Mayor Tiemann, honest and wealthy, personally bid in the city hall, the entire town laughed because Wood had threatened to buy the glorious architectural masterpiece to house his mercenary Mozart Hall Democracy. All's well when the people are merry.

Twenty-four hours after the election of 1871 the people were not merry. They had little, or nothing. The Ring had millions. They knew that these millions had come from their pockets, taxpayers and non-taxpayers alike. And so they redoubled their shouts for vengeance. In another twenty-four hours, a sop was thrown their way. Tom Fields, the Ring's agent in the state assembly, was arrested in a civil suit for some $500,000 which he was charged with having obtained by fraud and deceit from the city. Bondsmen had $200,000 ready when the sheriff called.

This arrest, with the promises to punish every one involved in the Ring's thievings, temporarily deceived the people into regarding the reform element as sincere. The reformers also promised to publish a complete list of all the sums of moneys paid out of the city treasury on the authorization of the Ring, and the names of the recipients. No guilty person would escape. But Tilden and his political allies had no such intentions.

A fortnight later, Slippery Dick was arrested in a civil suit. As in Tweed's case, bail was fixed at $1,000,000. This was the first manual arrest, for Connolly had no bondsmen. He languished in Ludlow Street jail till New Year's Eve, when he was released in the reduced sum of $500,000.

Connolly was the third of the Ring quadrumvirate to be arrested. There remained only Sweeny. But he did not wait for his arrest. He fled to Canada, thence to France, taking millions with him. And in Paris he was soon joined by Connolly, who took with him more than $6,000,000. How many millions Sweeny carried was never known. When Slippery Dick and the stolen millions reached France, he was met by a daughter—he had two—and her husband, once the proud owner of a wooden Indian and a little cigar shop on Canal

"Stone Walls Do Not a Prison Make" is the title of this prophetic cartoon of Tweed's escape from jail. The subtitle reads: "No prison is big enough to hold the Boss. In on one side, and out at the other." *Harper's Weekly,* January 6, 1872.

Street. Slippery Dick blossomed forth with a château and private yacht basin on Lake Geneva, and a mansion in Paris. He saw a granddaughter marry a French count. Most of Slippery Dick's millions, practically his entire loot, had gone to the ex-tobacconist's wife and to another daughter. After eighteen years of exile, his hair white, his body bent, his pockets almost empty, Slippery Dick died in Marseilles, an ignoble Lear.

While Tweed was on his way to the Tombs, he was haled before Barnard on a writ of habeas corpus and released in bail. Slippery Dick Connolly was later housed in Ludlow Street jail. Sweeny, at large, is shown peering from the City Hall at the "Amusing trick scene of 'Now you've got him, and now you haven't,' in the laughable burlesque of the 'Brazen Ring.'" Charles O'Conor is holding down the lid of the trunk. Mayor Hall is backstage with Justice, attired as a danseuse, then a synonym for bawd because of Fisk's association with opera and ballet. *Harper's Weekly*, 1872.

During Slippery Dick's imprisonment a grand jury indicted Tweed for felony. He was held without bail upon his arraignment on December 16, but before he reached the Tombs a writ of habeus corpus spared him this added shame. Barnard released him in $5,000 bond, as he was already under $1,000,000 bail. His case was not to be tried for more than a year.

These prosecutions, civil and criminal, save in the case of Tweed, were farcical. The Ring's thievings, as we have seen, were monumental—how much, only those in the know could say, and they never told. The first official audit, admittedly incomplete, put the Ring's loot for the thirty months ended on July 31, 1871, at $30,000,000. A later audit estimated that the Tweed Ring proper, which began in 1869, and its immediate forerunner had looted the city of between $45,000,000 and $50,000,000 in the three years and six months beginning January 1, 1868. Six years after the fall of the Ring, an aldermanic investigation raised the estimate to $60,000,000. This was only another guess. O'Rourke reckoned that the Tweed Ring and the lesser rings headed by Tweed despoiled the taxpayers of $200,000,000 between January 1, 1865, and July 31, 1871. This included fraudulent bond issues, the sale of tax reductions, and the disposal of franchises and other favors of an approximate worth of $125,000,000.

Tweed escaped conviction at his first trial, January, 1873, because the jury disagreed. On his second trial, ten months later, he was found guilty of fifty-one of the fifty-five charges in an indictment alleging neglect of duty. Each of the charges contained four counts. The maximum sentence was one year on each of the 204 counts. He was sentenced to twelve years in the penitentiary and to pay a fine of $12,750; but after serving a little more than one year on Blackwell's Island, the Court of Appeals held that the sentences were not cumulative, and freed him. He was rearrested on a new civil suit for $6,000,000 based on a retroactive act of the state legislature aimed at him alone. Unable to provide $3,000,000 bail, he was cast into Ludlow Street jail. But money bought him favors, including trips around town, and less than eleven months after this imprisonment, he escaped from his keepers while visiting his home on December 4, 1875. He fled to Cuba and thence to Spain, where he was as safe as Connolly and the other millionaire exiles. He could not be extradited. Nevertheless, he was arrested and immediately surrendered to the commander of Farragut's famed flag-ship, the U.S.S. *Franklin*, which sailed from Vigo with its prisoner of state. On November 23, 1876, Tweed was again in the custody of the sheriff of New York. Knowing his days were numbered, he was contrite and willing to surrender and tell all, if spared the crowning disgrace of dying in prison.

Immediately began a grim farce that did not end with Tweed's death in Ludlow Street jail, April 12, 1878. This farce represented a greater crime than any committed by the Ring. Of the millions stolen—all recoverable at law—only $1,353,410.96 found its way back to the city treasury, and this amount did not cover the expenses of the sham prosecutions. When Tweed offered to surrender all he possessed, and aid the people to recover the rest of the stolen moneys by a complete breast of everything, no one dared to refuse his offer coldly. It was at first accepted, pretendedly so. Tilden was governor. Tweed was a sick man. His brown hair was gray from suffering. He did not have many months to live. When it became apparent that his confession was not desired, he appealed to O'Conor, writing to him on December 5, 1876, repeating his offer of "unqualified surrender." He continued:

It is not my purpose to appeal or further resist the suits which you have against me in the name of the State or the People. I propose forthwith to place at your disposal a full surrender of all I have left of property or effects and respond at once to such examination in this connection as may assure you and the public of the good faith of the assignment as well as show the entire amount and disposition of all I have possessed as far as you wish it to be detailed.

I am an old man, greatly broken in health, and cut down in spirits and can no longer bear my burden, and to mitigate the prospects of hopeless imprisonment, which must speedily terminate my life, I should, it seems to me, make any sacrifice or effort. . . . I would not make this futile offer if I had not had some assurance through your published statements that the vindication of principle and the prospect of permanently purifying the public service was the object you have in view as being more desirable than the recovery of money. If in any manner you see fit to use me for such purposes, I shall be only too glad to respond, trusting implicitly to your high reputation and character. . . . I hope to have any matters affecting other persons restricted to your *personal* knowledge and discretion. . . . I only ask in qualification that your more reliable judgment shall take the responsibility of publication and the use of such matters only as may be necessary for the ends you may wish to advance. . . . I have no legal counsel. I shall not employ any except to aid in the spirit of this communication and conform to the usages of the courts.

O'Conor soon learned that the door Tweed's confession alone could open must remain closed. To open that door would disclose as grafters men who had served with Tweed in the legislature, now holding high place on the bench and as chief executives of towns and cities of the state. To open that door might precipitate runs on banks when some of their officers were exposed as accomplices of thieves. To open that door would injure the good name of many prominent men. But no one, not even Tilden, dared to tell O'Conor that the door must remain closed. O'Conor was never accused of lack of understanding, and had reason before this to suspect that strange things were happening. Tilden and the rest had lured him from his rustic retreat on the northern tip of Manhattan Island to direct the fight against the Ring. O'Conor had exacted only one condition: that he serve without pay. He had gained nothing materially from his labors. Tilden had obtained all he could possibly expect, politically. Some were now calling him President-elect. Well, O'Conor could go back to his country place, no richer than when he left, save in honor.

After O'Conor retired, Charles S. Fairchild, attorney-general of the state, pretended a willingness to accept Tweed's proffered confession. But Tweed realized there was little hope. They would let him rot in a debtor's cell for the $6,000,000 judgment he could not satisfy rather than injure a little army of silk-hatted thieves. They would not even dare put him on trial on any of the several indictments for forgery pending against him lest his testimony injure these worthies. Many others escaped because Fairchild delayed action until the statute of limitations threw its protecting arm around the crooks. And the honest jurist, Noah Davis, in condemning from the bench the farcical prosecutions of the Ring, said:

"The worst feature of it all . . . is that, notwithstanding all these crimes have been so clearly proven that no man can doubt their existence, nevertheless, the whole body of these conspirators against the city and its treasury go substantially unwhipped of justice."

But there was real tragedy in the farce, for those who compounded this grave crime had garbed themselves in the white habiliments of reform. One who sat through this tragic farce was the always amiable Colonel Asa Bird Gardiner, called the most brilliant judge-advocate of the United States Army. He was courtliness itself, and his scholarship is partly enshrined in several legal textbooks. He served in the Civil War, and was professor of law at the United States Military Academy until invalided out in 1888. He was assistant secretary of war under Cleveland and made his famous attack on reform and reformers as Tammany's successful candidate for district attorney.

Gardiner's double-barreled attack—he fired two blasts, one within and one outside a Tammany club-house in Harlem—had its roots in the sham prosecution of the Tweed Ring and the attendant disclosures. Gardiner was in jolly mood when presented to the members of the Wabatchie Club at their headquarters, 125th Street and Third Avenue. He began by recalling Tammany's defeat in the preceding election, and inquired if they remembered how Tammany was driven from office. Lest any had forgotten he proceeded to tell them.

"The cry was for reform," continued Gardiner scornfully. "We got it." After he had paid tribute to the personal honesty of William L. Strong, a Republican, the reform mayor of the city, he berated the reformers for increasing taxes and accused them of stealing a million dollars a year in cleaning the streets. "When any of these people talk to you about municipal reform," he shouted, "you can tell them—and I use strong language because I have been in the Army—to hell with reform!"

The peppery Colonel, long noted for his free tongue and soldier's oaths, was denouncing the knaves who wax rich in their professed devotion to reform, whose motto is: "Make money, rightfully if you can, but if not, in any manner possible." A few minutes later, speaking to an overflow meeting outside the Wabatchie Club, the Colonel made it clear that his targets were professional reformers, whom he called bastards. He had no sooner used this epithet than he half apologized for using the word in public by confessing he had had a cocktail. But one who had fought for the Republic would be pardoned for applying the ancestral taunt to its worst enemies—even without a cocktail.

18

HOW A JEST CREATED

A REPUTATION FOR BRAINS

COMPARE THE UNRELENTING PROSECUTION OF THE CONTRITE and dying Tweed with the friendly attitude of the reformers toward the other master grafters. Let us consider Sweeny, the most brazen of the lot. Some $7,000,000 stolen from the taxpapers was traced to him and he was sued for that amount.

Sweeny was in Paris when this action was brought. Yet, as Tweed was dying in Ludlow Street jail, Sweeny was permitted to return to New York, immune from molestation, upon payment of $394,594.28, leaving him with more than $6,500,000 of the stolen money.

An attempt was made to depict Sweeny as a hero, for, in compromising the claim against him, the reformers authorized him to say that the money was stolen by his brother James, and he was making restitution to clear his dead brother's name. A judge was party to this fraud, and volunteered from the bench that the settlement did not reflect in any way on Mr. Sweeny.

This judge was Theodoric R. Westbrook. We have an explanation for Westbrook's conduct in the impeachment proceedings vainly brought against him five years later by a new member of the assembly, Theodore Roosevelt, charging "corrupt collusion with Jay Gould and the prostitution of his high judicial office to serve the purpose of wealthy and unscrupulous stock gamblers." Gould was an old pal of Sweeny.

James M. Sweeny, who bore his father's Christian name, died of drink in 1875. He had been his brother's chief graft collector, and depended upon him for his debauches. Newspapers knew this, and condemned the shabby fraud. Said the New York *Evening Post* of June 7, 1877:

Of course, no one will be deceived by this disgraceful and offensive sham. The suit of the people was not against James Sweeny. He is dead. The proceeding was not against the estate. It is not believed that he had any estate. It is known that he lived by the breath of his brother, that he was a mere miserable tool and that nobody would have been more astonished than himself if it had been suggested that he should pay to the people of New York, or to anybody else, several hundred thousand dollars, or any other sum. James Sweeny is simply a lay figure upon which are to be hung the garments that are to rehabilitate with respectability the living person of Peter B. Sweeny.

This was typical of the criticisms of this hocus-pocus. Peter Bismarck Brains Sweeny was described by an aldermanic investigating committee this same year as "the most despicable of the gang." This was not an exaggeration. But it was poppycock to call him Tweed's evil genius, or the Brains of the Ring. He was neither. The erroneous impression that Sweeny was a one-man brain trust had its origin in an amusing incident. During the early assaults upon the Ring, a journalist humorously wrote that the middle initial of Sweeny's name stood for Bismarck. This sobriquet appealed to popular fancy, for Sweeny was noted for his domineering ways; thereafter he was described as Peter Bismarck Sweeny or plain Bismarck until the German element protested against pinning the Iron Chancellor's name on a notorious thief. So overnight Bismarck became Brains, and from that day Sweeny was a man of massive intellect in the eyes of the unknowing. He was the chief legal adviser of the Ring, nothing more.

Sweeny was a welter of contradictions—shy, bold, timid, brazen, cruel, kind. His one redeeming quality, kindness, was —so far as the record discloses—lavished wholly on his mother's brother, Thomas J. Barr, sometime Tammany leader of the Sixth Ward, and successively assistant alderman, alderman, state senator, member of Congress, and police commissioner. Barr was a member of the City Council of 1852, wherein the Ring had its origin. Tweed's first elective office was to this notorious body, which was called the Forty Thieves. Sweeny was then a lobbyist of at least three years' standing, handling bribes, principally for street-railway companies and other seekers after legislative favors. Barr, before going to Albany in 1854 as a member of the senate, made Sweeny public administrator. At the capital Sweeny and the Elegant Oakey became chums. Hall was a Whig, but both were lobbyists, which removed any political barriers. In 1858 Sweeny was elected one of the two leaders of Tammany Hall, there being two rival general committees, and that same year he succeeded the Elegant Oakey as district attorney. Both places Sweeny owed to his uncle, whose devotion to him began when Sweeny was an infant and Barr worked in the Park Row porterhouse of Sweeny's father. Until the overthrow of the Ring, the private life of Sweeny was a closed book. The people were prepared for anything that might be said of Tweed; they just shrugged their shoulders on reading that the Elegant Oakey's private life "would not bear looking into," and that Slippery Dick had to flee from Philadelphia in his youth to escape the consequences of an intrigue with a market woman. But when they read that Peter Brains Sweeny had as mistress an attendant in a Turkish bath, a journalist ventured that Peter Brains was an

Ottoman in disguise and had a harem. When Sweeny, Connolly, Hall, and Tweed were in the saddle, few dared even
to whisper a thing against them. And that their influence,
Tweed excepted, had not wholly waned with their fall is
manifest from the arrangements, secretly made, for Sweeny's
return from exile to enjoy the millions criminally filched
from the taxpayers and taxearners.

19

FISK INVOKES TOMAHAWK JUSTICE—

A MURDER TRIAL RESULTS

SHORTLY BEFORE THE ELECTION OF 1871, JOSIE MANSFIELD informed the town that she was no longer Fisk's favorite concubine by suing him for the return of $50,785. Of course, he owed her nothing; but this did not prevent her bringing suit and capping it with his arrest. A handy bondsman saved him from a cell. Presently the public sat in on a sordid triangle which was to have a most unexpected dénouement, for Thalia was to give way to Melpomene.

The proceedings were rooted in Fisk's jealousy of Edward S. Stokes, the son of wealthy parents who had financed him in an oil-refining enterprise in Brooklyn, which was profitable from the start. With the loss of Josie, Fisk began to squeeze his rival, deposing him as treasurer of the oil refinery and posting guards around the plant to keep him out. Stokes regained possession of his property through the courts. Fisk next abolished the Erie's low rates on the crude-oil shipments from the Pennsylvania fields and canceled the railroad's contract to buy oil from Stokes. Anticipating the end of the favorable rebates, Stokes planned to pipe oil direct from the wells to the plant. This involved grants from the New York and Pennsylvania legislatures.

While the necessary legislation was being drafted, Stokes was arrested on Fisk's trumped-up charge of embezzling $27,500 from the Stokes oil refinery. This was in the first

Fisk, garbed as Falstaff, save for his regimental cap, with bandaged ankle, regaling Long Branch with tales of his daring deeds in the Orange Riot. *Harper's Weekly*, August 5, 1871.

week of 1871, at the height of the Tweed Ring's power. Stokes was conducting his own fight. After a night in the Tombs, he was arraigned before Justice Dowling, whom we met earlier when he was denouncing blackmailing police. Neither Fisk nor Tweed, nor any other corruptionist, could influence Dowling, and he released Stokes in $28,000 bail— $500 more than the sum Fisk swore he embezzled. After three hearings, Dowling discharged Stokes and denounced Fisk for malicious prosecution.

Fisk had his inning when the New York legislature killed the pipe-line bill, and Stokes retaliated by writing an article revealing how Erie stockholders were swindled through rebates in freight rates to concerns in which Fisk or Gould, or both, had an interest. A court injunction restrained its publication. Stokes won the next inning, collecting $10,000 from Fisk for malicious prosecution.

Fisk should have learned by this time that Stokes was not the type to endure his tyranny. Yet soon after Josie brought suit against him, Fisk had Stokes indicted for blackmail. There was no more basis for this than for the arrest of Stokes as an embezzler.

Fisk next struck at Josie, publishing an obviously perjured affidavit by a butler she had discharged. The servant professed to have overheard Josie tell Stokes she would blackmail Fisk. Josie obtained a warrant for criminal libel, and Fisk appeared in Yorkville Court to answer the charge on November 25, 1871. He seldom appeared in public without either a military or naval coat. This day he wore an admiral's jacket of mulberry, gleaming with gold buttons bearing the monogram of his Narragansett Steamship Company. He was the self-styled admiral of its fleet.

Josie was escorted by Stokes and chaperoned by a cousin. Reporters vied with one another in describing her expensive charms and rich raiment. When her counsel objected to an embarrassing question, Fisk's lawyer declared: "I expect to show that Mr. Fisk found this lady without a dollar; that after lavishing upon her means enough to have satisfied Cleopatra herself, when the supply ceased, methods were resorted to to replenish her treasury, among others this very proceeding." Josie gave her age as twenty-four. She was, in fact, thirty-one. She wept demurely during the unfriendly cross-examination and was still on the stand when court adjourned. As she and Stokes left the chambers, the crowd cheered them as though they were another Baucis and Philemon.

The next hearing was on Saturday forenoon, January 6, 1872. Stokes followed Josie to the stand. He was still testifying when the case was again adjourned to the following week. A few hours later, at half-past four that afternoon, Fisk alighted from his carriage in front of the Grand Central Hotel, now the Broadway Central, and was ascending the staircase leading to the ladies' parlor on the first floor, when he saw Stokes, on the landing above, pointing a revolver at him. Two shots rang out, one tearing through the left arm, the second entering the abdomen. Fisk died eighteen hours later.

"The whole world rang with the reports of his preposterous transgressions," said the *Tribune*. "No name of any American was better known at home or abroad. . . . His four-in-hand usually conveyed more spotted characters than his own. His box in his own opera-house was shunned as if infected. . . . He was no hypocrite—if that is any praise. When he devoured the widow's substance he differed from so many of his associates in refraining from the pretense of long prayers." Unlike Fisk, Gould was notorious for his pious professions, and had Stokes killed Gould, he might have been elected mayor. But the mob that cheered him yesterday now threatened to storm the Tombs and lynch him, as Fisk's body, dressed in a colonel's uniform, lay in state in his opera-house. Death had transformed the poltroon into a hero.

Without blare of trumpets, the wealth of the Stokes family moved in to save Fisk's assassin from the gallows. But a year to a day after he had fired the shots, he was sentenced to be hanged. Money was also used by Gould and other accomplices of Fisk in his crooked deals to send Stokes to the gallows. They retained lawyers to assist the prosecution, and private detectives to aid the police.

The Court of Appeals granted a new trial, at which Stokes was pictured as a sacrificial offering of corrupt financiers and Tammany Hall. This twaddle impressed the jurors, who returned a verdict of manslaughter in the third degree. He was sentenced to four years in Sing Sing. But it was not close confinement, for Stokes kept a pair of horses in a livery-stable in the village, and drove through the rolling country-side at night, as newspaper readers learned from time to time. But nobody cared, and the nocturnal outings continued until his release.

20

THE LIBERAL REPUBLICANS
CHALLENGE THE SPOILS MACHINE

THE YEAR OF OUR LORD, EIGHTEEN HUNDRED AND SEVENTY-
two, was devoutly hailed by countless thousands
throughout the United States as the beginning of the Age
of Reform. In every state of the Union, leaders of thought
in both parties had been advocating for nearly four years
the burial of ancient hates that the nation might, in truth,
have a new birth of freedom. And when this seemed attain-
able only through a new party, that party was forthcoming.

The initiative had been taken by Republicans, including
many practical politicians, who knew the great objective
could be achieved only by destroying the four great evils
that had menaced the land far too long—rabid partizanship,
selfish factionalism, bigoted sectionalism, and political corruption. All four had grown to record size during the Grant
administration, and Republicans who never thought they
would see eye to eye again with Democrats, especially after
the Civil War, were conferring with them on ways and
means of accomplishing the task before them. Their task
was simplified, for all four evils were sheltered in that American harpy's nest—the national spoils machine which had
become almost incredibly venal and proportionately powerful during the administration of Grant, a great soldier but
an artless and gullible President.

Their plan, involving national fusion in a day of violent

party strife, was first regarded as impractical by leaders of varying shades of political faith who sympathized with the movement. These men had not been impressed when a group of Republicans united with the Democrats in Missouri two

Carl Schurz, as Richard III, declaiming "Now is the winter of our discontent," etc. *Harper's Weekly,* 1872.

years earlier and carried the state election; for, being politicians, they were awed by the national spoils machine with its tremendous power reaching into even the smallest village boasting a postmaster. But the overthrow of the seemingly invincible Tweed Ring, a year later, altered their opinion, and there emerged the most ambitious and unselfish coalition in American politics.

This was the Liberal Republican party which temporarily absorbed the Democratic party.

The Liberal Republican movement was an answer to the corruption of the Grant administration and its refusal to carry out its major platform pledge of 1868—general amnesty to southern whites. Like some other well-intrenched administrations since then, it was callous, indifferent, and corrupt. It ignored the fusion triumph in Missouri in 1870 and the vote on the three referendums. The first restored suffrage to former Confederates, and was carried 127,643 to 16,268. The second made the late rebels eligible to hold office; it won with 123,418 ayes to 18,008 noes. And on abolishing the test oath for jurors, the Missourians were even more emphatic, 131,490 voting yes and only 10,790 voting no. This fusion was precipitated by the refusal of the Republican machine leaders to heed the popular demand for justice for the quondam Confederates in this border state by repealing the local proscriptive laws enacted at the close of the Civil War.

The New York *Tribune,* in discussing the Missouri results, said:

That state has been the arena of a fierce and bloody Civil War—a Missouri Civil War. It was no "War between the States" there, whatever it may have been on the Potomac or the Tennessee, but a war of neighbor against neighbor, brother against brother. It broke out there at a very early day, and held on to the last. Hostile armies swept repeatedly across the state, leaving desolation in their track. Worse still: citizens were shot in the midst of their families by those who had been their familiar associates; green boys were shot as traitors or spies, on the sentence of court-martial, for no other offense than trying to reach a Union or a Rebel camp, to volunteer, across territory which was constructively held by the opposite party. Hundreds were waylaid and bored through with bullets by ambushed foes as they were quietly, unsuspectingly, traversing some public highway. The diabolic hate engendered by civil war was never more intense than in Missouri. And the Unionists, at the close of the struggle, disenfranchised and proscribed their beaten adversaries. . . .

And with the implication that states where no such horrors obtained would be even more inclined to grant general amnesty to those who fought for the Lost Cause, the *Tribune* asked: "Do we need any more of such bolting and such voting to convince us that the day for disenfranchisement and proscription has passed?"

The unspoken answer of the Grant administration was that of the managers of the Republican machine in Missouri: general amnesty must not be granted lest it impair Republican chances at the polls.

The Missouri fusion gave rise to considerable third-party talk, and the outstanding Republican daily of the West, the Chicago *Tribune*, on November 27, said: "The threats of a new party are natural enough."

In several southern states, the Republican and Democratic parties were both denounced as "too extreme" in a plea for reviving the Whig party.

The free-traders, or Revenue Reformers, hoped for a third party with their credo as its basis.

The fault did not lie with the Grant administration or any existing party, but with the people who had permitted the disgraceful conditions to develop through the years. This was emphasized by the Springfield *Republican*, in an academic discussion of governmental corruption:

"We ought to know by this time—we have had a sufficiently costly experience to teach us—that what good men will not do for the love of their country, bad men will do for the love of themselves, whether it be to run caucuses, or manage elections, or hold office."

Then followed this tragically truthful appraisal, which might also have been written any time during the last hundred years:

"The whole caucus system, from the ward meeting up to the national convention, has been converted into a machine to relieve the people of the task of governing themselves."

Dispassionate analyses of party methods and constructive and vitriolic discussions of the Grant administration were provoked by the results in Missouri. Although Grant had sorely tried Greeley's friendship by appointing Murphy collector of the Port of New York, the *Tribune's* founder had not broken with Grant openly. William Cullen Bryant's New York *Evening Post*, in admonishing the administration to heed the growing resentment against some of its policies, noted a like attitude on the part of the *Tribune* which it described as a most constant and zealous supporter of Grant. But it was not long before Greeley had publicly accepted the Murphy appointment for what it was intended—a gage of battle. Once Greeley unlimbered his batteries, he was the outstanding leader in the drive on the administration.

Months before Greeley opened up on Grant and his administration, he struck constantly at Murphy, the symbol of the Grant machine in the metropolis, and forced his resignation in November, 1871. Later in the month he denounced Murphy as "an unblushing liar" for asserting that he "always paid the money to run the party machinery out of his own pocket," and proceeded to make good his characterization. Four months after his appointment, Murphy had posted the following on the wall of the office of Alonzo B. Cornell, a subordinate:

Notice.—All persons employed in this Department will be taxed 2 per cent upon their salaries at the office of the surveyor.

Thomas Murphy
Collector of the Port

The surveyor was Cornell. In addition, Murphy had sent word to all employees to pay the assessment at Cornell's office. Two per cent was modest, for in the year Murphy posted his delightful bit of frankness, all court-house and city-hall employees in the higher brackets in the metropolis contributed one month's salary to Tammany Hall. A year later, under date of September 15, 1871, Tammany Hall sent a circular to city and county employees "requesting" a contribution equal to 2½ per cent of their yearly salaries. The sole exceptions were firemen—they had to contribute but $10, representing 1 per cent of their thousand-dollar salary. These assessments, as can be seen, ranged from one to 12½ per cent.

Political assessments, however much they may be deplored, have been levied through the years, and the practice will continue while we have party government with campaigns waged on private funds. These assessments are but one of three recognized sources of income upon which parties depend. The other two are contributions from candidates and seekers for office and other favors, and gifts from party patriots—those who seek nothing in return. A fourth source is tapped by some machines. This is the underworld.

In keeping with his traditional loyalty to his friends, Grant wrote to Murphy that his "unqualified confidence" in him was "still unshaken," although Murphy's administration of the custom-house at the country's greatest port of entry was a national scandal. Merchants complained daily of thefts of their imports by Murphy's appointees, who carried on a "general system of fraud and pilfering." These appointees, numbering 589 in all, constituted the backbone of the down-state wing of the Conkling-Murphy machine, and were known throughout the land as the Custom-House Gang.

When Grant appointed Murphy's lieutenant, Chester A. Arthur, as Murphy's successor, Greeley recalled how Murphy induced the legislature in 1867 to replace the New York City Tax Commission, composed of Greeley Republicans, with a bipartizan board consisting of Murphy Republicans and Tammany men. This was a windfall to both Murphy and Arthur, for Arthur was made counsel at $10,000 a year, and the new tax commission allowed Murphy $56,000 for damages sustained in a street extension although Murphy had asked for only $41,260.

"Chester Arthur," said Greeley, "is Tom Murphy under another name."

In a letter to John Bigelow, Whitelaw Reid wrote: "We drive Mr. Murphy out, and his counsel and personal representative takes his place." And as Reid added, even the enemies of the Grant administration scarcely suspected the depths of its corruption.

Reid's thought was shared by a group of Republicans and Democrats who assembled about this time in Cincinnati, Ohio, to consider a third party to be called the Honest Man's party. Save for this delightful name and the opportunity it afforded the stanchly Republican *Leslie's Weekly* to consider on January 13, 1872, the administration's weaknesses, the Cincinnati gathering was unimportant. Said *Leslie's Weekly*:

The public ear is daily startled by stories of defaulting officials in Washington. . . . Since the formation of this government there has never been such a series of frauds, defalcations and peculations, either in number or magnitude as have characterized the last three years. Should the stealings continue on a progressive ratio for the next eighteen months, even if we succeed in altering the people and the principles at the White House, it is to be feared we shall have little left to be saved except the national character. . . . And shall we have four years more of such misrule, such sordid self-seeking and greed—to crush out the very soul of this great and growing nation? God forbid. . . . Down with the Washington Ring!

On January 24, the anti-machine Republicans of Missouri, under the leadership of Carl Schurz, met in Jefferson City, and invited partizans opposed to the Grant administration to meet in national convention at Cincinnati on May 1. These Schurz adherents called themselves Liberal Republicans. The movement was off to a good start. For two years Schurz had been fighting to end the disenfranchisement and proscription of southern whites. He had introduced a general amnesty resolution in the Senate on December 12, 1870, more than two years after the platform on which Grant was swept into office had solemnly covenanted with the people to adopt such a measure. Three days later Schurz informed Congress that the split in the Missouri Republican party was on the question of general amnesty only. The machine managers, he explained, opposed amnesty because they feared they might lose the state.

As a result, the House acted favorably on a measure which granted almost universal amnesty, but no action was taken on Schurz's resolution in the Senate. At the beginning of the next session, Grant belatedly bowed to popular sentiment and advocated amnesty to all except "the great criminals," a phrase borrowed from Thaddeus Stevens. The exceptions were the bare handful who had directed the Confederacy. There had been some individual grants of amnesty, but tens of thousands were too proud to petition for rights and privileges they felt were theirs despite the unjust clauses of the Fourteenth Amendment. Just before the Christmas holidays of 1871, the Senate was about to pass the House amnesty bill when Sumner offered an amendment to banish Jim Crow from public carriers, theaters, schools, and elsewhere—an old proposal with Sumner. Sumner's anti-Jim Crow amendment was unpopular, and was passed only by the casting vote of the Vice-President. But as the civil disabilities imposed on southern whites could only be removed by a two-thirds vote of each house, the general-amnesty measure failed of passage although it received a vote of 33 to 19. A shift of two votes would have saved the day. And if Sumner had heeded friendly counsel to withdraw his amendment, the bill would have been passed unanimously.

This was the status of the general amnesty act when Schurz and his fellow Missourians issued the call for the Liberal Republican National Convention. In the tentative platform adopted at Jefferson City, Schurz and his fellows blundered in declaring for "a genuine reform of the tariff" —free-trade. Had they centered on corruption and amnesty, they would have done better, for they temporarily alienated many important Republicans of the industrial East, protectionists all, of which the foremost was Greeley. But minds met, and the irritation was allayed save among extreme free-traders whose faith was thus expressed by Bryant's *Post:* "The protectionist policy is a policy of war, by its very nature. It seeks the advantage of one nation at the expense of others." Schurz knew that governmental corruption and general amnesty were the overshadowing issues and acted accordingly.

A more appropriate champion of the proscribed southern whites than the picturesque Schurz would have been hard to find. He had fought to save the Union, as a divisional commander under General Franz Sigel. Among Americans of German heritage, Schurz ranked with the glorious Sigel

in their affections and high esteem. Like Sigel, he had
written his name indelibly in German history before settling
here in 1852. He was a junior in the University of Bonn in
1848 when he collaborated with Gottfried Kinkel, the poet,
in publishing a democratic newspaper. In the following year,
after an abortive local insurrection, he and Kinkel fled to
the Palatinate and joined the revolutionary army. Schurz
participated in the storming of the arsenal in Siegburg and
in defending the fortress of Rastatt. With Rastatt's surrender,
Schurz escaped to Switzerland, and Kinkel was captured
and imprisoned for life. Many of their comrades were executed.

Schurz did not forget the poet. In 1850, at the risk of
his life, he secretly returned and rescued Kinkel, whose
charming poems in his exile breathe a passionate longing
for the old scenes, and a prayer for the unity and greatness
of his race. For a short time Schurz corresponded in Paris
for German journals. Next he taught school in London for
a year, and then came to the United States, living first in
Philadelphia. In 1855 he moved to Wisconsin, and campaigned among his fellow Germans for the Republican
ticket in the presidential canvass of the following year. In
1857 he ran a losing race for lieutenant-governor. He was a
delegate to the convention that nominated Lincoln, and
was rewarded for his notable speeches in English and
German in the ensuing campaign with the portfolio to
Spain. Schurz resigned this post to join the colors. In the
summer of 1865 he made a tour of inspection of the South
for President Johnson to whom he reported that returning
Confederate soldiers found "their homesteads destroyed,
their farms devastated, their families in distress," and not
only conquered in "a political and military sense, but eco-
nomically ruined." During the winter of 1865-66 he was
Washington correspondent of the New York *Tribune,* and

in the ensuing summer founded the Detroit *Post*. In 1867
he became editor of the *Westliche Post*. This famed German
daily was published in St. Louis, but its influence was national.

Universal amnesty was the corner-stone of the Liberal
Republican movement. Schurz quarried the ashlar, polished
it and set it in place.

21

THE PRESIDENT RESORTS TO THE PURGE

ALL WHO SUPPORTED THE PRINCIPLES OF THE JEFFERSON City meeting were against a second term for Grant. Even his warmest admirers conceded he had failed as chief executive. "I think," wrote George William Curtis, when Grant had been in office some two years, "the warmest friends of Grant feel that he has failed terribly as President, not from want of honesty or desire, but from want of tact and great ignorance. It is a political position and he knows nothing of politics—and rather despises them." And James Russell Lowell, after a White House visit, said: "I liked Grant and was struck with the pathos of his face; a puzzled pathos of a man with a problem before him which he does not understand." George Frisbie Hoar, a younger brother of Grant's first Attorney-General, and a member of Congress during both of Grant's administrations, said: "Selfish men and ambitious men got the ear of that simple man and confiding President. They studied Grant, some of them, as the shoemaker measures the foot of his customer." And two years after his retirement from office, Grant himself said: "I did not want the presidency, and have never quite forgiven myself for resigning the command of the Army to accept it; but it could not be helped. I owed my honors and opportunities to the Republican party and if my name could aid it I was bound to accept."

In this frank avowal, Grant bears witness to the truth of Hoar's appraisal. The "ambitious men who got the ear of that simple man and confiding President" were the managers of the spoils machine, and they made him their tool, and subordinated every department of the Federal Government, including its armed forces, to their own selfish ends. To Grant, these men were—as they were in fact—leaders of the Republican party to whom he believed he owed "the honors and opportunities" he had won on the field of battle. As a consequence, the spoils machine, not Grant, was President. The basic need of a spoils machine is jobs. There was no job Grant denied it, from the smallest village postmastership to a cabinet post, and these appointments were revokable at the whim of the machine.

The three outstanding members of Grant's first Cabinet were Hamilton Fish, of New York, Secretary of State; Jacob Dolson Cox, of Ohio, Secretary of the Interior, and Attorney-General Hoar. All three were able and honest, yet Grant let the machine force out two of them. He asked for Hoar's resignation on June 15, 1870, to make a place for a Georgian, as a sop to the Senate clique which blocked Hoar's appointment to the Supreme Court six months before. Cox lost favor because he introduced civil service in his department, prevented the assessment of departmental employees for party purposes, and opposed a dishonest claim to mining lands in California. Cox escaped the ax by resigning. In a letter to Grant, he said: "My views of the necessity of reform in the civil service have brought me more or less into collision with the plans of our active political managers and my sense of duty."

Fish alone of the three remained, at Grant's earnest urging. In the summer of 1869 Fish tendered his resignation upon learning that Grant, without color of law, had sent a former member of his military staff, General Orville E. Babcock, now his assistant White House secretary, to Santo

Domingo to negotiate a treaty to annex the Dominican Republic.

Grant's reckless and imperious attitude in this affair drove many devoted supporters into the Liberal Republican move-

General Baez, the usurper President of Santo Domingo, about to drain graft from a coconut. From a cartoon by Bellew in *Leslie's Weekly,* April 8, 1871.

ment. After the Cabinet turned a cold shoulder on the illegal treaty, Grant again despatched Babcock to Santo Domingo, and he returned with another equally singular document, but on this occasion it was duly signed by our consular agent. Babcock had signed the first. The treaty obligated us to pay $1,500,000 to Santo Domingo, ostensibly to discharge her debts. But it was generally believed, and subsequently charged in the Senate, that the $1,500,000 was potential graft for a ring headed by Buenaventura Baez, the Negro usurper, who had obtained the presidency of the Dominican Republic in 1876 by a sanguinary revolution, and was maintained in office by three war-ships ordered by Grant to Dominican waters.

These charges were blazoned forth by the intrepid Sumner, the most distinguished member of Congress, as chairman of the Senate Committee on Foreign Relations. Until Grant's election to the presidency, Sumner and Greeley were the twin idols of the Republican rank and file.

The Santo Domingo affair was directed by "the White House hangers-on," of which Babcock was one. Despite its unpopularity, Grant tried to jam the treaty through the Senate even after the Foreign Relations Committee reported it adversely on March 15, 1870. Six weeks later, in a special message promoting the project, Grant said: "I have information which I believe reliable that a European power stands ready now to offer $2,000,000 for the possession of the Bay of Samaná alone, if refused by us." This was on a par with the yarn of an undisclosed American naval officer who reported having seen lots staked out in cocoanut groves on the shores of the Bay of Samaná, the stakes bearing the names of Baez and other Santo Domingo plotters, as well as those of Babcock and Grant. Other Washington despatches reflecting on the treaty made the rounds of the nation's press, and these persisted after the Senate, on June 30, rejected the treaty by a tie vote. Grant believed Sumner inspired these articles implying and charging fraud and corruption.

The day after the vote, Grant had Fish demand the resignation of John Lothrop Motley, the historian, as minister

to England. Motley, a friend of Sumner, was summarily removed some six months later. Grant had previously in-
trigued in vain to purge Sumner from the chairmanship of
the Senate Committee on Foreign Relations, a post he had
filled with honor for a decade. To Grant, there was nothing
repugnant in a purge, and he—or the machine—kept Sumner
on the purge list.

The word purge has been a synonym for tyranny
to the English-speaking races since Colonel Pride's purge
of the House of Commons in 1648. But the word was
alien to American political argot until 1870 when General
Alfred Howe Terry illegally expelled twenty-four white men,
Democrats and Conservative Republicans, from the Georgia
legislature to which they had been duly elected, so that the
carpetbagger-scalawag-Negro régime of Governor Rufus B.
Bullock might pack the legislature and "so shape affairs
that the state may fall helpless into their hands, for plunder
and oppression." This charge, which proved to be only too
true, was made by the victims of Terry's purge in their
futile pleas to Terry to exercise his powers and "rescue the
people of Georgia from the violence and outrage with which
they are threatened by boldly wicked men." They especially
petitioned him to remand the issue of their eligibility to the
courts, where it belonged. In their pleas, the legislators
vainly addressed Terry as a soldier of unsullied honor. He
was brave as well. But as the instrument of the radical Congress, he committed the first violation of legislative sanctity
in our history. Plunder was the lesser motive of this crime.
The dominant motive was to return the Radicals to power.

The active agent in this last was Henry Wilson, Sumner's
colleague from Massachusetts, who gloried in his bench-won
soubriquet, the Cobbler of Natick. Lowell described Wilson
as a more despicable demagogue than the Paphlagonian
tanner.

While Sumner was first on Grant's purge list, he was not alone. Schurz was on the list, but Grant did not dare force him off the Committee on Foreign Relations because of the German voters. A third was Senator James W. Patterson, of New Hampshire, who escaped for an undisclosed reason. These three, with Senators Simon Cameron, of Pennsylvania and Eugene Casserly, of California, had killed Grant's Santo Domingo scheme in committee. Grant's purge had for its immediate objective control of the Committee on Foreign Relations.

Grant tried a new tack when his purge was halted, and recommended the adoption of a joint resolution empowering him to name a committee to negotiate a treaty of annexation. This was in December, 1870. He painted imaginary riches in the Dominican Republic and informed Congress that if we abandoned the project, "a free port will be negotiated for by European nations in the Bay of Samaná." He did not say how many nations. His Congressional supporters told him the proposal would be defeated, and he compromised on a resolution to create a committee of investigation. As Sumner pointed out, no such authority was required, for Grant had the power to send investigators anywhere.

Grant's utter lack of training for any high civil post was especially demonstrated in this affair, for he even told Congress that annexation would open the way to canceling the national debt, a matter of $2,500,000,000.

Sumner said that the Dominicans were against annexation; that it would mean war; that Baez was not only an usurper held in office by our Navy, but a political jockey, a trickster, a conspirator willing to trade his country for a mess of graft.

These charges did not come from a disappointed or disgruntled party hack given to loose talk. Sumner was a scholar who abhorred ward politics, an idealist who cherished his dreams, a statesman who never sought preferment, an office-holder who served his country only. Sumner was wrong, and stubbornly so, at times; but now he was right, and the nation was with him.

The people, and politicians generally, had assumed that annexation had been abandoned after its decisive defeat in the preceding session of Congress. Only an army commander, accustomed to blind obedience, or a man utterly alien to political ways, would have pressed for further action.

The Senate debate on the resolution was set for December 21. Newspapers of that date carried an article inspired by the White House hangers-on which was designed to abort the plans of prominent Republicans to heal the rupture between Grant and Sumner. If these peacemakers had been successful, Sumner's representations to the President might have destroyed this White House ring of plunderers, in spite of Grant's stupidly blind loyalty to his friends, real or false. Sumner first saw the article in the *Daily Patriot,* published at the national capital. It related that "the President said . . . Mr. Sumner attributed dishonest motives to him, and if he were not President of the United States, he would hold Mr. Sumner personally responsible for the language and demand satisfaction from him." Babcock supplemented Grant with the declaration "that if he were not officially attached to the Executive he would subject Mr. Sumner to personal violence." Other newspapers, more specific, said Babcock threatened to pull Sumner's nose.

In a time when the code duello was still invoked, these threats from the White House, especially Babcock's, came with poor grace. Two of the known duels that year ended seriously, one in death. The first was fought on the afternoon of July 13 between Major Henry Keitle, a reporter on the St. Louis (Mo.) *Times,* and Captain L. D. Van. "The weapons were cavalry sabers," said a news despatch. "Major

Keitle received a slight wound on the forehead and a trifling cut on the hand. One of Captain Van's eyes was put out by a thrust.... The seconds are unknown.... The fight arose from reflections cast on the fighting qualities of the northern troops by Captain Van." The fatal duel was between "Captain Richard Francis Aiken, gentleman, and Mr. Ludlow Cohen, a merchant, equally well-known and respected," who left their homes in Savannah, Georgia, a little after dawn on August 19, accompanied by seconds and surgeons. The weapons were the traditional smooth-bore dueling pistols. Three-quarter-ounce balls were used. After four exchanges, both men still answered "No," when asked, "Are you satisfied?" At the fifth exchange, "Captain Aiken fatally wounded Mr. Cohen, who died almost immediately."

Grant's talk of "demanding personal satisfaction" may be dismissed as the expression of one goaded by the false reports relayed to him by the White House ring and other false friends in whom he placed his trust. But Babcock probably intended to intimidate members of the anti-Grant faction in Congress with his threat to pull their leader's nose.

This White House bravado was in keeping with Sumner's account of a visit to the Executive Mansion when Grant and Babcock threatened his life. The President and his secretary were just letting off steam. And the country chuckled as Sumner vowed Grant came so close he could smell the whiskey on his breath. Grant once said to Representative Hoar as they came abreast of Sumner's home on Pennsylvania Avenue: "That man who lives up there has abused me in a way which I never suffered from any other man living." Grant emphasized his feelings by shaking his clenched fist.

The article inspired by the White House was specific in one particular respecting the groundless charges against

Sumner: "The President said Mr. Sumner had attacked him in executive sessions of the Senate."

Sumner opened the debate by having the clerk read the

The victim of the first senatorial purge. The caption reads: "Washington, D. C. Removal of Hon. Charles Sumner from the Chairmanship of the Committee on Foreign Relations. Scene in Reception Room of Capitol; Mr. Sumner receiving the sympathy of his colleagues." *Leslie's Weekly*, April 1, 1871.

inspired story. He then called upon his colleagues to support his denial of "ever accusing President Grant of dishonesty" in any Senate session. He next made a sweeping denial of the entire White House accusation. And no one in the Senate or elsewhere made reply.

Sumner's speech, which lasted four hours, represents one of the noblest efforts of a life dedicated to country. More than once he was justly vituperative, but at no time was he slave to his eloquence. He had an unpleasant task to perform, and he did it as pleasantly as the circumstances allowed. At the outset, he said he would use strong language, "but only such as the occasion required." It was not Sumner's strong language that galled Grant's servile Senate supporters, but his condemnation of the use of our Navy to keep Baez in power, and his impassioned plea to Vice-President Colfax to visit Grant and warn him "not to follow the example of . . . Andrew Johnson; . . . tell him not to exercise the war power without authority of Congress; tell him there is a grandeur in justice and in peace beyond anything in war."

This allusion to Johnson, with its implied threat of impeachment, recalled the regrettable attempt of Sumner and other radical Republicans to remove Grant's predecessor, which happily failed, albeit by a lone vote. Sumner had been sincere, for he regarded Johnson's policy of dealing justly and realistically with the South as "the greatest and most criminal error ever committed by any government." Although Sumner had somewhat softened since then, Johnson was still to him "the successor of Jefferson Davis," and guilty of "treason." The frenzied passions of war do not vanish with peace.

Sumner denounced the resolution authorizing Grant to appoint commissioners as a device to commit Congress to annexation and "a dance of blood." Then he added: "Baez is now waiting to receive from the United States the money for the sale of his country in the expectation of being able to slip off to Europe, there to enjoy the proceeds." Newspapers reported that "the Santo Domingo plotters were to divide $3,000,000 to $4,000,000 among themselves," and that shippers and merchants stood ready to raise the difference between the anticipated $1,500,000 from the United States Treasury and the larger sum. Noting that Babcock, during his negotiations with the Dominican Republic, had "entitled himself aide-de-camp to U. S. Grant, President of the United States," Sumner observed that such an office was unknown in our history. He excoriated Babcock as a confederate of Baez and, recalling France's claims of 60,000,000 francs against the Dominican Republic, demanded: "Are we ready to enter upon this bloody dance? Are we ready to take up this bloody lawsuit?"

From noon until seven o'clock the next morning the debate continued, with brief interludes for consideration of other measures, and just before adjournment the resolution was adopted by a vote of 31 to 9. The burden of the arguments of Grant's defenders was that the resolution was merely one of investigation and that Sumner had attacked the President in a manner justifiable only in a Democrat. This was Sumner's great crime: criticizing one of his own party.

Conkling voiced the views of the machine when he said Sumner "stabbed the President in the back like an assassin." The House, ever more responsive to popular sentiment, added an amendment declaring that the resolution did not commit Congress to annexation. Grant appointed a commission, which might as well have remained at home, for Sumner had roused the nation against the scheme.

Sumner's detractors and Grant's self-appointed apologists have insinuated that Sumner's mind was now affected by the wanton bludgeoning inflicted upon him fourteen years earlier by Preston S. Brooks, of South Carolina. Sumner's speech and the contemporary comments thereon refute these false witnesses. Following his airing of the Santo Domingo plot, the New York *Evening Post* said: "Mr. Sumner used some harsh language yesterday, but he has ... been attacked in a very bitter and unscrupulous way by certain over-zealous hangers-on at the White House, from whose officious-ness the President occasionally suffers, and whom he would be wise to get rid of." The New York *Herald* said: "Grant was sore and pig-headed; Sumner stood on his dignity." And the next day it coupled further praise of Sumner with this attack on Grant: "He seems to have no faculty of ap-pealing to one's reason; so when patronage and plunder are powerless, as in Sumner's case, he is powerless."

But Grant was not altogether powerless, for he revenged himself on Sumner shortly after the new Congress met on March 4, 1871, prevailing upon a majority of job-hungry Republican Senators in the party caucus to depose the great-est among them from the chairmanship of the Committee on Foreign Relations.

Few imagined, until it was done, that Grant would invade a separate and coördinate branch of government by going through with his purge of Sumner. No act of Grant's created deeper or more justifiable indignation, and it provoked Schurz to declare that "another term of such arrogant as-sumption of power and wanton acquiescence may furnish the flunkies with a store of precedents until people cease to look for ordinary means of relief."

The shallow pretenses on which the purge was defended—that Sumner no longer maintained personal and social rela-tions with the President and the Secretary of State—de-ceived no one.

This purge was spoilsmanship at its worst. A short time

before, on the eve of the expected ouster of Motley, Bowles wrote in the Springfield *Republican:* "How long does the President suppose the people will patiently endure this dealing with high office as if it were a presidential perquisite, to be given away on his mere whim, without regard to the claims of the office? It was bad enough when he only dealt with the consulates and small post-offices; but now that he has come to foreign ministers and cabinet officers it is intolerable."

SPOILSMEN OPPOSE A SINGLE TERM

FOR PRESIDENT

HARD UPON THE PURGE OF SUMNER, THE MANAGERS OF THE spoils machine increased the potential strength of the Liberal Republicans by a new outrage—the Ku Klux Act. Its primary purpose was to bolster Grant's waning political fortunes in the South where the vicious carpetbagger-Negro governments had driven nearly all southern whites into the Democratic party. North Carolina was temporarily in the hands of her own people, and the same was true in Tennessee, Virginia, and Georgia. The Ku Klux Act was to complete the work started by the unconstitutional reconstruction acts of 1867—the unintentional conversion of the South to a one-party section of the nation.

A partizan majority report filed by Senator Oliver Perry Morton, of Indiana, and his radical colleagues set the stage for the bill's passage. "The Ku Klux Klan," read the report, "does exist and is composed of members of the Democratic or Conservative party, with a political purpose which is carried out by murder, whipping, intimidation, and violence." And they might have been equally informative had they recited that carpetbagger-Negro régimes also existed and were composed of members of the Republican or Radical party, with a political purpose which is carried out by murder, et cetera.

A Republican journal, the *Commercial,* of Cincinnati,

Ohio, commenting on the report, which grossly and wilfully exaggerated the number of offenses, observed with prophetic irony, that a message to Congress from the President might now be expected "on the necessity of additional legislation for protecting the loyal people in the southern states."

"The carpetbaggers are becoming important," continued the *Commercial.* "The President's possibility of renomination rests with the carpetbaggers. . . . The intense solicitude of the President for the safety of the loyal men in the South means anxiety to secure the carpetbag vote."

On the day the Ku Klux bill was passed, the Democratic members of Congress, in an address to the people, emphasized that the measure was designed "to place in the hands of the President the power to command his own renomination, and to employ the Army and Navy at his sole discretion as a means of subserving his personal ambition."

Morton incautiously disclosed the act's political purpose during debate on the bill. Said he: "Shall reconstruction be maintained, shall the colored people be protected in the enjoyment of equal rights, shall the Republicans of the southern states be protected in life, liberty, and property, are the great issues to be settled in 1872."

Many Republicans opposed the bill in both houses. They reflected the overwhelming sentiment of the party rank and file. But the handful running the machine were of a different mind, and were determined to enact the measure. Schurz assailed it as "an encroachment of the national authority upon the legitimate sphere of local self-government." Another Republican, Senator Lyman Trumbull, of Illinois, anticipating a Supreme Court decision of eleven years later, said he was not willing to invade the states to punish "individual offenses against their authority committed by one citizen against another."

Under its provisions, in the following October, the President declared nine counties in South Carolina in rebellion against the United States and suspended the writ of habeas corpus.

Some radicals, before drafting the Ku Klux bill, had considered placing the entire South under martial law. A restoration of bayonet rule would have insured a solid South for Grant in the next election.

The Ku Klux Act did not stop night-riding, but it did widen the gap between the Republican factions. Oddly enough, Sumner, once the radical of radicals, was now discussed as the likely contender against Grant. But Sumner was in frail health and had no ambitions for himself. When the *Tribune* advocated his candidacy, he wrote to Whitelaw Reid: "I beg you to believe that I do not consider myself a candidate for anything—unless it be the good-will of good men. . . . I have had enough of combat and am very weary." Sumner could not make the race, but he would help.

As the bolting Republicans of Missouri planned their Jefferson City meeting, Sumner introduced a constitutional amendment which would destroy the greatest source of power of the national spoils machine—the desire of a President to succeed himself. The first section of Sumner's proposal read:

"No person who has once held the office of President of the United States shall be thereafter eligible to that office."

While the amendment could not affect Grant's renomination, even if adopted, for it was not to be effective until after March 4, 1873, it was a blow at his second-term ambition, and so designed.

Conkling declaimed scornfully agairst the proposal as he led the successful fight against it. "In the name of civil-service reform," he said, "we are asked to advise the nation to tie its hands against ever availing itself of the services of that citizen who, having been once chosen President, has acquitted himself so well as to prove the wisdom of his choice, and to convince his countrymen that he is still the best and safest guardian of the trust." Then Conkling dragged in his pet villain, Jefferson Davis, waved the bloody shirt, and thundered: "Traitors and slaveholders, forming a confederacy, made the one-term dogma a tenet of their faith. . . . Slavery, and a denial to the people to reëlect presidents, or not, as they please, fitly became corner-stones in such a structure."

The single term—one of six years—had its birth in the original draft of the Constitution. Jackson and other illustrious Americans subsequently urged a single term, and Old Hickory's proposal was on all fours with the one-term clause of the Montgomery Constitution.

Conkling cited Jackson for his purpose. "Andrew Jackson," he said, "received and sought a reëlection, and he turned men out of office, too, and put in supporters of his administration." But he forgot to add that the spoils of office were not sold in Jackson's day.

Conkling made a splendid effort, although he did not squarely meet the issue raised by Sumner. Yet the speech had its eloquent passages; no address by Conkling lacked them. If Conkling had not been involved in the worst side of spoilsmanship, the barter and sale of public office, he could have delivered on this occasion an address worthy of any anthology of American orations. For his honor as a Congressman and his personal integrity had been recently impugned by Greeley, then being looked upon as a possible rival of Grant. Greeley had personally indorsed the ugliest charge ever lodged against Conkling by reprinting it, without comment, in the *Tribune*. The charge, which first appeared in the Rochester (N. Y.) *Union*, follows:

"This man Conkling is the most impudent fraud ever

palmed off on any people in the shape of a public man. He holds his seat in the Senate by virtue of bribery and corruption in the legislature at Albany. He entered Congress penniless and threadbare, but soon became a millionaire."

Tilden, as the reader recalls, had accused Conkling—although he did not identify him—of acquiring his Senate seat through bribery and corruption. But now Conkling was named, and the charge elaborated, without provoking even a denial. Weeks passed, and the charge remained unanswered as the Liberal Republicans assembled in Cincinnati on May 1: in fact, the charge was never answered. There is confession in silence as well as in flight.

23

A GREAT CONVENTION

AND SOME PETTY LEADERS

SCHURZ CALLED THE LIBERAL REPUBLICAN NATIONAL CON-
vention to order, and in his opening address committed
a political blunder of primal magnitude by describing
Charles Francis Adams, of Massachusetts, as the strongest
candidate the convention could name, and Greeley as the
weakest. Henry Watterson, whose Louisville *Courier-Jour-
nal* had been a stalwart supporter of the movement, said
Schurz's political management was "guided by the unpractical practicality of the littérateur."

Schurz, Watterson, Murat Halstead of the Cincinnati
Commercial, and Samuel Bowles of the Springfield *Republican,* comprised the original journalistic Quadrilateral of
the Liberal Republican movement, and the designation
stood when their number was increased by the inclusion of
Horace White, of the Chicago *Tribune,* and Whitelaw Reid,
who was there as Greeley's political manager. Reid was the
only one of the six who battled for Greeley's nomination.
Halstead had advocated Greeley's nomination a year before, but now professed an open mind. Watterson preferred
Adams, but like Reid, agreed to abide by the convention's
decision. The other three threw all their strength behind
Adams. Bowles defended his opposition to Greeley thus:
"Greeley has magnificent qualities and has done more for
political and social reform . . . than any man living. Then

he has more first-class weaknesses than any man, too." Thus was Bowles apologizing for opposing a man who should have had his unbroken support, for he next said: "There are risks in taking him, but compared to the benefits, they don't begin to be as great as those under Grant." Lyman Trumbull, of Illinois, was the second choice of the Adams supporters in the Quadrilateral. Had he been their first, it would have been understandable. But we must go back to Watterson's characterization, "the unpractical practicality of the littérateur," to explain the efforts of these journalists to force Adams upon the convention after the leading Democrats in Congress and throughout the country had advised the convention they would not accept him.

In a field of seven, Adams led on the first ballot, with 203 votes to 147 for Greeley. On the second, Greeley led Adams by two votes, their respective strength being: Greeley, 245; Adams, 243. On the third Adams topped Greeley with 264 to 258; he also led on the fourth with 279 to Greeley's 251. Greeley had a substantial lead on the fifth ballot, with 309 to 258 for Adams, and he was nominated on the sixth, with 332 votes, a bare lead of eight over Adams. But before the result was announced, there was a scramble to change votes in favor of Greeley, making the final tally for the two leaders: Greeley, 482; Adams, 187.

Greeley's fortunes rose because of the appeal of B. Gratz Brown, who had been elected governor of Missouri in 1870 by the nucleus of the new party. Brown was not a delegate and had no intention of attending the convention until advised by telegraph that Schurz was luring his ninety-five delegates to Adams. The fiery, red-haired Missourian arrived in Cincinnati as the balloting started. After the first ballot, a note was handed to Schurz; learning its contents, he announced that a gentleman who had received a large number of votes had a statement to make and courtesy demanded that he be heard. Brown ascended the platform and declared he would withdraw in the interest of Greeley—"the man most likely to win." After the wild cheering and boisterous applause ended, Schurz left the chair to urge the Missouri

Charles Francis Adams
Leslie's Weekly, August 26, 1871.

delegates to support Adams. Schurz then resumed his presiding post, called for the second ballot, still hopeful for Adams. Schurz never quite recovered from this rebuff to his political management and ascribed Greeley's nomination to a deal between the friends of Greeley and Brown.

Of all the candidates considered for first place, Trumbull and Greeley were the only ones with popular support. To have named Adams would have reduced the Liberal Republican party to little more than a factional opposition to Grant and doomed the movement to the rôle of a tertium quid.

Adams was able and exceptionally worthy, but he was obnoxious to Democrats because he had been the Free Soil candidate for vice-president in 1848. And he alienated many with his Olympian disdain for the men of the convention. "I do not want the nomination and could only be induced to consider it by the circumstances under which it might possibly be made," wrote the impractical Adams. The call for him must be unequivocal, based upon confidence in his "character earned in public life," and faith in his professed principles. And there was laughter on the Thessalonian eminence as Adams pronounced: "But if I am to be negotiated for, and have assurances given that I am honest, you will be so kind as to draw me out of that crowd." To show that he could be human, Adams vouchsafed: "If the good people who meet at Cincinnati really believe that they need such an anomalous being as I am (which I do not) they must express it in a manner to convince me of it, or all their labor will be thrown away." There was more of this political transcendentalism.

More astonishing than the letter was its widespread publication in the press by Bowles in the belief that it would win votes for its author. The condescending allusion to "the good people," and the offensive reference to "that crowd," would have injured any man's candidacy in a general election.

But "that crowd" was described by a staff correspondent of *The Nation*, which later supported Grant, as "respectable, honest, intelligent, and public-spirited." When it flopped to

Grant, this reform weekly told its readers the faces of Liberal Republicans were odious. What price reform?

Detractors of the movement have pictured the delegates as crude puppets of political tricksters, and have cited the New York delegation's adoption of the unit rule in favor of Greeley to support this baseless characterization. But they suppressed the fact that the unit rule was adopted overwhelmingly by the united voice of the two contesting delegations, the vote standing 126 to 27—better than four to one. Also, they failed to note that the rule would automatically cease to be binding if the New York delegates reversed their action, or the convention decided otherwise.

Two of Greeley's rivals were members of the United States Supreme Court, Chief Justice Salmon P. Chase and Associate Justice David Davis. Another, who received only a complimentary vote on the first ballot, was Pennsylvania's war governor, Andrew G. Curtin.

The balloting for the presidential nomination follows:

	1st	2nd	3rd	4th	5th	6th
CHARLES FRANCIS ADAMS, Massachusetts	203	243	264	279	258	324
HORACE GREELEY, New York	147	245	258	251	309	332
LYMAN TRUMBULL, Illinois	110	148	156	141	81	19
B. GRATZ BROWN, Missouri	95	2	2	2	2	
DAVID DAVIS, Illinois	92½	75	41	51	30	6
ANDREW G. CURTIN, Pennsylvania	62					
SALMON P. CHASE, Ohio	2½	1			24	32

The convention quickly disposed of the vice-presidential nomination, which went to Brown on the second ballot. His closest contender was Trumbull with 175 votes. The nomination was then made unanimous.

With the nomination of Greeley, Reid's convention work was but half done. There was still the Quadrilateral to hold together. He had anticipated a possible division in their ranks, if Greeley were nominated, and sought to avert it by arranging a dinner to be held at the close of the convention where all might discuss plans for the success of the ticket. Of his five colleagues, only one had a real flair for politics, which embraces all other arts and artifices of the great game of government. This was Marse Henry himself, the Democratic member of the Quadrilateral, who was to win fame in his party as a platform builder. Watterson talked Reid's language. So after Greeley was nominated, Reid said to him: "I have won, and you people have lost. I shall expect that you stand by the agreement and meet me at dinner tonight." In describing the dinner, Watterson said:

"Frostier conviviality I have never sat down to than Reid's dinner. Horace White looked more than ever like an iceberg; Sam Bowles was diplomatic, but ineffusive; Schurz was a death's-head at the board; Halstead and I, through sheer bravado, tried to enliven the feast. But they would have none of us, nor it, and we separated early and sadly, reformers hoist by their own petard." And Watterson also observed: "The Quadrilateral was knocked into a cocked hat. Whitelaw Reid was the sole survivor. He was the only one of us who knew what it was all about."

The platform and address to the people of the Liberal Republicans stand unexcelled for brevity and adherence to the issues. Together, they slightly exceed one thousand words. The address is a joint indictment of the administration, the machine, and the President. The counts against Grant are five:

The President of the United States has openly used the powers and opportunities of his high office for the promotion of personal ends.

He has kept notoriously corrupt and unworthy men in places of power and responsibility, to the detriment of the public interest.

This cartoon is typical of the baseless slanders on Greeley after his nomination for President. On a banner flying from Tammany Hall appears the untruth: "Tammany Ring Bailed by H. G."—Greeley's initials. Although Tweed had been driven from public life, Nast shows him and Greeley clasping hands. The caption reads: "Diogenes has found the honest man.—(Which is *Diogenes* and which is the *honest man?*)." *Harper's Weekly*, August 3, 1872.

He has used the public service of the government as a machinery of corruption and personal influence, and has interfered with tyrannical arrogance in the political affairs of states and municipalities.

He has rewarded with influential and lucrative offices men who had acquired his favor by valuable presents, thus stimulating the demoralization of our political life by his conspicuous example.

He has shown himself deplorably unequal to the task imposed upon him by the necessities of the country, and culpably careless of the responsibilities of his high office.

Administration supporters were charged with attempting "to justify such wrongs and palliate such abuses to the end of maintaining partizan ascendancy." Then followed more specific accusations, from which we cull:

They have kept alive the passions and resentments of the late Civil War, to use them for their own advantage; they have resorted to arbitrary measures in direct conflict with the organic law, instead of appealing to the better instincts and latent patriotism of the southern people by restoring to them those rights the enjoyment of which is indispensable to a successful administration of their local affairs, and would tend to revive a patriotic and hopeful national feeling.

They have degraded themselves and the name of their party, once justly entitled to the confidence of the nation, by a base sycophancy to the dispenser of executive power and patronage, unworthy of republican freemen; they have sought to silence the voice of just criticism, and stifle the moral sense of the people, and to subjugate public opinion by tyrannical party discipline.

The administration itself was accused of wanton disregard of the laws of the land, of usurping powers not granted by the Constitution, and of having acted "as if the laws had binding force only on those who were governed, and not for those who govern."

The indictment justly charged the Conklings, the Mortons, and the rest of the congressional clique with blocking necessary investigations and indispensable reforms, and with striving to maintain themselves in authority for selfish ends. Then followed the core of the Liberal Republican movement:

"Believing that an organization thus led and controlled can no longer be of service to the best interests of the Republic, we have resolved to make an independent appeal to the sober judgment, conscience, and patriotism of the American people."

A nobler platform has yet to be written. Two of its planks should be used for the faith and guidance of all administrations. The first of these, and the primal principle of the new party, read:

"We recognize the equality of all men before the law, and hold that it is the duty of government, in its dealings with the people, to mete out equal and exact justice to all, of whatever nativity, race, color, or persuasion, religious or political."

The second read:

"The public credit must be sacredly maintained, and we denounce repudiation in every form and guise."

And of the nation's great evil, in phrases that may be used unchanged to-day, the platform said:

The civil service of the government has become a mere instrument of partizan tyranny and personal ambition, and an object of selfish greed. It is a scandal and reproach upon free institutions, and breeds a demoralization dangerous to the perpetuity of republican government. We therefore regard a thorough reform of the civil service as one of the most pressing necessities of the hour; that honesty, capacity, and fidelity constitute the only valid claims to public employment; that the offices of the government cease to be a matter of arbitrary favoritism and patronage and that public station shall become again a post of honor. To this end it is imperatively required that no President shall be a candidate for reëlection.

To all these truths, the supporters of Grant countered with the charge that the Liberal Republicans had slandered our great country. But there was nothing novel in this. More than four hundred years before the birth of Christ, when the immortal critic of graft and corruption in the Grecian metropolis denounced public thievings and other vices of the demagogues, the mighty Cleon haled Aristophanes into court to answer the charge of having "slandered the city in the presence of foreigners."

24

"TO THE PRESIDENT'S FAMILY

BELONGS THE SPOILS"

THE OPENING SPEECH IN THE LIBERAL REPUBLICAN CAM-
paign was delivered in the Senate during the closing
hours of May. Sumner timed it for the Republican National
Convention which would meet in Philadelphia the following week. Realizing that no one could change the program
prepared for the stampede-proof delegates, he spoke for
what effect he might have on the country. Of the convention
he said:

"It may be an assembly—and such is my hope—where ideas
and principles are above all personal pretensions, and the
unity of the party is symbolized in the candidate; or it may
add another to the presidential rings, being an extension of
the military ring at the Executive Mansion, the senatorial
ring in this chamber, and the political rings in the custom-
houses."

Grant was "radically unfit" for the presidency, and had
done things more reprehensible, more unconstitutional, and
more illegal "than anything alleged against Andrew Johnson
on his impeachment." Then he voiced the irrefutable charge
that Grant used the presidential office "to advance his own
family on a scale of nepotism dwarfing everything of the
kind in our history." And with equal force he charged that
Grant, in the same spirit, conferred office "upon those from
whom he has received gifts or benefits, thus making the

country repay his personal obligations...; how the vast appointive power conferred for the general welfare has been employed at his will to promote his schemes, to reward his friends, to punish his opponents, and to advance his election to a second term." He likened Grant to Cæsar—"Cæsar with the Senate at his heels is not the fit model for our Republic."

Many called Grant both king and Cæsar.

The reader will observe two notes in Sumner's speech: the charge of accepting gifts and of repaying the donors at the nation's expense, and nepotism. One list showed forty-two relatives of Grant on the Federal pay-roll through appointment; another, thirteen.

"The rule of to the victor belongs the spoils could not fail to degrade any administration," continued Sumner. "But now this degrading rule is extended, and we are told that to the President's family belongs the spoils."

Sumner recalled that only one other President, John Adams, had appointed a relative, but he bowed to outraged public opinion, and wrote to another place-seeking kinsman on April 2, 1799: "You know it is impossible for me to appoint my own relations without drawing forth a torrent of obloquy."

"The judgment of the country," continued Sumner in his unanswerable arraignment of this prostitution of the highest office in the land, "found voice in Thomas Jefferson who, in a letter written shortly after he became President, used these strong words: 'Mr. Adams degraded himself infinitely by his conduct on this great subject.'"

Sumner next quoted Washington on gifts by way of answering the Grant apologists who had cited England's rewards to Wellington—a yearly pension of £2,000 for three lives when elevated to the peerage in 1809; another £2,000 in 1812; £7,000 annually in addition to his salary as commander in the field when made a marshal in 1813; £500,000 when made a duke in 1813, and the public subscription of more than £250,000 for a mansion and estate after his victory at Waterloo.

The attacks on Grant are symbolized by mud on the White House. *Harper's Weekly,* May 4, 1872.

Washington's financial affairs had suffered during the Revolutionary War, and the products of his estate had fallen off. His financial circumstances were known to his neighbors, and in 1785, two years after he ceased to be commander-in-chief of our armies, and four years before he became President, the Virginia Assembly voted him canal stock worth $20,000. In declining the gift, Washington wrote:

"How would this matter be viewed by the eye of the world, and what would be its opinion when it comes to be related that George Washington accepted $20,000? ... However customarily these gifts are made in other countries, if I accepted this should I not henceforth be considered a dependent?"

Jackson followed his predecessor's example and declined a horse and carriage.

It has been said in extenuation of Grant's acceptance of gifts, from whiskey, cigars, and horses to blocs of securities, that he knew to the last shilling the value of the gifts showered upon Wellington by England and her people. Conkling listed them in what may be regarded as Grant's reply to the charge. It was also pleaded in mitigation that Grant rated highly the possession of money because of his early struggles with poverty. And Conkling dealt in more of the same noxious balderdash.

25

A MUSHROOM PARTY POINTS THE WAY—

SCHURZ'S WILD PLAN

EIGHT DAYS BEFORE SUMNER'S ATTACK ON GRANT, THE MAN-
agers of the spoils machine had one of their mushroom
parties hold a meeting in New York City. This was called the
Workingmen's National party, and its convention is important because, after it named Grant for President, it renominated the Cobbler of Natick for Vice-President. Wilson's
nomination was a sign-post to the Republican National Convention which met two weeks later.

Vice-President Colfax and his friends did not accept the
decision meekly. They were part of the machine, and after
Grant was nominated by acclamation at Philadelphia, they
vainly tried to save Colfax. The vote on the first and only
ballot stood: Wilson, 364½; Colfax, 321½. Colfax was denied
renomination because it was being whispered he had shared
in the easy money lavished by the Crédit Mobilier on members of Congress. Not knowing how long the lid could be
kept on this scandal, the machine managers took no chances
and named Wilson.

Grant's running mate was born in 1812, the son of poor
parents named Colbath. His father, of Irish stock, was a
hired man on a New Hampshire farm. The son was chris-
tened Jeremiah Jones Colbath, but became Henry Wilson
by legislative act on attaining his majority. He worked successively as farmer, cobbler, teacher, and shoe manufac-

turer. Most of his adult years were spent in public office. For a time he embraced Know Nothingism. After his twenty-fourth birthday, with savings earned at a cobbler's bench, he attended an academy in his native state. Until then, he had had less than twelve months' schooling, snatched between farm chores from the age of nine to twenty-one, an average of one month per year.

Wilson had a rough-and-ready eloquence, and became an active Whig. He turned Free Soiler in 1848, bought the Boston *Republican,* and made it a Free Soil organ. He presided at the second Free Soil National Convention. After eight years in the Massachusetts legislature—for two years he was president of the state senate—he ran unsuccessfully in 1853 for governor on the Free Soil ticket. In 1855, through a coalition of Free Soilers, Know Nothings, and Democrats, he was elected to the United States Senate, serving continuously until the eve of his inauguration as Vice-President.

The platform adopted at Philadelphia thus summarized one of the few laudable achievements of the Grant administration: "Despite annual large reductions of the rates of taxation, the public debt has been reduced during General Grant's presidency at the rate of a hundred millions a year." The platform also boasted that the amnesty bill had become law at last, having been signed a fortnight earlier. This belated fulfilment of the party's pledge of 1868 was a triumph for the Liberal Republican movement. This act reënfranchised about 160,000 southern whites. Some 400 or so were excepted from the amnesty, all former high-ranking Confederate officers or officials—"the great criminals." But as the proscribed were elected to Congress or chosen for other offices, their disabilities were removed by special congressional acts until full amnesty was granted twenty-six years later.

There were weasel-worded planks on civil-service reform

and woman suffrage. The Liberal Republicans were silent on this last, for Watterson regarded extension of the suffrage as a great evil. He was outspoken against the female suffragists, and once called them red-nosed angels.

The Republican platform-makers stressed in their opening plank the party's "glorious record of the past" after it had waved the bloody shirt by recalling how "it suppressed a great rebellion, emancipated four millions of slaves," and so on. This might keep alive the hatreds of the war, now seven years in the distance, but it would make votes on Election Day. The administration was praised also because it had peacefully and honorably composed menacing foreign difficulties. This referred to a minor dispute with Spain and the war-fraught *Alabama* claims. Greeley or Sumner could have used the settlement of the *Alabama* claims to swing votes to the Liberal Republican ticket. But this would have meant playing the demagogue, an alien and reprehensible rôle to both; the high plane on which the Liberal Republicans waged the campaign is emphasized by their refusal to inject the *Alabama* claims into the canvass.

Yet Schurz tried to use the settlement of the *Alabama* claims in a mad effort to reconvene the Liberal Republican Convention and repudiate Greeley. The Geneva Tribunal's award of $15,500,000 indemnity against Great Britain for damages inflicted on our commerce by the *Alabama* and other Confederate sea-raiders built in England was but a token. Although it was all we pressed for, it did not fulfil popular expectations. The negotiations began in the second month of Grant's administration, shortly after the Senate rejected the Johnson-Clarendon treaty with but one dissenting vote. As Sumner said in the debate, the treaty not only failed to mention our claims, but neglected to express a word of regret for the causes of our "massive grievance." The $15,500,000 award was for the damages inflicted by the

Alabama and two other Confederate cruisers, the *Florida* and the *Shenandoah*. On a fourth sea-raider, the *Retribution*, the Tribunal decided by a vote of three to two that we had not made out our case, and unanimously held Great Britain not liable for damages done by the *Chickamauga, Georgia, Nashville, Sumter,* and *Tallahassee*.

Sumner voiced the national sentiment when he put our damages at more than $2,125,000,000, of which $15,000,000 was for direct damages inflicted on Union shipping by the *Alabama*. The balance represented indirect damages. Of this vast sum, Sumner estimated the nation suffered $110,000,000 in losses because our "commerce was driven from the ocean," and at least $2,000,000,000 for additional damages resulting from the prolongation of the war which "may be directly traceable to England." Recalling that the Civil War was suppressed at a cost of more than $4,000,000,000, Sumner held that "through British intervention the war was doubled in duration" and, therefore, Great Britain should pay the "additional expenditure."

"I conversed with the President before I spoke, and found his views to be in strict conformity with mine," wrote Sumner as the entire nation rang with praise for his speech. "Since the speech, he has thanked and congratulated me."

The most influential Republican Congressman at this time, next to Sumner, was Senator Zachariah Chandler, of Michigan, one of the party's organizers, chairman of its National Executive Committee, and later Grant's Secretary of the Interior. "If Great Britain should meet us in a friendly spirit, acknowledge her wrong, and cede all her interests in the Canadas in settlement of these claims, we will have perpetual peace with her," said Chandler. "But if she does not, we must conquer peace. We cannot afford to have an enemy's base so near to us. It is a national necessity that we should have the British possessions. I hope that such a negotiation will be opened and that it will be a peaceful one. But if it should not be, and England insists on war, then let the war be short, sharp, and decisive." Sumner never talked war, but he did suggest Canada be ceded to us in settlement of our claims.

Many Canadians of prominence had been talking for many years of independence, and in the early part of the seventies there were three important groups in Canada actively agitating for a political change, one for an autonomous state within the British Empire, another for complete independence, and a third for annexation to the United States of America.

Harper's Weekly characterized Sumner's speech as the most popular he had ever made, and Sir Edward Thornton, the British Minister, told his government that it had been received "with vehement applause by the whole of the Republican press." And Fish himself, who did not share Sumner's notion that the abortive Fenian raids on Canada were provoked by the presence of the British flag, and that Great Britain should withdraw wholly from the Western Hemisphere, did agree with Sumner's stand on Canada. When Fish urged upon Sir Edward Great Britain's withdrawal from Canada, the diplomat replied: "Oh, you know that we cannot do. The Canadians find fault with me for saying so openly that we are ready to let them go whenever they shall wish; but they do not desire it." Sumner went further than Fish: he urged the withdrawal of the British flag "from this hemisphere, including provinces and islands."

Sumner's stature increased with his stand on the *Alabama* claims, and nearly two years later, John Bigelow thus appraised him in a letter to Whitelaw Reid: "And yet of all our living statesmen, I don't think of one whom Americans will be so proud of as him when he has been buried as long as Jefferson." And no American then mocked Sumner's demand for $2,110,000,000 to cover our indirect damages. Grant waited until there was no danger of losing an election before characterizing it as humbug.

The settlement of this dispute was effected by Charles Francis Adams. He had scarcely started on the final phase of the negotiations when Schurz planned a new Liberal Republican convention to repudiate the work of the first by naming a ticket headed by Adams, or Cox, whose resignation from Grant's Cabinet had endeared him to civil-service reformers. Cox was no more eligible than Schurz for the presidency, having been born in Montreal, Canada. Schurz fancied the Democrats would reconsider their antagonism to Adams and accept him. But Reid persuaded him to abandon his utterly impractical scheme.

26

THE DEMOCRATS
BECOME LIBERAL REPUBLICANS

BEFORE THE DEMOCRATS MET IN NATIONAL CONVENTION ON July 9, numerous state conventions of the party had either instructed for Greeley or left the decision to the delegates. The uninstructed, with few exceptions, were inclined toward Greeley. From the Virginia convention emanated the phrase "to eat crow," on which the Grant supporters rang the changes throughout the campaign. The Virginians deliberated in Richmond on June 26 and 27, and on the second day, the Old Dominion fire-eater, Colonel J. H. Lacy, coined this picturesque expression. The delegates were all for Greeley save one. The venerable Extra Billy Smith, then in his seventy-sixth year, answered the lone malcontent with: "Give me Jew or Gentile, dog or devil, I care not which, so we can beat Grant." Smith commanded the Forty-ninth Virginia Infantry during the war, and served his state as governor in the closing months of the struggle—his second régime as chief executive, his first being from 1845 to 1848. As Extra Billy resumed his chair to the approving thunders of the convention, Colonel Lacy added his delightful bon mot—and thus the *Times* recorded it: "I kin eat crow, but I don't hanker arter it."

Despite the declaration of the Democratic State Conventions for Greeley, the hired men of the Grant machine in the Democratic party attempted to block his nomination.

The activities of this mercenary host reached its first peak on the eve of the Baltimore convention. The cry, "Anybody to beat Grant," had resolved itself into, "Anybody to beat Greeley." A favorite observation of politicians is that you can't beat somebody with nobody—you must have your man. And the man was Adams.

Adams lent himself to this movement, which could serve only to divide the opposition to Grant. The organ of the movement was the notoriously venal New York *World,* the leading Democratic journal in the East. When Adams was flirting with the Cincinnati convention, he played coy. That failed. Now he tried frankness. In a cable despatch to the *World,* dated London, June 21, Adams said: "I would accept a nomination by the Democratic convention at Baltimore if the platform was good and the offer of the candidacy was spontaneous on the part of the convention."

There was one other sentence in this brief interview, which led the *World's* first page. "I adhere," said Adams, "to the principles laid down in the Cincinnati convention."

Every one had known for weeks that the principles of the Liberal Republicans would be adopted *in toto* by the Democratic convention, and that the Democrats also planned to name both Greeley and Brown. This did not daunt the Grant managers. Conventions had been bought before. But this one was rendered unpurchasable late on July 8, the eve of the convention, by the Colonel Lacys, the Extra Billy Smiths, and other war-impoverished southerners who lined up the delegates in a stampede-proof phalanx behind Greeley.

The *World* maintained its opposition to the last, and in accepting Greeley, drove a knife into him by repeating its old cry that it had opposed Greeley not because he was a Republican but because of "his fierce invectives against the Democratic party." This was the cry of undercover Grant

After the Liberal Republican Convention, the Grant machine's strategy to prevent Greeley's nomination by the Democrats involved a drive on Whitelaw Reid, who had outgeneralled the opposition at Cincinnati. Nast shows Reid grinding an organ, with Greeley, as a monkey, begging Democratic support. Greeley's running mate is a tag on his tail. *Harper's Weekly*, June 8, 1872.

emissaries in the Democratic ranks. Southern planters were repeatedly told: "Greeley did more than any one else to free your slaves." To which one southerner answered: "That is the very reason why I want Greeley to try his hand at freeing southern white men."

The *World* quoted southern delegates as attributing the craze for Greeley to the South's desire for "peace and a true reunion." Countless southerners knew by heart the memorable sentence from Greeley's letter to the Cincinnati convention: "I accept your nomination in the confident trust that the masses of our countrymen are eager to clasp hands across the bloody chasm."

As the Democrats assembled in the convention hall awaiting the opening gavel, the result was no longer in doubt. They would ratify the work of the Cincinnati convention. The Liberal Republican platform would be adopted without the change of a comma. One plank is especially noteworthy: "We pledge ourselves to maintain the union of these States, emancipation, and enfranchisement, and to oppose any reopening of the questions settled by the Thirteenth, Fourteenth, and Fifteenth amendments of the Constitution." The Civil War and its aftermath were over—for all save the Grant managers.

It was a novel gathering. Union Democrats, including many who had led commands against Confederate forces, fraternized with leaders of the rebel armies. If there had been no women arrayed in summer finery in the boxes and balconies, these Johnny Rebs alone would have lent an unusual touch of color to the scene.

These southern delegates possessed two outstanding characteristics—culture and poverty. This last was apparent in their garb, and northern journalists noted that the older men "were curiously dressed in black clothes with large linen cuffs to their shirts." Many cuffs dangled on empty sleeves. Some of the younger ones, with their hand-me-downs, also reflected the fashion of another day. But young and old carried themselves as though they wore the products of the most stylish drapers in America.

When the band struck up the "Star-Spangled Banner," veterans of the war, both the Blue and the Gray, were first on their feet, and as the last bar was played, the entire audience loosed an exultant cheer. The cheering was renewed for "Yankee Doodle," and then for "Dixie." To paraphrase Greeley, all were eager to clasp hands across the bloody chasm. They were Americans all. But there were votes to be won by keeping them apart.

The heat was intense. It was one hundred degrees in the hall. While waiting for the gavel to fall, some delegates removed their coats. Spectators and journalists followed suit. "Perspiration rolled down the backs in rills," wrote the New York *World* correspondent. The musicians, attired in heavy regimentals, worked with little pause. During a lull in the music, a small group from the South began singing. It was a war song a few years back—a war song of the North. The bandmaster, catching the air as it soared above the tense drone of a convention waiting to begin its labors, raised his baton, and presently thousands were singing with religious fervor:

> *The Union forever, hurrah, boys, hurrah,*
> *Down with the traitors and up with the Stars,*
> *For we'll rally round the Flag, boys, rally once again,*
> *Shouting the battle-cry of freedom.*

Ladies dabbed their eyes with dainty handkerchiefs as the stirring strains awakened memories of heroes now at rest. The men, being of the stronger sex, did not dab their eyes, but they did wipe the perspiration from their faces with most extraordinary care.

When the objectives of a national convention are agreed upon in advance, roll-calls are listless, save for the occasional cheer as some favorite casts his delegation's vote. What ordinarily passes for enthusiasm under such conditions is carefully rehearsed. But there was no stage-manager at Baltimore, and so the cheering squads, the claques, and other convention mummery were missing. The *World* correspondent said that during the roll-call for the head of the ticket there was the typical cheering, some real and some plain buncombe. Greeley had 686 of the 732 votes cast. Seven were blank. The remaining thirty-nine—from Pennsylvania, New Jersey, Delaware, and Ohio—were divided among three Democrats who had not sought the honor. When the result was announced, a Pennsylvanian moved that the nomination be made unanimous. "The proposition took the fancy of the majority," the *World* recorded, "and the ensuing tumult would have overwhelmed any protest even if any had been offered ... flags and handkerchiefs were waved ... delegates shouted as if they would split their throats."

Greeley's *Tribune* noted that while "shouts of applause went up at every mention of Greeley's name," the applause "was not so uproarious as at the Philadelphia convention because there were no well-drilled choruses to hurrah at the word of command ... but there was plenty of enthusiasm of a spontaneous and hearty kind." A political historian, De Alva Stanwood Alexander, who as a delegate to the Philadelphia convention voted for Grant, has written that "the response to Greeley's nomination was disappointing," and that the New York *Tribune* of July 11 "attributed it to the intense heat and the exhaustion of the delegates." The very contrary is the truth. Ordinarily eminently fair, Alexander provides us in this instance with a typical example of how Greeley has been decried that Grant might be praised. The *Tribune* of July 11 did speak of the intense heat and of the exhaustion of delegates in describing the reception of Greeley's nomination. But it did so in this wise: "Weary and exhausted delegates sprang up and waved hats and fans and handkerchiefs as vigorously as if the overpowering heat was not felt." And the *Tribune* emphasized, and correctly so, that this was "the strongest evidence of the enthusiastic temper of the convention."

When the uproarious approval which greeted the motion to make Greeley's nomination unanimous was at its height, the chairman first silenced the band and next the audience. Then he put the motion, which was answered by a roar of ayes. But there were two noes, so the motion was lost.

Brown was also named on the first ballot, polling 713 votes. Thirteen ballots were blank and six were cast for an astonished Kentuckian. The Liberal Republican platform was adopted by 670 to 62.

The morning after the nominations, above the *Tribune's* lead story was a woodcut of hands clasped in fellowship—across the bloody chasm.

27

"A WAR OF MUD"—

AND A WHITE HAT AND COAT

THE GRANT CAMPAIGN WAS FORMALLY LAUNCHED IN NEW York City by Conkling on July 23. This early date betrays the apprehensions of Grant's supporters. Greeley enthusiasts predicted Grant and his followers would be swept from office by a "great tidal wave." We have additional evidence throughout Conkling's lengthy address of the administration's fears. This speech is an ideal pattern of the stereotyped address of the demagogue, for its thin veneer of truth would deceive the unwary. No one could challenge his declaration that Grant, a "man to whom the nation's gratitude and benedictions are due, is made the target for ribald gibes and odious, groundless slanders." But there were also odious things said which were tragically true. "Why is all this?" asked Conkling. Then he callously answered: "Simply because he stands in the way of the greed and ambition of politicians and schemers . . . the sordid and the vile, who follow politics as the shark follows the ship."

"A war of mud and missiles has been waged for months," he continued. "The President, his family, and all nearly associated with him, have been bespattered, and truth and decency have been driven far away. Every thief and cormorant and drone who has been put out, every baffled mouser for place and plunder, every man with a grievance or a grudge, all who have something to make by a change, seem to wag an unbridled tongue or to drive a foul pen."

Conkling conceded that some honest men opposed Grant, but they were the gullible victims of greedy politicians, schemers, thieves, and the like.

It was in this speech that Conkling defended Grant's acceptance of gifts by telling how other nations rewarded their heroes of the battle-field. But he might have answered some of the oft-repeated charges. A few days before, on July 12, the New York *World* said: "The truth is that the Grant organizations in all sections of the country are run on the theory of public plunder. They have taken their cue from their master to get all they can, from loans to bullpups, or Seneca Sandstone stock." Grant was reputed to own $25,000 worth of these securities. The stone was used in public buildings in the national capital. Babcock and another of Grant's secretaries, and Grant's brother-in-law, General F. T. Dent, each held $10,000 worth of the stock, while five other administration officials possessed securities valued at $54,000. The governor of the District of Columbia, another Federal appointee, was the company's promoter. He had $240,000 of the Seneca stock. He alone of this group was said to have invested cash in the enterprise. It had also been charged, and was to be repeated in the press throughout the campaign, that General Dent received $1,000, and his brother Louis, $2,500, from William D. Farrand to have Grant appoint him Consul at Callao. Grant made the appointment. But Conkling ignored the specifications, resting content with a general denial.

Conkling bid for Democratic support by quoting some of Greeley's wanton partizan attacks, such as: "...every one who chooses to live by pugilism, or gambling, or harlotry, with nearly every keeper of a tippling house, is politically a Democrat...."

These cullings made the rounds of the Grant journals, and

were shouted, with embellishments, from the hustings. While the outer fringe of the Greeley oratorical squads answered in kind, no leader of the Liberal Republican movement manned a mud battery.

The day before Conkling made his address, Schurz spoke in St. Louis and held to the record. "No president, save perhaps Washington himself, was elected under more flattering auguries, and there is probably not one whose performance stands in more glaring contrast to his opportunities," said Schurz. He recalled Grant's empty professions of civil-service reform, and how "the whole office-holding force" had "engaged in pulling wires to dragoon the party into renomination of the President," and how "at this moment the whole civil service of the country, from the cabinet minister down to the humblest postmaster, is converted into a vast political agency to secure the President's election. . . . Never has the political conscience of office-holders been more despotically controlled."

But the spoils machine, under the masterly direction of Conkling & Co., did not stop with the mere use of office-holders. They had their agents at Cincinnati; and at Baltimore, the machine sponsored a rump Democratic convention. It was inconsequential in itself, for its largest attendance, including journalists, spectators, and a handful of delegates, numbered some threescore. The nominal organizer of the movement was Colonel Blanton Duncan, a Democrat. Their slogan was "Democrats on a Democratic platform." They issued a call for a national convention in Louisville, Kentucky, on September 3. It was charged that "the movement has been set up by friends of the administration and that the money to pay for the expenses come from Washington."

This group called themselves Straight-out Democrats and

Taproot Democrats. Greeley supporters dubbed them Blanton Duncan's Bourbons. They faked an editorial assailing the chastity of southern womanhood and falsely attributed it to Greeley. Senator Thurman wrote to Tilden of a rumor in Washington "that O'Conor is willing to accept the nomination of Blanton Duncan's Louisville convention." Thurman urged Tilden to prevail on O'Conor to decline, and added: "I have a very high opinion of O'Conor, and would be much distressed should he give the use of his great name to the Louisville movement, which is wholly in the interest of Grant." The Bourbons named O'Conor for President, and John Quincy Adams, of Massachusetts, for second place. O'Conor immediately wired his declination, whereupon James Lyons, of Virginia, was substituted. Then Lyons declined, and the unscrupulous Bourbons again put O'Conor at the head of their ticket and adjourned sine die.

Another convention, also inspired by Grant's managers, had nominated O'Conor for president in Philadelphia about two weeks earlier. But they accepted O'Conor's declension. This gathering was the aftermath of a convention held by the Labor Reform party, in Columbus, Ohio, which nominated Associate Judge Davis, of Illinois, and Governor Joel Parker, of New Jersey. After they declined, the Grant machine had a handful of delegates reassemble in Philadelphia on a sultry summer day. They named no one in place of Parker, and when O'Conor refused to stand, the farce was finished.

Another group met in a hotel room in New York City. They made up in zeal and dissension for their lack of numbers. They were free-traders and included Democrats and Liberal Republicans. A majority favored either passive action or open support of Greeley. The irreconcilables, headed by Parke Godwin, of the *Evening Post,* bolted and organized the Liberal Republican Reformers party, and nominated William S. Groesbeck, of Ohio, for President, and Frederick Law Olmstead, of New York, for Vice-President. Their platform denounced the congressional caucus method of nominating national tickets as one of "flagrant corruptions, secret intrigues, bargain and sale, and utter disregard of the popular will," and the convention system, which succeeded it, as having "led to even greater evils" through taking "the nomination and choice of their rulers out of the hands of the people" and committing them "to a machinery which is controlled by self-appointed leaders and their trained band of dependents." The platform proposed a constitutional amendment for "spontaneous nominations" by the people, and the direct election of the President and Vice-President; conventions and other intermediary bodies between the people and the ballot-box were to be outlawed. This glorified town-meeting as a substitute for a national convention was neither practical nor new. Godwin wrote the platform, which was his alibi for deserting the Liberal Republican movement.

Godwin had been riling free-traders against Greeley, and he tried to induce William Cullen Bryant to run for President. In denying any such thought on his part, the poet-editor recalled his years, now seventy-eight, and said: "I should not commit the folly of accepting it." Godwin and his crowd canted about their opposition to Grant. But their opposition to Greeley resolved itself into a pro-Grant movement, nothing else, and no one realized this better than Bryant's assistant. At a free-trade rally in Steinway Hall, Bryant and other speakers were received with the shouted chant, "Greeley! Greeley! Give us Greeley!"

Still another minority made its national début in this canvass. This was the Prohibition party, which met in Columbus, Ohio, and nominated James Black of Pennsylvania for President, and John Russell, of Michigan, for Vice-President. The politicians ignored the Prohibitionists who polled in the November election but 5,608 votes out of a total of 6,456,402 cast.

There were two other presidential candidates in this election. One was George Francis Train, of distinguished New England stock, who amassed a huge fortune in shipping before he turned to railroading. He was one of the backers of the Union Pacific Railroad and the sponsor of the Crédit Mobilier of America, but was forced out of both after being fleeced of part of his wealth. Train's erstwhile associates next turned to robbing the stockholders of millions and the government of millions more through exorbitant prices paid to dummies of the Crédit Mobilier for building the road. Train had been in France during the Commune and returned to espouse Communism, Fenianism, and woman suffrage. After spending freely on these causes, Citizen Train decided to spend some on himself. He organized the Train *Ligue*, which nominated him for President, and then he toured the country in his own behalf. During the first week of September Train was happy, as Dana's *Sun* showed "how the Crédit Mobilier bought its way into Congress"—to borrow part of the first day's caption. Oakes Ames, a House member from Massachusetts since 1863, had bribed his corrupt colleagues.

It was charged in the press, and repeated on the stump, that $9,000,000 was paid to a group of Congressmen to insure the success of Ames's schemes. This slush fund consisted of 30,000 shares of Crédit Mobilier stock actually worth $300 a share. Twelve Congressmen were accused of having "sold out to the Crédit Mobilier at $20,000, each." The names of these and four others were published. The accused made denials that convinced no sane person.

The spoils machine remained silent until September 18,

exactly two weeks after the *Sun* published its opening disclosure of the most infamous national scandal since the Jackson and Van Buren administrations when Biddle's Bank of United States bought Congressmen as a housewife purchases cabbage heads, with this difference—the Congressmen

Oakes Ames
Harper's Weekly, February 15, 1873.

were bought with other people's money. On September 18 Ames lied like a lord, and his false statement, nominally given to the Boston *Journal,* appeared simultaneously in every Grant journal of consequence throughout the country. "I never gave a share of stock, directly or indirectly, to any member of the Congress," said Ames. Others culpably involved made similar denials throughout the campaign.

Two congressional investigating committees, friendly to the accused, found that Ames did bribe some of his colleagues by "selling" them stock "to be paid for through dividends...with the intent...to influence the votes and decisions of such members in matters to be brought before Congress." Ames testified that the Crédit Mobilier earned $10,000,000 in building the road. He defended his bribery of Congressmen on the theory that he merely sought to make friends for the railroad, the building of which he regarded as an act of patriotism. His apologists have emphasized that all railroads were then built with bribery and corruption, and Ames was merely doing what others were doing. Therefore it was eminently proper for Ames and his associates to bribe Congressmen, rob stockholders of the road of $10,000,000, and saddle a debt of $6,000,000 on the road while looting it of the government subsidies.

How many Congressmen were bribed is not known, for the friendly investigating committees—their hearings were behind closed doors until the country demanded an end of the star-chamber sessions—did not probe too deeply. Some Congressmen to whom it was offered declined to touch the bribe-tainted stock. Several who took it said they saw nothing wrong in paying for the securities out of the rich dividends. Three Congressmen returned their holdings, together with the dividends, when they received returns of 60 per cent in cash and 80 per cent in stock, a total of 140 per cent, within a year. One of them was Wilson, Grant's running mate. Some to whom the stock and dividends were traced denied receiving either stock or dividends. All these were given the benefit of the doubt. The investigators found only three culpable to such a degree as to recommend expulsion. One was Senator Patterson, of New Hampshire. His term expired March 3, 1873, and this date passed without a vote on the recommendation to expel him. The investigators also recommended the expulsion of Oakes Ames, and James Brooks, of New York. Every one else received coats of whitewash. The House crowned this burlesque by refusing to expel Brooks and Ames, and then solemnly and mendaciously resolved that "grave doubts exist as to the rightful exercise by this House of its power to expel a member for offenses committed by such member long before his election thereto, and not connected with such election." The House was enacting an unwritten statute of limitations—perhaps to save others, for Brooks was not the sort to play the scapegoat. But the House had to do something to appease public clamor, and so it adopted resolutions in which it "absolutely condemns the conduct" of Brooks and Ames.

But there was one noble spirit in the House of Representatives who had the courage to shout: "Stop thief!" Why didn't they propose the impeachment of Vice-President Colfax? True, his term had only a few weeks to run. But wherein did Colfax differ from Brooks? The difference was merely one of degree. But the honor of the country demanded his impeachment for high crimes and misdemeanors and his removal from office. And the valiant champion of the people did not fail his faithful constituents back in little, old New York, for he moved the impeachment of Colfax. This hero who would not be swerved from his painful duty was our thieving old acquaintance, Fernando Wood, the friend of the people.

Colfax was ruined before the friend of the people spoke. The disclosures shortened the life of Wilson, who suffered a stroke from which he never recovered. He died November 22, 1875. Ames and Brooks were also stricken, Brooks dying within four months after the investigation started, and Ames eight days later.

Train had no running mate. Neither had Victoria Claflin Woodhull, whose candidature stemmed from Mary Wollstonecraft's *Vindication of the Rights of Woman*, the feminist answer to the *Rights of Man*. Our first woman candidate for President was a soothsayer, and the ablest of the suffragist spellbinders. She had daily training in public speaking from childhood. She began with a traveling medicine show, vending quack nostrums compounded by the older members of her family, telling fortunes and communing with spirits for the coins of villagers and townsmen of her native Ohio. As Homer was her birthplace, it was but natural that her visitants from the dim meadows were immortal Greeks. Demosthenes was her guide and guardian. Her bilking of yokels ceased when she was sixteen and married a quack named Woodhull. She bore him two children; but the years with the medicine show on wheels had steeled her heart even to the tug of an infant at her breast. She had ambitions, but in this she was not selfish, for she took her younger sister, equally beautiful, as a partner. They became clairvoyants extraordinary. The younger sister called herself Tennie, and added a middle initial, C. Some said her given name was Tennessee. It might very well have been Ohio, which signifies "beautiful." What is important is that she had also played spiritualist, fortune-teller, and hawker of nostrums with the traveling medicine show. They worked the sister act in Chicago and other western cities before coming to the metropolis in 1868. Although Victoria still talked of Demosthenes, it is more likely her familiars now were Aspasia and others who wore the sheer silks of Amorgos and invoked Aphrodite Colias. In 1869, Commodore Cornelius Vanderbilt, then in his seventy-fifth year, first heard of the pair. The hard-headed founder of the Vanderbilt millions leaned toward spiritism. The three met, and a curious friendship ensued. He made money in the stock-market for his new mediums, and the bobbed-haired Victoria found time to preach suffrage, thereby gaining grace with Elizabeth Cady Stanton, Susan B. Anthony, and other serious advocates of the cause. Early in 1871 Victoria presented to Congress the petition of the Woman's Rights Association. The little girl of the traveling medicine had arrived. She now had a new husband, Colonel James H. Blood, who had accompanied the sisters to New York; and she founded the Victoria League, as powerful politically as Godwin's Liberal Republican Revenue Reformers party. Victoria's party also had its organ—Woodhull and Claflin's *Weekly*.

The stage for Victoria's nomination for President had been set by Theodore Tilton, journalist, lecturer, radical Republican spellbinder, and superintendent of Henry Ward Beecher's Plymouth Church Sunday-school. Tilton wrote a fanciful sketch of Victoria to lure the gullible to her offices in the heart of the financial district. For the Claflin girls were now bankers and brokers. They were no longer mediums, save to Commodore Vanderbilt. Tilton produced a turgid elaboration of Victoria's patter to the Ohio rustics. Demosthenes had "prophesied to her that she would rise to great distinction; that she would emerge from poverty and live in a stately house; that she would win great wealth in a city crowded with ships; that she would publish and conduct a great journal; and that, finally, to crown her career, she would become the ruler of her people." She was ineligible for the presidency on the score of age, lacking a year of the constitutional minimum. The major object of Tilton's sketch was to represent Commodore Vanderbilt as her backer in stock-market speculations. Tilton had a wife; Victoria had a husband. But neither circumstance prevented her from publicly holding up Tilton as her paramour. Tilton introduced her to his wife and to his pastor. Mrs. Tilton was editor of the suffragist organ, *Revolution*.

The introduction of Victoria into Tilton's home circle led to the public airing of the Beecher-Tilton affairs. Victoria's speeches and lectures reeked with a prurient defense of free love which made her notorious. As a consequence, she was driven from one "stately house" after another until there remained only one respectable hotel in New York from which she had not been ejected. This was the Gilsey House, and as had happened elsewhere, patrons objected to her presence and she was ordered out. She wrote unavailingly to Beecher to save her from ejection. She retaliated by publishing in the preëlection issue of her crim. con. weekly the still disputed story of Beecher's relations with Tilton's wife. They also maligned a broker in the same issue, and the Claflin girls and Blood were imprisoned for criminal libel and uttering obscenities. The Beecher-Tilton scandal had been bruited for two years in suffragist circles; but as the daily press ignored it, the scandal was kept from the general public for another two years when Tilton's accusations echoed throughout the civilized world.

The Claflin girls remained in New York until Commodore Vanderbilt died in 1877. There was talk of contesting the will, but shortly after this the sisters sailed for Europe with some Vanderbilt gold. They left Blood behind, Victoria having divorced him in 1876.

The sisters did well abroad; Victoria married into an English banking family; Tennie became Milady. As they embarked for Europe, they could say of the metropolis—as Demosthenes might have told them had been said of Athens—"this city of simpletons."

Shortly before the soothsaying suffragist attacked Beecher, the managers of the spoils machine made their most effective response to the attacks on Grant and his administration. This was the Soldiers' and Sailors' Convention held in Pittsburgh. The principal speaker was the President's running mate, a little the worse from a newspaper encounter with Reverend Charles W. Denison and other temperance advocates over Grant's drinking, which has been perverted into the baseless charge that he was a drunkard. Wilson started it. Denison quoted him as having said: "General Grant drinks too much. I have told him so." Denison and Wilson were friends. Wilson might have held his peace, for the tales of Grant's drinking had long been public property. Instead, Wilson gave the lie to the cleric. Here he might have stopped, but being the typical demagogue, he needs must proclaim his own virtues. He, too, was a temperance worker, and he discussed Grant's drinking, but he had merely regretted that Grant used "any intoxicating liquor" and admitted that he said: "I wished he would take the pledge, and that I had a mind to ask him to join the Congressional Temperance Society." Friends of Denison seized upon Wilson's manifestly false denial and his explanation that stamped it as such. Wilson deprived posterity of a delightful anecdote in not inviting Grant to sit on the congressional mourners' bench.

The Soldiers' and Sailors' Convention was held on September 17 and 18 while Greeley was swinging through Indiana, Ohio, and Pennsylvania, which elected their state tickets on October 8. North Carolina had been carried by the Radical Republican state ticket in August; and on September 3, Vermont, where the Greeleyites were hoping to regain lost ground, was also carried by administration state candidates. While these reverses boded ill for Greeley, the huge throngs that greeted him wherever he spoke alarmed the Grant managers, who knew that Greeley's personal popularity had not yet been evaluated. Greeley frequently reviewed thousands in picturesque torch-light processions, each man wearing a duplicate of Greeley's familiar long white coat and white high hat, made of oilcloth, to prevent the drip of their coal-oil flares from ruining their clothes. This campaign costume was the answer of Greeleyites to Nast's caricatures of the editor-candidate's eccentric garb. In these marching legions, leaders of thought rubbed elbows with workers at lathe and bench, and tillers of the soil. For

The Liberal Republican defeat in North Carolina was noted by *Harper's Weekly*, August 31, 1872, with the above, and the following heading: "Eclipse of North Carolina. Will be visible throughout the U. S., Nov. 5, 1872."

Greeley was one of them. He had been a farm boy, a printer's devil at fourteen, and now he was their standard-bearer. He symbolized their hope and faith. Occasional men reached the heights through poverty's thorny path in other lands, but here it was commonplace. Few of his supporters could match Greeley's boyhood in suffering—unless they were city-bred. For the poverty of the country-side does not know hunger, and Greeley never lacked food. At ten he saw his father flee their little New Hampshire farm to escape imprisonment for debt. The farm was theirs no more and the elder Greeley became a hired man. As a youth away from home, Horace Greeley acquired an unsought reputation for eccentricity. He wore clothes that should have been discarded, and went sockless in well-mended shoes. But new shoes and socks and clothes would have meant less help for his sisters, a young brother, and his parents.

Greeley embraced many of the isms of the day, and died poor. What were these isms? To begin with, he championed throughout his life a just distribution of wealth. As a means to this end he advocated labor reform before the phrase was coined or mouthed by demagogues. His *Tribune* was the Whig organ of the land, yet he opened its columns to the socialism of Fourier, which he temporarily cherished. Years after, when the Whigs gave way to the party of Lincoln and Greeley, and the *Tribune* was the leading journal of the new party, this same freedom was observed, and Karl Marx contributed to its columns for a time. Was there a festering sore in his party? Greeley was the first to bare it and suggest a remedy.

When Greeley founded the *Tribune*, he announced it would be Whig in politics, but "removed alike from servile partizanship on the one hand and gagged and mincing neutrality on the other." Such a policy involved the occasional shattering of popular idols. And Greeley never flinched from iconoclasm.

He was fanatical on two isms. One was a belief that public office should not be a thief's vantage. The other was drink. He went to the extreme of advocating force to ban intoxicants. He had seen at first hand the havoc liquor wrought—in his childhood home, among his fellow workers, and among the poor.

For a time he advocated woman suffrage. But even after

The paterfamilias staggers into his cellar home. Greeley made the war on drink popular in journalism. Drawn by W. L. Sheppard. *Harper's Weekly*, January 7, 1871.

he struck this article from his credo, he gave the cause a fair field in the *Tribune*. Typical of the treatment of suffragists in other leading journals, is a despatch dated South Framingham, Mass., July 14, 1870, in Bennett's *Herald:* "The bold labor reformers, woman-suffrage advocates, spiritualists, and free and easy lovers, had their customary jamboree in Harmony Grove to-day." Some newspapers bracketed suffrage with prostitution. The *Tribune* was the only daily of consequence to treat suffragists as decent women. Yet at the Baltimore convention they fumed against Greeley. Susan B. Anthony avowed that nothing would delight her more than to have the convention "cram suffrage down Horace Greeley's throat as he had forced Negro suffrage upon the South."

Greeley's isms were never concealed. And he did not pay mere lip-service to his beliefs. He dramatized his faith. This kept him poor. He nearly destroyed his journal and beggared himself by his fairness to the South and its imprisoned leader. He did not capitalize on this during the campaign in New England, or subsequently in the three October states, for to have done so would have been demagoguery. The spoilsmen misunderstood his silence, and when he was touring Pennsylvania they had a heckler denounce Greeley during his Lockhaven address for signing the bail-bond of Jefferson Davis. Greeley answered the heckler: "I believe, in going bail for the only prisoner left of the war, after he had been confined in jail for two years, with nobody desirous of giving him a trial, though he sought it, that I performed a generous as well as a genuine service to this American Republic." But then there were protests when the iron shackles had been removed from the Confederacy's leader.

Greeley was patient with the Lockhaven rustic. But when a group of the Republican élite of the metropolis called a meeting of the Union League Club to consider his expulsion for signing the Davis bail-bond, Greeley wrote them:

I shall not attend your meeting this evening. I do not recognize you as capable of judging or even fully apprehending me. You evidently regard me as a weak sentimentalist, misled by maudlin philosophy. I arraign you as narrow-minded blockheads, who would like to be useful to a great and good cause, but do not know how. Your attempt to base a great, enduring party on the heat and wrath necessarily engendered by a bloody Civil War is as though you should plant a colony on an iceberg which had somehow drifted into a tropical ocean. I tell you here that, out of a life earnestly devoted to the good of humankind, your children will recollect my going to Richmond and signing the bail-bond as the wisest act, and will feel that it did more for freedom and humanity than all you were competent to do, though you had lived to the age of Methuselah.

Greeley added that he asked no quarter. But the Union Leaguers decided the wisest and only thing to do was to swallow Greeley's censure and wash it down with copious drafts in the club's taproom.

Greeley's reception in the three October states heartened his side, and his journalistic supporters redoubled their attacks on Grant and his administration. They sought to overcome the insidious propaganda in the South by stressing the huge debt imposed on the states of the Confederacy by the carpetbagger-Negro governments. Many published the following:

"Before the war, the total debt of the ten states was $76,416,890.

"On January 1, 1872, the debt of these states was $291,-626,015.

"On January 1, 1872, the total debt of the other twenty-seven states was nearly $88,000,000 less, or $203,872,552."

This increase of more than $215,000,000 in the southern states' indebtedness was largely waste and graft. But it was not all, for the salaries and fees paid to the carpet-baggers were not represented in this.

A direct charge, also unanswered, which appeared both in cartoon and type, disclosed Grant's running mate taking the following oath in a Know Nothing lodge in 1854:

"I will not knowingly vote for, appoint, or elect, any person of foreign birth, or a Roman Catholic, to any office." There was more of the same tenor.

The Grant managers, while thoroughly alarmed, were counting heavily on the fear they had instilled in the business man that a change in administrations would not be helpful. They were also relying on the effect in the North of the Soldiers' and Sailors' Convention. On the surface, this convention was partizan but patriotic, and it warned all patriots against intrusting the national government to elements but recently hostile to all it stood for.

As Greeley said in a Pittsburgh speech two days after the veterans adjourned, a stranger who had read of the convention's transactions would imagine "that we were still at war."

"They talk about rebels and traitors!" he exclaimed in his next sentence. "Fellow citizens, are we never to be done with this? We demanded of our adversaries in the great Civil War that they surrender their arms and go to their homes, and they surrendered them. We demanded that they abandon slavery, and they abandoned slavery."

After enumerating other conditions imposed on the South, all of which had been met, Greeley stressed that "the party that shouts for Grant and Wilson alone asks for proscription.... No other party requires that any human being should stand proscribed on our soil for a rebellion that ceased seven and a half years ago."

He denounced the Grant managers for instigating the Soldiers' and Sailors' Convention in order that they might "further and further separate and divide the American people," and added: "They hold essential to their triumph that hatred should continue, that distrust, suspicion, and alienation should continue."

Greeley's soul was in this extemporaneous address.

"We had a great, a terrible, a bloody and destructive Civil War," he continued. "Our success was perfect. The defeat of the adversary was more complete than any defeat recorded in history. They have suffered much. Cannot we afford to be magnanimous at least?"

He characterized the elections held under the proscriptive restrictions imposed upon the South as "war in another aspect."

He apostrophized the North through Pittsburgh, and said: "Now I appeal to her business men, I appeal to her merchants, I appeal to her manufacturers to stop this war. It has gone far enough. You cannot afford to teach a part of the country to hate you, to feel that your success, your greatness is identical with their humiliation."

Greeley concluded with an appeal to northern men to grasp the hands of the southerners, and say, "Brothers, we differed, we fought, the war is ended, let us again be fellow countrymen and forget that we have been enemies."

But the business men, merchants, and manufacturers to whom Greeley appealed were pouring money into these three October states, and into the other thirty-four, to defeat him. They were influenced by Grant's reduction of the national debt, and their fear of Greeley in the White House. They were also influenced by the country's prosperity, a false prosperity, but real enough for the election. The Grant campaign fund was prodigious, to which all administration beneficiaries contributed. The Whiskey Ring and every other sordid combination, north and south, parted with a share of their plunder to reëlect the President. One of the ring's leaders, with money diverted from government coffers, paid $2,400 for a diamond for Babcock, whose pockets jingled with more of this stolen gold. Some Republicans of national prominence, to save their self-respect, abandoned his administration; former admirers now disliked Grant, and

George W. Julian voiced the sentiments of many when he said his dislike had grown into "disgust and contempt." Julian, now a Representative from Indiana, and a Greeley supporter, was the Free Soil candidate for Vice-President in 1852.

When the administration tickets carried the three October states, sanguine adherents of Greeley abandoned hope. It had been generally expected that the Greeley men would carry Pennsylvania and Indiana and reduce the Grant strength in Ohio. But Greeley had only a passive interest in the results, for when he returned home, wearier than he had ever been before, he found his helpmate of the years in her last illness. He remained constantly at her bedside until her decease on Wednesday, October 30.

The following Tuesday the poll showed Grant with a popular majority of 763,007, the vote standing: Grant, 3,597,132; Greeley, 2,834,125. For the unwilling O'Conor, 29,489 votes were cast. The Prohibitionists polled 5,608, all in six northern states, an occasion for jest in the South, which was later to give prohibition its greatest strength. Of the thirty-seven states, Greeley carried only Georgia, Kentucky, Maryland, Missouri, Tennessee, Texas. These six had only 66 of the 352 votes in the Electoral College.

For a campaign so rife in bitterness, Election Day passed quietly, especially in New York City, usually good for several notable free-for-alls. But the metropolis had for its major disturbance the boisterous efforts of a few suffragists to vote. The noisiest of the lot was their soothsaying presidential candidate who tried to vote for herself. In the western part of the state, fifteen Rochester women, Miss Anthony at their head, wheedled election officials into letting them vote on the plea that they were qualified under the Fourteenth and Fifteenth amendments. This was all part of a feminist farce staged simultaneously in New York and four other states by a few silly Sallies, as Colonel Watterson dubbed these law-flouting extremists. Mrs. Virginia Moore of St. Louis sued election officials for $10,000 in Missouri for refusing to enroll her as a voter. At Norwalk, Connecticut, the selectmen administered the oath of citizenship to Mrs. Sarah M. Huntingdon but declined to register her. Hartford selectmen allowed two women to register but rejected them as voters. In Detroit, Michigan, Mrs. Mannette B. Gardner, who had been permitted to vote in 1870, was refused a ballot this year. Mrs. Gardner was the first woman to vote in the United States. Her vote was illegal, but it was counted. To keep peace in an Oregon polling booth, the officials let Mrs. A. J. Dunniway and three other women vote; but after the quartet departed, their ballots were thrown out.

Ordinarily, all this would have evoked a joyous editorial from Greeley. For the lady who talked of cramming something down his throat at the Democratic convention, and her fourteen female followers, with the obliging election officials, were arrested on Federal warrants. All had voted for Grant. They escaped imprisonment by posting $500 bail. Miss Anthony was fined $100, but she declared she would never pay a cent of it. The authorities, declining to martyrize her, overlooked her contumacy. Greeley was back on the job, his white hat and coat on their customary peg in the *Tribune* sanctum. But little humor was left him. He was fagged out; his old insomnia had become acute; and he was still smarting from the wounds of the campaign. Grant complained he had been "the subject of abuse and slander scarcely ever equalled in political history." Yet Grant invited many attacks, some well founded, from patriotic men to whom the party meant more than it did to Grant. Typical of these was Representative Austin Blair, a party founder, sometime governor of Michigan, who said of Grant: "Surrounded by an army of bold, brazen corruptionists, he is as powerless as was Samson in the hands of Delilah." The attacks on Greeley were groundless and almost limitless in their viciousness. He wrote to Colonel Mason W. Tappan, a former Republican Representative from New Hampshire, that he had been assailed so bitterly that he hardly knew whether he "was running for President or the penitentiary."

Greeley had a member of his staff compile the worst utterances of his campaign calumniators. They accused him of being a bribe-giver in Washington and head of the lobby in New York's capital; of participating in schemes for robbing the national treasury; of sharing in the Tweed Ring's thievings; of defending Tweed's rascalities and intriguing to restore the Ring to power. Other fabrications depicted him as a slave-trader, a secessionist, a friend of the Ku Klux. He was also accused of having promised to pay the Confederate debt and provide pensions for rebel soldiers. Calumny was not a novelty to Greeley. Thirteen years earlier he noted that he had been called atheist, infidel, communist, and traitor.

Only Reid and other intimates knew how the recollection of these vilifications tore Greeley's heartstrings as he analyzed his defeat. To Julian he said: "I was an abolitionist for years when to be one was worth as much as one's life in New York; and the Negroes have all voted against me." This was understandable: an old Negress cursed the heroically unselfish Greeley because he had sold her baby downsouth before the war! The tragedy was that the slavery-bereaved mother believed this one of countless fictions invented by village postmasters and other agents of the spoils machine. Greeley recounted how he had devoted his talents and energies through the years to the protection of American manufacturers, and added: "And the manufacturers have expended millions to defeat me." Then Greeley continued: "I even made myself ridiculous in the opinion of many whose good wishes I desired by showing fair play and giving a fair field in the *Tribune* to woman's rights; and the women have all gone against me." But Greeley would do all these things over again, for he came honestly by his white hat and white coat. Even in his great grief, Greeley found solace in the knowledge that those who knew him honored him. He wrote to Tappan: "In the darkest hour my suffering wife left me, none too soon, for she had suffered deeply and too long. I laid her in the ground with hard, dry eyes. Well, I am used up. I cannot see before me. I have slept little for weeks and my eyes are hard to close. . . ."

Greeley's repudiation at the polls occurred November 5. Before the month was over, the entire nation did him reverence. He died November 29. The Stars and Stripes were half-staffed throughout the Union; he lay in state in the city hall; and President Grant, accompanied by the Vice-President and Vice-President-elect, rode in the funeral procession to Greenwood. Now communities hastened to adopt Greeley's name; parents used it at the baptismal fonts; the metropolis called a square after him, where he contemplates the hurrying throngs with the wisdom of pity and understanding; and in the older part of the town, which often echoed to his footfalls when the city slept, stands another enduring bronze of this true reformer, whose faults, minor ones all, sprang impetuously from a crusading heart.

28

CONCERNING FOUR RING JUDGES

IMMEDIATELY AFTER THE NEW YORK LEGISLATURE ORGAN-
ized in January, 1872, Tilden, now an assemblyman, and
O'Conor, began their uphill fight against the more offensive
Ring judges. Charges had been prepared by the Association
of the Bar of the City of New York against Barnard, Mc-
Cunn, Cardozo, and Ingraham; but the Ingraham indictment was not pressed, influential friends pleading he was
an old man whose term was about to expire. One group of
legislators sought to block all impeachment lest it build up
the ambitious assemblyman. Other legislators became advocates of the accused at the first whisper of a huge slush
fund. In the restrained and cumbersome circumlocution of
the over-cautious Tilden, "a large fund was attempted to
be raised." The bribery plan never advanced beyond the
talking stage because Cardozo declined to contribute in
advance, offering to pay his share if and when acquitted.

The assembly judiciary committee began its investigation
of the charges in the Fifth Avenue Hotel. Cardozo was the
first of the accused on the scene. He was slender, lithe, with
"the eyes of a serpent looking from the face of a corpse."
In a day when most men wore mustaches or beards, Cardozo was smooth-shaven, revealing an "almost livid" skin.
He looked younger than his forty-two years. A contemporary study said "his darling dream was to secure a seat on
the bench of the Supreme Court of the United States." He
was at his villainy as late as October 31, 1871, on the eve

of the Ring's rout at the polls. On that day a dummy bought ten shares of the Mercantile Fire Insurance Company for $375, and had the transfer of the stock immediately recorded. Half an hour later Cordozo signed an order adjudging the company insolvent and appointing his nephew, Gratz Nathan, receiver. In the four years ending December 31, 1871, Cardozo gave Nathan more than eight hundred receiverships, some of them netting him $10,000 for ten days' work—$1,000 a day.

Cardozo made a general denial through counsel. Nathan, who was his uncle's bagman, testified he could not produce his check-books or bank-books, which, it was believed, he had destroyed. But the missing books did not hamper the inquiry, for bank officials and accountants traced the telltale deposits from Nathan's bank accounts to Cardozo's. Large sums, such as $8,707.50, $2,404.50, $1,017.50, and smaller sums, from $245 up, were withdrawn from Nathan's bank account, and the identical amounts transferred one or two days later to Cardozo's bank account.

The smaller sums were said to represent the payments of thieves and other petty criminals for jail deliveries. One charge against Cardozo was that he conspired with the shyster firm of Howe and Hummel to free from Blackwell's Island penitentiary convicts able to pay the price. Howe and Hummel numbered the most notorious bawdy houses among their clients. One night the police raided six dens and arrested the keepers and eighty-three girls. Howe and Hummel appeared as counsel for all.

McCunn and one of his brothers-in-law were accused of conspiring to rob Binninger and Clark, wholesale wine importers, of $200,000 through a fraudulent receivership. They made a perfect job of this. Another McCunn receivership involved the Fenian Brotherhood, which had some $16,000 in gold on deposit with August Belmont. The legislature could find no trace of the gold after it left the banker's possession. Sweeny's uncle, Thomas J. Barr, was receiver in this case.

"Making an Example of Two Naughty Boys," reads the caption on Bellew's cartoon of Cardozo and Barnard after their impeachment. Barnard wears the sign, "A Bad Boy," etc., while Cardozo, surnamed the Machiavelli of the Bench, is plain "Dirty Hands." *Harper's Weekly*, May 25, 1872.

It was estimated that Cardozo and Barnard made more than $1,000,000 each through Fisk and Gould alone. Barnard was the one bright spot in the dismal proceedings. He did not seem the intimate of harlots and other underworld characters until he loosed his tongue. One of the articles of impeachment amused him: that he used coarse, obscene, and indecent language in court. At his first appearance before the assembly investigators, he startled every one with the announcement: "I am going to scratch myself." As he set out to perform the task, he exclaimed: "Take notice!" Having scratched himself, he mused aloud: "I suppose that will make the 101st article of impeachment."

Barnard thought so well of this after seeing it in print, that at his next sitting of court he interrupted the lawyer arguing a motion to say: "I beg pardon—I don't wish to interrupt you; but I desire to say that if there is any member of the Bar Association here, he can have an additional specification in the charges against me, for I am going to scratch my—head." And all laughed heartily as he clownishly scratched his poll.

On Wednesday, May 1, the assembly received the first of the impeachment resolutions. It read: "Resolved, that Albert Cardozo, a justice of the Supreme Court of this state, be and he hereby is, impeached for mal and corrupt conduct in office, and for high crimes and misdemeanors." This had been reported out and signed by the following members of the judiciary committee: L. Bradford Prince, chairman; Robert H. Strahan, William W. Niles, Charles A. Flammer, Albert L. Hays, F. W. Tobey, Samuel J. Tilden. David Bennett Hill, later governor, concurred in the impeachment for mal and corrupt conduct in office, but opposed impeaching Cardozo for high crimes and misdemeanors.

In an effort to prevent the resolution from coming to a vote on the floor, Hill rose to a question of high personal privilege, an extraordinary use of this prerogative, which is invariably the prelude to a legislator's defense of himself or his conduct. When recognized, Hill merely read a letter from Cardozo resigning from the bench. As Cardozo had resigned before the assembly acted, his prosecutors did not proceed with his trial.

The next day Tilden and other assemblymen denounced Cardozo from their seats. They had planned to star him in their show, but he had run out on them. Their language was confined to parliamentary phrases. No such inhibitions had stayed the brimstone vituperation of Barnard in the metropolis where he excoriated Cardozo as "a cowardly liar unworthy of Hell." Barnard had a just grievance. Two days before Cardozo sent his resignation to the secretary of state, Barnard, hearing of his intentions, called on the "Machiavelli of the Bench" and stormed and threatened. Cardozo heard him through with mock astonishment.

"Your resignation will be a confession of guilt and compromise us all," said Barnard in a calm moment.

Cardozo replied he had not considered resigning, and moreover, would not do so. Barnard departed after apologizing for suspecting Cardozo of treachery to his fellow thieves of the bench.

Cardozo's resignation was regarded as a confession of guilt, and it stiffened wobbly legislators on whom Barnard and McCunn relied.

The legislature was controlled by the Conkling faction of the Republican party, that is to say, the Grant faction. The senate stood 24 Republicans and 8 Democrats; the assembly, 97 Republicans and 31 Democrats. And the Conkling-controlled lower house ignored Tilden and other aggressive foes of the accused in naming the managers of the Barnard impeachment trial.

Control of the impeachment managers would not ensure the success of the scheme. They must also appoint counsel who would scuttle the case.

Tilden learned of the plot and checkmated it by forcing

the legislature to adopt his proposal empowering the Bar Association to select the counsel. For this was the purport of the Tilden measure, although it merely provided that counsel must be satisfactory to the Bar Association, which looked to Tilden and O'Conor for leadership.

McCunn was placed on trial first. He was found guilty on all counts save one, and his removal decreed by unanimous vote. The trial broke his heart, and he died three days after the verdict.

McCunn's case had been referred to the senate by the impeachment managers because of the simplicity of proving the major charges of embezzlement, fraud, and theft. But Barnard was a tougher nut to crack. There was no doubt of his financial corruption, but proof was concededly difficult in his case. The High Court of Impeachment, composed of the senate and the judges of the Court of Appeals, held that Barnard's hands were "unstained by bribery" but found him guilty of all other charges. With two dissenting votes, the court disqualified him from ever holding and enjoying "any office of honor, trust or profit, under this state."

This automatically removed Barnard from the bench, who celebrated the event by getting drunk. This was the beginning of a series of sprees that continued until his death seven years later.

Cardozo so far was scot-free. He was without official stigma. He could practise law, or buy another judgeship and go back into his old business again when times got better. But after Barnard's conviction the Bar Association proceeded with Cardozo's expulsion from the practice of law. "He pitifully pleaded against expulsion . . . and promised to leave New York immediately and settle in the West." The Bar Association relented, as it had in the case of Ingraham. But Cardozo lied to the association, as he had to Barnard. For we read a few weeks later:

Just after the formal opening of the Court of General Sessions yesterday some little excitement was manifested among the spectators when the first case on the calendar being called, ex-Ring Judge Albert Cardozo rose as counsel and asked for trial. The case in which this notorious person thus made his first appearance since his resignation was that of John Smith and James Tully, two young men charged with the murder of William Brown on the night of the 9th of June as he was returning from the Bowery Theater with his wife....

For some reason, the Bar Association did not carry out its plan to disbar Cardozo, and he remained in the metropolis engaged in defending disreputables.

We will meet Cardozo later on, as a reformer in politics.

29

THE REFORM OF TAMMANY

AND THE METROPOLIS

O**N NEW YEAR'S DAY,** 1873, **THE METROPOLIS WAS RETURNED** to the rule of an honest mayor, William F. Havemeyer, elected by a fusion of the reformers with the most corrupt local Republican machine in the North, the Conkling-Murphy organization. The Elegant Oakey Hall was no more, politically. But like Cardozo and Ingraham, he had escaped punishment. Or to be exact, he had been declared innocent ten days before by twelve jurors during the season which softens the stoniest hearts. Hall, his own counsel, had made a most emotional plea for freedom: he too looked forward to spending Christmas with his family, et cetera. His voice broke, he sobbed, the jurors wept. All had a good cry. It was his third trial. The second ended in a disagreement, the jury standing 7 to 5 for conviction. The first was a mistrial because of a juror's death. After his acquittal, the Elegant Oakey presided over the destinies of the city he had looted until Havemeyer restored the integrity and dignity that once was associated with the title—His Honor, the Mayor of the City of New York.

The new mayor had inherited a fortune from his father, a sugar refiner; he made another in the refinery and in banking before he was thirty-eight, and then retired from active business—at least he thought he did. This was in 1842. But he might as well have attempted retirement from politics.

Politics and business, each in its separate sphere, were part of Havemeyer's life.

Havemeyer had all the makings of an excellent chief executive, save two. He was obstinate, and he could be easily

William F. Havemeyer
Harper's Weekly, December 12, 1874.

provoked into a quarrel. He had lived intensely, and devoted most of his adult life to successful civic-betterment movements. When he succeeded Hall, he was six weeks short of sixty-nine years, having been born February 12, 1804. Havemeyer did not seek the mayoralty, and, in fact, declined the nomination. But powers behind the Committee of Seventy, which managed the fusion campaign, needed him and forced the nomination upon him.

The nomination of Havemeyer was a coup of the Grant supporters on the Committee of Seventy. They needed Havemeyer to carry New York for Grant. Had the Committee of Seventy been honest with the good people of the city, whose self-appointed agent it was, and honest with its own professions to indorse all worthy candidates, regardless of political labels, it would have supported Abraham R. Lawrence, one of their number and their legal adviser. It was a close shave for Havemeyer, who won by only 5,898 over Lawrence. Yet Greeley carried the city by a majority of 22,759 over Grant.

Greeley's sweep of the town was due primarily to Honest John Kelly, the new boss of the Hall, which was held up to the world as a reformed Tammany. The purification began February 20, 1872, when Augustus Schell, as Tweed's successor, was installed Grand Sachem, with conventionalized Indian rites at the Great Wigwam; and the Elegant Oakey, Slippery Dick Connolly, and Peter Brains Sweeny were replaced as Sachems by Tilden, O'Conor, and Seymour.

Some two months after his installation, Schell gave way to a triumvirate from which Kelly emerged as boss.

In his brief career as boss, Schell made political history. With the overthrow of the Ring, Tammany was divided in four factions—the surviving lieutenants of Tweed and their followers; those who acknowledged Tilden as leader; the adherents of Morrissey; and the supporters of Kelly.

Schell's first act as boss was to appoint a committee to reshape the political structure of the organization. A highly desirable reform effected was the relegation of the Sachems to their proper functions as trustees of the Society of Tammany or Columbian Order. They were no longer to usurp the political powers of the general committee, as they had been doing for more than two decades. Another important change increased the membership of the general committee by abolishing the twenty-two ward organizations and allotting one committeeman or delegate to each election district. The outgoing general committee consisted of sixty-six delegates, three from each ward. The new one, chosen at the primary on April 10, 1872, numbered 384.

The Tweed remnant controlled about fifty delegates in the new committee, scattered through most of the twenty-one assembly districts. The Eleventh Assembly District was typical of many. Here, among its fifteen delegates, we find Schell, Morrissey, and Peter Brains Sweeny's uncle, Thomas J. Barr, still commissioner of police under the Elegant Oakey.

In abolishing the ward system, Tammany was again setting the fashion, for its adoption of the assembly district as the major unit of representation was copied by other large city machines, and soon the state committees of both parties followed suit.

Tammany's new general committee assembled on the night of April 27, 1872, to elect officers for the ensuing year. There were not quite 150 in attendance, because the slate had been agreed upon days before. Yet early in the meeting the chair declared a fifteen-minute recess to enable the nominating committee "to select suitable candidates." Tweed never staged a more cut-and-dried meeting. Out of the magic hat popped John Winthrop Chanler as chairman of the general committee. He was an estimable lawyer, but utterly ignorant of political management, as he frankly confessed in his first address as the nominal leader of the Democratic party of the metropolis. But all present knew he was to share the leadership with Kelly and Morrissey. Then the other nominees were also unanimously elected, men without history save one, Abram S. Hewitt, Tammany's new treasurer.

The rule of the unofficial triumvirate was short, and when the Democrats met in national convention some ten weeks later, Kelly was there as the lone Tammany chief. Loyalty, a prerequisite to successful political leadership, was an outstanding trait of Kelly. His word was reliable, another indispensable attribute of leadership.

Kelly had represented the Fourteenth Ward in the Board of Aldermen in 1854. That same year he was elected— on the face of the returns—to the House of Representatives. He was reëlected without any cloud on his title, and resigned to begin his first term as high sheriff of the City and County of New York on January 1, 1859. After the lapse of a term, he was again elected sheriff in 1864. Four years later, after Tweed denied him further honors, Kelly organized a reform party which nominated him for mayor. Kelly now measured his wealth in six figures, and could afford a campaign. To the amazement of the town, he suddenly withdrew from the contest, pleading ill health, and was still visiting Europe's spas when the Tweed Ring scandals broke. The Elegant Oakey, his Tammany opponent for mayor, boasted that he was the physician who ordered Kelly to leave on the next boat for Europe for his health. Kelly celebrated his fifty-first birthday the month he began his fourteen year reign of Tammany Hall.

While Kelly's able generalship saved the city for Greeley, it was Schell's money that made it possible. The amount of Schell's generous contributions to the Greeley canvass were never disclosed; but friends said they would have made many men rich. This was probably true, for in the Democratic presidential campaign of 1868, foredoomed to failure from the start, his initial gift to the Seymour war chest was

$10,000, an amount matched at the same time by Tilden, O'Conor, August Belmont, and Schell's older brother, Richard.

Schell's princely gifts to the Greeley campaign were expected. He had been elected chairman of the Democratic National Committee to succeed Belmont, and as such, was the Democratic manager for Greeley.

30

THE THIRD TERM—

THE COLLAPSE OF THE REFORM—

A FORGOTTEN COMMITTEE OF SAFETY

IN THE SUMMER OF 1873, SCHELL AND OTHER INTIMATES OF Tilden wished him God-speed on his first trip to Europe. But to none of them did Tilden confide that he was secretly nursing a presidential boom—his own. He regarded Grant as his likely opponent, believing that the spoils machine would overcome, in the convention, the deep-rooted prejudice against a third term. But he did not think they could overcome the prejudice, as old as the nation itself, and born of the fear of tyranny, in a campaign. The feeling against a third term is more than a prejudice; it is a tradition. Savage tribes have their taboos. This tradition is the taboo of civilized peoples.

This talk of Grant for a third term, while redoubling the cries of "King!" and "Cæsar!" did not abate the drive of the well-drilled office-holding class to keep him in the White House for four years more. For those who spurred on Grant were concerned only in saving the spoils machine which gave them easy living, and they saw in the soldier-President their only possible salvation. He was an idol of the mob. No mere man could have emerged triumphant from the torrent of ugly charges of the Greeley campaign.

One of Grant's intimates who did not encourage the third-term movement was Conkling. He had his own presidential boom. But like Tilden, he kept it quiet. To have announced it would have had his enemies in his own party accusing him of disloyalty to Grant. Conkling publicly professed his readiness to support Grant if he ran for a third term.

A month before Tilden sailed for Europe, Chief Justice Chase died. Grant offered this exalted post to Conkling, who promptly declined. Despite the criticisms of Democratic and independent journals, predicated largely on Conkling's relations with machine politics, Grant vainly tried to persuade him to reconsider his declension. "I could not take the place, for I would be forever gnawing my chains," observed Conkling.

Tilden bared his presidential ambition in a letter written from Geneva, on an unnamed day in August, to Honest John Kelly, with the customary initial coyness of a seeker for high office. Tilden's primary object in writing was embraced in his opening sentence: "As I shall not be able to return home in season to take part in the political canvass of this fall, I desire you to request the delegate to the state convention who will be chosen from my district to say for me that I decline a reëlection as member-at-large of the state committee and as its chairman."

Then followed some fifteen hundred words including a summation of the evils of the body politic, an extremely partizan arraignment of the Republican party, true in the main, and a fanciful picture of Jefferson and his accomplishments. In this last, Tilden was addressing an imaginary audience of cheering partizans. This letter did not reflect the cautious Tilden, but a Tilden unknown to the crowd, a demagogue of the hustings, the spouter, the spellbinder. Tilden was letting himself loose. He was already campaigning against Grant. There were, as Tilden knew, but two parties in Jefferson's day, the Federal and the Republican;

yet he said: "Thomas Jefferson founded and organized the Democratic party." That was good for two applauding interruptions with any Democratic audience—Jefferson's name and the party's. It would not have served his purpose to quote these noble passages from Jefferson's first inaugural address:

"We have called by different names brothers of the same principle. We are all Republicans; we are all Federalists. If there be any among us who would wish to dissolve the Union or to change its republican form, let them stand undisturbed as monuments of the safety with which error of opinion may be tolerated where reason is left free to combat it."

Instead, Tilden described another Jefferson. He might have said that Jefferson left office impoverished, actually apprehensive of arrest as a debtor. But Tilden was rich, and that would not do. So he said: "He refused to appoint relatives to office. He declined all presents. He refrained, while in public service, from all enterprises to increase his private fortune."

In the last four paragraphs of this letter, Tilden pictured himself as a leader seeking to restore "Jeffersonian democracy" and striving ever "to prepare the Democratic masses to act their part in a general movement for reform in all the governmental institutions of the country."

Instead of a signature, Tilden penned a Latin phrase which may be rendered, "More to follow." But after thinking it over, he decided his boom could wait, and he tucked the letter away in a trunk, and despatched a brief note resigning the state chairmanship. He subscribed himself Kelly's friend. The Tammany chief demonstrated his friendship by ignoring the resignation, so Tilden was unanimously reëlected chairman at the close of the Democratic State Convention in Utica on October 2.

The convention's most conspicuous accomplishment was to nominate a Republican, Thomas Raines, of Rochester, for state treasurer. Although he had ably and honestly administered his office, Raines was denied renomination by the Republican convention, which met in Utica a week earlier. Raines had offended them by supporting Greeley. Conkling did not attend the Republican convention because of the reprehensible work he had allotted to it.

The rejection of Raines could be defended by the Conkling machine on partisan grounds; but no defense could have been offered for not renominating Attorney General Francis C. Barlow, the best-informed official in the state on the thievings of the Canal Ring. This ring was composed of state employees and contractors, Republicans chiefly, who had swindled the state through fraudulent charges for work on the Erie Canal. Barlow was actively prosecuting them. This made him objectionable to the upstate wing of the Conkling machine, and was the immediate cause for turning him down. As attorney general, he was in charge of the prosecution of the Tweed Ring. O'Conor praised him for his austere integrity, and for like reason, the metropolitan wing of the Conkling machine condemned him. Barlow stood high in the life of the metropolis. He had served under Hancock and Grant, and bravery and distinguished service won him a brigadier-generalship.

The Conkling machine expected resentment over the rejection of Barlow and Raines, but were relying on the popularity of Grant and their well-drilled corps to save the ticket; they were also counting on the support of the reform Democrats in the metropolis, the Apollo Hall Democrats, led by "the notorious James O'Brien," as the *Tribune* designated the state senator and ex-sheriff. O'Brien was accused of having sold his followers to the Conkling machine in the

1872 campaign at so much per head, which was probably true, for O'Brien's was a trading organization.

Conkling was not gambling on an entire state ticket; Governor John A. Dix and Lieutenant-Governor John C. Robinson had another year to serve. The offices to be filled, besides attorney general and state treasurer, were secretary of state, comptroller, canal commissioner, state engineer, and prison inspector.

The Liberal Republicans indorsed the Democratic ticket save the nominees for comptroller and prison inspector. Here they supported the Republican candidates as more desirable.

A week after the Utica convention, O'Brien set out to pin the double cross on Honest John Kelly's breast by proposing a fusion between Tammany and Apollo Hall. All O'Brien asked was a place or two on the judiciary and county tickets. Kelly decided to beat O'Brien at his own game, and without betraying that he suspected him of being a secret ally of Conkling, appointed a committee to confer with the Apollo Hall group. After several conferences, Kelly publicly broke off the negotiations. On the same day, he declined the German Democratic Reform League's offer to support Tammany for the price of one coroner and the county clerk.

This was October 14. Immediately thereafter O'Brien began trading openly with the Conkling Republicans, with Chester A. Arthur as chairman of the Conkling conference committee. In ten days the results of the deliberations were announced. The metropolis was to elect two Supreme Court justices, two Superior Court justices, two Marine Court justices, sheriff, county clerk, and three coroners. Each of the contracting parties shared alike on the judicial nominations. The candidates for sheriff and one coroner were to be O'Brien men, while those for county clerk and two remaining coroners went to Conkling Republicans. There were also some swaps on the local candidates for the senate and assembly.

The Liberal Republicans indorsed most of the Tammany candidates, and Tammany reciprocated in kind. The Tammany-Liberal Republican coalition elected all six judges, the three coroners, sheriff, county clerk, four of the six candidates for the state senate, and the bulk of the twenty-one assembly nominees. The New York City vote for local candidates was overwhelmingly against the Conkling-O'Brien fusion, the Tammany-Liberal Republican candidates sweeping into office with majorities of more than fifteen thousand to nearly thirty-one thousand in a total vote of a little more than one hundred thousand.

The vote in the metropolis and elsewhere for state officers surprised the Conkling machine. A year before, Dix had been elected governor by a majority of 45,491 over Francis Kernan. Now the Democratic-Liberal Republican alliance overturned this splendid majority and elected their candidates with majorities ranging from 9,893 to 14,702. These were Diedrich Willers, secretary of state; Thomas Raines, treasurer; Daniel Pratt, attorney general; Sylvanus H. Sweet, state engineer. And by way of rubbing salt into the wounds, the Liberal Republicans saved the two candidates on the Conkling ticket they had indorsed: Nelson K. Hopkins, comptroller, who was elected by a slender majority of 4,065; and Moses K. Platt, prison inspector, with a still smaller majority—3,760. Conkling's only consolation in the returns was that he still controlled the legislature, but by reduced majorities in both houses. In the senate, he had a bare majority of one.

In this election the Liberal Republican voters demonstrated their capacity for knifing candidates. Each man they failed to indorse was defeated by intelligent cutting.

Straw votes indicated the closeness of the contest. On the day before election, Kelly learned that the Conkling machine had bargained with O'Brien to steal votes in several senate and assembly districts in the metropolis. The frauds were to be committed at the polls, by outright thefts and ballot-box stuffing, and at Police Headquarters by switching the count on the tally sheets. Kelly manned the polls with trusted men, and he sent five men to Police Headquarters to protect the count.

Kelly called these five watchers the Committee of Safety, a name hallowed by the nation's struggle for independence, when committees of safety governed the new-born states until they had organized their own civil governments. A few saw a note of humor in Kelly's device, but to the many, it was irrefutable proof that Honest John had restored Tammany to its pristine, patriotic purity, and that its opponents were ballot-box thieves, and worse.

Wags had it that Kelly created the Committee of Safety to fill the void caused by the evanescence of the Committee of Seventy which sang its swan-song while the Conkling Republicans and the O'Brien Democrats were agreeing upon a common ticket. The Committee of Seventy recalled it was formed to rescue the city from desperate conspirators, and cited the municipal campaign of 1871, with the defeat of the Tweed ticket, as the climax of its labors. But it bemoaned its failure to obtain a satisfactory new charter for the city because of "the corrupt influence of the great army of office-holders and the machinations of politicians together with the hostility of the then Executive."

The truth is that the Committee of Seventy had degenerated into an annex of the Conkling machine. The state legislature which had refused to enact the charter proposed by the committee was Republican in both branches, but the committee studiously refrained from saying so. The "then

Executive" referred to by the committee was Hoffman, Tweed's man. But the legislature of 1873 was also Republican, and Governor Dix was of the same faith. The Committee of Seventy would have embarrassed the Conkling machine, which controlled both, to press its demands for charter reforms such as it desired, and it meekly accepted the amendments passed by the 1873 legislature and signed by Dix. To continue the committee's swan-song:

In one important respect, the charter of 1873 has ... disappointed our hopes, and under the name of reform, was an outrage upon that much abused cause, in that it compromised with corruption in office, and expressly continued in office certain leading heads of departments who had been placed where they were by the expiring efforts of the discarded Tammany leaders, and were known to be more or less in sympathy with them. The triumph achieved in this one respect by corrupt and selfish politicians over the virtue of the legislature was a fatal obstacle to the thorough renovation of the city government.

But nowhere did the Committee of Seventy indicate the political complexion of the legislature or the governor who were jointly responsible for this triumph over virtue. One ignorant of the facts would have concluded from the committee's farewell that Tweed's governor and Tweed's legislature still ruled. But the committee fooled no one, as the election returns demonstrated.

31

HARD TIMES PACK

THE ALMSHOUSE OF THE WORLD

THERE ARE OCCASIONS WHEN THE METROPOLIS IS THE PULSE of the nation. This was true on New Year's night, 1874, when hundreds of homeless men and women slept on pine boards in out-of-the-way corners of police stations, usually in the cellars. The exact number for the night is not obtainable, but the total number of lodgings for January was 30,774, a marked increase over the corresponding first month of 1873. Some two-thirds of these homeless were classified as habitual station-house lodgers.

No child used these shelters unless accompanied by a mother, or father, or both. The homeless children crawled into stables, barns, hallways, and vacant dwellings. But they weren't particular, for an empty packing-box, or hogshead, or anything else would do, provided it protected them from the rain and snow and icy blasts. Children are proud spirits, and like some birds, they cannot survive a cage. To a child, a police station would still remain a cage if stripped of its iron bars.

The increase in the station-house lodgers, estimated at 20 to 25 per cent, had not been unexpected, for health-department inspectors in making their rounds late in November, 1873, found that cellars condemned and vacated during the preceding eighteen months as unfit for human habitation, were reoccupied, chiefly by unemployed mechanics and their families.

The reoccupation of the condemned cellars was tangible evidence that hard times, which had been anticipated by

The Panic of '73 as seen by Nast. Historic old Trinity at the head of Wall Street moralizes, "I Told You So." *Harper's Weekly,* October 11, 1873.

the well-informed for some time, had set in. The first major symptom was discernible on September 18, 1873, and a metropolitan journal of the next day said:

"The 'Street' is indulging in the costly luxury of another

panic. Yesterday two large firms, one of them probably the best known of our banking houses, Messrs. Jay Cooke & Co., and Messrs. George Opdyke & Co., yielded to nearly identical influences. Both had advanced money largely to new railroads, and both were caught by the feeling of distrust of this class of enterprises which has come over the community."

The failure of Jay Cooke was to Americans what the closing of the Bank of England would be to Britons. Other banking houses shut their doors for the last time. Stock prices tumbled so rapidly on September 19 that the Stock-Exchange was closed on the following day for the remainder of the month. Money was unobtainable at any price. Banks pooled their resources, and clearing-house certificates were used for the first time. Grant and his new Secretary of the Treasury, William A. Richardson, conferred with bankers in New York. The government temporarily eased the currency scarcity by recalling its securities to the value of $13,000,000. But this was all it could do. It was clear that nothing could be done to stem the panic or avert its consequences. Inefficiently, improperly, or corruptly managed financial institutions went to the wall. Railroad and building construction was crippled for lack of credit, and factories and workshops became silent. Business insolvencies became commonplace.

Crooked banking and speculation had again brought another period of prosperity to an end.

With the dawn of 1874, some thought conditions might be as bad as the panic of 1837 which lasted all through Van Buren's administration, with disastrous backwashes in the succeeding régime. They proved to be worse. Bankruptcies increased with each passing month and year, reaching their peak in 1878, when 10,478 business houses failed. Even then, no one attempted to foretell the end of this depression.

They had thought it was ending in 1876, but its effects were still observable in the 1880's.

This depression has been erroneously described as dating from the crash of the banking houses of Jay Cooke and George Opdyke. It was with us in January, 1872, twenty-one months before these two failures. These industrial and financial crises are first felt in the big cities, and at the beginning of 1872 journalists noted the unusual number of job-seekers who surged into New York, and the extraordinary rise in station-house lodgers. New wooden horses and new pine boards were purchased to increase the length of the rough platforms in the station-houses on which the homeless slept. One night seventy-five men slept in the Oak Street police station where Captain Anthony J. Allaire was commander; in the room reserved for women, thirty-four women, young and old, stretched themselves out on the pine boards. Allaire had a breakfast fund for his guests.

The color line was sharply drawn in the metropolis in the seventies. There were Jim Crow public schools; but hard times made black and white equal, at least on the pine-board beds. We find "two Negroes packed down with whites" in the Mercer Street station-house one winter night in 1872. With the arrival of warm weather, stoves were dismantled, and many station-houses cleaned up their coal bins to give the homeless a little more privacy.

Free lodgings were provided at the police stations all through the seventies. But in the summer months, there was more sleeping out—to use the euphemism of the homeless. The sleeping out was confined almost exclusively to the men. The women preferred the pine boards the year around.

Let us take a typical year, 1876. In the first quarter—January, February, and March are the coldest months—78,788 lodgings were provided; less than one-third that number, 27,167, in the third quarter. But toward the end of Septem-

A snowstorm greets the homeless after a night in a New York police station. Drawn by Miranda. *Leslie's Weekly*, February 10, 1877.

ber, the police began to protest against housing all comers, and requested permission to provide quarters only for the deserving. Accordingly, a general order was issued to arrest "indolent and dissolute habitual lodgers as vagrants." This resulted in a decrease of a little more than 43 per cent in the final quarter of 1876 compared with the fourth quarter of 1875, when 63,386 lodgings were provided. Less than one-third of the homeless women came under the classification of indolent and dissolute.

The quarterly statistics of station-house lodgings for 1876 follows:

	1st	2nd	3rd	4th
MALE	58,748	25,651	8,594	21,598
FEMALE	20,040	19,432	18,573	14,240

This represented a total of 186,876 for 1876. This was the last year the station-house lodgings were tabulated. The figures were first compiled in 1871, and the totals for this and the ensuing years follow: 1871, 136,743; 1872, 147,215; 1873, 183,854; 1874, 221,968; 1875, 217,552.

Another indication of the depression being in full swing nearly two years or so before the Wall Street panic was the extraordinary number of beggars, especially children. *Leslie's Weekly*, on February 10, 1872, said: "We have been affected in our chief avenues by an inundation of child beggars." These were part of the city's vast army of vagrant and neglected children. No one knew the number of these unfortunate little ones, although rough guesses were made throughout the years. On July 2, 1871, when the population of the city was about one million, we are told that "vagrant and neglected children if placed in double file, three feet apart, would make a procession eight miles long." This would give us 28,610 innocent ones clad in rags. Back in the late 1850's, and during the Civil War, estimates ranged from 10,000 to 30,000.

Whatever their number, these children, with comparatively few exceptions, had fled from drunken homes. The exceptions were mostly adventurous youths from the country. Girls too young to be prostitutes, rescued from this army of

The homeless seeking shelter in a police station on a winter's night. Drawn by Sol Eytinge, from a sketch by Thomas Worth. *Harper's Weekly*, February 4, 1871.

juveniles, often told of fleeing the parental roof to avoid a life of thievery. Girls of thirteen and fourteen took to the highroad rather than sell themselves.

How did these children live? In the spring they gathered the first violets from wooded stretches of the metropolis, and the wild iris from the city's marshes; in the summer, these marshes yielded large blueberries, and it was a rare year when blackberries were not abundant on many a patch of wild-wood where the sun fell freely. And open field and marshy meadow provided some of these youngsters with a way out of the abyss.

The most extensive bog in the seventies stretched from Third Avenue to the East River and from Ninety-second Street to 110th Street, a pitiful reminder of the Harlem Marsh, and Manhattan's noblest fresh-water stream, the Harlem Kill, which was fed by five brooks that drained the watershed embracing sections of Bloomingdale, Manhattanville, and Harlem.

The Harlem Kill had its inception in Central Park west of Fifth Avenue and 109th Street. In crossing Fifth Avenue, the Kill covered most of the present roadway from 108th to 106th streets, and then flowed, as straight as a creek can go, until it roared into the East River at 107th and 108th streets. Throughout its turbulent course it averaged more than four hundred feet between banks; from Madison to Third avenues, its width was nearly eight hundred feet, and yachts were moored at this point in the early seventies. All there is to remind us of the Harlem Kill is the pond in the northeastern corner of Central Park, and the marshes it nourished are but memories. In the late seventies the creek had been filled in to Second Avenue, but from here on it still flowed bravely, and the only bridge spanning it was a rude plank structure at First Avenue. But bridge, creek, and marsh have given way to the massive piles of brick and steel and stone that heralded the twentieth century.

The few remaining patches of neglected woodland were harvested by the homeless children in the fall, first for the chestnuts, butternuts, and hickory-nuts, and then for the faggots. Most of the timber was second growth, and little remained of the forest that once covered the upper part of the island. The largest stand of old trees was in Jones's Wood, long the city's favorite picnic ground, and advocated by many in 1850 for purchase as a city park instead of Central Park. The woodland that once stretched to north and south of the Jones homestead on the bluff overlooking the East River at the foot of Sixty-ninth Street, had dwindled in 1877 to the plot bounded by Sixty-eighth and Sixty-ninth streets, the East River, and Avenue A, now York Avenue.

Overripe vegetables and decayed fruit provided another source of income. These squashy missiles were in high demand when some unpopular actor or melodrama held the boards. These children dealt in anything involving little or no capital, from shoe-strings up.

The authorities ignored these homeless children until they violated some law, or were found half-frozen of a winter night, and taken to a hospital, fortunate if they lost only a toe. For many of these boys and girls went through the winter shod like Washington's troops at Valley Forge. The callous indifference of officialdom toward these youngsters was reflected in the police designation for them—street rats.

It was an old name for these little ones. But one man of the cloth, Charles Loring Brace, had decided some years earlier that "Suffer little children to come unto me" had use outside of a sermon. Brace had labored among prisoners on Blackwell's Island and among the poor of the Five Points before he founded the Children's Aid Society in 1853. Twenty-one years later he had four lodging-houses for boys in the metropolis, and lived to see his movement adopted in every civilized nation.

The boys called these establishments lodges. A clean bed in a warm room cost five cents, and the same sum bought a good meal. The largest of these lodges, at 49 Park Place, was named the Newsboys' Lodging-House. More than two hundred slept here nightly, mostly newsboys, "sharp, ready, light-hearted, quick to act, quick to understand." A *Times* reporter attended Sunday evening service at this lodge on December 4, 1870, and saw "many rows of little street arabs, bright-faced, intelligent lads, poorly clad, more than half of them barefoot." Barefoot—in December.

While more than seventy-three thousand beds were made up in the course of the year at the Park Place lodge, those who passed through it in a year numbered slightly more than eight thousand and the average length of stay was nine days. Many of the boys found homes on farms and with artisans in other cities.

In the lodge on Rivington Street, near Goerck, once a public school, the winter patrons were steady. These were boys who worked on the canal-boats when the waters were navigable. During the winter, these canallers, as they were called, turned street merchant or did any odd job that turned up.

What became of this vast army of homeless boys and girls? Many were rescued by Brace and others like him, unknown beyond their own little circles. Some were snared by pickpockets, thieves, and pimps.

The metropolitan Department of Charities and Corrections did not include these children in its statistics of 1872, which set down one in every thirteen of New York's first million as a pauper. This was an increase of 900 per cent in forty years, while the increase in population was about one-tenth of this ratio. The pauper ratio—7.69 per cent—was high, when compared with England's, which was one in thirty, or 3.33 per cent, and represented 76,923 paupers in the metropolis, exclusive of the homeless children. Across the East River, in the old City of Churches, when Brooklyn's Superintendent of the Poor announced one in every nine of the population was on relief, the cry went up that this ratio—11.11 per cent—was false and fraudulent.

"Station House Lodgers"

From a drawing by Winslow Homer. *Harper's Weekly*, February 7, 1874.

A phrase, long current and common in the press of the seventies, was this redundancy: "New York is the almshouse of the poor of all nations." This phrase described a condition dating back to the early 1830's. And once again protests were being regularly lodged with diplomatic representatives of countries which dumped their paupers and felons on us.

However, the dumping was not confined to New York. All large cities were similarly afflicted. Year in and year out, newspapers described the shameful conditions, which reached the proportions of an international scandal in 1855. In January of that year, New York City lodged a complaint with President Franklin Pierce, through its mayor, who informed him that "there can be no doubt that for many years this port has been made a sort of penal colony for felons and paupers by the authorities of several of the continental European nations." The problem was an old one to Congress. It was before the body in 1838, and in 1874. There was much talk, and some investigating. But little was done to check the pollution. Frequently, the alien beggars and criminals were arrested as they landed. But able lawyers were mysteriously retained, and almost invariably obtained the admission of these undesirables to our shores.

These protests reached a climax on September 11, 1879, at a meeting in Saratoga of the State Board of Charities. The board accused European nations of sending "blind, crippled, insane, and other paupers to the United States," and forwarded these charges to the Department of State with a plea that these "pauper shipments be stopped." Most of the paupers "come to the port of New York and a majority become a burden on the state. . . . Cities and towns in foreign countries relieve themselves in this way of a tax upon their resources." Also we find in this protest: "The State Board of Charities has sent back many and thinks it is time to stop the evil at the source."

In the previous month, an imbecile woman with two illegitimate children arrived in New York from Switzerland. She was sent back—at the expense of New York. The Swiss poorhouse authorities of Berne decided to make an example of a rebellious and dissolute inmate, an ex-convict, sixty-one years of age, so they sent him penniless to New York. He was returned. When the New York Commissioners of Emigration learned that the Berne officials were about to send the convict-pauper on a second voyage to the metropolis, this time with a draft on a New York bank for four hundred francs, they protested to the Department of State. Under date of August 7, 1879, William M. Evarts, successor of Hamilton Fish as Secretary of State, wrote that "Mr. Fish has laid the matter before the Swiss Government."

Local officials in England, Italy, Holland, and other countries were equally guilty. Protest followed protest. The governments apologized. But still the paupers and criminals came in, and were "given charity at Castle Garden," then the office of the emigration commission and now the Aquarium.

"The emigration commissioners feel that if this state of things continues," said the New York *Tribune* on August 26, 1879, "the burden upon the state will become so great that there will be a demand for relief through a national law on immigration. This has been sought by the commissioners in years past, but now the people are aroused to the fact that this country does not need for its population paupers and criminals from other shores."

The commissioners of emigration were not talking loosely. Of the outdoor poor aided by the municipality in the seventies six in every seven were foreign-born. In 1872, while the Tweed appointees were still in power, 5,541 families, averaging four to a family, received relief. Of this number, 811 were born in the United States, and 4,730 in foreign countries.

These figures, published by Tweed's Superintendent of the Poor, are reliable, for Tweed and his followers surpassed their predecessors in cultivating the good-will of the foreign-born. All males over twenty-one meeting the color test, provided they were not criminals, could be made voters overnight—fuel for the spoils machine. This was one reason why protests by the commissioners of emigration went unheeded. Another was that passengers meant profits to ship-owners. A third was that immigrants provided cheap labor. It would be easy for spokesmen of any of these powerful groups to raise the cry of bigotry, if their immediate interests were menaced. And so New York and other cities continued to be the almshouses of the world.

32

THE ORIGIN OF THE SLUM OF SLUMS

THE PRINCIPAL DORMITORY IN THE LEADING ALMSHOUSE OF the world was the Five Points. There were others, mostly scattered along the water-front, but the Five Points was the symbol of things vile, from the depravity of many of its inhabitants to the criminal neglect of those who governed. Yet the authorities favored it above all other slums, for its streets were the first to be cleaned with the passing of winter. Once the cold weather set in, no attention was paid to the mean streets, and the submerged stood on the curb before their homes and threw into the gutters all things undesirable; "When the snow melted, ridges three feet high of garbage, human excrement, and ashes" were commonplace in these streets as noted in a metropolitan journal on March 13, 1871. The Five Points was outwardly cleaned after the first thaw because it was the backyard of the city hall. With the continued hard times, health-department physicians became unusually apprehensive of this first American slum. On May 12, 1874, they reminded the city how "smallpox clung in this locality with remarkable tenacity," and sounded this warning: "Unless steps are taken promptly to improve conditions in this locality, it will become a hotbed for cholera and kindred diseases."

The physicians were striving for action before the end of June, for mortality is ever high in July and August among New York's poor. They knew that pestilence would stalk through the city if it obtained a foothold in the Five Points,

275

the geographical center of the populous part of the city. To emphasize the danger to all, the doctors recalled that "half the population of the metropolis lived in tenement-house basements [cellars], attics, and huts [shanties]."

Dreaded most were the disease-breeding cellars which constituted a city in themselves, with their own restaurants, bar-rooms, gambling dens, dance halls, lodgings for all types, including special accommodations for tramps. The immediate objective of the doctors were the plague spots, above and below ground, which they had succeeded in having condemned as "unfit for human habitation" immediately after the rout of the Tweed Ring. These places, as the reader knows, were taken over by the poorest of the poor in 1873. The vast majority of these unfortunates were worthy unemployed and their families, strangers to the city, who had seen their slender stores dwindle till they were plunged into the depths of the Five Points or some other abysmal slum. Americans whose roots were in the nation's earliest settlements shared these pest holes with newly arrived immigrants, chiefly Irish and German. An occasional pioneer of our present Chinatown gravitated to a condemned house of the Five Points.

The police could have vacated these condemned houses on their own initiative, if they desired, for they had sealed them. On the morning of July 1, 1872, fifty policemen emptied some of the vilest rookeries in the Five Points, first descending upon a four-story tenement in the rear of 52 Mulberry Street, called the White House, because its red brick had once been painted white.

Upon entering the White House, the police found the men away, either working or hunting for work. "Many of the women lay on the dirty floors insensible from death-dealing rum and whiskey which can be purchased in the neighborhood at six cents a quart."

The police next emptied the adjoining house, No. 50, a two-story wooden structure. Then they swung west one block, to the five wooden buildings in the rear of 35 and 37 Baxter, known as Carey's Alley. Two of the alley tenements had been workshops, one of three stories, the other, two; each floor housed four families—and their lodgers—in two-room apartments. The other dwellings were two-storied, with two rooms to a floor. In all five houses the monthly rent was $3 to $4.50 per room. "There literally was no yard to these premises," wrote a journalist accompanying the police, "the space between the front and rear houses being covered by a number of shanties used as stables for horses, goats, and dogs."

The cellars in the two-story dwellings in Carey's Alley were not tenanted by humans—this being a recent concession to the health officials. One cellar was a stable, another a junkman's storehouse for putrefying bones and foul rags, and the third a lumber warehouse. After evicting the tenants, the police pried into the shanty shelter of dogs, goats, and horses. Said the *Times*:

"In one of the stables were found two women, both prematurely old, rolling in the refuse in a state of semi-insensible intoxication, their stockingless feet and legs begrimed with the manure of horses, dog, and goats."

These two women, once laughing, carefree little girls, continued their troubled sleep while the police noisily removed all household furnishings to the sidewalk from the condemned houses. After nailing boards across all windows and doors, the invaders departed, leaving the rum-stupefied pair to sleep it off. They were habitués of the Five Points, as their scant garb and their choice of the filthy floor of a rear stable for a couch attested.

These rear stables afforded free lodgings to chronic drunkards, as stablemen in such places were unknown. Only those familiar with the neighborhood knew of their existence, for all that could be seen from the street was an unbroken row of weather-beaten dwellings. A stranger would learn of these stables if he chanced by at the end of a day and saw an empty wagon drive up to a parking space, the horse unhitched and led through a tenement's narrow doorway which opened on an equally narrow hallway floored with rotting boards. It was not uncommon for a peddler or a truckman to find one of his uninvited guests dead of a morning, especially in winter.

Carey's Alley was but one of hundreds of its kind in the city's scattered slums where thousands of tenements, unfit for human habitation, were occupied to the last room in the summer of 1874. The continued depression had increased the number of homeless.

There were dwellings in the Five Points where sordid poverty reigned in good times and bad, where parents spent their all on rotgut, and on the drainings of beer barrels, called swipes.

These tenements were of brick or clapboards, and had housed the successful of an earlier day. These old homes could readily be repaired; but those built since 1817, on filled-in ground, were beyond restoration. Most of these newer dwellings consisted of two stories and attic, and were erected on substantial stone foundations that made for spacious cellars. Each floor had two large rooms. By 1870 the old cellar walls had settled, always unevenly, tilting the houses at rakish angles. Some houses were two to five feet lower at one end than at the other. These, and other small houses, had been built for workers in the neighborhood factories, with their wide variety of products, from candles, soap, and buttons, to the fabrications of brass and iron foundries. These factories multiplied with the city's abnormal growth, and the density of population, especially in the Old Sixth, increased commensurately. The higher paid workers moved out of the dwellings on filled-in ground, for water from the old marshes and ponds seeped into the cellars in wet weather.

Distributing free ice-water in New York's Printing House Square, upon which the *Tribune* and *Times* buildings fronted. Drawn by E. A. Abbey, later R. A. A woman rag-picker has just been served. On the left is a newsboy, and in the immediate foreground are a girl street-musician, a youthful pedler of fans, and a little bootblack. *Harper's Weekly,* July 27, 1872.

Such was the demand for living quarters by neighborhood factory workers in the Old Sixth that by 1853 most of its houses had a double, or rear tenement, as indicated by the monumental survey published that year by William Perris, showing all structures in the city, their size and use, and every inch of lawn or yard. But Perris found yards and no lawns in the Old Sixth, and by 1870 it was a rare dwelling that did not have a double. In many instances the front tenement was the true double, for it stood on the former lawn and garden of what was now the rear house.

The cellars of houses out of plumb which were deep in water in the spring and early summer, were the only shelters not used as dwellings the year round. Families crowded those cellars where only mud oozed through cracks of the flooring, winter and summer, for mud is removable.

Besides the abnormal growth of the metropolis, and civic indifference, there was a natural cause for the Sixth Ward outranking all other slums. This was its topography before it was changed to meet the growth of the metropolis. The ward began, or ended, in a point formed by the junction of Broadway and Park Row. If the reader will take a map and draw his pencil northward from this point along Broadway to Canal Street, thence along Canal to the Bowery, and down the Bowery to Park Row—a continuation of the Bowery—and to the point of beginning, he will have described the Sixth Ward, the Bloody Old Sixth of fights and riots, political and religious. The reader will note that his pencil has made a crooked shield, the base comprising the Park and the city hall.

This crooked shield may be said to have been the municipal coat of arms for nearly a century. On the dexter, or Broadway side, from Chambers Street north, minor marts of commerce and an occasional old home successfully held out as the slums besieged Broadway from 1830 on. The sinister side, north of Chambers Street, to Canal Street, surrendered by 1850, and the Civil War saw the entire Sixth Ward, north from City Hall Park to Canal Street, and from the Bowery west, to within a block of Broadway, practically a solid slum.

33

A FORGOTTEN CRUSADE

THE FIVE POINTS SOON BECAME THE SYMBOL OF THE SLUMS
of the United States, and after people stopped talking
in the terms of Kent—that the population of New York was
"rapidly swelling into the burdensome pauperism of a European metropolis"—they considered the reality. Greeley had
aroused them and led them. He became intimately acquainted with the Five Points as chairman of the Sixth Ward
Relief Committee during the winter of suffering among the
poor that followed the financial panic of Van Buren's first
months in the White House. No one was more alert than he
to the menace of the slums to the American experiment in
government. These urban crucibles refine and destroy. They
have produced business leaders, industrialists, clerics, physicians, skilled artisans, statesmen. But these are not the
run of the slums, for the run of the slums are the weak, the
depraved, the embittered, who gravitate to the gambling
den, the bagnio, the prison, and the soap-box. The soap-box
is the protest against the slum, against the wrongs that create
it. All soap-boxes are not of foreign make. Greeley sought
escape in Fourierism after his harrowing experiences in the
Five Points, but realizing that Utopia is not reached in an
overnight journey, he set out on a long, patient drive.

The germ of this forgotten crusade is in the *Tribune* of
January 21, 1854, when Greeley praised the extension of a
dead-end street and urged that another be "opened through

two blocks of wretched old houses" in the heart of the Five Points:

Here at Orange [renamed Baxter] Street he will find an old frame house directly before him. That is the end of Anthony [now Worth] Street. If that old frame house were removed, and a few more buildings of little value, he would have an open way right into Chatham Square, opposite Oliver Street. . . .

There is another point of view in which this improvement would be beneficial; that is the change to be worked upon the class of people who inhabit that street. . . . Will our City Council back this much-needed improvement?

The old frame house confronting one in walking through Worth Street from Center Street constituted one of the five corners, or points, which gave the neighborhood its name. This dwelling stood on the northeast corner of Baxter and Park streets until the fall of 1868, when Greeley's suggestion was adopted and Worth Street was cut through to Chatham Square. These five corners, or Five Points, opened on a plaza, where two scraggly trees grew in a triangular plot of grass. A wooden fence kept out the goats and served as drying racks for the rag-pickers. This triangle received the mocking name of Paradise Park from the humorous councilmen. Another of the Five Points was the apex of the park, formed by the junction of the end of Worth Street with Park Street. This point was flanked by two others, the southwest corner of Baxter and Park streets and the northwest corner of Baxter and Worth. The fifth point was the southeast corner of Baxter and Worth. The base of Paradise Park was Little Water Street, a narrow alley of vile tenements and stables. Little Water began at Park Street and, after crossing Worth, formed a cul-de-sac midway between Worth and Leonard streets. On Park Street, fronting on Little Water, was the Old Brewery.

Greeley returned to his slum-clearance crusade three months later while discussing the opening of the eighth school established by churchwomen to rescue children from lives of crime by teaching and feeding them. Soon there were scores of these schools, and twice a day, at noon and at evening, poor women went to them with empty pails and returned home with thick soup or stew and loaves of bread. On Fridays, fish and clam chowder were also served. The first of these soup schools was founded in 1853, and was patterned on London's Ragged Schools, where any child, no matter how poorly clad, was welcome. On October 30, 1868, we find one at 110 Center Street, "exclusively for Italian children—the little organ-grinders and bootblacks of the city." Our tax-supported public schools in the cities would not admit a barefoot child. This snobbery has not tainted our country schools where children cast aside shoes and stockings—if so minded—with the advent of warm weather.

"The state has duties in this matter which it has never recognized," said Greeley, in noting the opening of the eighth soup school. "There should be a cure which should go to the source of our social evil in the great cities. . . . A Ragged School—or better named, an Industrial School—is opened, where the children who are too poor for the public schools are taught a common-school education and a means of livelihood. A soup kitchen is connected with the establishment."

After praising the women volunteers in these schools, Greeley, who had a virile concept of what constituted good works, continued:

This is no rose-water philanthropy. . . . And as our men, our legislators and politicians, and comfortable millionaires, look at this devotion and self-denial of the most refined women of the city to remove evils which they ought themselves long ago to have been administering to, they may happily be persuaded at

Homeless children in New York City. This unsigned sketch from life is significantly entitled: "School or Jail?" *Harper's Weekly,* January 21, 1871.

least to open their pockets to the cause. The Industrial School needs money as well as laborers. And possibly, after a term of those efforts, we shall have society doing as a whole what is now so laboriously undertaken by individuals; and government may at length, on a broad scale, fulfil the function of blessing as well as of punishing.

When cholera visited the city later in the spring, Greeley drove home the lesson of the slums. On June 19 he noted that of the fifty-seven cholera fatalities in the past week, "deaths in most instances were the result of the filth by which the victims were surrounded," and added:

The plague spots in which the seeds of cholera so rapidly and fatally fructify are the tenement-houses, the old rookeries, and blind alleys into which the poorer classes crowd or are crowded with the most reckless disregard of health, comfort or decency. ... It was in one of these that the cholera first appeared in 1849, and in such barracks as it now exists.... Of the localities most infested by cholera in the city, we may name the Five Points, the low grounds near the East River, the emigrant boarding-houses in the First Ward, the overcrowded tenements in the Seventeenth Ward, and the filthy shanties far up the island.

The Civil War temporarily halted the fight against the slums in which many newspapers had joined. But it was not until the late seventies that there was any systematic opposition, outside of newspaper offices, to the well-intrenched tenement landlords, who insisted Greeley and his kind were incapable of the truth. Moreover, lies sold newspapers.

Let us visit Baxter Street, north of Worth, and inspect a typical row of houses, Nos. 33 to 39. It is a summer day in 1871. Each of the four tenements consists of two stories and an attic. A *Times* reporter points to the gable-roofs and observes: "The shingles are split and rotten and admit the rain like a basket.... The roof and floors have sagged down five feet from the level. . . . All timbers are decayed." In the rear are more hovels; "six goats roam the yard and four women are stretched out in the July sun, dead drunk." Where these drunken women came from was never a matter of speculation, but many errors arose respecting these and other goats on Manhattan Island. The prevailing notion was that the thousands roaming the streets were the stock of a few imported after the Revolution; but Manhattan's goats boasted ancient pedigrees that stemmed from six proud animals brought to the colony in 1633 by de Vries, a gift from the governor of Virginia to the governor of New Amsterdam.

Across the street from the goats and the drunken women was a six-story tenement in the rear of 38 Baxter. Although the dirt here was not extraordinary, the house was unfit for human habitation. On the second floor, an Italian organ-grinder was gouged $14 a month for two rooms. The furnishings consisted of a stove, some broken chairs, chipped crockery, and three cots.

This Italian was a capitalist. To begin with, he owned his barrel-organ. Ordinarily, organ-grinders either hired the instruments or were employed by *padroni*. In addition, he had eight lodgers, *paesani* all; six of them paid 75 cents weekly to sleep on straw shake-downs, and two paid $1.00 each for real beds. This brought in $6.50 weekly, so that he lived rent free, and had a few dollars to boot at the end of the month. All nine kept the place fairly clean, and foraged for their fuel, so that the *padrone* only bought kerosene and an occasional few handfuls of straw. The apartment also housed a cat and a monkey.

Every morning, before faring forth on his rounds, this immigrant-capitalist put a gaudy Austrian army officer's tunic on the monkey, as most of his kind have done since the close of the Austro-Italian war in 1866. That year marked the beginning of native competition, for many wounded Civil War veterans had their choice between organ grinding and begging. The Italians left the heart of the town to the veterans, who could not hobble far on a wooden stump, and some were grievously maimed. Most of these men wore their faded uniforms, and on their hurdy-gurdies were signs reciting their engagements. Some sold matches and shoe laces.

Hardly a tenement-house in Baxter Street, or in any other slum street, was fit for human shelter. The health-department physicians were too few to cover more than a small fraction of the slums. Their reports resulted in orders to vacate the worst of these tenements. The press published the orders—and that, almost invariably, was the end of it. It did not matter whether a Tammany or a reform administration was in power—the landlords won out.

Let us consider the first year of the reform administration ushered in by the fall of Tweed & Co., when tens of thousands lived in cellars. On April 23, 1873, the Board of Health announced that of 549 cellar lodgings inspected in the previous week, 450 were unfit for human habitation. Of these 450, sixty-six were south of Houston Street, mostly in the Five Points. This represented the work of four physicians. In the week ended March 12, Dr. E. H. Janes inspected 176 cellars and found 137 unfit for humans. All these 176 were in the ward just to the southeast of the Five Points, the Fourth, which fronted on the East River, from Peck Slip to Catherine Street.

All these cellars were crowded to capacity, and four out of five were loathsome menaces. Men, women, and children ocupied these underground lodgings, quite often consisting of one big room where "many of the inmates cook, wash, smoke, and perform all their physical functions." Some of these cellars "have thin drapes between the beds, which are

ranged alongside of each other, and others have none at all."
One cellar-dwelling family of seven had ten lodgers, a total
of seventeen in one long room. In some of these places, no
children were ever admitted.

"The greater part of this ward being originally swampy
or marshy ground," Dr. Janes reported, "it was seldom that
any subcellar or open space beneath the floor was found,
and the floors, resting directly on the ground, were rotten
and bad. The only floors in good repair were those of the
dance cellars."

Dr. Janes and his fellows had no jurisdiction over dance
cellars as such. Moral filth was not their official concern.
There was not a dance hall among the 137 cellars ordered
vacated and closed. As if in grim jest, the Board of Health
set the closing day for April 1! The Janes report ended with
the observation that great good will be established "by closing forever these filthy dens of immorality and disease."
This last referred in part to the cellar bagnios, where the
average inmate was syphilitic.

A cellar lodging, at 378 Water Street, always passed
muster. It was kept by Mrs. Mary Hurley. She also had
lodgings on the floors above. The Hurley lodgings were of
the better sort. Rude beds, each fitted with a tick and nothing more, were the only accommodations. It was patronized
chiefly by families down on their luck. They kept their belongings, including fragments of food, in baskets, stowed
under the beds at night. Like the lodgers, the house could
stand improvement. There was not a wall or ceiling in the
place where broken plaster did not bare the lath. On a bed
lay a mother with her six-year-old boy, "both specklessly
clean." A candle guttered on a box that served as a table.
The child, she admitted, did handicap her a little in getting
work, but she managed somehow. When it was suggested
that the boy be put in the city home on Randall's Island,

the woman looked fondly at her sleeping son as she replied softly, so as not to waken him:

"And have some one adopt him in three months if I left him there that long? And never see him again? You do not know what it is to have nothing on earth but a child. Take him from me, and it won't make much difference where I sleep."

That day a man and wife and their two children—it was winter—were dispossessed down the street. Neighbors took in their few belongings, and Mrs. Hurley gave the penniless family a small room with one bed. The mother and the younger child occupied the bed, the father and his son slept on the floor.

Unlike the cellar of the Hurley lodging-house, many of the cellars on Water Street, and the two thoroughfares between it and the East River, Front and South streets, had not been used since the houses were constructed, save by small boys. All of South Street, except for the three blocks from Whitehall to Broad Street, is filled-in ground, as are most of Front and Water streets. When the tide was high, the water from the East River converted these cellars into ponds, which small boys navigated on rafts. This remained a favorite East Side pastime long after the turn of the century.

Advocates of slum improvement centered their attention on the cellar lodgings immediately after the panic of 1873. Early in the summer of 1874 they protested against the continued occupancy of places constantly condemned. By way of appeasement, a platoon of police staged a spectacular show early Sunday morning, June 28. They started at 149 Chatham Street, now Park Row, and awakened "seven girls who were sleeping off a night's debauch," drove them to the streets and threw the beds and other furnishings after them. This was one of several cellar lodgings for women

within the shadow of the city hall. The cops next went down
the street to No. 53, routed ten men and women, and put
the furniture on the sidewalk. They then invaded 29 North
William Street—another women's lodging-house—and repeated the performance. Other places raided were 13 Oak
Street, 14 Dover, 336, 338, and 337½ Water Street. This
last was kept by Cockney Joe, a retired costermonger, whose
cellar was divided into four rooms, reached through a bar
where he served whiskey only.

There was hardly a cellar dance hall or lodging without
its bar, and in many of them the favorite drink was swipes.
The gathering of swipes became a profitable industry after
the Civil War, and toward the end of the seventies it was
monopolized by "certain Italians who go out early in the
morning and sweep out lager-beer saloons or help the
drivers of beer wagons and get the dregs in payment," as
the *Tribune* related on July 8, 1879. The police attributed
"two-thirds of the misery found in these squalid tenements
to the stale-beer traffic." In a rear Baxter Street tenement,
in a basement room 10 by 12 feet, the reporter and his
police escort "counted twenty men and women seated on
dirty beds of straw; two or three were lying on the floor
overcome by liquor." At the lone table "four men were playing cards, with pennies for stakes. The door, the only means
of ventilating this stinking hole, was closed. In one corner
sat an Italian keeping guard over a cag of stale beer and
doling out pints at two cents apiece." In an adjoining cellar
bar and lodging-house "besotted women lay as they had
fallen, half in the middle of the floor and half under a bed."
On entering this dive, "in the dim light could be seen the
legs of a woman who lay on the damp stones; the head and
shoulders were hidden behind a barrel."

On this stretch of Baxter Street, on the east side, between
Worth and Bayard, was the filthiest row in the city. Here

"Shelter for the Homeless—Night Scene in a New York Station House"
Harper's Weekly, December 13, 1873.

dwelt the depraved and the meanest of petty criminals, and here gravitated the baser tramps of every nationality. But the vilest tenement in all the town was on the block immediately to the south. It was nicknamed Mulberry Hall. Its address was 5 and 7 Mulberry Street, rear.

Mulberry Hall was once an architectural gem of the Sixth Ward. It was then a church, and stood sixty feet back from the sidewalk on a gentle slope. A gravel walk led through a shaded lawn to peaceful portals that knew William Colgate and others who are part of the glorious side of the story of New York. From 1809 to 1850 it was a house of prayer, first as the Mulberry Street Baptist Church, and from 1839 on as the Tabernacle Baptist Church. When the congregation moved uptown, the old trees were cut down and the lawn vanished as the new owner erected a five-story tenement almost flush with the façade of the church which he had converted into a wooden barracks of five floors. This transformation was not novel in the Five Points, for in 1837, Coulter's brewery, built in 1792, was turned into a rookery, and three years later became the most notorious dwelling in the land. The tenants entered by alleys at each side of the building; one was called Murderer's Alley, the other, the Den of Thieves. As if to atone for the profanation of the church, the Ladies' Home Mission of the Methodist Episcopal Church converted the Old Brewery into the Five Points Mission House in 1852.

Let us follow a reporter and his escort of two detectives into Mulberry Hall, for this was one of many places where even a policeman did not venture alone. The day is July 1, 1871, and 170 men, women, and children are packed within the foul walls. One of the detectives recognized a young, flaxen-haired, blue-eyed girl. As he grasped her arm, she timidly inquired:

"Do you want me—what have I done?"

"Ragpickers' Court, Mulberry Street" is the title of this drawing by
W. A. Rogers of metropolitan slums. *Harper's Weekly*, April 5, 1879.

"We don't want you, Mag," said the detective. "But what are you doing here? Do you live here now?"

"No, sir. I only stayed here this morning. I don't live anywhere. I only stay, you know. I was out all night, and Mrs. —— let me lay on the straw for a little sleep."

"Why don't you go home, Mag?"

"Home! Pshaw! What's the use? Please let me go."

An old woman's story of the girl, vouched for by the detectives, was thus summarized in the *Times:*

"She was a good, nice girl, once. She came here from the country for work. She was looking for lodgings at night when two men told her to come in here and they would show her a cheap boarding-house. When she got in a dark place they knocked her down. She couldn't make much noise, and you can guess the rest, sirs. These two devils left her most dead faint, and she's gone from bad to worse."

Dr. Roger S. Tracy of the Health Department described Mulberry Hall as dangerous to life and detrimental to health. He continued:

The walls and floors are saturated with offensive effluvia, the accumulation of years. The inmates are all pallid, thin, and delicate. The areas on all sides of the house are exceedingly filthy with excrement, urine, garbage, and rubbish thrown there by the inmates of the house. At night nearly all the adult tenants are drunk.... The tenants are of the lowest type...throwing filth of all kinds out of their windows and into the windows and yards of adjacent houses.

In Mulberry Hall and its kind, the death-rate averaged 96.7 per 1,000 in 1872. There were some sixty houses where the annual death toll in each was 6 to 11. Most of the victims were children. The death-rate in the metropolis in 1872 was 32.6; London, England, with its own share of slums, was only 21.4, while our own Buffalo was 17.3, and

San Francisco 17.2. The death-rate to-day in a city with fairly decent living standards hovers around eleven. So about eight in every nine of these deaths were wanton and possible only because it profited grafting officials and callous landlords to continue these death-traps.

In the winter of 1878-79 the movement to reform the slums assumed aggressive, well-organized proportions. A private group, the State Charities Aid Association, served as the planning agency for all concerned. The objective was remedial legislation. The campaign was admirably planned. First, a survey of the tenements was to be made by a committee of eight laymen and the distinguished physician, Dr. Richard Henry Derby, whose namesake son married a daughter of Theodore Roosevelt. Derby would give the movement the required impetus, and no one could cry him down as a sensational journalist, as they had Greeley, if he demanded that owners of foul tenements be forced to recognize that they owed more than shelter to their tenants. Next, on the fourth Sunday in February, 1879, the churches were to aid through sermons at the regular services and at evening meetings. The following Friday, a rally was to be held in Cooper Union. Then the fight would shift to the legislature. Every move was made according to schedule.

The principal meeting was in the Madison Square Presbyterian Church where Derby spoke. His opening sentence was a confession: his professional labors did not give him time to inspect all the slums that his colleagues had. He had selected for inspection "a few of the houses they had visited as types of their class." He described a six-story tenement with four middle sleeping-rooms on each floor, all windowless, and "so dark that a light had to be procured to see in them in daylight." In another, of five stories, were thirty-two dark rooms. This was not overcrowded as tenements go, for only ninety-two dwelt here, including fifty-one children;

of the children only twenty-two went to school. In one tenement were five bar-rooms where swipes alone was sold.
He then introduced his listeners to the tramp lodging-
houses where men and women slept on the bare floor, one
batch at night, another during the day. The physician said:

Many houses are provided with what is known as a tramp
room. A typical one was below ground, 10 feet long, 14½ feet
wide, and 7 feet high, and bare of furniture except for a stove
in the center. The room was filled with men and women, all
intoxicated. The proprietor was a young man of decent appearance who paid $5.00 per month rent and let lodgings at 5 cents,
and sold stale beer at 2 cents a pint. His customers were people
without occupation who lived on charity and petty thefts.

Derby visited this tramp room in the daytime, when he
found five men and four women, and again at night, when
six men and five women patronized the dive.

Derby found a room upstairs occupied by two Italian
men and three women; in another just over the tramp room,
of similar dimensions save that it was half a foot higher,
were five settles for sleeping, for which 10 cents was
charged. When the settles were full, lodgers were taken for
the floor at the same rates. Men and women lived together
promiscuously.

Derby continued:

Across the way was a house inhabited by rag-pickers. In a
room 10 by 16 feet lived nine men. They paid $6.00 a month
rent. The room was filled with the evidence of their calling, and
horribly filthy. The entire house was in a condition of criminal
neglect. The roof leaked, the floors and stairs were unsafe. There
were here 87 men, 18 women and but 13 children. . . .

In a basement near-by were nine men and four women sodden
with beer, sitting amid a pile of bones and rags. The stench
was intolerable. In an attic room, lighted by one small window,
were four women and five men. . . .

It is only right that a demand should go up to blot out such pest-houses.

Derby ended with this thought:

"The remedy will be found in an enlightened public opinion which will force landlords to recognize that they owe more than shelter to tenants."

From the same pulpit, Charles Loring Brace uttered this truth: "They [tenement-house dwellers] are the tools of designing demagogues, and without this ignorant class, such gigantic frauds as were perpetrated by Tweed would not have been possible."

In the Church of the Covenant, the Reverend Dr. Marvin R. Vincent noted that the first tenement-house was built in 1839—two years after the Old Brewery became a rookery. "In the first ten years," he said, "7,041 tenements were built. There are 21,000 of these houses to-day." There was no tabulation of private homes, stables, workshops, and other structures converted into tenements prior to or after 1839, nor of the shanties.

At the Cooper Union meeting, after Joseph H. Choate and others spoke, Mayor Edward Cooper appointed a committee to draft the required legislation. They drafted a most progressive measure. No building hereafter constructed was to occupy more than 65 per cent of the plot, the remainder to be yard or court. The bill struck at existing evils by requiring each room to be lighted and ventilated by at least one window of not less than twelve square feet opening on street or court, and most important of all, they provided for adequate tenement-house inspection.

Save on rare occasions, the Department of Health, because of lack of funds, could not assign more than five sanitary inspectors—physicians all—to inspection of tenements. It was essential that the legislation creating the new corps of tenement inspectors should also provide for their salaries.

Sketches in Bottle Alley. This Five Points slum derived its name from a dealer in old bottles. Drawn by William A. Rogers. *Harper's Weekly,* March 22, 1879.

This was to be done by a yearly tax of $3.00 on each tenement.

Instantly the tenement-house lobbyists invaded the state capitol. First the lobbyists—they are frequently more effective than legislators—struck out the clause imposing a $3.00 yearly tax, thereby crushing all hopes of adequate inspection. Then they modified the light-and-air provision by empowering local officials to find a substitute for the window opening on yard or street. This substitute is called an air-shaft. In reality, it is a cesspool, and a death-trap for children.

The tenement owners argued that most of their tenants came from European slums and would befoul any property they inhabited. That they had no intention of spending anything to clean their property, so long as no law required them to do so, was indicated by the following description of a Mulberry Street tenement from the *Tribune* of July 22, 1879—less than two months after the legislation was emasculated:

"The rickety stairs have not been swept or even shoveled off in years, and the boards of the steps are not only hidden, but their very form is lost under the accumulation of trodden dirt."

There were four of these dwellings, two front and two rear, each three stories in height, and all equally filthy. They housed two hundred people whose entire water supply "consists of a single hydrant in the court."

A little diversion now is in order, so let us forget the vile tenements and their viler landlords, and see the most popular sport of the day, a sport now forgotten. This invitation does not include the ladies, for reasons presently apparent.

34

RAT-BAITING SUCCEEDS BEAR-BAITING

THROUGHOUT THE WORST OF THE HARD TIMES, THE INDUSTRY
least affected was commercialized sports. In New York
the better class of dance halls would dispense with music at
least once a week to cater to the sporting fraternity. Only
major prize-fights were held outside these gathering places
of the slums. The contests between men, wherever held, were
as fairly conducted as those between birds and beasts. Prize-
fighting is to-day the only money-making sport of the seventies that has been legalized. Men may now lawfully
maul and maim one another provided they possess an
immunizing license from the state. Politicians and sports
promoters could not make millions in fighting birds or animals because of the relatively small room in which such
contests are held, so they have been outlawed. One could
attend a prize-fight in a dance hall in the seventies for 50
cents tops. But to see a cocking-main or a dog-fight—these
were held in pits—cost as high as $2.00. Several dog-pits
flourished clandestinely in the metropolis until the late nineties and received the personal attention of Theodore Roosevelt when he was police commissioner. One who later held
high office in the city was tipped off that T. R. planned
to raid his pit on East Sixteenth Street, near the East
River. When T. R. arrived there was not even a hair
of a dog in sight. The future President was angry as the
future city official greeted him with a bland "Good evening,

Commissioner." Part of T. R.'s explosive response was: "I'll get you yet!" But he didn't, because some of his higher ranking subordinates were patrons of the dog-pits, as were many outstanding public men. While both dog-fighting and cock-fighting may be said to have ceased as national sports in the United States with the passing of the nineties, they are far from being lost arts. Commercialized dog-fighting and cocking-mains have continued to hold their popularity in many of the smaller cities where urban boundaries and farm lines blend.

Cock-fighting, like dog-fighting and pugilism, has its literature. But there was a fourth sport, a variant of the bear-baiting which flourished in England for seven centuries, which has been wholly neglected in the field of letters.

This was rat-baiting, the most popular indoor sport of the seventies, at least in the metropolis.

Rat-baiting is a topsy-turvy variety of bear-baiting. In the latter, a lone bear, muzzled, was chained by a hind leg to a stake in the center of a pit into which several English bull-dogs or Irish wolfhounds were thrust simultaneously to harry and destroy him. This cruel pastime was outlawed by Parliament in 1835.

There were several varieties of rat-baiting, but in each, the rats outnumbered the dogs from 5 to 1 to as much as 100 to 1.

Rat-baiting differed from bear-baiting, dog-fighting, cock-fighting, and prize-fighting in that there must be at least two bouts.

Sometimes two fox-terriers would be placed in a pit with twenty-five or more rats; when this bout was over, a like number of rats would be placed in the pit against two other terriers. Fox-terriers were used exclusively.

But in the rat-baiting classic, one hundred full-grown rats were matched against a lone fox-terrier. When the dog had disposed of his hundred, the pit was cleared for another terrier and another hundred rodents.

Frequently a dog had to be rescued from the rats.

Pit-dogs, both rat-baiting terriers and fighting bulldogs, were the proud possession of the average New York politician who boasted a stable during the seventies.

We have a measure of the popularity of rat-baiting in the admission fees where the sport was commercialized. Where not more than fifty rats were used in a bout, the price was seldom lower than $1.50. It cost from $2.50 to $5.00 to witness a rat classic. This price kept out hoi polloi.

As in prize-fighting, rat-baiting called for trainers, handlers, timekeepers, and referees. Another functionary was the rat-catcher. Still another, unknown to pugilism, was the enumerator. Men who served in these several capacities contributed their full knowledge of the art of honest rat-baiting, which they always preferred to the brutalities, frauds, and swindles of the prize ring.

Newspaper readers of the seventies who never saw a rat-pit identified them with water-front dives where dog-fights and rat-baiting were added lures. These dens had dog-pits only, which were so low that they had to be covered with escape-proof wire netting when used as rat-pits.

Rat-pits are never screened. Each of the four wooden walls is 4½ feet high, 8 feet long, and lined with tin or zinc. These pits are of the take-down type, clamped at the corners. In the early days, the rat classic was held in a bear-pit. New York had several bear-pits prior to the Civil War. The spectators sit on bleachers, and the show begins as the referee calls out, "Are the enumerators ready?" Receiving the proper response, he shouts, "Let in the rats!" A low flat wooden cage, lined with metal, is now thrust over the edge of the pit, and the rat-catcher opens the cage door. As the rats begin leaping into the pit, the two enumerators, represent-

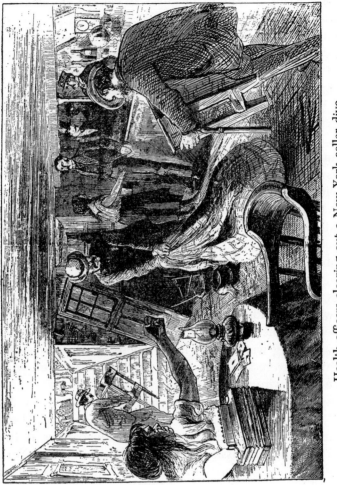

Health officers clearing out a New York cellar dive
Harper's Weekly, July 12, 1873.

ing the owners of the rival dogs, silently count until the last rat has left the cage. "How many, gentlemen?" inquires the referee. And each replies, "One hundred." Whereupon the referee, who has also counted the rats as they squealed out of the cage, says: "The count is correct—one hundred rats."

For a full five minutes there is a craning of necks as the rats scurry around the bottom of the pit, vainly seeking escape. Some scale the highly polished metal walls, only to lose their hold before climbing four feet. If one reaches the top, the flange around the edge prevents escape. This five-minute period enables all concerned to inspect the rats, for each one must be sound. The occasional weak or injured rat is removed with a tongs and another substituted. The primary purpose of this pause it to "let the rats get their ease," and once they are running around freely, the referee shouts, "Ready!" Instantly the handler of the dog approaches the pit—the handler is usually the dog's master—and speaks soothingly to the terrier which is clasped gently in his arms. The handler watches the frantically weaving mass beneath, for when the word is given, he must drop the dog on the patch of floor where the fewest rats are at that important moment.

As the referee begins counting, the handler shifts his hold on the terrier. The dog seems to know the slow "One! Two! Three!" and at the word "Drop!" the dog is thrown gently toward the spot selected. Before the terrier hits the floor, the timekeeper rings the bell. Encouraging shouts of approval fill the hall as the first rat is tossed high in the air or hurled with a thud against a wall of the pit.

But it is never one-sided, for there are moments when the dog is barely visible as rats fasten themselves to his face, ears, head, back, and legs. Save for an occasional shake, the dog ignores the fang-fastened rodents, for their hold is brief.

His attention is ever centered on his immediate opponent, and this disposed of, he methodically seizes the nearest rat, and so on until the bell proclaims the end of the hundred. Now the muffled growls in the pit give way to triumphant yelps. Attendants quickly open a side of the pit to admit the terrier's master, and while the spectators continue their cheering, the referee solemnly announces: "Gentlemen, we will now have the usual half-hour for refreshment."

The spectators use the half-hour chiefly in thirst-slaking. Additional bets are made, and some money changes hands, as bets were laid on the time the dog would remain in the pit. The attendants use the half-hour in preparing the pit for the final bout.

The average well-trained terrier could dispose of a hundred rats in thirty to forty-five minutes. The champions cut this time by about half, and several dogs, during the seventies and the succeeding decade, went the full hundred in less than twenty minutes. No dog lowered the time below fifteen minutes until Billy Fagan's champion of champions, Jack Underhill, killed one hundred rats in 11½ minutes, at Secaucus, New Jersey. This was fifteen years after our decade ended. Every Republican and Democratic politician in the metropolis, to whom rat-baiting was the king of sports, witnessed this classic, and thousands of dollars changed hands. Fagan was a house-painter, and resided on East Thirteenth Street, between Avenues B and C. Some two or three years later a terrier owned by a Brooklyn Navy Yard official made away with one hundred rats in 13 minutes in a near-by saloon on Jay Street.

Rat-baiting was familiar to all America. We find it referred to in a Senate debate in the spring of 1879. Conkling introduced it tauntingly to describe the metropolitan "graduates of the nurseries of modern so-called democracy" as thugs, shoulder-hitters, carriers of slung-shots, dirks, and bludgeons, and "all the fraternity of the bucket-shops, the rat-pits, and the slums." Senator Benjamin H. Hill, of Georgia, and others participated in the debate, but none rose to a point of information respecting the rat-pits. Hill himself repeated the words. Journalists, in writing of rat-pits and rat-baiting, never even attempted the briefest description of them. Every one was familiar with the sport.

When and where did rat-baiting originate? The known facts point to Manhattan as the place of origin. It started shortly after England outlawed bear-baiting. In its infancy, rat-baiting was a crude sport, serving only as an added attraction where bear-baiting was the prize event of the evening. Bear-baiting flourished in New York City until the Civil War, a quarter of a century after it was outlawed in England. In the infancy of rat-baiting, men as well as dogs, fought the rats. The dogs used their teeth; the men, wearing stable boots, used their feet. McLaughlin's bear-pit at 155 First Avenue, was the scene of one of these contests on Saturday night, January 27, 1855. In describing the event, the *Tribune* reporter quite properly called it a rat-killing, for it was unworthy of the noble designation of rat-baiting. On this occasion a bag of rats was emptied into the pit, and "men and dogs jumped in and kicked up a general mêlée." The journalist neglected to cite either the number of rats or how many men and dogs were pitted against them. The custom was to match two men and two dogs against one hundred rats. Wagers were made on the time it took to kill the rats. In the bear-baiting on this night, five dogs baited the bear, and "he caught them in his paws and crunched them half to death." English bulldogs were generally used in bear-baiting, but the breed or breeds in McLaughlin's pit on this January evening were not named. There was a third bout, between a dog and a raccoon. "The 'coon caught the dog by the nose," and this contest was soon over. Any good dog

will fight a 'coon. This was not a clandestine card, for Mc-
Laughlin advertised the show, a circumstance that especially
galled the *Tribune* reporter.

Rat-baiting and its unscientific predecessor, rat-killing, un-
doubtedly owe their inception to the primordial swamps of
Manhattan. The reclamation of these swamps began in the
1830's. The fill was rubbish and garbage, and each dump
became a breeding place for rats. These dumps began as
private ventures, but gradually the city established its own
dumps and in the seventies operated thirteen on the marshes
bordering the East and Hudson rivers. The law provided for
the dumping of garbage at sea, and contracts were let accordingly. A pretense of legal compliance was made by towing the garbage-laden scows from the Manhattan shores. A
scow on the West Side would be towed across the Hudson
to Jersey City and dumped there; garbage from East River
docks was dumped on the Brooklyn shore. In 1877, Brooklyn
officialdom lodged formal protest, and was joined by Governor R. D. Hubbard, of Connecticut, who said the beaches
of his commonwealth were also being polluted. Before being
loaded on the scows, the garbage was raked over for bottles,
rags, metal, and bones by trimmers who lived in shanties at
the edge of the dumps. After assorting the junk, these men
and women piled it just outside their shacks. Work ended at
dusk. Then the rats invaded the mounds of bones for scraps
of meat. A cat or ordinary small dog who ventured on the
dumps after twilight was devoured by the rats. But fox-
terriers made these dumps their hunting-grounds. So did
youths of twelve to twenty. Unlike the terriers, they did not
destroy the rats, but caught them in home-made traps, or
with a pair of tongs having grasping ends about four inches
square, and light slender levers a yard in length. These rat-
tongs were fashioned by friendly blacksmiths who always
exacted a penny from their juvenile patrons. This was for

luck. A juvenile expert caught 232 rats with such tongs one summer evening in 1879. The price for live rats ranged from five cents to twelve cents. The rat-catchers usually worked in pairs, especially when they put their catch in burlap bags, as the bags were shaken from time to time to prevent a hole being gnawed which might give freedom to all.

It is now time to return to the dance hall, for the half-hour is up, and the bleachers are filled to the last seat. All are curious to know the number of paid admissions—there are several obvious deadheads in the audience—for one-half of the gate goes to the owner of the place, and the remainder is divided between the owners of the rival dogs, one-third to the loser and two-thirds to the winner. It was a poor night when there were fewer than one hundred paid admissions at $2.50 upward per head, which meant the sharing of a purse of $125 or more. After the purse was announced, the second bout started, and the same ritual observed as before, save that instead of announcing a period of refreshment at the finish, the referee proclaimed the winner.

But no rat-baiting devotee imagined that pugilism would be legalized and his favorite sport outlawed, its followers driven to New Jersey and Long Island towns to witness the killing of plague-bearing rodents, and secretly at that. Henry Bergh's Society for the Prevention of Cruelty to Animals, incorporated by the New York legislature in 1866, paid no particular attention to rat-baiting until the late eighties.

And no injured prize-fighter ever received more attention than a pit-terrier after a bout with the rats. The dogs always required treatment, for some would fall into a dead faint—to use a phrase of the rat-pit. The rat bites always caused infection, and sometimes it would take three days to reduce the swelling of head and body. But the most badly bitten dog would be his old self once the lacerations had healed.

The veterans of the rat-pit were scarred on head and legs

and body. A distinguishing feature were the ears, which hung in irregular shreds, like the tattered fringe of an old crocheted lambrequin. But the pugilist has cauliflower ears, and dogs have never been driven insane from the grueling they underwent in the rat-pits. Prize-fighters lose their minds from oft-repeated head blows, and physicians use the jargon of pugilism in diagnosing this dementia—slap-happy. This is a misnomer, for occasionally the slap-happy fighter becomes melancholic and homicidal. The rat-baiting terrier confined his killing to rodents.

These terriers were trained from puppyhood. As soon as the sturdiest and most agile of a litter showed his ability to bowl over the others in play, he was chosen. Then began a most rigid training. He was kept from other dogs. Daily the pup was taken out on leash, always muzzled, so that he would associate the muzzle with his daily exercise in the open. In near-by fields the muzzle was removed. His food was fresh, raw meat. But he had to work hard for his meal, as he had to gnaw the flesh from the bones. This was to strengthen his teeth.

From the day he was separated from the rest of the litter, the future ratter had one eating place—a miniature rat-pit set up in yard, barn, or stable. This pit was more than an eating place. It was home. He was taught to resent intrusion. This was done in a strange way. We have observed that he was kept away from other dogs. But dogs, especially when young, must have playmates. The pup had one the first day he was in his new home. It was a full-grown rat, as big as himself. But the rat must not bite the pup, for this would make him afraid of rodents. And so before the rat was put into the pit, its teeth were extracted. After several minutes in the pit, the rat was removed with a tongs. This occurred twice a day during the first month of training, immediately before the pup's only meals—morning and evening. The pup learned to bark for a rat, because it was a prelude to food. In the second month of training the pup's daily playmates could put up a weak defense, for they had teeth in the upper jaw. Thereafter the pup avoided the jaws of the rat. When the pup could kill with a few shakes, the daily appetizer was gradually increased until he disposed of five rats before feeding time.

When six months old, the pup was tried out on a full-toothed rat. But instead of the rat being thrown to the dog, the process was reversed, and the dog was dropped into the pit for his first real rat-baiting. Soon the dog was placed in a regulation-size pit with two rats, then three, and the number was gradually increased to ten.

A dog was usually a year and a half old before being entered in a contest. Ten or fifteen rats were the maximum a novice might bait. A dog remained in the novice class until his second year. Some never got beyond this class, for many a dog would quit after several rats attacked him simultaneously. This ended his career in the rat-pit.

Rat-baiting enthusiasts always regarded the sport as less brutalizing than watching a prize-fighter with longer reach, more ably trained, and with more telling blows, tear the cheeks and close the eyes of an outclassed opponent while the mob clamored for a knockout. Then, too, the masters of rat-pit terriers were decent men, and not, like the owners of many prize-fighters, brothel graduates and their kind, who waxed rich and powerful.

35

HAVEMEYER RESTORES THE GOOD NAME

OF THE METROPOLIS—HIS REWARD

O N JANUARY 1, 1874, THE CRITICS OF THE AMERICAN EXPERI- ment in democracy could no longer hold up the metropolis as their horrible Exhibit A.

Havemeyer, the city's chief executive, had wrought the change. He had supplanted corruption and misgovernment with an efficient, honest, and economical administration.

In one year he had reduced the cost of government by nearly 25 per cent, a mere matter of $8,000,000 at that time. Havemeyer's reduction did not impair any important municipal function. On the contrary, all were improved, notably the public schools.

He did these things despite the Ring tools still fastened upon the city by the old Tweed charter, and the refusal of a Republican legislature and a Republican governor to heed either his pleas for honest charter revision or his protests against the state's interference in the purely local affairs of the city. He had protested against the charter they forced upon the city in 1873 which empowered heads of departments to create jobs and fix salaries, and rendered them immune from removal by the mayor without the governor's written approval.

These protests and pleas had irritated the Conkling machine which controlled both the executive and legislative branches of the state government.

As the reader knows, this corrupt machine's minions on the Committee of Seventy had induced Havemeyer to run for mayor against his will. Their sole interest then was to use an outstanding Democrat whose name symbolized honest government to help them carry New York for Grant. After astonishing his sponsors by winning, they had a new interest in him—patronage. But Havemeyer repeated his performances of nearly a generation earlier, when he had twice served the city as mayor, by making appointments regardless of party or faction.

This also irritated the Conklingites, for Havemeyer rejected some of their number, and named Liberal Republicans and members of Tammany Hall. He gave little to the minority Democratic faction, the Apollo Hall group.

Like all executives with many places to fill, Havemeyer was imposed upon. But the same man did not fool him twice. Honest John Kelly played him a sharp trick, but thereafter the Tammany chief was unwelcome at the city hall.

Havemeyer was the mayor and the country knew it. He heeded suggestions, but ignored orders. This was in keeping with his record.

A more honest man did not exist, yet no mayor of the metropolis has been more shamefully and unjustly pilloried.

He was commendably callous to clamor, as the Conklingites learned when they tried to bludgeon him into making his administration an annex of their spoils machine. With their first failure, they loosed their mud batteries. On January 28, 1874, when Havemeyer was within a fortnight of his seventieth birthday, the *Times* thus bespattered him:

"Almost all his appointments or recommendations have been about as bad as Tammany, in Tweed's day, could have suggested."

This was followed by another venomous outburst, more deliberately mendacious than the first. It follows:

"New York was never cursed with so dishonest and disreputable a mayor as we have at this moment in Havemeyer.... We can only regret that he is not being taken care of in some good asylum instead of being free to create a new scandal every other day and to fill the city offices with riffraff."

And again:

"Honest men cannot see in what respect Havemeyer is one whit better than Oakey Hall."

The despicable part of these malignantly untruthful attacks was that they were believed by those unfamiliar with the background of his newspaper assailant, who knew it only for its fight on the Tweed Ring.

In the preceding election Havemeyer had given especial offense to machine politicians of both parties by insisting on an honest vote and an honest count. He controlled both to the extent that he controlled the police board, consisting of five commissioners, three Republican and two Democratic. One of these was his friend, Oliver Charlick, a Democrat, whom he had appointed in June, 1873. A recent law provided that "all inspectors of elections and poll clerks shall hereafter be selected and appointed by the board of police." The law further provided for bipartizan election boards. This entailed reliance upon the leaders of the two parties to designate honest men for inspectors of elections and poll clerks. Part of the police board was a survival of the Tweed days, and protected from removal by the crooked Tweed charter. Charlick overcame this by having the board adopt a resolution empowering him and two others to pass on election inspectors and poll clerks. One of these was Commissioner Hugh Gardner, an uncompromising Republican and an intimate of Charlick. The two did splendid work, Charlick doing most of the explaining when political leaders protested against the turning down of some of their designees.

Charlick later testified that he had "trouble" with the Tammany chief because "Mr. Kelly wanted me to let Tammany make the appointments, and I declined." But despite all the vigilance Charlick and Gardner exercised, some smart lads, Republicans and Democrats—"notorious in character" was Havemeyer's description of them—were named to the election boards. Just before the 1873 election, Havemeyer received information which he immediately relayed to Charlick. As a consequence, affidavits were presented to Charlick and Gardner on Election Day, and they forthwith removed seven election inspectors and poll clerks accused of being various types of vote manipulators. All were adherents of Honest John, and one had been arrested as a repeater in 1872. Under the law the accused could not be removed except upon trial after due notice. Observance of this joker in the law would have let the seven serve out the day in their respective polling-places. But Charlick and Gardner ignored the joker, thereby committing a technical violation to which no legal defense could be interposed. And on the charge of removing an election inspector without due notice, the two police commissioners were indicted, tried, convicted, and sentenced to pay a fine of $250 each! This was tomahawk justice with a vengeance.

This had been anticipated by Havemeyer, who knew that the two machines planned his ouster so that a pliable police board might be appointed for the next fall election. Friends of Havemeyer consulted Governor John A. Dix, an honest man with a highly developed presidential urge. Dix advised that the two police commissioners resign, which they did on June 27, 1874. Knowing they had done nothing wrong, although guilty of a technical legal violation, Havemeyer determined "to do something to save these men from the appearance of disgrace which they might ... wear in the eyes of the unreflecting crowd," as he subsequently ex-

John A. Dix

From a photograph by E. W. Bogardus. *Harper's Weekly*, January 18, 1873.

plained to Dix. Havemeyer could speak publicly of the unreflecting crowd as he had never cared a hoot whether he offended it or not. On July 2, Havemeyer lent the affair the proper touch of burlesque by appointing Gardner to Charlick's former commissionership and Charlick to Gardner's.

In the meantime, Honest John had written an impertinent letter to Havemeyer, who said he would answer the Tammany chief in due time. The reappointment of Gardner and Charlick gave Honest John an opportunity he had long sought, and he promptly had a resolution introduced in the board of aldermen requesting the governor to remove Havemeyer for abuse of the appointing power. On July 7, learning that Honest John, with the aid of Conkling Republicans, had the necessary votes to adopt the resolution, the two police heads again resigned. Honest John should have called off the aldermanic hounds at this point, but he urged them on, and the board petitioned the governor to remove the mayor. And Honest John supplemented the indictment with accusations of his own in which William H. Wickham, the rich diamond merchant and Honest John's neighbor, joined.

A corrupt executive would have removed Havemeyer without a qualm, for a governor may depose a mayor—and there is no appeal from his act—for good reason, or for none at all. Those who really knew Dix believed he would dismiss the trivial charges without ceremony; but, instead, he asked Havemeyer to file an answer.

In his answer, the accused mayor said the necessity of confining himself to the record presented by his assailants imposed upon him a constraint which at some not-far-distant date he might think it suitable to break. On September 14, two days before the Democrats were to meet in Syracuse at their state convention to name a ticket, Dix dismissed the charges in a decision of some three thousand words. While praising Havemeyer's unimpeachable record, he mildly censured him for reappointing the two police commissioners, which had "surprised the citizens."

"This is richness!" exclaimed Havemeyer to a reporter, as he laughed at some of Dix's observations. "I've surprised the

citizens? Well, I'll surprise them more before I get through."
Then he confided that the surprise would be his long-de-
ferred reply to Honest John's open letter, and said it would
be ready at five o'clock the following afternoon. Then he
inveighed, and justly so, against Dix's moralizing. Noting

Colonel William T. Pelton
Leslie's Weekly, March 1, 1879.

Dix's praise of his management of the city's finances, Havemeyer exclaimed: "What had the charges against me to do
with the finances?"

While Havemeyer's reply was being manifolded for the
press the next day, Tilden sent his nephew, Colonel William
T. Pelton, to plead with Havemeyer to ignore Honest John,
or at least to withhold the letter until after the Democratic

convention adjourned, lest it destroy Tilden's chances for the gubernatorial nomination. As an old friend of Tilden, Havemeyer agreed to defer publishing the letter until after the nominations. Tilden knew Honest John's shady past, which was then being hinted at in the press by Democrats supporting Sanford E. Church, chief judge of the Court of Appeals, for the nomination.

Until a week before the convention, Church seemed certain of heading the ticket. His preconvention campaign manager, Joseph Warren, secretary of the Democratic State Committee, had persuaded all other aspirants, save Tilden, to withdraw in favor of Church. On September 8, Tilden met Warren by appointment and rejected Warren's suggestion that he also withdraw. If Warren had any doubt of Tilden's unquenchable ambition for high place, it was dissipated within the next forty-eight hours.

After his meeting with Warren, Tilden conferred with Honest John. In a fair fight in the convention, Church might defeat Tilden for the nomination. Church's strength was wholly upstate where the party was dominated by the Canal Ring, which also ruled the upstate Republican machine. Tilden's chief strength was Tammany and its downstate allies. The object of the conference was to wreck Church's candidacy. The cold-blooded ruthlessness in which it was done shocked decent politicians, for they knew that the average voter would be unable to appraise the attack on Church at its true worth.

The attack appeared in the New York *World*, the organ of the Democratic party in city and state. Honest John first described Warren and others active in Church's behalf as members of the Canal Ring which, he said, was plotting to nominate Church. "They have always been very friendly to Judge Church and of great assistance to him personally," continued Honest John. The same could have been said of

Tilden, for without the votes controlled by the Canal Ring in the Democratic State Committee, he could not have been elected chairman when he began his upward climb. And Honest John emphasized that the Tweed Ring—he called it the defunct Tammany Ring—had worked with the Canal Ring.

Typical of the criticisms of the attack was the *Herald's*, which read: "This atrocious Tammany libel on Judge Church will rouse the indignation of every honest Democrat in the state." Newspapers praised Church as "the most honored Democrat in the state" and denounced Tilden for inspiring the attack. In his own paper, the Buffalo *Courier*, Warren said: "Tammany Hall under Honest John Kelly is exactly the same as Tammany Hall under dishonest William M. Tweed." And as the Democratic delegates assembled in Syracuse, Warren supplemented the charge with the accusation that Honest John, while sheriff, had robbed the city treasury in the manner of the Tweed Ring.

Seymour and other Democratic leaders silenced the party-harming exchange. Tilden chose Manton Marble, editor of the *World*, for Chairman of the Committee on Resolutions. And to appease Church's many friends, the convention adopted a resolution censuring the *World* and its editor for publishing Honest John's withering blast at Church. Although Tilden was nominated on the first ballot with 252 votes, more than a third of the delegates, as a further protest against the attack on Church, cast 126 votes for Amasa J. Parker, twice the party's nominee for governor, and 12 votes for five others. For lieutenant-governor, they named William Dorsheimer, a Liberal Republican, who had resigned as United States Attorney for the Western District of New York to follow Greeley. The Liberal Republicans had held their convention a week earlier, but did not nominate, intending to support the Democratic nominees.

The day after Tilden's nomination, Honest John returned home to find Havemeyer's reply the talk of the town. Havemeyer specifically accused him of stealing $84,482 from the city treasury by means of false and fraudulent bills during his shrievalty.

"I think that you were worse than Tweed, except that he was a larger operator," continued Havemeyer. "The public knew that Tweed was a bold, reckless man, making no pretensions to purity. You, on the contrary, were always avowing your honesty, wrapped in the mantle of piety. Men who go about with the prefix of 'honest' to their names are often rogues."

Honest John had to sue for libel or quit politics. So he sued.

The Republicans renominated Dix along with the rest of their successful ticket of two years before. Dix had carried the election in 1872 by 53,451 votes. His reëlection in the face of the depression and the sentiment against the third term would have made him the logical nominee for President in 1876. But he lost by 50,317 votes, the tally standing: Tilden, 416,391; Dix, 366,074. After his defeat, Dix accused Conkling and his lieutenants of throwing the election to Tilden. This charge was first made a fortnight before the Republican State Convention by the *Herald*. On September 10 the newspaper noted that "there have been rumors of an intention on the part of the administration Republicans to defeat Governor Dix at the polls since they have found it impracticable to prevent his renomination.... The vigor with which Mr. Samuel Tilden is being pressed by the new Tammany Ring against the wishes and judgment of the Democracy is due to this expected treason..." The *Herald* attributed the treachery to Conkling's plan to remove Dix from the presidential picture and said that Dix "bears about him no taint of congressional jobbery, from which

Conkling, with all his good fortune, may not be entirely free."

A switch of some twenty-five thousand votes would have reëlected Dix and the Republican ticket. This might have been done with a vigorous campaign upstate, for Conkling and his lieutenants could have capitalized the unanswerable charges of two outstanding Democrats, Havemeyer and Warren, against Honest John, who made Tilden's nomination possible. They could also have capitalized the resentment among Church's friends. But they did nothing, bearing out the charge that Conkling and Honest John had entered into a deal. In the metropolis the Conkling machine was silent on the fact that, with the exception of a few respectable figureheads, Honest John's candidates for local office had been top-rankers in the Tweed Ring. Ten of his 15 aldermanic nominees were Ring satellites and one was awaiting trial on a swindling charge. Tammany's nominee for register, James Hayes, had been a Tweed lieutenant and possessed more than half a million dollars made by grace of the Ring. Hayes lost to Patrick H. Jones by 11,647 votes. Had the Republicans fused on an outstanding independent Democrat for mayor, they might have defeated Wickham, Honest John's neighbor and mayoralty nominee. Their candidate, Salem H. Wales, was put up to be knocked down. He polled 36,953 votes to the 70,071 cast for Wickham. While the Republicans controlled the state senate—it had been elected in 1873—by a comfortable margin, the Democrats broke the Republican hold on the assembly, electing 75 members to the 53 chosen in Republican strongholds. The senate stood 18 Republicans, 12 Democrats and 2 independents, giving the Democrats a majority on a joint ballot.

The first effect of this was seen on January 21, 1875, when Kernan was chosen United States Senator to succeed Fenton —another bit of balm for Conkling. With Fenton and Dix re-

William H. Wickham
From photograph by C. D. Fredericks. *Harper's Weekly*, November 21, 1874.

moved from his path, Conkling became the undisputed Republican boss of New York. The Liberal Republicans no longer constituted a formidable faction. Conkling realized that his title would be of little value without some successful fence-mending throughout the nation, for the election of November, 1874, gave the lower branch of Congress to the Democrats for the first time since 1856. The determining factors were hard times, carpet-bagger-Negro government, national corruption, and the third-term threat with its attendant charge of Cæsarism. Desperate Republican congressional candidates had visited Washington in a vain attempt to persuade Grant to deny any third-term pretensions in an effort to save themselves. The consequence was the unexpected upheaval in the House. In the forty-third Congress the Republicans had 198 Representatives to 88 Democrats, 4 Liberal Republicans and one Independent Republican. But in the forty-fourth Congress the Republican seats dwindled to 110. The Democrats had 168 seats, and the Liberal Republicans and independents held 14.

For this rout, the Grant journals offered puerile explanations. The *Times,* in discussing the Tammany victory in the metropolis, put the blame on its familiar target, saying: "We owe the utter and ruinous collapse of the reform movement very largely to Mayor Havemeyer."

The honest Havemeyer ignored this calumny as he put the finishing touches to his answer to Honest John's libel action. In his reply, published November 18, Havemeyer began by admitting the libel as charged, and added:

The defendant further admits that he meant in and by certain parts of the letter to allege that the plaintiff had defrauded the City and County of New York out of large sums of money, that his bills as sheriff contained fictitious and fraudulent charges; that he had perpetrated small frauds as well as great ones; that his conduct has been criminal; . . . that he has made false oaths to fraudulent bills presented by him against the county; that by such conduct the plaintiff has greatly disgraced himself; that his guilt was graver than that of Garvey or Ingersoll, other well-known depredators upon the public treasury, because the plaintiff was the incumbent of an office of high public trust . . . ; that he was also worse than Tweed, another well-known depredator upon the public treasury, because the plaintiff was a hypocrite, and he was falsely assumed to be a man of honesty and piety; . . . that the plaintiff has made frequent avowals of his great honesty, in consequence of which he was commonly known as Honest John Kelly; that he was also reported to be a man professing great piety; that his character in these reports was far different from that of William M. Tweed, and that therefore the fraud and dishonesty practised by the plaintiff was of greater culpability because it was more injurious upon others.

Havemeyer itemized Honest John's fraudulent bills; some were sheer inventions. The trial was set for Monday, November 30, a month before Havemeyer's term of office would end. But Havemeyer was late at the city hall on the trial day. He arrived at twenty minutes before noon, muffled to the chin. After removing his wraps, he sat in front of the blazing open fire. He had spent part of the week-end with his former police commissioner, Oliver Charlick. A police commissioner is a reservoir of contemporaneous historical arcana. Havemeyer told an attaché he had had to walk nearly three miles after his train had met with an accident. He seemed weary as well as cold. At ten minutes past noon, half an hour after he arrived in his office, this noble and consistent foe of corruption breathed his last; and the half-masted Stars and Stripes above the city hall told Honest John that he had been spared the public ordeal of a trial at which Havemeyer would have stripped him of his tattered mantle of piety.

36

HONEST JOHN SNATCHES CROKER
FROM THE HANGMAN

ON JANUARY 1, 1875, HONEST JOHN KELLY WAS FITTINGLY acclaimed the hero of the twin inaugurations—of Tilden as governor of the most populous state in the Union, and of Wickham as mayor of the metropolis of the western hemisphere. He had taken hold of a discredited Tammany in 1872 and led it to victory in 1873, and again in 1874, save for the loss of one major municipal office, that of register. While the national victories of 1874 were part of a country-wide revolt against Republican misrule and corruption, the Tammany chief received all the credit for the local victories from the unreflecting crowd, which also credited him with foiling the putative plot to send Richard Croker to the gallows for the murder of John McKenna, a horse-car conductor and a follower of James O'Brien, Tweed's old enemy. And what Honest John did that election day in 1874 on behalf of his lieutenant, soon to be his chief aide and destined to succeed him as boss of Tammany, was thus criticized by the *Times* two days after the killing: "Kelly was ordering coroners and judges to do his bidding, just as Jim Fisk used to command the corrupt judges. That the people of New York should openly and voluntarily revive the scandalous system which prevailed here for so long prior to 1871-72, is a phenomenon which will necessarily attract much attention throughout the civilized world, and for which it would be hard to find an explanation complimentary to the voters themselves."

Croker was one of the city's three coroners, having been elected in 1873. This office has primary jurisdiction over violent and suspicious deaths. If Croker had not long borne a reputation as a versatile election thug and a ready brawler, it is doubtful if he would have been indicted for murder after Honest John had finished "ordering coroners and judges to do his bidding," for Croker was guiltless of this crime. But then, had Croker been other than what he was, he and his companions would not have gone to the polls with guns. There was ingratitude in Croker's presence at the polls, an ingratitude common to machine politics. Ex-sheriff O'Brien, who had made him politically, was the congressional candidate of his Apollo Hall Democrats and the Republicans in the Tenth District. The Tammany nominee was Abram S. Hewitt, metallurgist, philanthropist, and friend of Tilden and Honest John. Croker could have told George E. Hickey and some of his other pals when they asked him on the morning of November 3 to help put down some rough work by the O'Brienites that he was now a coroner, and order was his middle name. Or he could have whispered to Hickey that they both owed much to O'Brien, and might leave it to O'Brien and Hewitt to fight it out. But this would not be politics.

O'Brien befriended Croker when his fondness for gaming on horses and pit-dogs had stripped him of the little he had and could borrow. Croker had pawned his watch, and had sold his two fighting bulldogs to a liveryman on Murray Hill, when O'Brien started him on his upward climb which brought him a stable and a Derby winner, and a kennel of blooded bulldogs.

The principal objectives of the O'Brienites were the Hewitt electioneering booths where Hewitt ballots were

distributed. Each candidate then had his own ballots, paid
for their printing, and distributed them at sentry-like boxes,
accommodating one or two election workers, which stood
on the sidewalk, close to the curb, a few feet from the official polling-booth. A wealthy candidate would have at
least two of these wooden booths flanking each polling-
place. Small boys and youths of the neighborhood collected
the electioneering booths at the close of the voting for their
election-night bonfires. Hewitt had a minimum of two booths
at each polling-place, and his managers, with ample funds
at their disposal, had purchased peace from most of the
local election bullies the night before. The Tenth Congressional District embraced nearly all the territory between
Fourteenth and Fortieth streets, from river to river. O'Brien's
lads began their work at the lower end, where the slums of
the gas-house district rubbed elbows with the brownstone
fronts of fashionable Stuyvesant Square and Gramercy Park,
routing the Hewitt workers and overturning and smashing
the Hewitt polling-booths. But it was not all one-sided, for
Hewitt plug-uglies were mauling O'Brien workers and
wrecking O'Brien booths. Some of these guerrilla bands
were armed, the favorite weapons being short serviceable
lengths of lead pipe. A few carried heavy navy revolvers,
but most of them depended on their fists.

Croker and his fellow roughs to the number of six or
seven witnessed a Hewitt booth overturned with its occu-
pant inside. The O'Brienites had advanced into the upper
end of the district at this time. O'Brien was walking down
Second Avenue when he saw Croker and his little mob at
the corner of Thirty-fourth Street talking to two of O'Brien's
followers, including Billy Borst, a scion of an old New York
family. Croker had just ordered Borst out of the district.

There are two versions as to what happened when O'Brien
approached the group. One is that O'Brien asked Borst,

"Billy, what is that damned loafer saying to you?" and that when Croker denied being a damned loafer, O'Brien repeated the impeachment with embellishments and added that Croker was a repeater. This last Croker did not deny. The other story, as related four days later in the Yorkville Court when O'Brien was arraigned on a charge of striking Croker in the face with his fist, calls for a word of explanation. Croker had told friends some time previously that O'Brien had tried to patch things up with him, or, as he phrased it, "he came sucking around me." The police-court testimony is that as O'Brien neared him, Croker ordered O'Brien on his way with the taunt: "We don't want any suckers around here!" To which O'Brien loudly retorted: "Get out! I don't want any repeaters around here!" McKenna, soon to fall with a bullet in his head, was standing near O'Brien as Croker called him a damned thief. O'Brien met the reflection on his honesty by replying in thunderous tones:

"You're a damned cur! I picked you out of the gutter, and now you're supporting a rich man like Hewitt against me for Congress."

Croker and O'Brien now exchanged blows, and presently several shots were fired, and McKenna fell mortally wounded. A policeman who knew the dying man bent over him and asked: "John, who shot you?" McKenna muttered: "Dick Croker." These were his last words. O'Brien had previously accused Croker of firing the shot, and when Croker was placed on trial for his life, O'Brien testified that he said to Croker, as McKenna fell: "You murdered that man." Three other witnesses testified they saw a pistol in Croker's hand. One said the pistol was slightly elevated, another that he saw it after he heard the first shot, a third that Croker was the first person in whose hand he saw a pistol. A fourth witness for the prosecution said he saw something in Croker's hand but did not recognize it as a pistol. Counsel for Croker produced more than a dozen witnesses who denied he had a pistol in his hand. Others swore he never carried one in his life.

Immediately after Croker's arrest Honest John Kelly drove to the police station and ordered the captain not to put him in a cell. The captain obliged with a private room. Then Kelly had Croker released in $2,000 bail by Coroner Henry Woltmann, who hurriedly summoned a jury which found that McKenna had come to his death from a gunshot wound fired by a person unknown. Croker was a free man within a few hours after the murder.

When no one was apprehended for the killing, the press demanded that the crime should not go unpunished. Croker and his companions knew who fired the fatal shot, but all held their peace. Honest John also knew, which explains his wire-pulling on behalf of the man the town regarded as the slayer. Twelve years after he delivered the charge to the jury which many felt would mean Croker's conviction, Supreme Court Justice George C. Barrett said he also knew that Croker did not fire the shot. Croker was then leader of Tammany Hall. After Croker's death, one of his counsel, General George L. Wingate, said that Hickey fired the shot, thinking Croker's life was in danger. Hickey was at Croker's side when the fatal shot was fired.

After Croker's arraignment in Yorkville Court on an assault charge the Saturday following Election Day, the animus of O'Brien was evident. The next case after Croker's was that of Hickey, accused of shooting at O'Brien. The court interrupted O'Brien's testimony, and indicating Hickey, asked: "Did he fire the shot?" Ignoring this direct reference to Hickey, O'Brien pointed to Croker, and said: "He [Croker] didn't fire at me, but at McKenna."

Nine days after the police-court proceedings, Croker,

Hickey, and John Sheridan, another Croker adherent, were indicted and arrested. Croker was cast into the Tombs on a murder charge. Hickey was indicted for firing a pistol at McKenna, while he lay mortally wounded, with intent to kill, and with feloniously assaulting, with intent to kill, Patrick Craig, who ran to pick up the dying McKenna. Sheridan was charged with shooting at O'Brien with intent to kill. Besides the murder charge, Croker also was indicted for attempting the life of O'Brien. All three had the same eminent counsel, and on their motion, Sheridan and Hickey were released in $5,000 bail. Kelly was a daily visitor to the Tombs until Croker went on trial for his life a month and four days after the murder.

Many always regarded Croker as the slayer because of McKenna's ante-mortem statement. But before the policeman had asked who fired the fatal shot, he had urged McKenna to tell how it happened. McKenna answered with a fervent, "For God's sake, give me a glass of water." He was then expiring. It is possible that he was trying to tell how it happened when he named Croker in response to the blunt demand to name the assassin. He may have been delirious as he muttered Croker's name in his dying breath. Croker's political foes, outside of the immediate O'Brien directorate, never doubted his innocence. The many who persisted in believing him guilty, after the trial, did so largely because of his checkered background. At the age of fifteen he began work in a machine-shop. Handy with his fists, he quickly rose to a commanding position among the neighborhood roughs, the Fourth Avenue Tunnel gang. Like most gangs, Croker's outfit was useful at election. His career as a machinist was cut short in the summer of 1863 by his victorious fist-fight with an East Side pugilist. This encounter settled a personal difference which had its origin at a picnic in Jones's Wood, and it led to Croker's entrance into the prize-ring, then an antechamber of politics. Five years later, we read that "a hundred metropolitan bandits under the notorious Dick Croker, all well armed and spoiling for a fight," had entrained for Philadelphia to help swing an election there. Croker at this time was court attendant under Cardozo, Barnard, and Ingraham, having been appointed at the instance of O'Brien in 1867. This netted Croker $1,200 annually until 1870, when he served about four months as alderman, and drew from this a little more than $1,000. The same year he was made superintendent of market rents and fees with a salary of $3,000. In 1873, Honest John and Morrissey lost out with Havemeyer because they had wheedled him into appointing Croker a city marshal in charge of personal taxes. Beginning January 1, 1874, Croker's fees as coroner brought him between $20,000 and $30,000 annually.

Croker's trial lasted three days. When both sides rested, it was obvious that a first-degree murder verdict was impossible, the weight of evidence favoring Croker. The prosecution therefore asked for a verdict of murder in the second degree or manslaughter. But the jurors failed to agree, six holding out for acquittal. Croker was soon released in $15,000 bail, and later the indictment was quashed on motion of the prosecutor who said the city should not be put to the expense of a second trial because "it would be more difficult to convict than at the first."

Many attributed the result to perjury and political chicane. There was plenty of both. The charges and countercharges of assault were dropped. When Croker's assault charge against O'Brien was called after the murder trial, neither appeared and the case was dismissed. "Does this mean," inquired the *Herald*, "that there has been an arrangement, and that we are to hear no more about the indictment against Croker? Are the people to understand that a citizen can be killed in broad daylight and no one called upon to answer for the crime?" But politics did not influence the prosecution of the murder charge, for the Republican district attorney was bent on making a reputation throughout the state by convicting Croker, if possible. The presiding

Honest John Kelly
Harper's Weekly, January 20, 1877.

judge owed his place on the bench to O'Brien's Apollo Hall Democracy, and his address to the jury was called a hanging charge. Many lawyers, regardless of their opinion of Croker, felt the court had gone too far, and drafted a bill restricting charges of judges in criminal cases; but it died in the legislature.

Croker had been out of the Tombs about three months when word spread that one of his old gang had shot Justice

John A. Stemmler of the Seventh District Court, to provide another place for Tilden to give to Honest John. The canard was invented by the O'Brien crowd to create another laugh on Tilden and Honest John. A short time before, the Tammany chief had informed Tilden that Stemmler was dead, and suggested J. Fairfax McLaughlin for the vacancy. Tilden immediately announced the appointment of McLaughlin. Typical of the reception in the metropolitan press of this intelligence was the following:

Mr. J. Fairfax McLaughlin, who was yesterday appointed to fill the supposed vacancy in the judgeship in the Seventh District Court, is a native of Maryland, where he practised law for ten years before coming to New York about four years ago. He has practised law in this city, but is at present a clerk in the county clerk's office. He has the reputation of being an elegant gentleman and scholar, speaking several languages. Judge Stemmler, however, is still alive.

Honest John immediately penned his apologies for the blunder, to which Tilden replied that he "need not be disgusted by the awkward accident about McLaughlin, for though a trifle ridiculous, it is not serious." Tilden knew this blunder would make the rounds of the Republican press, and anticipated that it would be seized upon to lend color to the report that he made the appointment while drunk or in one of his mad moments, as his letter to the Tammany chief disclosed. Said Tilden:

A small coterie of rogues, who, when they first recovered from the subduing effect of the election, started into a life of whispers, first circulated the rumor that I had a softening of the brain; next, that I had suffered a stroke of paralysis; then, that I went to bed drunk every night; and at last came to the statement that I had lost my snap—that I had not decision or energy to make proper removals or appointments, and, indeed, had become physically unable to make up my mind about anything.

These whispers appeared in unfriendly newspapers which seized upon anything that might tend to ridicule. Tilden was in office less than two months when this paragraph began the circuit:

"Sam Tilden felt and looked ten years lonelier directly after his interview with the girls at Vassar College. The saucy creatures made fun of him. One wanted a list of his wrinkles, another a plaster cast of his left cheek, and still another a lock of his hair cut exactly from the top of his venerable head...."

But before another month had ended, Tilden dramatically assumed the offensive, and there was no more ridicule, nor talk of drunkenness or softening of the brain.

37

THE TRIUMPH OF REFORM

TILDEN'S OFFENSIVE, DIRECTED AGAINST THE CANAL RING, was embodied in a special message to the legislature on March 19. Although governor but eleven weeks, his message, with its revealing tables prepared by engineers and accountants, indicating the theft of millions, represented the labor of nearly five months, for which Tilden paid out of his own pocket. But it was well worth-while, for it took him again before the nation in the crusading rôle that made him famous, this time as champion of the Erie Canal, the principal scene of the upstate depredators, which had been the country's pride, its foremost public work, for half a century.

Tilden's attack opened with this disarming announcement: "I have received a petition from forwarders, boatmen, and others engaged in transportation on the canals of this state, representing that the depressed state of their business called for legislation, and necessitates a reduction of tolls; and requesting me to look into the condition of canal commerce, and to make such recommendations to the legislature as will lead to measures of relief."

Respectful consideration was due to the owners of about six thousand canal-boats, their thirty thousand employees, and twenty thousand others indirectly employed by them. The state owned and managed the canals and had a common interest in preserving the joint business and should "listen to the rightful complaints of our people against the extreme burden of our present taxation and the prodigal and wasteful expenditure in connection with the canals, which is one of the main causes of such taxation."

Tilden knew where the waste went. It had been political gossip for many years, but he had long remained silent on it, as he had on Tweed and his Ring. He had been the political beneficiary of both, but had publicly ignored them until he stood to benefit by striking. Many had denounced looters of the metropolis before he had taken a hand; others, through the years, had assailed the Canal Ring and forced legislative investigations that ended in a whitewash.

Like all bands of public plunderers that flourish through the years, the Canal Ring was bipartizan. Tilden had first acknowledged its existence six months before when it stood between him and the governorship, and he was now using it as a span to the White House.

Tilden's charges of canal graft covered the five years ended September 30, 1874. Some hundred contracts for repairs and maintenance had been hastily examined, and ten of these had been publicly awarded to one contractor, for $424,735.90, and then secretly increased to $1,560,769.84, representing an estimated theft of more than $1,136,000. Another contractor's pap included $150,337 for work never performed. This sort of thing was of common occurrence. The principal frauds were committed through collusive bids. Tilden illustrated this with a case where an honest contractor bid $7,102.50 on the official estimate of work and material required. The ring contractor underbid him by nearly $5,000 with a $2,104.50 bid. After the ring member received the contract, corrupt officials secretly raised the award to $28,098, a steal of more than $20,000.

The entire annual loot during the five years, approximately $1,000,000, was trivial compared with the thievings in the metropolis. Little was stolen in the work on the twelve small canals—the Erie Canal was the chief source of graft. Tilden subsequently appointed a commission of two Democrats and two Republicans to investigate and report.

While the Canal Ring was bipartizan, it was dominated by Republicans. But it so happened that the indictments, arrests, and suits to recover the stolen money involved Democrats almost exclusively. Of the ten indicted men, only three were Republicans; eight of the indicted were state officials and ex-officials, including two former members of the legislature. No one could accuse Tilden of making scapegoats of Republicans.

Tilden had dramatized the scandal so effectively that he became an idol of the crowds the country over. Journals that derided him in the spring, praised him before the summer was well under way. Yale, his alma mater, conferred on him the degree of Doctor of Laws. Record-breaking throngs cheered him on a speaking tour of the principal communities along the Erie Canal in August. Even the Republican press carried his onslaughts on corruption, and while some applauded, others impugned his sincerity, ascribing his assault on the Ring to his presidential ambition. He described this battle as the symbol of the popular demand for reform. In his Buffalo address after recounting that he had reduced canal tolls between $500,000 and $600,000, decreased taxes by some $1,750,000, and had remedial measures enacted, he said:

"There is something higher, more important, more noble, more deeply concerning human society than even these material advantages. We have lifted the standard of public and official morality in the country; we have awakened a sense of justice and duty in the people, and we are rousing public opinion to demand better government and purer administration everywhere."

This was "the great reform" which "the people are impatient to consummate." There was a little conscious exaggeration in his assertion that opponents of reform "will fall, not to rise again," and in the following:

"I know there are men of selfish interests who have not yet learned that the old age has gone out, and the new age has come in. There are public men who still think that the way to success and honor is to combine selfish interest—to pile Canal Ring upon Tweed Ring and so rule the people of this free state."

Tilden was too worldly wise to believe this. But some weeks later, in addressing farmers at the Syracuse fair, he told of an age that was, indeed, gone, when farmers "formed two-thirds at least, perhaps three-fourths, of the whole mass of voters," and governed the state "completely and exclusively." Tilden had seen that age pass—he fixed it at "thirty and forty years ago." And in the same speech occurred this sentence, which should be memorized by our school children:

"The evils of corrupt government are not confined to the money that is taken from the pockets of the people to enrich those who are not entitled to its enjoyments; but the growth of such a system saps all public virtue and public morality, and at last, government of the people, by the people, and for the people will cease to exist, as other republics in ancient times have perished, from the general demoralization and corruption of the people."

Tilden appealed for the election of "sound" legislators who would serve the people's interests, and added:

"What concern have you by what name a man is called who goes to misrepresent your interests and duties? Is it any satisfaction to a Republican that that man is called a Republican, or to a Democrat that he is called a Democrat? Does it make any difference what livery he wears to serve the devil in?"

Tilden was bidding for Republican support, and doing it effectively.

The Republican State Convention met at Saratoga, on September 8, and followed the example of their partizans in Pennsylvania who had convened in Lancaster on May 26 and eliminated Grant from the presidential contest. The Pennsylvania Republicans did this with a plank pledging "firm and unqualified adherence to the unwritten law of the Republic, which wisely and under the sanction of the most venerable examples, limits the presidential service of any person to two terms," and added: "We, the Republicans of Pennsylvania, in recognition of this law, are unalterably opposed to the election of any person for a third term." Grant acknowledged the warning, and wrote on May 29 to General Harry White, chairman of the convention, that he "would not accept a nomination if it were tendered him, unless it should come under such circumstances as to make it an imperative duty—circumstances not likely to arise." The third-termers still had their hold on him.

The New York Republicans, with Conkling as boss, pledged "unalterable opposition to the election of any President for a third term." But Conkling was not defying Grant, for the President had signified to him, as John Bigelow subsequently wrote to Whitelaw Reid, that he would not accept a third-term nomination. Bigelow also informed Reid that Grant was "grateful for Conkling's forbearance, until he, Grant, withdrew." Conkling was not openly in the race for the Republican nomination, and his entire state platform breathed reform, lauded all "honest" efforts for the correction of public abuses, promised support to secure "pure government," and declared for "honesty, economy, and efficiency, in every branch of the state and national governments." As neither a governor nor a lieutenant-governor was to be elected, the state ticket would be headed by the nom-

inee for secretary of state. Conkling offered the honor to
Bigelow who, next to Tilden, was most prominently identi-
fied with the fight on the Canal Ring. Bigelow, a lifelong
Republican, and former minister to France, was chairman
of the bipartizan commission investigating the canal frauds.
He declined the nomination.

When the Democratic convention met in Syracuse the following week, Bigelow renounced his Republican faith to
head the Democratic ticket as Tilden's candidate for secretary of state. The most conspicuous Democrat on the commission headed by Bigelow was John D. Van Buren, Jr.,
grandson of President Van Buren. He was instructor in
engineering at the United States Naval Academy, and Tilden drafted him for state engineer. The other Democratic
member of the commission was Daniel Magone, Jr., a lawyer. Tilden made him chairman of the Democratic State
Committee to end, temporarily at least, the Canal Ring's
influence in the committee. Also, on Tilden's order, the convention named for attorney general, Charles S. Fairchild,
counsel to the commission.

The Democratic wing of the Canal Ring openly and co-
vertly opposed the Tilden ticket. The Republican press,
with rare exceptions, joined in the attack. Both assailed
Tilden as well. He was a political trickster; he had been a
respectable figurehead for Tweed's political machine; he
had shared in Jay Gould's loot of the Erie stockholders.
This last charge was based on a $10,000 retainer Gould had
given him in 1869.

The mud batteries were in full blast when the New York
remnant of the Liberal Republican party convened in Albany, on September 22, and, in lieu of a ticket, urged the
electorate to vote for candidates "who will earnestly and
efficiently coöperate with Governor Tilden in his work of
administrative reform."

The ineffectiveness of the attacks upon Tilden became apparent when he took the stump, for the crowds at his meetings in the key centers of population were larger than his August audiences, and more enthusiastic in approving his demand for economical and clean government.

"You cannot preserve your present system of government unless you purify administration and purify legislation," he told twenty-five thousand cheering voters at Utica. And he voiced another truth when he said the cost of government could be halved if the voters would but elect "the right men."

In leading the Republican spellbinders, Conkling adopted Tilden's strategy of four years earlier, when Tilden sought to remove the stigma of Tweedism from the Democratic party with the specious charge that Tweed and his crew were creatures of Republican legislation. Conkling accused the Democrats of having given birth to the Canal Ring. He said that Republicans appreciated the "little" Tilden had done for reform, and warned the people against selfish and hypocritical reformers. He likened a campaign pamphlet of Tilden's speeches on reform to "an accordion, something of the kind upon which mendicants (not political) play upon street corners."

"It contracts and expands easily," he continued. "It appears to have been issued by Tilden & Co., medicine men; it states that its content is a cure wholly vegetable; that it is a remedy for everything from cholera infantum to cerebro-spinal meningitis."

Conkling was making the best of a poor issue.

The crowds that thronged from farms to the upstate cities to hear Tilden were not reflected in the election returns. Bigelow lost upstate to Frederick W. Seward by 4,850 votes, the tally standing: Seward, 325,787; Bigelow, 320,937. The vote was substantially the same for Bigelow's and Seward's running mates. But Bigelow and the rest of Tilden's state ticket were saved by New York City's vote on which Conkling had pinned high hopes. Bigelow carried the metropolis by a majority of 29,660, polling 79,274 votes to Seward's 49,614. The total state vote gave Bigelow 14,810 majority, the count being: Bigelow, 390,211; Seward, 375,401. The others on the Tilden ticket were elected by like majorities.

Conkling's machine carried both branches of the legislature overwhelmingly. The senate stood twenty Republicans and twelve Democrats; the assembly, seventy-one Republicans and fifty-seven Democrats. In the metropolis a fusion of Republicans and anti-Tammany Democrats swept the city, defeating Honest John's candidates for district-attorney, recorder, surrogate, judge of the Superior Court, judge of General Sessions, judge of the Marine Court, and coroner. Honest John also lost four of his five senatorial nominees, and thirteen of his assembly candidates.

The triumph of Tilden's state ticket in the city astonished all, for never before had there been so many substantial Democratic factions warring among themselves. Honest John had a badly torn and tattered Tammany behind him; Mayor Wickham led a small faction of local office-holders; John Morrissey commanded a formidable group; and O'Brien marched at the head of his Apollo Hall Democracy. These factional rows began taking shape nine months before the election and led to the organization of a new local Democratic party, called from its meeting place, the Irving Hall Democracy. In the November election it fused with the Republicans on local candidates, and earlier it had nominated its own delegates to the state convention. This delegation, led by Morrissey, was denied seats in the convention, the Tammany delegates being seated on Tilden's orders. There were personal feuds as well. Tilden and Wickham had parted company over legislation. Subsequently, Tilden's political partnership with Honest John was dissolved. They differed over patronage and party control. Tilden insisted that he, not Honest John, was the state boss. To add to the dissension, Honest John broke with Wickham for appointing General Fitz John Porter as commissioner of public works without consulting him.

Honest John loyally supported the Tilden nominees despite his quarrel with the governor. A deal with Conkling, and Tilden's ticket would have lost, as a switch of 7,425 votes would have changed the result.

The Republican victory in the legislative canvass emphasized Tilden's personal triumph in the election of his state ticket, and Democratic leaders generally attributed his victory to the popular concept of him as a St. George engaged in slaying the dragon of corruption, of spoilsmanship. These leaders saw him as their presidential nominee in 1876. But some leaders opposed him for this honor, notably Honest John, who had done more than any other man to set Tilden on his pedestal.

38

THE CURTAIN RISES ON OUR MOST
DRAMATIC PRESIDENTIAL CONTEST

HONEST JOHN'S ANTAGONISM TO TILDEN PROVIDED THE colorful opening scene in our most tensely dramatic presidential contest. The Tammany chief realized his justifiable opposition would probably be futile. He had no alternative. To begin with, he had eliminated the one man who blocked Tilden's path to the governorship. But Tilden had failed to consult Honest John on nominations to both elective and appointive offices, although he owed his election to the Tammany chief, more than to any other man. In short, Tilden was ambitious to be state boss, a part which Honest John properly looked upon as his very own.

Tilden's flouting of the Tammany chief was deliberate. Honest John symbolized Tammany, and Tammany had become a synonym for political corruption with the fall of the Tweed Ring. And as soon as Tilden publicly gazed toward the White House, he acted as if he had never been an important cog of the Tammany machine, and, for a time, its boss and its Warwick.

The folly of Tilden's hypocrisy became apparent when the New York Democrats met in Utica, on April 26, 1876, to name delegates to the national convention. The metropolis again sent two delegations to the state convention, one headed by Honest John, and another, labeled reform, led by Morrissey. Through patronage and other powers of his office, Tilden controlled a majority of the state convention, and although his lieutenants had promised to seat the Morrissey delegates, they seated Honest John and his followers instead. Tilden knew that without Tammany's aid, he had little chance of carrying New York. Resolutions were adopted commending Tilden's candidacy for the presidential nomination to the Democrats of other states for the "arduous work of national regeneration and reform." The Tilden majority did not dare press a resolution instructing the New York delegates to the national convention to vote for him. To have done so would have precipitated a fight on the floor. For Honest John and other anti-Tildenites stood ready to offer resolutions instructing the delegates for Church and for Seymour, despite Seymour's advocacy of Tilden for the presidency. This opposition in his home state increased Tilden's popularity elsewhere, and the ire of northern Republicans over Grant's continued indifference to the unclean types around him emphasized the desirability of the New Yorker's candidacy.

As both parties prepared for their national conventions, two new major scandals involving the President's immediate official family were brought to light, making the Republican outlook gloomier than ever. The first of these was the Whiskey Ring frauds. Yet this shameful mess could have been capitalized by the Republicans if the machine had been so minded. For the prosecutor of these frauds was a Republican, Benjamin H. Bristow, of Kentucky, Secretary of the Treasury, whose fight against the corrupt members of his party had won him a national reputation for aggressive honesty.

Bristow began his duties as Secretary of the Treasury in June, 1874. He had been in the Cabinet hardly a fortnight when the Freedman's Savings Bank and Trust Company, with its main office in Washington, failed because its Republican managers had stolen more than $3,000,000 from the freed

"Calling in Frauds" is the title of this Whiskey Ring cartoon. But once the Republican machine put a quietus on the prosecution, Nast lost interest, for *Harper's Weekly* was rabidly partisan. From its issue of November 20, 1875.

slaves—$3,000,000 that the thrifty among them had saved from their meager wages. Of course, no one went to jail for this. Bristow soon learned that his own department took the palm for corruption, sheltering the Whiskey Ring, which had been started in 1870 by Brigadier-General John McDonald, whom Grant had placed in charge of the Treasury Department's revenue office in St. Louis. Missouri's two Senators had vainly protested McDonald's appointment, but Mc-

Donald and Grant had been friends since the Vicksburg campaign, and friendship with Grant outweighed any protests. In February, 1875, Bristow obtained evidence showing that McDonald organized rings in St. Louis and other whiskey-making centers of the West. These rings, composed of crooked distillers and corrupt officials, had fleeced the government in the ten months preceding May, 1875, through thirty-two western distilleries, of $1,650,000 in unpaid whiskey taxes. It was estimated that the aggregate sum stolen was about $10,000,000. The crooked officials divided some $2,500,000 in graft among themselves, the remaining $7,500,000 being shared by the distillers. McDonald said that more than $30,000 cash and expensive presents went to General Babcock, Grant's secretary, who was indicted, along with others, by a Federal grand jury in St. Louis for frauds upon the revenue and conspiring to burglarize a safe containing incriminating documents. United States secret-service agents assisted in the burglary. Before his indictment, Babcock and others involved tried to hamstring the prosecution. A St. Louis banker wrote to Grant that John B. Henderson, special United States Attorney, was prosecuting men whose only offense was loyalty to the administration. This was as true as the plea of the Whiskey Ring thieves that they used all their graft in 1872 to help reëlect Grant. On July 29, 1875, Grant forwarded the letter to Bristow with the admonition: "Let no guilty person escape." There was more of the same noble tenor.

Henderson had served Missouri in the United States Senate, and was known for his brilliance, integrity, and fearless tongue. He had seen his witnesses systematically silenced or spirited away, evidence tampered with or vanish, and Federal officials, bound by their oaths to aid him, intimidated into passive or active hostility against him. During the trial of a Whiskey Ring member, later sentenced to two years' imprisonment, Henderson cast caution aside and dragged in the President. Referring to Babcock's attempts to influence a Federal commissioner, Henderson said: "He [the commissioner] was bound to listen to no dictation, from the President, Babcock, or any other officer." After the trial, Henderson was removed from office. This damaging blow to the prosecution was followed by one far more crippling. An order was issued by the Attorney General which, in effect, prevented the government from obtaining evidence or testimony by promising immunity or leniency to witnesses. This was done shortly before Babcock was placed on trial. Bristow and others regarded this order as dictated by Grant himself, and designed to save Babcock. More astonishing still, Grant submitted a deposition to be read at Babcock's trial. The deposition was thick with whitewash, as witness the following interrogatory and the President's answer:

Q. Have you in any form observed or learned anything in connection with General Babcock's conduct which has tended to diminish your confidence in his fidelity and integrity, and is that confidence in his fidelity and integrity still unimpaired and undiminished?

A. I always had great confidence in his integrity and his efficiency, and as yet my confidence in him is unshaken; I have never learned anything that would shake that confidence; of course I know of this trial that is progressing.

The deposition was published February 18, 1876, and Republican journals revolted at the spectacle. Typical of their resentment was this comment in Whitelaw Reid's *Tribune:* "The President is anxious to clear General Babcock." The *Tribune* noted that a subtle attempt was being made to force out Bristow "who has done so much by his splendid fidelity to make this administration respectable," and added that months ago, when the President did not believe that General Babcock or any other personal friend could be indicted, he wrote, "Let no guilty person escape"; and that Bristow "remains in the Cabinet to-day, not because the President desires the unsparing prosecution of offenders, but because he does not dare openly to arrest it...."

Babcock was cleared by a jury's verdict of "not guilty." He called at the White House, and two hours thereafter departed, no longer Grant's secretary. But he had a new government job, Superintendent of Public Buildings. Grant would not let down a friend.

Bristow next moved the trial of Grant's other friend, General McDonald. But lacking a presidential deposition, McDonald was convicted, sentenced to three years, and fined $5,000. McDonald, who had presented Grant with a pair of blooded horses two years before, blackmailed himself out of jail after serving six months of his term, extorting a pardon from Grant under threat to break the silence he had maintained during his trial if kept in prison. Grant also remitted the $5,000 fine.

McDonald was sentenced on April 13; Babcock was acquitted on February 24. But a scandal greater than either broke within a week after Babcock's acquittal. This was the unanimous impeachment of Secretary of War Belknap for "high crimes and misdemeanors," offenses involved in the sale of a post tradership at Fort Sill in October, 1870. Every Republican in the House voted with the Democratic majority, a circumstance which occasioned no astonishment, for Grant had lost favor with his own partizans in this popular branch of Congress as was signally demonstrated December 15 when all but eighteen Republicans voted with the Democrats for a resolution denouncing the third term as "unwise, unpatriotic, and fraught with peril to our free institutions."

Because he had obtained the indictment of General Babcock, Grant's private secretary, in the Whiskey Ring frauds, ex-Senator Henderson was summarily dismissed as Federal prosecutor. J. Keppler depicts Babcock as a whimpering boy in Grant's lap as Henderson announces: "Here's a lady come for you, Master Babcock." Grant consoles Babcock with: "Don't cry, Pab. She shan't have you. I discharge you, Henderson, and I don't want to be bothered by that lady any more." *Leslie's Weekly*, January 8, 1876.

There was no question of Belknap's guilt, and it was proven that he had received $24,450 graft for this particular appointment. His impeachment was voted on March 2, and he sought to escape trial by resigning. Grant accepted the resignation in an attempt to save the party further shame on the eve of the presidential canvass, as implied by George F. Hoar, a Republican manager for the House in the impeachment trial. Hoar called Belknap "the great public criminal," and said this "high Cabinet officer, the constitutional adviser of the Executive" fled from office "before charges of corruption." When Grant failed to save Belknap from impeachment, a move to postpone the trial until after the election was blocked by Hoar and other impeachment managers. On August 1, thirty-five Senators voted guilty, and twenty-five not guilty. This acquitted Belknap of the charge, as a Senate rule provided that "if the impeachment shall not upon any of the articles presented be sustained by the votes of two-thirds of the members present, a judgment of acquittal shall be entered." Belknap was saved by one vote. One of the twenty-five voting "not guilty" was Conkling, and he and others apologized for their "not guilty" votes with the plea that the Senate lacked jurisdiction, holding that having resigned from office before the House acted, Belknap could not be impeached. The House had decided otherwise, and unanimously held that Belknap was doubly within the jurisdiction of Congress: he was in office during the investigation, and for part of the day of his impeachment. It was whispered in his behalf that he had turned grafter to gratify his wife's extravagance. But Belknap's wife was not answerable to Congress for her spendthrift habits; and the Senate, in acquitting Belknap, to borrow the language of Hoar, "treated the demand of the people for its judgment of condemnation as a farce, and laid down its high functions before the sophistries and jeers of the criminal lawyer." But it was all part of the slimy pattern of the machine-ridden administration. Hoar reminded the Senate that he had not been long in Washington—a matter of seven years—and added:

But in that brief period I have seen five judges of a high court of the United States driven from office by threats of impeachment for corruption or maladministration. I have heard the taunt from friendliest lips, that when the United States presented herself in the East to take part with the civilized world in generous competition in the arts of life, the only product of her institutions in which she surpassed all others beyond question was her corruption. I have seen in the state in the Union foremost in power and wealth four judges of her courts impeached for corruption, and the political administration of her chief city become a disgrace and a byword throughout the world. I have seen the chairman of the Committee on Military Affairs in the House . . . rise in his place and demand the expulsion of four of his associates for making sale of their official privilege of selecting the youths to be educated at our great military school. When the greatest railroad of the world, binding together the continent and uniting the two great seas which wash our shores, was finished, I have seen our national triumph and exaltation turned to bitterness and shame by the unanimous reports of three committees of Congress . . . that every step of that mighty enterprise had been taken in fraud. I have heard in highest places the shameless doctrine avowed by men grown old in public office that the true way by which power should be gained in the Republic is to bribe the people with the offices created for their service, and the true end for which it should be used when gained is the promotion of selfish ambition and the gratification of personal revenge. I have heard that suspicion haunts the footsteps of the trusted companions of the President.

39

GRANT'S DARK HORSES:

ONE FAILS TO FINISH,

THE OTHER DOES NOT START

THE RIGGED TRIAL OF BELKNAP HAD BEEN IN PROGRESS LESS
than two weeks when the Republicans, meeting in national convention in Cincinnati, on June 14, denounced the
Democratic majority in the House as traitors, and for good
measure, indicted the entire Democratic party on the same
count. Conkling had written the plank three months before
for the New York Republican State Convention. Save for a
minor verbal change, it was incorporated *in toto* in the national platform. "We charge the Democratic party," read
Conkling's plank, "with being the same in character and
spirit as when it sympathized with treason; with making its
control of the House of Representatives the triumph and
opportunity of the nation's recent foes; ... with thwarting
the ends of justice by its partizan mismanagement and obstruction of investigation." This last was a joyous Cleonian
outburst, for it was the Democratic majority in the House
which had impeached Belknap.

Fear ruled the convention—fear of a Democratic triumph
in the fall. The Republicans could no longer rely on a corrupt electoral vote, garnered with bayonets, from the southern states. The Democrats predicted a united Democratic
South in the impending presidential election, although the

phrase, the Solid South, did not become part of our political jargon until later in the campaign. And the Republicans, seeking to offset a Solid South by a Solid North, adopted a plank designed to inflame the North, especially Union veterans, against all Democrats. This plank read:

We sincerely deprecate all sectional feeling and tendencies. We therefore note with deep solicitude that the Democratic party counts, as its chief hope of success, upon the electoral vote of a united South, secured through the efforts of those who were recently arrayed against the nation; and we invoke the earnest attention of the country to the grave truth that a success thus achieved would reopen sectional strife and imperil national honor and human rights.

But the machine omitted even the lip loyalty to civil service of its 1872 platform. It could not consistently do otherwise, for the administration had repudiated civil-service reform after Grant himself had made an excellent start toward depriving the machine of some of the spoils of office. He had acted on a rider attached to an appropriation bill on March 3, 1871, authorizing him to prescribe regulations to determine the "fitness of each candidate in respect to age, health, character, knowledge, and ability for the branch of the service in which he seeks to enter." The President was empowered to "employ suitable persons to conduct such inquiries, prescribe their duties and establish regulations for the conduct of persons who may receive appointments." Grant lost no time in appointing our first civil-service commission, with George William Curtis, chairman. This seemed the realization of the dream of the nation's pioneer civil-service crusader, Thomas Allen Jenckes, a Representative from Rhode Island, who introduced a bill on December 20, 1865, to "regulate the civil service of the United States." But the machine had a second thought on civil-service reform and in two years forced Curtis to resign, and then abolished the commission by refusing an appropriation for its work.

Conkling and other machine managers had snuffed out the commission. But when the convention got down to the order of balloting for a presidential nominee, Conkling learned how effectively the despised reformers had destroyed his ambition to head the ticket. The drive against Conkling had been launched three months before at the state convention of New York Republicans. Under the leadership of Curtis, the anti-Conklingites forced the gathering, although Conkling's Custom-House Gang controlled it, to withdraw a resolution naming Conkling as New York's favorite son and accept a substitute, calling upon the national convention to name "a tried and true Republican whose character and career are a pledge of a pure, economical, and vigorous administration of the government." This was followed by the Fifth Avenue Hotel conference where Henry Cabot Lodge, William Cullen Bryant, and other Republicans from seventeen states, formulated an "Address to the American People" which opened with this truthful indictment of the Republic's greatest menace:

"Every student of our political history knows that since the spoils system was inaugurated, corruption has steadily grown from year to year; and so long as this system lasts, with all its seductions and demoralizing tendencies, corruption will continue to grow in extent and power, for patriotism and true merit will more and more be crowded out of political life by unscrupulous selfishness."

And there was this direct repudiation of Conkling and other bosses of the spoils machine: "We shall support no candidate, no matter how conspicuous his position or brilliant his ability, in whom the impulses of the party manager have shown themselves predominant over those of the reformer; for he will be inclined to continue that fundamental abuse—the employment of the government service as a machinery for personal or party ends."

The effect of the reformers' drive on Conkling was noticeable on the first roll-call when he polled but thirty votes outside of his own state, and these due chiefly to his congressional friendships in ten scattered states. Curtis, alone of New York's seventy delegates, refused to vote for him—even on this obviously complimentary ballot. Another manager of the national spoils machine, Morton of Indiana, and, next to Conkling, closest to Grant, lined up ninety-five southern delegates for himself besides Indiana's thirty delegates.

Yet in striking contrast was the candidacy of Bristow who had no organization support. Curtis stressed his antagonism to Conkling by seconding Bristow's nomination in the name of Republicans "who have seen that reform is possible within the Republican party." Bristow polled 113 votes on the first ballot. His support, which came from seventeen states and one territory, disclosed only part of his popularity, for the machine had put pressure wherever it could to prevent any sizable demonstration for this foe of corruption.

There was a fourth contender of national reputation for head of the ticket, Blaine of Maine, who lacked only ninety-three votes of the required majority on the first ballot, and led the field on the first six ballots. Morton and Conkling, each with less than half of Blaine's vote of 285 on the first, lost steadily after the first. Bristow outdistanced Morton on the third ballot, forging ahead to second place. Governor John F. Hartranft, of Pennsylvania, and Governor Rutherford B. Hayes, of Ohio, were the favorites among the five dark horses. Hayes increased his lead appreciably on the fifth ballot, and shoved Bristow out of second place on the sixth with 113 votes to 111. But while Blaine still held first place, with almost three times the votes of Hayes, the Ohioan had nearly doubled his own vote since the fourth ballot. One of the dark horses, Postmaster-General Marshall Jewell, of Connecticut, dropped out after the first ballot. Another, a New York member of the House, William Almon Wheeler, of Malone, known to his colleagues for his personal charm, sterling integrity, and legal attainments, received three votes on both the first and second ballots. And thereafter, at the suggestion of George F. Hoar, two delegates from Massachusetts kept Wheeler before the convention on each roll-call. On the second ballot, one vote was cast for Elihu B. Washburne, of Illinois. His top was four votes, on the sixth ballot.

Conkling became aggressively active as the seventh and final roll-call started and delegates began switching to Hayes; he helped defeat Blaine by throwing his delegates to Hayes. But Curtis and other foes of Conkling also threw their strength to the Ohioan, thereby preventing Conkling from taking credit for Hayes's nomination. The balloting follows:

	1st	2nd	3rd	4th	5th	6th	7th
BLAINE	285	296	293	292	286	308	351
MORTON	125	120	113	108	95	85	
BRISTOW	113	114	121	126	114	111	21
CONKLING	99	93	90	84	82	81	
HAYES	61	64	67	68	104	113	384
HARTRANFT	58	63	68	71	69	50	
JEWELL	11						
WHEELER	3	3	2	2	2	2	
WASHBURNE			1	1	3	3	4

Conkling sought to soften his defeat by capturing the vice-presidential nomination for General Woodford, who ran for governor of New York in 1870. But no man with a Conkling label, whatever his merits, stood any chance. The reformers were on the warpath. Luke P. Poland, of Vermont, a friend of Hoar, nominated Wheeler, who was seconded

by S. H. Russell, of Texas. Wheeler had few friends or acquaintances in the convention outside of the New York
delegates and his fellow Congressmen, and he was disliked
by Conkling who once tried to enlist him in his Custom-
House Gang, saying Wheeler might aspire to anything
within the gift of New York. Wheeler replied: "Mr. Conkling, there is nothing in the gift of the state which will
compensate me for the forfeiture of my own self-respect."
Wheeler had served in both branches of the New York
legislature after several years as district attorney of Franklin
County. He was president of the state constitutional convention of 1867-68, and he was now rounding out his ninth
year in Congress.

Before New York was reached, Wheeler had 366 votes—a
few short of a majority—against a scattered field. Fourteen
other delegations were yet to be called. At this point Conkling withdrew Woodford; other candidates were also withdrawn, and Wheeler's unanimous nomination ensued.

A more downcast delegation did not leave Cincinnati on
June 16 than Conkling's Custom-House Gang. Their departure was a sorry contrast to their jubilant arrival four
days before with banners flying, their yellow silk toppers at
rakish angles as they paraded behind a military band, bliss-
fully unaware of the impression they created among the
delegates from other states. One curbstone spectator observed that it was "a mystery to him where the Custom-
House got bail for all those fellows." Reid's *Tribune* identified the cynic as a Pennsylvania delegate.

There was no solace for Conkling in the ticket—two dark
horses, one from his own state and that one a foe. Grant had
expected a dark horse would head the ticket after the outstanding candidates, Conkling, Blaine, and Morton, had
killed themselves off; but in his puerile concept of politics
he had imagined that Washburne or Hamilton Fish would

be the nominee for President. Fish, in whose behalf he had written a letter to be used "at the proper time," was never before the convention; and Washburne's peak vote, as we have seen, was 4 votes in a total of 756. Washburne, minister to France, was little known outside of Illinois, although he had served sixteen years in the lower branch of Congress. But he was Grant's unselfish friend, and to Grant, that qualified him. Fish was objectionable on three grounds: as a member of the Cabinet, his nomination would make the Grant administration a dominant issue; the machine managers regarded him as not amenable to their aims; and his election would lead to the reorganization of the party in New York and the deposal of Conkling. But if all Grant's appointees had been cast in the mold of Fish and Washburne, he would not have had to plead in his last annual message to Congress that he had entered the White House "without any previous political training," and to charge most of his mistakes—this was his euphemism—to men he had appointed to office "upon the recommendation of the representatives chosen directly by the people"—the congressional agents and managers of the machine.

40

PICKING UP $10,000 AT A CONVENTION

THE DEMOCRATIC CONVENTION OPENED IN ST. LOUIS ON
June 27; but leaders from the larger states had been on
the scene for a week or so. One of the first to arrive was
Augustus Schell, who was there in the dual capacity of
chairman of the Democratic National Committee and manager of the anti-Tilden forces. Some of Tilden's foes from
New York were armed with galley-proofs of articles, which
subsequently appeared in the New York *Evening Express*,
wherein Tilden and four others were accused of having
mulcted the St. Louis, Alton & Terre Haute Railroad Company of more than $1,000,000. The charge was based on a
suit pending in the United States Circuit Court of the
Southern District of New York. Tilden and his codefendants
were asked for an accounting, the road having been sold to
them at auction for $800,000; and thereafter, as the incorpo-
rators and directors of the road, the defendants issued stocks
and bonds of a par value of $10,450,000—more than thirteen
times the purchase price. This was done on the recommendation of Tilden, as counsel. The complaint alleged that
Tilden and his companions presented themselves with $250,-
000 in common stock without authority from themselves or
anybody else, and described a fee of $20,000 to Tilden as
extravagant. The charge, in sum, was that Tilden and his
little group had indulged in a highly profitable game of
stock-watering and melon-cutting. It was estimated that
Tilden made more than a quarter of a million dollars in the

transaction. One newspaper article said: "Of the weak points in Mr. Tilden's railroad career, we know more than we care to publish." Tilden ignored the newspaper attacks on his personal and professional integrity, and instead of replying promptly to the suit, filed his answer in mid-September, after obtaining several postponements. All five denied that the railroad company had any right to ask for an accounting, emphasizing that they had sold the property to the complaining railroad as individuals, not as trustees. They specifically denied that their acts had made the road liable for more than $1,000,000 "or any other amount whatever," or that they had unlawfully retained or divided any bonds or stocks among themselves. Which was another way of saying that the stocks or bonds they retained or divided among themselves—no one outside of the five knew the amount—were technically within the law. Tilden, in the answer, said his $20,000 fee was for services over a period of years.

The attacks failed to halt Tilden's political progress, for railroads were unpopular because, with few honorable exceptions, they corrupted legislators, local, state, and Federal, fleeced the government, swindled the stockholders, defrauded farmers and other small shippers, and paid little better than starvation wages to their employees.

Two days before the convention opened, all the New York delegates being in St. Louis, Honest John Kelly called his followers together, and the meeting deputized a committee of five to inform delegates from other states that New York's thirty-five electoral votes would be lost if Tilden were nominated, and that only a western man could beat Hayes.

Tilden's agents ignored the attacks. Being confident of the nomination, their strategy was to avoid friction, especially with Honest John. They were equally confident of winning the election, for there seemed to be no let-up in the scandals in the national administration, the most recent being the forced resignation from the Cabinet of Bristow, the man who had done so much to make the Grant administration "respectable."

Kernan directed the Tilden high command, aided by Dorsheimer, Hewitt, and Honest John's neighbor, the diamond merchant, Wickham. Hewitt was a member of Congress, and Wickham mayor of the metropolis, by grace of Honest John.

An hour or so after Honest John's committee of five began its labors, the Tammany leader entered the dining-room of the Lindell House. Wickham was drinking champagne at a table with several friends. Honest John had to pass the table, and as he neared it, Wickham rose ostentatiously and offered his hand.

"I don't shake hands with you, sir!" exclaimed Honest John.

"Why, old gentleman, ain't you going to speak to me?" countered Wickham, smiling blandly as he essayed the rôle of "one of the boys."

"I'll take the opportunity to speak to you plenty at another time," said Honest John meaningly. This sobered and silenced Wickham. Honest John passed on.

Unaware of Wickham's misadventure, Hewitt shortly thereafter called at Kelly's suite in the Lindell House, and extended the hand of friendship.

"I don't care to shake hands with you, sir," said Honest John with studied formality.

"Why, Mr. Kelly, I don't understand this," stammered the astonished Hewitt. "I have a message for you—a letter from Speaker Kerr, given me for you by Mr. Cox."

"I don't choose to receive any message through you, sir, or any letter from your hands," said Honest John.

Hewitt made as graceful an exit as the circumstances permitted.

The New York delegation convened the following day. Of the seventy delegates, all but two were present, and fifty-two declared for Tilden. One absentee was a Tilden man, the other followed Honest John. Of the sixteen opposed to Tilden, Honest John had twelve use Tilden's intimate, Horatio Seymour, for a stalking horse, and he had the other four vote for as many candidates—Chief Judge Church, former Governor Hoffman, United States Senator Thomas Francis Bayard, of Delaware, and General Winfield Scott Hancock, of Pennsylvania.

Working zealously in Tilden's behalf, in his own way, was John Morrissey. He was there with a batch of anti-Tammany delegates, all pledged to Tilden, and ready to vote for him—if the convention seated them. On the convention eve, when word flashed that Tilden would be nominated, with Governor Thomas A. Hendricks, of Indiana, as his running mate, Morrissey encountered a party of Honest John's adherents, including Edward Kearney, a rich contractor, in the Lindell lobby. After hearing them repeat Honest John's prediction that Tilden could not carry New York, Morrissey assumed a strictly professional tone and said:

"I'll bet any of these gentlemen [from] $10 [up] to $100,-000 that Tilden can carry New York if this convention nominates him."

Kearney took $10,000 of the $100,000, and both he and Morrissey posted a forfeit of $5,000 cash dug from their pockets. The balance was to be put up after the nomination.

"Now," continued Morrissey, "I'll bet $100,000 on the same event."

Receiving only smiles, Morrissey continued:

"Well, I'll make it $50,000 then."

He waited a few moments, and then resumed:

After John Morrissey's famed wager of $10,000 on Tilden at the St. Louis convention, Nast showed the gambler-statesman and the Democratic nominees for President and Vice-President, Tilden and Hendricks, in this effective cartoon. "I'll bet $10,000 that this is the greatest deformed (reformed I mean) animal going," says Morrissey; "$10,000 that it is going to lick everything in the field; $10,000 that this double-faced tiger can be turned any way to gull the American people." *Harper's Weekly*, July 22, 1876.

"Well, gentlemen, I'll try to make it worth your while. I'll bet you $100,000 to $80,000, or $50,000 to $40,000, that Samuel J. Tilden, if the nominee of this convention, will carry the state of New York."

There being no takers at these odds, Morrissey offered to lay $5,000 to $500 that Tilden would be nominated.

Morrissey had this group intimidated, but he failed to make the slightest impression on the Committee on Contested Seats, for they recognized Honest John's Tammany contingent; had they done otherwise, the convention would have been a cut-and-dried affair. For Tilden had more than four hundred delegates pledged, and it was only a question of a second or third ballot when he would gain the additional votes to round out the required two-thirds, barring, of course, a surprise. Honest John was resolved to spring the surprise if he could. When New York was reached in the alphabetical roll-call of the states, he rose to oppose Tilden's nomination.

A tumult ensued. All recognized the shrewd, bearded face and massive head of the Tammany chief. Hundreds tried to howl him down. Scores applauded and shouted encouragement. Above the din rose the voice of Kernan crying for order, which was repeated at rhythmic intervals until the uproar subsided. Kernan had nominated Tilden, and his demand for a respectful hearing for Honest John was heeded.

The Tammany chief came quickly to the point. The presidential nomination should go to a westerner, and his choice was Hendricks of Indiana. As he paused, a Tilden follower roared: "Three cheers for Tilden!" When the last cheer was chorused, Honest John protested Tilden's nomination on behalf of himself and sixteen other New Yorkers. Jeers and cheers greeted him as he finished.

Of the 744 votes on the first ballot, Tilden had 404½.

His opponents included the two Ohioans, Allen G. Thurman and William Allen; Thomas A. Hendricks, of Indiana; Winfield Scott Hancock, of Pennsylvania; Joel Parker, of New Jersey; James Overton Broadhead, of Missouri, and Thomas Francis Bayard, of Delaware. On the second and final ballot, all but Parker and Allen lost votes to Tilden. When the tally showed him with 535 votes, 39 more than the necessary two-thirds, his nomination was made unanimous. The vote on the two ballots follows:

	1st	2nd
TILDEN	404½	535
HENDRICKS . . .	140½	60
HANCOCK . . .	75	59
ALLEN	54	54
BAYARD	33	11
PARKER	18	18
BROADHEAD . . .	16	
THURMAN . . .	3	7

Hendricks was unanimously named for Vice-President on the first ballot.

When the convention adjourned sine die, Tilden's managers were relieved, for they had feared a devastating outburst from Honest John, whose whisper squads had spread the charge that delegates had been bought with Tilden money. But it was not until long after the campaign, when he broke openly with Tilden, that he publicly made the accusation. Then he said (and no one denied it):

"With reform as a cloak, Tildenism has bought delegates in a Democratic National Convention."

Entire state delegations have been bought and sold, like so much merchandise, at many conventions. This form of political corruption neither came nor ended with Tilden.

41

THE INDIAN RING DEFEATS CUSTER

O N JUNE 26, THE DAY BEFORE THE OPENING GAVEL FELL AT the Democratic Convention, five troops of the Seventh Cavalry under General George A. Custer were annihilated on the Little Big Horn by a force of Sioux outnumbering them more than ten to one. The exact number of Custer's command is not known, the estimates varying from 204 officers and men to "about 250." The considered estimate is 225 or so. Besides the soldiers, Mark Kellogg, of the Bismarck *Tribune*, the only correspondent with Custer, and three other civilians, were slain. Military experts far from the scene gave no credence to the first intelligence of the disaster, for like the other commanders directing operations against Sitting Bull and his three thousand hostiles since early in the year, Custer had won his first laurels in desperate Civil War encounters. But in eleven days hope fled as the verified report of the tragedy reached civilization. Whether Curley, the Crow scout, was in the battle and escaped, or witnessed it from a safe vantage, or whether the sole survivor was Comanche, the horse of Captain Miles W. Keogh, is not our concern. For this is not another history of the Custer Massacre, ever to be half veiled in myth and mystery, but an outline of the more recent villainies of the Indian rings responsible for it and other clashes between redskins and whites. The wrongs committed by the rings— not the rush of gold-seekers to the Black Hills, or a railroad's penetration of their hunting-grounds—made Crazy Horse,

Rain-in-the-Face, and other young chiefs pliable tools of
their medicine man. Had there been no rings, or broken
treaties, Sitting Bull would have gone on obscurely "making
medicine." Red Cloud alone prevented the entire fighting
strength of the Sioux nation, some twelve thousand braves,

SITTING BULL.

The chief of the Siouan hostiles
Harper's Weekly, December 8, 1877.

from taking the war-path. This is the same Red Cloud we
heard in Cooper Union six years earlier reminding the
whites that only the frontier Indians, not the entire race,
had been "corrupted and demoralized by the white man's
whiskey," as he approved Red Dog's plea to send honest
men, not men who "think only of filling their pockets," to

run the Indian reservations. In sum, as the reader recalls, these Siouan chiefs pleaded for justice.

This lack of justice was attested by General Philip H. Sheridan shortly after Red Cloud returned home, in reporting the murder of a harmless old Piegan and another inoffensive Sioux, a boy of fourteen. Both were wantonly shot down in the street at Fort Benton. Sheridan wrote to the War Department: "I think I can arrest the murderers, but I doubt very much if I can convict them in any court. . . . Nothing can be done to ensure peace here until there is a military force strong enough to clear out the roughs and the whiskey sellers."

From 1870 to 1874 the administration did nothing. Then it yielded to public opinion and appointed an Indian commission. Within a year the public had lost faith in it, despite its respectable window-dressing, and in 1875 a special commission was appointed to investigate the Red Cloud agency, admittedly one of the worst. The investigators found the Ring still there engaged in the customary twofold task of swindling the Indians and the government. Here, as at any other agency, the Ring was composed of Federal officials at the agency, local politicians, and contractors. While these officials, in the main, were Republicans, the Ring, like all rings, was essentially bipartizan, for the contractors who sold foodstuffs to the reservations were evenly divided politically.

The investigators cited a few of the Republican and Democratic contractors for fraud, and recommended the dismissal of Dr. A. J. Saville, Indian agent at Red Cloud, for incompetence. The commission's report, made directly to Grant, was generally denounced as whitewash. Newspapers named a Congressman as a Ring member, but the commission did not.

The whitewash was expected. Two years earlier the Indian Bureau suppressed an official report disclosing corrupt conditions at the Red Cloud and Whetstone agencies. Corn-meal, selling at near-by Omaha and Cheyenne for $1.50 per hundred-weight, was being bought by the agencies for $2.26⅔ per hundred-weight.

At the beginning of his first term, Grant made a brief attempt to reform the Indian agencies by appointing army officers to run them. But the spoils machine quickly restored the old order of graft and loot. Belknap was Secretary of War, and any disclosures of corruption made by army officers never saw the light of day through the War Department, or any other agency of government. Any officer foolhardy enough to interfere with the order of greed and graft quickly found himself in disfavor.

Custer himself had a taste of this. He learned from the Sioux how they were swindled by the Indian agents but this was beyond his control. He saw his own soldiers charged exorbitant prices for supplies by the post trader at Fort Abraham Lincoln. Prior to Belknap's administration of the War Department, these post traders went by the ancient and more descriptive name, sutlers, and were appointed by the post commandant after a conference with his officers. Belknap changed this, and profited thereby. Custer stopped the gypping of his soldiers—at least for a time—by having his troop commanders buy supplies at Bismarck and resell them at cost at the post. The post trader complained, and Belknap issued an order which restored the monopoly. Custer refused to accept eight thousand bushels of forage sent to the post in bags bearing the sign of the Indian Bu-reau. It was obvious that the same supplies had been sold twice to the government, once for the ponies of the Indians, and again for the horses of the cavalry. But this was not novel, for whole boatloads of Indian supplies were transported into the Sioux country and sold to traders in the Indian Ring.

Custer related what he knew before a congressional committee after Belknap's impeachment. He said the post trader had told him, after Belknap's impeachment, that he had paid $1,000 a month graft and thought some of it reached Belknap. Custer, his heart set on rejoining his command for action against the Sioux, found himself a prisoner-at-large in Washington after his testimony. Appeals to General Sheridan were in vain, so he called at the White House where for three days he sat in an anteroom in a futile attempt to see Grant, the commander-in-chief of the nation's armed forces. Custer took the situation into his own hands and started west, to be halted at Chicago by an order from the War Department. But newspapers had taken up his cause and he was permitted to rejoin his regiment.

Army officers, in discussing the graft of the Grant administration, generally did so anonymously. Even when retired, they preferred anonymity to reprisals. A year before Custer testified, an unnamed retired colonel related his experiences as an Indian agent in New Mexico to the New York *Tribune*. He had 250 Utes and Apaches to provision; but his civilian predecessor, with the same number to look after, had received rations for 900 Indians, and also received consignments of bar iron to shoe the ponies of Indians, although Indians never shod their mounts. Under the colonel's supervision, the Indians were content, for he gave them full rations of cattle, meal, and other supplies. They were no longer being cheated, nor was the government being swindled.

The superintendent of Indian agents visited the agency, but the responsible head-men of these 250 Utes and Apaches refused to talk with him. He bribed young bucks with tobacco to complain of inadequate supplies, which enabled him to ask for an additional appropriation of $20,800.

A favorite swindling method of the ring contractors, whether cattle-dealer, provision-dealer, or what not, was to deliver only a portion of the supplies charged on the bill. Another common device was to falsify vouchers for supplies presumably rationed to the Indians but actually sold to civilians. An army officer on his arrival at a New Mexico

This visit of Sitting Bull to an Indian Agent is wholly imaginative, but it symbolizes the truth, as did the fictive dialogue printed beneath the cartoon in *Leslie's Weekly*, September 16, 1876: "Indian Agent—'You are very welcome, Mr. Bull. What can I sell you today?' Sitting Bull—'Pale face soldiers all down South now attending election. Next spring all come North to visit Sitting Bull; so give me plenty goods and powder, that I may be ready to receive them warmly.'"

agency was offered $5,000 cash to certify fraudulent vouchers.

Army men looked upon handouts to the Indians as the most degrading feature of Indian life. "The Indian," said the retired colonel, in the *Tribune*, "has been pauperized by the system of giving him rations. He will not hunt game as long as he is fed by the government, and spends his time drinking, gambling, and lounging about the agencies."

Degrading the Indians with doles after despoiling them of their hunting-grounds was cynical consistency.

When Sitting Bull led a quarter of the fighting men of the Sioux nation on the war-path, the demand to transfer control of the Indians to the War Department was vigorously renewed. After Sheridan was assigned to direct the military operations against the hostiles, his primary object was to return the Indians to the reservations, without bloodshed, if possible. General George Crook, commanding the column of which Custer's regiment was part, had asked friendly Indians to aid him in getting the hostiles back to their reservation, with some promise of success. But the Indian Ring sent a key man to the Red Cloud and Spotted Tail agencies to influence the Indians against Crook's peaceful move. Newspapers reported that even Sitting Bull had "expressed a willingness" to aid Crook's plan, which the Ring destroyed.

A peaceful return of the hostiles to their reservation would give an impetus to the demand to place the Indians under military supervision, thereby putting an end to the Ring, which at this time was accused of supplying Sitting Bull's 3,000 bucks with guns, revolvers, and ammunition.

Nearly four weeks before the Custer Massacre, the New York *Tribune* correspondent wrote from Cheyenne that travel on the road from Fort Laramie to Custer City was unsafe, except in large parties or with soldier escort, because

of murder and theft committed by hostiles "directly traceable back to the Red Cloud agency, from which the Ring
had been supposedly supplying them with ammunition."

This ugly charge is tragically corroborated and elaborated
by both officers and men who fought Sitting Bull. "Came
Sheridan himself," wrote Charles King, "with orders to stop
the flow of warriors, arms, and ammunition from the Red
Cloud agency to Sitting Bull and his triumphant camp."
King was a lieutenant in the Fifth Cavalry when his regiment took the field against Sitting Bull. After the surrender
of Indians who participated in the Custer Massacre, they
told King and other army men that Custer's men had in-
ferior ammunition, and described some spending their last
moments vainly trying to remove shells which had jammed
in their carbines. King himself noted that the Indian agencies had supplied the Sioux "with superior weapons for
frontier warfare." No one had to tell King and his companions this; they knew it from bitter experience, and some,
like King, although severely wounded with one of these
"superior weapons," lived to tell the tale.

42

NO HOLDS BARRED

AFTER THE PEOPLE RECOVERED FROM THE SHOCK OF THE Custer Massacre, the presidential contest again engaged their attention. Impartial opinion conceded victory to the Democrats. Tilden was the logical answer to the prayer for governmental reform which was emphasized throughout the Democratic platform memorable for an unparalleled recital of national shame. Nine planks opened with the ringing refrain, "Reform is necessary." The first was a blanket indictment of "the abuses, wrongs, and crimes" of "sixteen years' ascendancy of the Republican party" and read:

Reform is necessary to rebuild and establish in the hearts of the whole people the Union, eleven years ago happily rescued from the danger of a secession of states, but now to be saved from a corrupt centralism which, after inflicting upon ten states the rapacity of carpet-bag tyrannies, has honeycombed the offices of the Federal Government itself with incapacity, waste, and fraud; infected states and municipalities with the contagion of misrule, and locked fast the prosperity of an industrious people in the paralysis of hard times.

Another of these reform-is-necessary planks demanded "a stop to the profligate waste of public lands, and their diversion from actual settlers by the party in power, which has squandered two hundred million acres upon railroads alone, and out of more than thrice that aggregate has disposed of less than a sixth directly to tillers of the soil."

A. B. Frost was inspired by an amusing campaign song published in the Chicago *Inter-Ocean* entitled, "A Call for Tweed," then a fugitive from justice. The first verse, sung by Tilden, of course, ran:

> "William, dear William, come home to me now,
>   Your Sammy is feeling forlorn;
> He misses your hand, and he misses your voice,
>   Which he knows would be raised for reform."

Harper's Weekly, August 19, 1876.

Following the example of the Republicans, the Democratic platform straddled the financial question. Both parties were alarmed by the recent formation of the inflationists into the Independent National, or Greenback, party, which had met in Indianapolis on May 18, and nominated for President our old acquaintance, Peter Cooper, the New York philanthropist, and General Samuel F. Cary, of Ohio, for Vice-

President. A Democratic straddle, on the basis of political expediency, was understandable; they had not been attacked. But the Greenbackers had accused the Republicans of conspiring with bondholders to compel the payment of government securities in coin, thereby making this paper more valuable than the depreciated dollar bills which had started down the toboggan with the suspension of specie payments in the first months of the Civil War. The Republicans, in their last days of control of both branches of Congress, had thrown a sop to the inflationists in the Resumption Act of 1875 by postponing the resumption of specie payments to January 1, 1879. But this law, like the currency straddle, pleased neither inflationists nor sound-money men.

Hayes saw the blunder of the straddle and atoned for it in his letter of acceptance by flouting the timid Republican managers with a promise to approve every appropriate act to resume specie payments. In this he outgeneraled the overcautious Tilden who masked his own firm belief in sound money in a verbose letter of acceptance.

Both candidates promised a civil-service reform, and Tilden's observation that "the public interest in an honest, skilful performance of official trust must not be sacrificed to the usufruct of the incumbent," earned him the sobriquet of Old Usufruct.

Hayes also scored with his courageous thrust at the heart of the spoils system by declaring for a single term for President. Said he:

The declaration of principles by the Cincinnati convention makes no announcement in favor of a single presidential term. . . . Believing that the restoration of the civil service to the system established by Washington, and followed by the early Presidents, can be best accomplished by an Executive who is under no temptation to use the patronage of his office to promote his own reëlection, I desire to perform what I regard as a duty, in stating now my inflexible purpose, if elected, not to be a candidate for election to a second term.

After the letters of acceptance, interest centered in the New York state conventions, for it was generally accepted that without New York's thirty-five electoral votes Tilden would have little chance.

The Republicans convened in Saratoga on August 23, and got off to a good start. The bolters who had followed Greeley four years before took seats in the convention. But harmony ended here. Conkling planned to name Alonzo B. Cornell for governor, to emphasize Tilden's intimacy with the Tweed machine. When Cornell was nominated, the convention was reminded how he had been robbed of the governorship in 1868 through the fraudulent count plotted by Tweed with the use of Tilden's name.

The attempt to use Cornell to retrieve the fortunes of the Conkling machine was doomed by Curtis and other reform leaders. They attacked him as boss-ridden, compelling Chester A. Arthur and other Conkling lieutenants to withdraw him before the balloting; subsequently, when Cornell was nominated for lieutenant-governor, he was again withdrawn after Curtis said his nomination would imperil the ticket.

The Conkling managers evened the score by defeating the reform faction's choice for governor, William M. Evarts, statesman, diplomat, and scholar, and nominating Edwin D. Morgan, twice governor, as the lesser—to them—of two evils. The tally stood, Morgan 242; Evarts, 126; scattering, 43. Morgan's running mates, although lesser known, were good men all.

A week later Tilden met Conkling's fate when he attempted to dictate to the Democratic State Convention at

Saratoga. His program was to build up German support throughout the nation by nominating Dorsheimer for governor. Dorsheimer's record as lieutenant-governor entitled him to the promotion; but when his name was presented, the

Edwin D. Morgan

From a photograph by Kurtz. *Harper's Weekly*, September 9, 1876.

Tilden adherents were hopelessly outnumbered by a vociferous Tammany and its upstate allies. Referring to Dorsheimer's Republican background, some of them shouted, "Give us a Democrat!" while others yelled, "Seymour! Seymour!" Anticipating this, Tilden had Seymour telegraph Kernan that he could not be a candidate because of his health. The telegram was read to the astonished delegates by the chair. But Honest John and his faction were prepared for this move; and Representative George M. Beebe informed the delegates that on his way to the convention he had visited Seymour who assured him he would accept the nomination if it came to him by acclamation. Seymour's unanimous nomination immediately followed. A committee of ten was appointed to wait upon Seymour that evening, and it reported the following morning that Seymour would run. The convention then renominated Dorsheimer for lieutenant-governor, named the rest of the ticket, and adjourned sine die.

Honest John now regarded himself as the state boss.

But on September 5, five days after the committee reported, newspapers published a letter from Seymour declining on the score of health; eight days later, the party, meeting again in state convention, saw the absent Tilden name Lucius Robinson for governor over Honest John's candidate, Clarkson N. Potter, with a bare majority of 1½ votes.

Tilden was still the boss—and an artful one.

Robinson symbolized the finer things in a public servant. He had been elected state comptroller in 1861 as a Democrat. Two years later, when his party rejected him because he supported the war, the Republicans nominated him and he was reëlected. In 1865, the Republicans turned him down at the end of his second term for criticizing the Lincoln administration's infringement of individual rights; and when the Democrats welcomed him back and made him their choice for comptroller, Greeley eulogized him as "a genuine Democrat, a true Republican, a hearty Unionist, and an inflexibly honest and faithful guardian of the treasury."

Honest John and his followers returned to their homes conscious that Old Usufruct had outwitted them. (The Tammany chief privately called Tilden by this name months before using the epithet publicly). But as the campaign got under way, the Republicans assailed Tilden in a manner to satisfy his worst enemy. They catered to southern prejudices by dubbing him Barnburner and recalling his activities in the Free Soil campaign of 1848 which cost the Democrats the presidency. They appealed to northern passions with the taunt of Copperhead, citing the irrefutable record of the arch Copperhead group, the Society for the Diffusion of Political Knowledge, of which Tilden was a founder and director. They quoted his inflammatory speech on the eve of the draft which was then interpreted as the inception of a revolutionary intrigue to rid the country of Lincoln. Nor did they overlook his definition of Lincoln in 1863 as "a man whose whole knowledge and experience of statesmanship was derived from one term in Congress, a long service in the county conventions of Sangamon, a career at *nisi prius* in the interior of Illinois, and some acquaintance with the lobby at Springfield." They proved Tilden a persistent tax-dodger, showing that during a fifteen-year period there were eleven years when he filed no return. Sometimes the tax appraiser guessed at his income and Tilden then paid the tax, plus a penalty. In 1860 and 1861 Tilden made no return and paid no tax; from 1864 to 1872 he let the appraiser arbitrarily assess him. They compared his income-tax returns with those of another rich man, Morgan, the Republican nominee for governor. Morgan was poor compared to Tilden, yet he paid income taxes during these years on $915,000, more than double Tilden's return on $435,000. In 1862, when Tilden received one railroad fee of $20,000 he filed a return on an income of only $7,118, although his taxable income was at least $89,000. Government agents sought evidence on which to hang an indictment; in the closing weeks of the campaign,

John Morrissey, professional gambler and ex-pugilist, as a leader of Tilden's reform wing of the Democratic party, announces: "Whoever says that I am not a Reformer, I'll lam him." *Harper's Weekly*, July 29, 1876.

George Bliss, United States Attorney for the Southern District of New York, thought he had Tilden. Bliss had information that in 1869, for which year Tilden paid income taxes on only $17,000, he had received a fee of nearly three times that amount—$50,000—from a railroad. Bliss was denied permission to examine the books of the road, and Tilden escaped indictment. Tilden ignored every accusation save his purported clandestine compact with southern leaders to pay the Confederate claims which ran well above $2,500,000,000. In a letter to Abram S. Hewitt, his campaign manager, and successor to Schell as chairman of the Democratic National Committee, Tilden wrote: "... No rebel debt will be assumed or paid. No claim for the loss of any slave will be allowed. No claim for any loss of damage incurred by disloyal persons in the late war ... will be recognized or paid...."

Tilden's managers were not alarmed by the charges. The trend of sentiment was reflected in the preponderant numbers at Democratic meetings and in the relative size of the rival torch-light processions. Moreover, there was a religious fervor to all large assemblages of Democrats, whether marching thousands with bobbing petroleum flares or mass-gatherings in armories and halls, in open fields and public parks, for all sang campaign songs set to familiar music. The favorite, to the tune of an ever popular hymn, had for the opening stanza:

> *Ho! Reformers, see the signal*
> *Waving in the sky;*
> *Reinforcements now appearing,*
> *Victory is nigh.*

The chorus ran:

> *Hold the fort, for we are coming,*
> *Hear the people cry;*
> *Wave the answer back with fervor,*
> *By your help we'll try.*

The extraordinary success of this song was due to its truthful recital of the campaign issues and to the fact that

"Tammany Reformer—'This 'ere ain't no ordinary political issue, this ain't! What we need is reform, and we're a-goin' to have it, if we kick every black Republican out of office.'" Drawing by A. B. Frost. *Harper's Weekly*, August 26, 1876.

revival meetings had made the stirring original a household hymn. Two stanzas follow:

> *See corruption boldly stalking,*
> *In our Congress Hall,*
> *In our presidential mansion,*
> *Tainting great and small.*

> *See the host of office-holders,*
> *Honest be they can't,*
> *For if honest, faithful, worthy,*
> *They're turned out by Grant.*

The song is preserved in a dime phamphlet entitled, "The Tilden Illustrated Campaign Song and Joke Book." One of the jokes read: "That explains where my clothes-line went to!" exclaimed an Iowa woman when she heard there was a Republican meeting in town.

Republican writers and orators emphasized Tilden's wealth and described the Democratic campaign fund as Tilden's Barrel, or Uncle Sammy's Barrel. They had real fears of the barrel's influence in northern cities where elections are frequently carried by the side with the most money. They were equally apprehensive of a solid southern vote through the open intimidation of the remaining carpetbagger-Negro régimes. "The shotgun policy South, the barrel policy North," was a Republican epitome of the Democratic strategy. The Democrats needed only New York, New Jersey, Connecticut, and the Solid South, to win, as Dorsheimer had reminded the St. Louis convention in seconding Tilden's nomination. The three northern states were conceded to Tilden, and only the most sanguine adherent of Hayes doubted the fulfilment of the Democratic prediction of a Solid South. But the Republican machine was not surrendering the little hold it still had on the South without a struggle. The Republicans could boast the most unscrupulous machines in the country in the three southern states where they still clung tenaciously with the aid of bribery, corruption, and violence. Both sides looked to the South to decide the issue. Neither side asked for quarter from the outset of this unprecedented campaign, in which no holds were barred. The Republicans seemingly had no new strategy. The Democrats had. They asked for the South's undivided suffrage for Tilden not because of his achievements or professions, but because he was a Democrat. It was a new note in politics, this plea for a Solid South.

43

THE SOLID SOUTH—HOW IT WAS MADE

THE SOUTH HAS KNOWN TWO EMANCIPATIONS. THE FIRST freed the blacks. The second liberated the whites. The world has forgotten the second which was accomplished through another revolt of southern whites, this time against the carpetbagger-Negro tyranny imposed on them by the Radical spoilsmen who took over the Republican party after the assassination of Lincoln. One of the last measures to bear his signature created the Bureau of Refugees, Freedmen, and Abandoned Lands—the Freedmen's Bureau.

The major functions of the bureau were to relieve distress in the war-devastated regions, regulate the labor of Negroes, administer justice among them, establish Negro schools, and manage abandoned and confiscated property. As this work could be completed within a year, the life of the bureau was restricted accordingly.

The bureau was scarcely organized when the spoilsmen saw its possibilities as a political machine. They had little in the shape of an organization in the South outside of the Union or Loyal Leagues, into which old-line Whigs and other opponents of secession gravitated during the war. But these groups were too conscientious to be of use. The Freedmen's Bureaus was the thing; how to extend its life into the next presidential campaign was the spoilsmen's problem.

The problem was resolved by southern legislatures, in their first post-bellum sessions, by replacing the old black codes with laws designed to meet the unparalleled conditions created by some four million ex-slaves enjoying a freedom as strange to them as the alphabet. Elder statesmen warned against these codes or any other measures likely to enrage northern sentiment. Texas alone heeded this sage counsel. The readmission of the eleven seceding states to the Union, and other momentous questions affecting southern welfare, were being discussed quietly in the North. But the black codes touched off the big guns, editorial and oratorical, and the South was accused of seeking to reëstablish slavery by statute. While the objectionable features of these codes were eliminated or modified within a year, the evil had been done.

With the black codes as an excuse the Radical, or Republican, spoilsmen passed a bill extending the bureau's life two years and broadening its scope. Johnson vetoed it. The House overrode the veto with the requisite two-thirds, but it lacked the needed votes in the Senate. Five months later, in July, 1866, with Congress and the President in open conflict, the bill was again sent to Johnson. In his second veto message, Johnson said the Freedmen's Bureau had become a political machine. This time both houses overrode the veto. With the Freedmen's Bureau good for another two years, the spoilsmen planned to make the South solid for the Republicans.

The advent of Negro suffrage in 1867 made this possible. The machine annexed this new vote through agents of the Freedmen's Bureau and their sinister oath-bound solidarity of ex-slaves, which had been fashioned out of the remnants of the Union, or Loyal, Leagues. The only white men in these revived Loyal Leagues were carpetbaggers and an occasional scalawag. More than seven hundred thousand ex-slaves were entitled to vote; and these, plus the carpetbaggers, could outvote southern whites, for one reconstruction act disenfranchised Confederate soldiers and all civilians who sided with the Confederacy. Ignorant blacks, to whom marriage was practically unknown, could vote, while the finest products of southern civilization were denied the ballot.

Besides the Freedmen's Bureau and the Loyal Leagues, the carpetbaggers had another formidable ally—the Negro militia. These soldiers terrorized members of their own race who refused to vote the Republican ticket, and forced unwilling blacks into the Loyal League lodges where they were taught that the government would give each Negro a mule and forty acres of land.

The lodges were held in lonely cabins and abandoned buildings. The blindfolded candidate was led into the incense-laden lodge, his conductor making the required responses to the various officers of the lodge. At a rude altar where a bowl of myrrh and alcohol flared, the candidate swore to obey all orders of the league under pain of receiving up to one hundred lashes on the bare back for a minor infraction, and death for revealing any password, grip, or other league secret. He also swore never to vote for a Democrat lest he be enslaved anew. Death to an unworthy Loyal Leaguer would be by bullets in his back, fired by a lodge member secretly appointed for the grim task. After assuming the obligation, the blindfold was removed from the candidate, who was then invested with the grips and passwords. Each Loyal Leaguer fixed his own dues, usually ten cents per month.

The presiding officer of the lodge was invariably a Freedmen's Bureau agent. The bureau was the sole judge in disputes between the ex-slaves and their former masters, and as it was to the interest of the bureau chiefs to stir up racial antagonism, and to impress the blacks with the helpless position of the southern whites, many judgments were rendered accordingly. Two white men accused of striking freedmen were strung up by the thumbs. White housewives charged with rudeness to black servants were fined five to ten dollars. These were typical.

The bureau heads had a simple method of filling their pockets. They induced freedmen to prefer fictitious claims against white employers; when such a case came before them they acquitted the accused for a price. If the graft was not forthcoming, a fine would be imposed, and if it were not paid, cotton would be seized and sold to irresponsible persons who made a pitiably small return, as decided in advance by the one-man judge and jury. But he always collected the fine.

Southern sentiment toward the bureau was voiced in this Mississippian outburst:

> *Breathes there the man, with soul so dead,*
> *Who never to himself hath said,*
> *God—— d——— the Freedmen's Bureau.*

This variation of Scott adorned the masthead of the Panola *Star*.

The Freedmen's Bureau was widely supported in the beginning by northern sentiment, but only fanatics and spoilsmen ever approved the use of the black troops, whose presence inspired a constant fear of a Negro uprising. At the close of the war, while still in command of the Army, Grant warned Congress against them. Said he:

The presence of black troops, lately slaves, demoralizes labor, both by their advice and by furnishing in their camps a resort for the freedmen for long distances around. White troops generally excite no opposition, and therefore a smaller number of them can maintain order. Colored troops must be kept in bodies sufficient to defend themselves. It is not the thinking men who would use violence toward any class of troops sent among them by the general government, but the ignorant in some places might; and the late slave seems to be imbued with the idea that the property of his late master should belong to him, or at least should have no protection from the colored soldier.

Grant ended his warning with this prophecy:

"There is danger of a collision being brought on by such causes."

Unfortunately, Grant forgot all this when he became President. Had he remembered, there would have been little or no bloodshed.

All during the decade that followed Grant's warning against using colored troops, these soldiers and all others of their race in the South were systematically taught by the carpetbaggers that the land of their former masters, and all the appurtenances thereon, were rightfully theirs. Another lesson drilled into them was hatred of their former owners, and this found expression in every form, from insolence to murder. Political meetings of whites were frequently disrupted; ostracism, torture, and death, were meted out to freedmen who voted the Democratic ticket.

None of these offenses went unpunished, for the oath-bound blacks had more than their match in the Ku Klux Klan and its lesser known counterparts, the Pale Faces, Knights of the White Camellia, Red Strings, White Leagues, Knights of the Black Cross, Heroes of America, Robinson Clubs, and numerous others. Each club, lodge, and den had its kangaroo court. The rituals of these organizations varied, but all were portentous of the grim nature of their work, as witness the method whereby members of the Robinson Clubs made themselves known to one another:

"Do you know Robinson?"

"Which Robinson?"

"Squire Robinson."

"Where did you meet him?"

"In the lodge room."

"What did he say?"

"Mississippi Ku Klux in the disguises in which they were captured. From a photograph." So reads the caption on this drawing by S. Fox in *Harper's Weekly*, January 27, 1872.

"Death."

"Unto whom?"

"Tyrants."

In carrying out the death penalty, members of allied groups from distant parts of the country were used; as a further precautionary measure, the executioners were usually unknown to one another. By 1870 these desperate night-riders had terrorized so many counties that outrages began to wane, and slowly the whites began to make themselves potent politically.

But it was an uphill fight, for deeply rooted in the freedman was a new-born sense of supremacy, especially in the black counties, where their race held nearly every office. Intelligent Negroes, whose prominence assured them immunity from harm, told their people they had been plunged into a new bondage, and that all of them, including the highest ranking Negro office-holders, were slaves of the carpetbaggers. This truth was first given public utterance in 1875. The Negro cleric, J. G. Johnson, appealed to his people in Mississippi newspapers to unite with the whites to "redeem" the state from "the despoilers of our common country." Another Mississippi Negro divine, Hiram H. Revels, the first of his race to sit in the United States Senate, astonished many abolitionist friends who had financed his educational work in the North before the war by making a like plea. Revels made this plea when the nation knew that the whites of his own state planned to carry the election by every conceivable form of fraud and intimidation as the only way to redeem the commonwealth from barbarism and corruption.

The 1875 elections redeemed all the southern states but three—Florida, South Carolina, and Louisiana. Democrats controlled the lower branch of the legislature in Louisiana. Many Negro leaders lent a hand in bringing this about. All were loyal Republicans, like the most outspoken northern critics of the pseudo-Republican régimes of the South. The most aggressively critical were Reid and other editors of leading Republican dailies. These journalists and their intelligent black southern partizans knew that the return of white supremacy would probably result in the election of a Democratic president. But there are times when decent people put country above party.

Two years before the presidential election of 1876, the Republican New York *Times* sent a staff correspondent to Alabama. He reported that "murderers and other criminals" were candidates on the Republican ticket, and that many Republican office-holders were "thieves and scoundrels." "A plain unvarnished statement of the frauds committed by such men would fill volumes," he added. This could have been said truthfully of any southern state. The reporter visited Montgomery, and was escorted to "a dark room over a saloon," by Mark D. Brainard, secretary of the Alabama Republican State Committee. Brainard was a carpetbagger from New York. Brainard kicked on a door. A Negro appeared and inquired:

"What is the ge'men goin' to drink?"

Brainard ordered champagne. The reporter said he preferred lager. Brainard then changed his order to a whiskey toddy. As they drank, Brainard offered to obtain railroad passes, saying:

"No way to travel—paying your own expenses."

The reporter declined the gratuity. Brainard thought he understood. So he talked at first of a little bribe, "a hundred or two." When this was spurned, Brainard was sure he could "fix things up."

A bribe was the most natural thing for a carpetbagger to suggest. Money came easily to them. They sold privileges and stole public funds. Their thefts became so enormous that they had to raise tax rates to a point approaching confiscation or else stop thieving, which they had no intention of doing. There was not a southern state where the extortionate rates did not often result in land and homes being sold for taxes; frequently the proceeds of these sales were stolen. No state was more beset than Mississippi.

In 1874 the state tax rate in Mississippi was 14 mills, a fourteenfold increase in five years of carpetbagger-Negro rule. A piece of property on which the state tax had been

$100 in 1869 was $1,400 in 1874. There were local taxes as well. A property owner in Vicksburg, the seat of Warren County, who was assessed $1,400 by the state, paid another $1,400 in county taxes and $2,150 in city taxes, the local rates being 14 and 21½ mills respectively. There was also a madly mounting debt and a constantly increasing host of Negro office-holders. The combined debt of the county and city in 1869 was $13,000, which had multiplied more than a hundredfold in five years. The city debt of Vicksburg in 1874 was $1,400,000. Warren was one of the black counties where Negroes drew the color line. They put a taboo on white men in public office. Although whites paid 99 per cent of Warren's taxes, Negroes assessed and collected taxes and spent and stole the proceds. All but one of the supervisors were blacks, and there were only two other white office-holders in the county before the Vicksburg municipal election in August of 1874.

After this municipal election, a grand jury composed of ten Negroes and seven whites returned indictments against some public plunderers, Negroes all, including T. W. Cardoza, state superintendent of education, the former clerk of the chancery court. Cardoza was the second-highest ranking black in the state, being topped only by the droll Alexander K. Davis, lieutenant-governor. It was unthinkable that the heads of the local Negro spoils machine should go to jail. And so the boys—black boys this time—put their heads together, and the evidence upon which the indictments had been found vanished from the offices of the sheriff and the clerk of the chancery court, two other cogs in the machine. When the theft of the evidence became known, the taxpayers met and adopted resolutions charging the clerk and the sheriff with this crime and with "stealing and plundering our substance" and demanding their resignations. The clerk of the court of chancery fled to parts unknown. The illiterate sheriff, Peter Crosby, was loathe to resign, for he received about $20,000 annually in fees. In addition, he was the chief tax collector, a source of rich graft. Even more profitable was the Court-House Ring which sold justice for whatever it would bring. Crosby was its boss. But a visit of five hundred irate whites created a change of heart, and he laboriously scrawled his name to his resignation. All this happened without violence, and again the nation was indebted to Mississippi for a grim laugh.

During the summer and early fall, the merriment was at the expense of Governor Adelbert Ames, a carpetbagger who left the affairs of state to the Negro lieutenant-governor while he went north. In his first few weeks as acting governor, Davis dismissed all employees in the capitol beholden to Ames to make places for his own cronies. He voided the governor's judicial appointments and installed his own followers on the bench. He established a profitable pardon-mill. Upon his return, Ames dismissed all the Davis appointees and reinstated his own men. When Ames took his fall trip, Davis let the jobs alone, but reëstablished his pardon-mill, opened a few county and state jails, and again turned loose criminals awaiting trial. What Davis obtained for his sixty-nine pardons is unknown, but he could not hide $800 he took to pardon a convicted murderer. Ames might have uncovered this corruption of his lieutenant-governor, but he did not. He was not an illiterate freedman, but a West Pointer who rose from first lieutenant to brigadier-general during the war in which he displayed more than ordinary heroism. But carpetbag politics and the love of power had dulled his finer sensibilities. No one ever accused Ames of personal corruption; but the Mississippi legislature solemnly charged that he pardoned a man serving a life sentence for rape. Two friends of Ames who had interceded for this felon collected $3,000.

Ames had returned from his second holiday when Crosby resigned his shrievalty. Ames sent him word he was still sheriff and to call out a posse comitatus. An inflammatory handbill, bearing Crosby's name, was circulated among the blacks, and hundreds of armed Negroes, on foot and on horseback, descended upon Vicksburg from three roads on December 6. One invading force took up positions in the old intrenchments outside the city. Vicksburg was prepared. Its two companies of citizen-soldiers included all able-bodied veterans in the city, Union and Confederate. Although greatly outnumbered, the whites routed the Negro troops after two hours of fighting. Twenty-nine blacks and two whites were killed. Of the scores wounded, nearly all were Negroes, as was usual in these racial conflicts.

Ames vainly appealed for Federal troops, and his carpetbagger legislature supported his appeal. Grant contented himself with a proclamation commanding all "disorderly and turbulent persons" to disperse.

Grant's refusal to send Federal troops was a new note, in consonance with the national protest recorded in the congressional elections of the preceding month against the misuse of Federal troops and other blunders, and, worse, of his administration.

Outside of the congressional contests, the Mississippi canvass was confined to local elections. Here, as elsewhere in the South, the whites in this campaign announced their determination to replace carpetbaggers and ignorant blacks with intelligent southern whites by all means short of actual violence, and were fairly successful. In Columbus, Mississippi, they published a card promising all Negroes who voted with them protection "in every sense of the term," and warned that freedmen who voted Republican would "vote the bread and meat out of the mouths of their wives and children." Then occurred this frank avowal: "You have driven the white man to the verge of ruin, and he has determined to draw the color line; if you can stand it, he can."

In Louisiana, where the lower branch of the state legislature was chosen in this canvass, this type of campaigning resulted in the election of a Conservative, or Democratic, majority of twenty-nine. The victory was stolen by the Republicans through the crooked returning board which rejected the actual count from many polling-places on charges that violence had prevented a fair election. There had been no violence.

Louisiana shared with Mississippi and Alabama the tragic distinction of having suffered most from the barbarism and corruption of carpetbagger-Negro régimes. But the people had no intention of letting this latest election theft go unchallenged, and the nation was with them. Moreover, the Democrats would control the lower house of Congress after March 3, and Louisiana did not fear a repetition of the usurpations that followed the 1872 election when Grant recognized the Republican ticket headed by William P. Kellogg, carpetbagger, one of the two pretenders to the governorship. The other was John McEnery, who had been elected—as honestly as any man could be in the ever crooked Louisiana canvasses—by a fusion of Democrats, Liberal Republicans, and Independents. The rival gubernatorial claimants were duly inaugurated, and each side saw its own legislature installed and organized. Each side also had its own state militia, the McEnery forces far outnumbering the Kellogg armed guard. A Federal circuit judge illegally held that Kellogg was elected. At the solicitation of local Republican bosses, including J. F. Casey, Grant's brother-in-law, the President sent Federal troops to protect the Kellogg government. Members of the McEnery legislature were arrested, and the people had their choice of fighting Federal troops or submitting to the Kellogg administration. They submitted. Congress saw the shame of the situation and proposed a new election. But there was no legal warrant for this, and Kellogg and his followers continued as the de facto government. In many sections the Kellogg administration was not accepted peacefully, riots ensued, and at Colfax, about seventy were slain, of whom only two were whites. Occasionally a few were killed in other parts of the state, Republicans as a rule. But these minor riots had become commonplace during reconstruction, and attracted little attention.

During the 1874 campaign, D. B. Penn, chosen lieutenant-governor on the McEnery ticket, issued a proclamation calling upon the McEnery militia to arm and drive the usurpers from the state capital. More than ten thousand troops responded. With Penn at their head, they captured the state-house in New Orleans along with the city hall after a battle in which more than twenty were slain, chiefly the defending policemen. On September 17, after holding the public buildings three days, the McEnery militia peacefully surrendered them to Federal troops, and then marched away unmolested.

The McEnery government gained control of the state house of representatives in the November election. But in six weeks the magic of the Republican returning board transformed the Democratic majority of twenty-nine into a Republican majority of three, with five seats doubtful. In some instances, decent Republicans who had been defeated refused to accept the fraudulent certificates of election.

On January 4, 1875, the Louisiana Democrats nullified the Republican election theft by a legislative coup. Within a few hours, however, despatches to the nation's leading newspapers read that "a legislative body, peacefully assembled, has been broken into and dispersed by the Federal troops acting under orders from the President of the United States."

This description of Grant's second legislative purge is from the call for a protest meeting in Cooper Union signed by William Cullen Bryant, Whitelaw Reid, and other distinguished New Yorkers.

Nothing in all of Grant's stormy eight years created more resentment or greater excitement than this blow at the very foundation of our republican form of government. All the murderous riots of reconstruction rolled in one could not have provoked a louder popular uproar.

It should be remembered that a legislature, or either branch thereof, is a judge of its own acts, and that these acts are not reviewable or punishable outside of the chamber of origin. No one may enter the floor of a legislature while it is in session except its members, employees, and designated representatives of the press—save by express invitation. Nor should it be forgotten that the most jealously guarded right of a legislative body is its exclusive jurisdiction over its membership.

Yet all these rights and privileges were violated by Federal troops under color of an order from the de facto governor. The Democrats had prepared for everything but the purge.

The Louisiana house was convened at 12:45 P.M. When the roll-call started there were present fifty Democrats, or Conservatives, forty-two Republicans, or Radicals, and about twenty claimants of seats. The house could organize with fifty-six members, a quorum. As the names were being called drum-beats echoed ominously in the chambers. Encamped within easy call, at the custom-house and on the levee, were the Thirteenth Infantry, four companies of the Third Infantry, Troop H of the Seventh Cavalry, and Company L of the First Artillery. At the conclusion of the roll-call, after fifty Democrats and fifty-two of the fifty-three Republicans certified by the crooked returning board had answered, a

Democrat nominated Lewis A. Wiltz, later governor, for
temporary speaker. Wiltz was declared elected amid noisy
protests. He ascended the rostrum, took the oath of office,
and then swore in the five Democratic claimants to the seats
declared doubtful by the Republican returning board. This
gave the Democrats a majority of three and they now nominated Wiltz for permanent speaker. The opposition entered
Michael Hahn, Federal governor of New Orleans and vicinity in 1864 when the rest of the state was held by the Confederates. It was to Hahn that Lincoln wrote that "some of
the colored people" be given the vote—"the very intelligent"
—and those who had fought in the Union ranks. The vote
for speaker stood: Wiltz, 55; Hahn, 2; blank, 1. Most of the
Republicans had refrained from voting. But two more than
the required quorum had voted, and neither Wiltz's election
nor the seating of Democrats in the doubtful seats could be
challenged outside of the chamber.

Before the Republicans recovered from their astonishment
at the next move, Wiltz had appointed sergeants-at-arms
and assistants who suddenly emerged from the crowd of
spectators wearing their badges of office. The Republicans
took alarm, for these men were officers of the oath-bound
White League, the Louisiana counterpart of the Ku Klux.
Wiltz instantly ordered a close call of the house. Under a
close call no member may leave the chamber without express permission from the presiding officer. At least a score
of terrified Republicans rushed precipitately for the doors,
drawing pistols, revolvers, knives, or whatever weapons they
possessed. The sergeants-at-arms and their assistants drew
murderous navy six-shooters, but these men were cool-
headed, and had been chosen because they were immune to
panic. Their commanding voices alone prevented bloodshed.
After a little scuffling at the doors, the Democrats were alone
in the chamber.

Some three hours later, Brigadier-General Philippe Régis de Trobiand invaded the hall of representatives at the head of thirty Federal soldiers with fixed bayonets. This was a violation of legislative sanctity. He stationed the infantrymen at the rear of the chamber, and strode to the speaker's rostrum, a further affront to the house. He committed a third offense when he began speaking, and asked that two documents which he presented to Wiltz be read to the house. Wiltz spurned them. One of Kellogg's adherents read them aloud. This done, de Trobiand ordered Wiltz to retire from the speaker's desk, and commanded the five Democrats he had duly sworn in as members of the house to leave the chamber.

Wiltz answered that the United States troops could not legally remove him from the rostrum, but could remove him only by force. He ordered the five Democrats not to leave except at the point of a bayonet. Presently the chamber rang with military commands and the tramp of marching soldiers. Two soldiers, with fixed bayonets, took up their positions beside the chairs of the Democrats marked for the purge. The commanding officer marched to the seat of the venerable Thomas Vaughn, whose head of silver hair made him the most conspicuous figure in the chamber. De Trobiand was speaking so softly, as he placed his hand on the old legislator, that he could not be heard a foot away. De Trobiand removed his hand as he finished his muted speech, and Vaughn arose and said to the house:

"A general of the United States Army has placed his hand on my shoulder and commanded me to leave the floor of this house. As a member of this body, duly elected by the people of Caddo Parish, and as an American citizen believing that the rights of American freemen are not yet all dead, I desire to enter my solemn protest against this outrage."

Then the representative of a sovereign people was summarily marched out of the chamber flanked by soldiers with fixed bayonets.

This was repeated with the other four Democrats on the floor. Then it came Wiltz's turn to be forced from the rostrum at bayonet's point.

The Silver-Haired Thomas Vaughn protests his expulsion by Federal soldiers from the Louisiana Hall of Representatives in one of Grant's legislative purges. *Leslie's Weekly,* January 23, 1875.

All else was forgotten while an angry Congress debated the purge. The Democratic Senators forced through a resolution calling upon Grant for all information in his possession. The Republicans tagged on a face-saving rider in which Grant was asked if there was an armed organization hostile to the Kellogg government and determined to overthrow it by force.

Grant admitted that the interference of the military was "perhaps a debatable question," and that a purge was "repugnant to our ideas of government." But these admissions were lost in a welter of self-serving, partizan truths and half-truths, from which emerged a defense of his recognition of the Kellogg government two years before. With respect to whether Kellogg or McEnery was elected, Grant said:

"It has been bitterly and persistently alleged that Kellogg was not elected. Whether he was or not is not altogether certain, nor is it any more certain that his competitor, McEnery, was chosen. The election was a gigantic fraud, and there are no reliable returns of its result. Kellogg obtained possession of the office, and in my opinion has more right to it than his competitor."

Grant held this opinion, absurd on its face, because Casey *et alii* had wheedled him into accepting it when they induced him to recognize Kellogg.

Also in Grant's message occurs this provocative paragraph, designed partly to lure back the Republicans and independents who had deserted the party in the preceding November, and partly to befog the issue:

"To say that the murder of a Negro or a white Republican is not considered a crime in Louisiana would probably be unjust to a great part of the people, but it is true that a great number of such murders have been committed and no one has been punished therefor."

Grant also made much of another circumstance, equally unrelated to the purge—the publication in leading journals of the Democratic threat to carry the election "at all hazards." He quoted advertisements from Shreveport newspapers, wherein leading citizens announced they would not employ supporters of the Radical ticket or "advance any supplies or money to any planter who will give employment or rent land to laborers who vote the Radical ticket."

Grant's message satisfied no one outside of the spoils machine directorate. The Republican investigators sent to Louisiana by Congress found that the election had been fair and peaceful, and branded the acts of the returning board in upsetting the election as arbitrary, unjust, and illegal.

Under an extralegal pact, formulated by Representative Wheeler, whom we left after his nomination as Hayes's running mate, the Democrats were returned to control of the house. Wheeler's ingenious plan provided that rivals for disputed seats should submit their claims to a congressional committee and abide by its decision: they were to do this voluntarily and as private individuals. The Democrats, upon being restored to power, were not to attempt an impeachment of Kellogg or any other Republican office-holder. On the theory that half a loaf is better than no bread, the Democrats readily assented, for their control of one branch of the legislature would check public plundering and extortionate taxation.

This settlement, reached on April 14, 1875, sprang from the Liberal Republican campaign when Greeley and his valiant crusaders pleaded for a real end to the Civil War, a plea now echoed in countless northern journals and pulpits, once bitterly hostile to the South.

This northern sentiment was the South's greatest moral asset, and the major problem of its Democratic chiefs was to restrain the poor whites from organized violence in the forthcoming fall elections, lest this asset be impaired. No one expected the campaign to be waged without bloodshed, for too many ferments agitated the masses, black and white.

Nowhere was the problem more acute than in Mississippi. On the day of de Trobiand's purge, Mississippi taxpayers held a state convention and covenanted to refuse to pay taxes until assessments were lowered; they further agreed to restore white supremacy, by force of arms if need be. They had tried everything short of violence in the preceding election, but without the desired result. Armed taxpayers' leagues were formed in all seventy-four counties to carry out this program of desperation, with the result that half the adult male population of the state was under arms.

This all-powerful taxpayers' movement compelled the Democratic State Committee to take a similar, if somewhat milder, stand. The committee adopted a resolution binding all employers to dismiss one-third of their workers if the carpetbagger-Negro candidates triumphed at the polls. Other measures, in keeping with the revolt of the taxpayers, were secretly adopted.

This program, which was called the Mississippi plan, became the pattern of all campaigns in 1875 where the overthrow of carpetbagger-Negro régimes was the primal objective. Lincoln's "very intelligent" Negroes approved it, although one feature called for converting the Negro masses to the Democratic cause by argument if possible, by intimidation or trickery where necessary. Counterfeit ballots were printed for Negroes who insisted on voting Republican, and who could not be kept from the polls in the preponderantly black counties. These ballots bore the names of Democratic candidates under the word Republican. While it was the rare freedman who could read and write, all had been taught to recognize two words, Democrat and Republican. Once they could make this distinction, the ex-slaves were regarded as educated by the average carpetbagger who went south to rescue them from semibarbarism. A third feature of the Mississippi plan called for stuffing ballot-boxes in the black counties.

There was an ostentatious display and use of firearms throughout the campaign; anvils, cannon, and shotguns

were fired to herald a meeting of whites, and election eve
was noisier than any Fourth of July celebration ever held.

The Mississippi campaign was not as one-sided as some
Democrats would have wished, for the resourceful Alexander Warner, the Republican State Chairman, refused to be
intimidated. A few who were apprehensive of the result
because of Warner's tactics decided to assassinate him. The
Democratic State Chairman was James Z. George, jurist
and statesman, and a hero of the Mexican and Civil Wars.
George fortunately heard of the plot against Warner and
telegraphed trusted aides to "see by all means that he is not
harmed." George was rewarded for his work in the campaign with a seat in the United States Senate.

Few state campaigns in the South have been better
financed, for the almost impoverished Mississippians contributed unstintingly. They chartered special trains, hired
detectives to watch Negro leaders and carpetbagger chiefs,
engaged bands for meetings and parades, depleted the
stocks of flags and bunting, and kept printing-presses busy.

The Mississippi plan emphasized the importance of Negro
meetings. These were addressed by "very intelligent" blacks
and noted whites. One of the most popular and picturesque
Mississipians was General Reuben Davis, who could command a crowd anywhere. He began his career as a physician,
but gave up medicine for the law. Back in 1842 he had been
on the High Court of Appeals, but had resigned after four
months, unable to stand the quiet of the bench any longer.
He was a colonel in the Mexican War, and a brigadier-general in the Civil War. He surrendered a seat in Congress to
follow the Stars and Bars. Speaking before a Negro meeting
in Blackwell's Chapel, after an excellent dinner, Davis said:

Colored men and fellow citizens ... I understand the Democratic state committee has recommended to the planters to turn
off one-third of the laborers unless they vote the Democratic

ticket. . . . I understand you to say you don't give a damn whether they turn you off or not and that you will never vote the Democratic ticket. . . . Who are your best friends, colored men? The white people of the South are your best friends. The damn Yankees took their ships and brought your ancestors to this country and sold them to the southern people. . . . Colored men, do you think the white people are a set of fools to feed and clothe you and then let you vote for the damn carpetbaggers?

After Davis shouted the last rhetorical question, a deaf freedman in the front row, a loyal Democrat, filled in the ensuing pause with a fervent, "Yes, sir!"

Davis reached for his navy six-shooter, but did not draw because a white on the platform explained the Negro's infirmity and his good intentions. A little later the general took umbrage at a question and drew his revolver. This ended the meeting, for most of his audience vanished through the windows.

In Clay County, some young wags forced J. W. Caradine, a Negro representative, to accompany them in a buggy to several Negro rallies where this unflinching Republican lawmaker urged his astonished audience to vote for Democratic candidates, including his own opponent. Not to be outdone in clownish canvassing, Democratic blades in near-by Grenada County kidnapped William Price, a carpetbagger senator, and had him spout at Negro meetings in behalf of Democratic victory.

Burlesque gave way to tragedy at a colored meeting in Yazoo City, where the carpetbagger sheriff, A. T. Morgan, fled for his life after three Negroes and one white man were slain in an exchange of pistol shots. Here the aggressors were Democrats, and only the poor light of a kerosene lamp and a few small tallow dips saved Morgan from death. When he reached the capital, Ames urged him to return, offering him an escort of three hundred Negro troops. Ames knew the white citizen cavalry patrolling the highways would wipe out any force that might accompany Morgan. Ames was accused of trying to incite civil war, and Mississippi papers reprinted from the Mobile (Ala.) *Register* that "if the tocsin of war is sounded by Ames, he will find men, money, and arms trooping across the border." He also knew that every county in the state was ready to assist the Yazoo whites. Morgan declined the martyr's rôle.

Ames was not stupid. He knew a race war would lead to the occupation of the state by Federal troops, whose presence at the polls could alone prevent a rout of his carpet-bagger-Negro candidates.

On September 4, three days after the Yazoo City affair, a sanguinary race conflict at Clinton gave Ames another opportunity to appeal for Federal troops. This clash occurred at an open-air debate between W. Calvin Wells, later a judge, and H. T. Fisher, carpetbagger editor of the Jackson *Pilot*, before an audience of about seventy-five whites and twelve hundred Negroes. For hours before the meeting, more than one thousand mounted Negroes, all armed, paraded the streets of the little college town. Most of the riders were grotesquely garbed, and their horses were extravagantly beribboned in red, white, and blue. At the head of the column rode an elder of a Negro chapel from near-by Edwards, his stovepipe hat surmounted by a black ostrich plume. He was modestly armed with a cavalry saber which dangled from his waist. Negroes later told Wells that the Loyal Leagues throughout Hinds County had ordered them to go to Clinton prepared for a fight. This runs counter to the grand jury presentment which described the riot as unpremeditated. There is also conflicting testimony as to whether a white or a black fired the first shot. The fact is that a Negro policeman shot a young white man, who killed his assailant with a ball in the temple. Thereafter the firing became general. Within the next two or three minutes one Negro was killed and five wounded; three whites were shot, one knifed and his head beaten "to a jelly." Another white man was killed a quarter of a mile from the barbecue ground, and one was slain in his own yard. Wells himself was shot through the hand. The Negro policeman's slayer, fleeing from the scene, was overtaken and disemboweled, and a finger severed for its gold ring.

Shortly after the first exchange of shots, the Negroes broke. Their leaders rallied them as snare-drums beat a sustained roll. The Negroes now divided themselves into bands. Eleven whites, huddled together, retreated along the bank of a stream, warning the Negroes to stand back. The local state senator, Charles Caldwell, Negro Republican boss of Hinds County, had two killings to his credit long before the Clinton riot; but on this occasion he was everywhere trying to restrain his people. He saved these eleven whites from slaughter as the frenzied blacks yelled, "Kill the damned whites! Run over them! God damn them! We did not come here to let no God-damned white trash run over us! This is our day!"

During the riot, Vicksburg and other near-by communities were telegraphed for aid, and some two hundred white citizens stood guard until reinforcements arrived.

"Throughout the county, for several days, the Negro leaders, some white and some black, were hunted down and killed," said Wells.

The casualties are unknown, and the contemporary published guesses of the slain ranged from ten to fifty.

Ames seized upon the riot as an excuse for an appeal for Federal troops. But Grant refused, saying he was tired of the autumnal appeals for troops. His stand was determined by the resentment created throughout the nation by the Louisiana purge, and the sound advice of Senator James

Lusk Alcorn, head of the Republican faction opposed to Ames. Alcorn himself led a white citizen corps to repulse Negro adherents of Ames who menaced Alcorn's home town of Friars Point during the canvass. Six Negroes and two whites were slain in this conflict. Illinois-born, Alcorn had been a resident of Mississippi since 1844, and was one of many old-line Whig-Republicans who fought on the Confederate side.

Rebuffed by Grant, Ames announced he would order out the Negro militia. But the Democratic leaders outwitted Ames in this fresh threat of civil war. They called on him and said it was up to him to prevent the impending catastrophe, and told him to disband his Negro militia and let the white Democratic armed bands preserve order. Southern newspapers were hurling at the carpetbagger governor such taunts as "Murderer Ames!" There was an insurrection in the making, and Ames saw it. Abandoned by Grant, Ames had no choice but to surrender. He disbanded the Negro militia, and turned over the policing of the state to the successors of the Ku Klux Klan. And Ames, on behalf of the state, and the Democratic leaders, on behalf of the insurgents, formally signed a peace agreement on October 15. In signing this pact, Ames knew he was signing the articles of his own impeachment. The Democrats were planning to oust him from office if they carried both branches of the legislature.

Mississippi enjoyed peace until Election Day, when the customary fraud and intimidation ruled nearly every polling-place. It differed from earlier elections of reconstruction in that it was the whites, not the blacks, who systematically violated the election franchise. In some communities there were no Republican candidates because the Radical politicians either had been afraid to nominate or had been forced to withdraw their nominees. Comparatively few Negro Re-

publicans voted. Most of them had been thoroughly intimidated by the almost continuous discharge throughout the
campaign of all sorts of weapons from a single-barrel der-
ringer to a cannon; and in many places the less timid, who
ventured forth to vote, had a second thought on beholding
silent whites, many of them Union veterans, armed with
rifles, shotguns, and side-arms, patrolling the streets leading
to the polls. This silent patrol was a survival of the Ku
Klux. In Aberdeen, Monroe County's capital, a cannon, attended by four cannoneers, was trained all day long on the
polling-place. White Leaguers from Louisiana invaded Amite
County, forced the election inspectors to resign, and drove
from the state the sheriff and superintendent of education,
carpetbaggers both. This invasion alone prevented the
Republicans from carrying the county, which the Democrats put into their column by the scant majority of ninety-
four votes.

Yet with all its violence and corruption, it was a fairer
and more peaceful election than Mississippi had known
during reconstruction. Only twelve of the seventy-three
counties elected Republicans; in the lone statewide contest,
W. S. Hemmingway, Democratic candidate for treasurer,
defeated G. M. Buchanan, Republican, by 30,441 majority,
the vote standing: Hemmingway, 96,596; Buchanan, 66,155.
In this vote is seen the extent of the fraud and intimidation.
In Tishomingo County, the official tally showed only twelve
Republican votes. Yazoo and Pearl River counties did better, each reporting but seven Republican votes. The honors
of the day went to Jones County, which returned four Republican votes!

The whites carried both houses of the legislature overwhelmingly, the joint strength being 126 Democrats and 32
Republicans.

Every "very intelligent" Negro supported this movement

to restore white supremacy, and in explaining this support
to Grant, Revels wrote:

Since reconstruction, the masses of my people have been, as it
were, enslaved in mind by unprincipled adventurers who, caring
nothing for country, were willing to stoop to anything, no matter
how infamous, to secure power to themselves, and perpetuate it.
My people are naturally Republicans, but as they grow older in
freedom so do they in wisdom. A great portion of them have
learned that they were being used as mere tools, and, as in the
late election, not being able to correct the existing evil among
themselves, they determined, by casting their ballots against these
unprincipled adventurers, to overthrow them.

As soon as the new legislature convened it proceeded to
take over the entire government by impeaching the carpetbagger-Negro state officers. Ames refused to recognize the
legislature as legally constituted, saying it came into being
through a revolution. He wrote subsequently that his "impeachment is progressing and my Winchester-rifle friends
will vote me out." Davis, the Negro lieutenant-governor,
was also impeached, as was T. W. Cardoza, the colored
state superintendent of public education. Ames alone of the
three was not accused of personal corruption. The most
serious charge was that he had caused the fatal race conflict
at Vicksburg. He escaped conviction and removal by resigning on the eve of trial. The senate also permitted Cardoza
to resign. Davis brazened it out, and was found guilty on all
five articles of impeachment. Six of the ten Negro senators,
Republicans all, voted for his conviction.

The Democratic legislature demonstrated to the nation
how an honest body of lawmakers can reduce extravagant
salaries, abolish needless jobs, and eliminate waste and graft
in the maintenance of institutions and in other governmental
enterprises. These reforms reduced the cost of government

from $1,130,192 in 1875 to $547,816 in 1876. These savings were reflected in taxes.

Mississippi was redeemed. In fact, all the late Confederate states, save Florida, Louisiana, and South Carolina, were in the control of the whites in 1876, and the entire South looked to the Hayes-Tilden election to perfect the redemption, to make the South solid for the Democratic party.

44

THE SPOILS MACHINE
STEALS A PRESIDENTIAL ELECTION

THE MORNING NEWSPAPERS OF NOVEMBER 8TH, IN RECORDING the election of Tilden and Hendricks over Hayes and Wheeler on the previous day, noted Democratic victories throughout the South, with the possible exception of South Carolina and Louisiana. But the unexpected Democratic triumph in Indiana, the home of Hendricks, more than offset the loss of these two states, assuming they had gone Republican. Tilden had carried the northern states on which the Democrats had relied, New York, New Jersey, and Connecticut. A few Republican journals still hoped for a Hayes victory, but nearly all accepted the reported verdict of the polls unquestioningly. The New York *Tribune*, which loyally supported Hayes, summed up the results in the caption, "Tilden Elected." The basis of the Republican hopes was that the carpetbagger-Negro régimes controlled the election machinery of not only Louisiana and South Carolina but Florida as well. It was one thing to steal state elections, but they would not even attempt the theft of the presidency— so the people thought. And this belief became conviction when the complete returns were tabulated, showing a decisive Tilden victory in the Electoral College and in the popular vote. He had carried both Florida and Louisiana, and if we give South Carolina to Hayes, which was claimed

416

for him by a majority of 974, Tilden led Hayes by more than a quarter of a million votes. The popular vote stood:

TILDEN	.	. .	4,300,590
HAYES	.	. .	4,036,298

This majority of 264,292 was reflected in the electoral vote:

TILDEN	.	. . . .	196
HAYES	.	. . . .	173

No campaign had attracted more attention, for Tilden enjoyed a world-wide reputation. Moreover, the nation was celebrating its hundredth anniversary, and visiting European journalists had interpolated their despatches about the Centennial Exposition at Philadelphia with dramatic incidents of the canvass. Now they told of the peacefully successful revolution against the eleven long years of misrule and maladministration, of political chicanery and corruption, that followed hard on the death of Lincoln. A politically minded delegation of French workers, their expenses paid by popular subscription, took an exceptional interest in the canvass. Before embarking for America, these men had attended a meeting in the Château d'Eau, and heard Victor Hugo, from whose peroration we quote:

The future is already dawning, and it clearly belongs to democracy, which is purely pacific. Your own delegates at the Philadelphia Exposition are the dim outline of the unification of the United States of America and of the United States of Europe. Go, workingmen ... go and bear the good news; go tell the new world that the old is young. You are going ... with the torch of civilization from the land where Christ was born to the land which beheld the birth of John Brown ...

But it was not long before these workers, to whom the overthrow of a government objectionable to the majority had hitherto signified civil war, and the whole civilized world, gasped as they beheld Tilden's election nullified by the crowning crime of American machine politics—the theft of the presidency. Men talked of civil war to prevent its consummation. But fortunately the whispers of an army of 145,000 well-disciplined southern troops marching on Washington, and Watterson's published appeal for 100,000 unarmed petitioners to invade the seat of government and prevent the usurpation, ended in words. Yet the situation was sufficiently grave for Grant to increase the troops in and around Washington as a precaution against transforming the nation into another southern state with a dual government.

It was to the Second Republic and Louis Napoleon that Tilden turned to find an analogy for this crime. To understand the comparison, a summary of events, familiar to those of his day, is in order. Louis Napoleon, President of the Second Republic, becoming irked in his third year in office at the constitutional ban on a President succeeding himself at the end of the four-year term, tore up the constitution, purged the National Assembly, imprisoned some of its members, banished and killed others, massacred the people, increased the presidential term to ten years and the presidential salary to 12,000,000 francs—$2,400,000: all as a prelude to destroying the Republic and raising on its ruins the Second Empire, with himself as Emperor. Said Tilden:

The increase of power in the Federal Government during the last twenty years, the creation of a vast office-holding class, with its numerous dependents, and the growth of the means of corrupt influence, have well-nigh destroyed the balance of our complex system. . . . If this tendency is not arrested, its inevitable result will be the practical destruction of our system. . . . The experience of France under the Third Napoleon shows that, with elective forms and universal suffrage, despotism can be established and maintained.

Neither the tendency nor the evils have been checked. Both have steadily increased under successive spoils machines.

In considering the theft of the presidency, we need only examine Florida and Louisiana, with a combined electoral vote of twelve. Louisiana had eight votes, Florida, four. They would have given Hayes a majority of one electoral vote over Tilden. To pluck victory from defeat is the function of a political party. To transmute defeat into victory is the function of a spoils machine. And seeing that the twelve votes of Louisiana and Florida would put Hayes in the White House, the machine obtained them by rank perjury, wholesale bribery, and unrestrained corruption. The ever obedient carpetbagger-Negro returning boards rejected the votes of preponderantly Democratic precincts to create Republican majorities for Hayes. When it was too late to be of any practical use, S. B. McLin, chairman of the Florida returning board, confessed that Tilden had carried Florida, and that promises of Federal jobs corrupted some of the board. Money was also used where necessary. Hayes appointed McLin associate justice of New Mexico, but the Senate refused to confirm the appointment. This was the only case where the machine failed to make good its promise to a corrupt agent. By shifting the twelve votes, Tilden's 196 electoral votes were reduced to 184, and Hayes's 173 were increased to 185. Tilden had carried Florida by a slender majority of ninety-four votes; his lead in Louisiana was substantial—6,549. The frauds in these two states cut Tilden's popular majority by 12,068; but even the fraudulent Republican count gave him a lead over Hayes of more than a quarter of a million votes. The tally stood:

TILDEN	4,285,992
HAYES	4,033,768
TILDEN'S MAJORITY . .	252,224

But the majority of the lone electoral vote outweighed the popular majority.

The crime has been erroneously attributed to Zachariah Chandler because he telegraphed implied orders to steal the presidency the morning after Election Day. Chandler only set in motion the actual operations of the year-old plot. Zack, as he was known to his intimates, was the nominal head of the spoils machine by virtue of his chairmanship of the executive committee of the Republican National Committee.

The conspiracy took shape when the state elections of 1875 indicated white control of the southern states in the presidential election. It was as certain as anything can be in politics that New York, New Jersey, and Connecticut would line up with the South, thereby assuring a Democratic victory.

Such a victory could be nullified by two separate operations. The Republicans must first steal the elections in the three southern states where Federal troops kept their carpetbagger-Negro régimes in power. Then they must have the stolen votes accepted by Congress.

This last involved changing the law—the congressional rule for counting electoral votes. The Constitution merely provided that "the President of the Senate shall, in the presence of the Senate and the House of Representatives, open all the certificates and the votes shall then be counted." Congress justly provided that if the two Houses failed to agree upon a return from a state, they were to decide the dispute in joint session.

This provision was the Twenty-second Joint Rule, adopted in 1865 when the Republicans ruled the Senate and the House.

The Twenty-second Joint Rule would block the steal be-

Zachariah Chandler
From a photograph by C. A. Bell. *Harper's Weekly,* November 22, 1879.

cause the Democrats now had a majority of more than sixty votes in a joint session of Congress.

A joint rule governs the deliberations and acts of the Senate and the House on those rare occasions when they sit as a single chamber.

A joint rule had the attribute of inviolability, for, once adopted, it remained as a beacon to illumine obscure passages in our parliamentary system.

The Senate wing of the Republican machine abolished the Twenty-second Joint Rule on January 10, 1876, after an innocuous discussion of parliamentary procedure. The Democrats were caught napping. The concurrence of the Democratic-controlled House was not required, for each chamber is a judge of its own acts.

Having abolished the method of counting a disputed return, the machine provided no substitute.

They had destroyed the beacon, leaving unmarked the abyss in which anarchy lurked.

This was a minor concern. The machine had stolen elections in southern states and maintained usurpers in office by the mere presence of Federal troops. Why couldn't this be done on a national scale? The repeal of the Twenty-second Joint Rule paved the way for Chandler's telegrams eleven months later. To Daniel E. Chamberlain, carpet-bagger governor of South Carolina, he wired: "Hayes is elected if we have carried South Carolina, Florida, and Louisiana. Can you hold your state? Answer immediately."

The telegrams to Louisiana and Florida seemed equally innocent in content. None disclosed the design to buy the election canvassers in these three states. Chandler was also apprehensive of Nevada and Oregon, although both were safely in the Republican column. The Oregon telegram read: "Without Oregon Hayes defeated. Don't be defrauded. Hasten returns. Answer."

Chandler was only trying to keep the election pure: he didn't want Uncle Sammy Tilden's Barrel to tempt the Republicans. In each telegram, Chandler wrote after his name, Fifth Avenue Hotel, which was the temporary abode of himself and the Republican Campaign Committee.

Chandler sent the telegrams to Western Union by a trusty who, finding himself without money, asked that they be charged to the Republican National Committee. As the committee had no account, the receiving clerk suggested charging them to the New York *Times*. And the *Times* paid the charges.

Chandler performed his part gladly, for he believed the South unworthy of a voice in the nation's councils. He owed allegiance to two flags. One was the bloody shirt. From 1857 till his death in 1879, he represented Michigan continuously in the Senate save for his brief service in Grant's second Cabinet. He taunted southern colleagues in the Senate before and after the war. In his last important speech, which was typical of him, he shouted at the southern senators: "You are to-day as you were then [just before the outbreak of the Civil War] determined to rule or ruin this government, and you cannot do either." The South ever remained to him "a confederation of traitors."

Chandler did conceive, so far as the record discloses, the plan of sending Republican leaders from the North to South Carolina, Florida, and Louisiana, although Grant was then regarded at the author of this scheme. These were the "visiting statesmen," and Democrats aped the Republicans and sent their own watchers—who were permitted only to watch from a safe distance. The ostensible duty of the visiting Republicans was to prevent fraud; but their real purpose was to lend aid and comfort to their respective partizans in committing fraud. Nearly all the Republican "visiting statesmen" were rewarded with Cabinet places, diplomatic posts, and offices of less distinction. Nor were the small fry forgotten, places even being found on the public pay-roll for known suborners of perjury.

Republican opponents of the steal were punished. A Republican member of Congress from Florida, Representative

William J. Purman, said Tilden had carried his state. Purman had a sister employed in the Treasury Department. She was summarily discharged.

The presidency was stolen under a cloak of pseudo-legality. The Republican returning boards threw out returns from Democratic strongholds under one flimsy pretext or another, or on the perjured testimony of Negroes and carpetbaggers, many of whom admitted their crimes two years later, when they could serve only the historian. In Florida, Tilden's majority of 92 in a total vote of 48,774, was transformed into a Hayes majority of 922. In Louisiana, a Tilden majority of 6,549 votes was topsyturvied into a Hayes majority of 4,807.

Before the Electoral College met on December 6, it was known that nothing could prevent the apparent election of Hayes and Wheeler by a single vote unless a Republican elector voted for Tilden and Hendricks. Tilden supporters looked to James Russell Lowell, long known for his independence, to give them the needed vote. Lowell wrote to one of them: "In my own judgment I have no choice, and am bound in honor to vote for Hayes, as the peolpe who chose me expected me to do. They did not choose me because they had confidence in my judgment, but because they knew what that judgment would be. If I told them that I should vote for Tilden, they would never have nominated me. It is a plain question of trust." At the meeting of the Electoral College, the spurious count gave 185 votes to Hayes and 184 to Tilden.

One Hayes elector was Orlando H. Brewster, surveyor-general for the District of Louisiana, by appointment of Grant. The Constitution decrees that "no ... person holding an office of trust or profit under the United States, shall be ... an elector." Brewster was disqualified when elected, but when his vote was challenged, the "visiting statesmen" assured him he was an elector de facto. He voted. A shallow device was adopted to lend the appearance of legality to Brewster's vote. Brewster "resigned" his Federal office after the election in a letter predated November 4—three days before the election. This letter was to Grant, and did not reach Washington until November 15 or 16. On the latter date, Chandler as Secretary of the Interior wrote to Brewster's immediate superior, to "inform Mr. Brewster that his resignation has been accepted by the President to take effect November 4"—eleven or twelve days before the resignation reached Washington. On December 6, when the corruptly chosen Louisiana electors met, Brewster momentarily absented himself, thereby creating a vacancy, and was immediately thereafter chosen to succeed himself.

Another counted-in Hayes elector, A. B. Levisse, was disqualified because he was clerk of the United States Circuit Court for the District of Louisiana. He qualified as an elector through the same rigmarole. Both were "reappointed" to their Federal jobs after voting for Hayes.

The same pattern was repeated in Florida. Here the Democrats, through their candidate for governor, George F. Drew, appealed to the Supreme Court, which held the doctored count to be illegal and fraudulent, and ruled that the returning board's functions were ministerial, not judicial, and that it had no power to eliminate votes. The board bowed to the court decision and certified Drew's election. The Tilden electors proceeded against their opponents in the nature of a quo warranto, and the court adjudged the Hayes candidates for electors "mere usurpers" and the Tilden nominees the true electors. After having done everything possible in the courts to right the wrongs, the people of Florida, through their legislature, passed two measures in January, made law by Governor Drew's signature. One law prescribed a new count of the votes for electors in accordance with the Supreme Court's interpretation of the returning board's duties, and the other declared that the Tilden electors had been duly elected. This second law also directed the Tilden electors to meet, and commanded the governor to give them certificates of election pursuant to the recanvass and to forward the returns to the President of the Senate at Washington—the recipient of electoral votes. All these things were done.

On the day the fraudulent Hayes electors met in the carpetbagger-Negro states, the duly chosen Democratic electors also met and voted for Tilden and Hendricks.

When the Electoral College acted, Congress had been in session two days. Congress would have to pass on the disputed returns, but the Democrats in both houses were without a program. Before going to Washington, their leaders called on Tilden to learn what his plans were in this chaotic situation. They visited his Gramercy Park home with an ardor for his cause at fever pitch, and left it so many icebergs. They looked for leadership, and found none. They sought his confidence, but went away without it. Even Hewitt, his chief spokesman in Congress, did not have his complete confidence. No one did. The task Tilden assigned to Hewitt called for profound knowledge of practical politics, not metallurgy, Hewitt's field. Hewitt was a stranger to public life until nominated in 1875 for a seat in the House. Yet he showed Tilden one way he could force the Republicans to abandon their conspiracy to steal the presidency. This was a personal appeal to the people, followed by mass-meetings throughout the nation. Tilden disapproved the mass-meetings lest they inflame the public. He approved the appeal, but never issued it. Tilden never courted a fight. When Senator Thurman asked him if the Democrats in Congress should fight, back down, or arbitrate, Tilden answered: "Arbitrate."

The Electoral Commission, which consummated the theft, was the result of arbitration. When the Democrats were committed to it, Tilden offered belligerent opposition. He was in fighting mood at last. But he restricted his belligerence to confidential telegrams to his partizans in Congress. So far as the public was aware, he acquiesced in everything.

Tilden could not openly oppose the commission, which was the product of bipartizan conferences. He had been advised of every important move leading to its creation. No fairer mechanism could have been devised, and the composition of the commission was fairness itself. It consisted of five Senators, five Representatives, and five associate justices of the United States Supreme Court. The Congressmen, chosen by their respective houses, were divided evenly politically, five Democrats and five Republicans. The act named four of the five justices, two Democrats and two Republicans, and empowered them to choose the fifth jurist.

The selection of this jurist—the fifteenth member of the commission—increased the hair-trigger tension. Unknown to the public, a gentlemen's agreement provided for the selection of Associate Justice David Davis. He had been a Whig, a Republican, and was now an independent with Democratic leanings. Tilden and his managers regarded him as favorable to their cause. So certain was Tilden of Davis that he included him in his list of tentative Cabinet members. But seven days before Congress began counting the votes, the Illinois legislature elected Davis to the United States Senate, whereupon Davis declined the commission appointment, although its labors would be finished before he could take his Senate seat. Justice Joseph P. Bradley, Republican, was named in his stead. The commission now stood eight Republicans and seven Democrats.

Tilden's circle regarded the Davis affair as part of the Republican intrigue, and accused Senator Morton, who took the initiative in abolishing the Twenty-second Joint Rule, of eliminating Davis.

This wholly unexpected move shattered the morale of the Democratic Congressmen more than Tilden's indecision and secretiveness. Incredible stories were whispered, and the impossible happened. Southern leaders had looked to Tilden to complete the redemption of the South by driving the carpetbagger-Negro governments from South Carolina and Louisiana. With his chances diminished by the changed complexion of the commission, they were ready to listen to Republican overtures. And so we find the ablest southern Democrat in either house, Lucius Q. C. Lamar, Senator from Mississippi, actively aiding the Republicans when Tilden's cause seemed doomed. To one Louisiana Democrat who inquired if the fight for the electoral votes of the state was to be abandoned, Lamar replied: "If we should lose the national government, we may be able to save Louisiana." To another, Representative E. J. Ellis, he wrote that Stanley Matthews, Senator from Ohio, and brother-in-law of Hayes, had said Hayes would not recognize S. B. Packard, the latest carpetbagger pretender to the governorship of Louisiana, and added:

Now, Ellis, this is the first thing I have ever heard as coming from Hayes, directly or indirectly, that is worth acting upon by any southern man. We do not want offices, but we do want to get our states and our people free from the carpetbag government. Ought you not, if an available opportunity offers you to serve your state and people, to spring forward at once and see if you can't free your state? I think you should at once see Mr. Stanley Matthews and ask him if Governor Hayes will give you some assurance that he will not nominate Packard in his domination of your people.

Through Matthews and others, Hayes promised to withdraw the Federal troops and recognize only the Democratic claimants for the governorships in South Carolina and Louisiana. This would write finis to the carpetbagger-Negro reign of terror. This deal between the Republicans and the southern Democrats is understandable, for an ancient maxim cherished by politicians is that half a loaf is better than none.

The counting began at one o'clock on the afternoon of February 1 when Congress convened in joint session in the House of Representatives, with Thomas W. Ferry, of Michigan, President of the Senate, in the chair, and Samuel J. Randall, Speaker of the House, seated on his left. At the clerk's desk sat four tellers, two Senators and two Representatives, and in the galleries were the diplomatic representatives of every civilized nation. The certificates of the votes from each state, starting with Alabama, were opened and read in alphabetical order. When Florida was reached, Democrats in both houses filed objections to the certificate of the Hayes electors. Republicans immediately countered with objections to the two Tilden certificates, the second certificate being in compliance with the special law. After congressional advocates of each side had been heard, the dispute was referred to the Electoral Commission, where Charles O'Conor made the chief argument for Tilden, and William M. Evarts for Hayes.

The Republicans contended the Tilden certificates were null and void; that the certificate of a state was conclusive; that to go behind the returns would involve an investigation which would postpone indefinitely the result and lead to the anarchy which the commission was created to avert; that the commission must not hear testimony or accept evidence to prove the Democratic charge of "a fraudulent and corrupt conspiracy to cheat the State of Florida out of its rightful choice of electors."

O'Conor characterized the picture of a protracted investigation as "a raw head and bloody bones to frighten this commission and the whole country from its propriety," and "a common plea among persons who set up a falsely and fraudulenty contrived title." He argued that the power of Congress to count the votes necessarily involved the power to distinguish between true and fraudulent votes. To quote him further:

... there is no limit to the power of investigation for the purpose of reaching the ends of justice, except such as a due regard for public convenience and the interests of public justice and society at large may impose in the exercise of this discretionary authority. ... We are told that here we stand, in the second century of the Republic's existence, in such a condition that there is no possible remedy against the most palpable fraud and forgery that could be perpetrated, or against any outrageous acts in violation of the rights of the people of the respective states and of the whole nation; that Congress must sit by, blind and silent, and permit an alien to be counted into office as President of the United States; they must sit by, and permit a set of votes plainly and palpably fraudulent—votes given by individuals not only disqualified for want of having been chosen by the states, but being themselves absolutely disqualified by the Constitution from acting in the office or casting the vote—and must permit the usurpation contemplated to take place ...

After days of argument, the commission, by a strict party vote of eight Republicans to seven Democrats, decided not to go behind the returns. On the following day, February 9, again by the same party vote, the commission sanctified the fraud by deciding that the votes of the Hayes electors must be counted.

The decision shocked the Democratic leaders who had learned the night before that Bradley had written an opinion favoring Tilden and would vote to count Tilden's electoral votes. But that night Republican insiders also heard of Bradley's intention, and sent Senator Frederick T. Frelinghuysen, a member of the commission, and George M. Robeson, Secretary of the Navy, to plead with him.

There were reports of venal railroad lobbyists calling on Bradley that night, and other ugly charges were whispered. Tilden told Bigelow he could have bought a vote in the commission—which would have given him the presidency—for $200,000. When shown an anonymous letter accusing Bradley of having received $100,000 for changing his mind, he cynically observed: "$200,000 seems to be the standard price." Bradley denied the nocturnal calls of railroad lobbyists, but did not deny he had originally written an opinion favoring Tilden. Some newspapers demanded Bradley's impeachment. No suggestion exists of Bradley's corruption stronger than Tilden's implied charge recorded by Bigelow, which may be dismissed. In sending Robeson and Frelinghuysen to change Bradley's mind, the machine had selected two friends to whom Bradley was indebted. All three hailed from New Jersey; it was Frelinghuysen and Robeson who induced Grant to appoint Bradley to the Supreme Court seven years before. Bradley repaid this debt with his good name.

As expected, the Republican-controlled Senate voted to accept the decision by a party vote, and the preponderantly Democratic House, in like manner, voted to reject it. Then the two chambers reassembled in a joint session of Congress where Ferry announced that "the two houses not concurring in ordering otherwise, the decision of the commission will stand unreversed, and the counting will now proceed in conformity with the decision of the commission." The vote of Florida was then credited to Hayes and Wheeler, and the counting was resumed without incident until Louisiana was called.

The Democrats offered to prove that the final canvassing and fraudulent shifting of votes which gave Louisiana to

Hayes had been done by criminals, one under indictment for murder, another for obtaining money under false pretenses, and three for subornation of perjury. But the commission, by the same party vote of eight to seven, rejected the offer, and decided for the Hayes electors by the same partizan division.

The Tilden managers were not downcast, for Conkling planned to lead a revolt of eight or nine Republican senators who would join the Democrats and reverse the commission in the Louisiana case, thereby giving the presidency to Tilden.

The Senate voted on February 19. But at two o'clock that morning a Republican Senator told Conkling that he dared not go through with the plan lest his political and personal fortunes be ruined. What else Conkling learned has never been revealed, but in the language of George Hoadley, sometime governor of Ohio, and counsel to Tilden in the proceedings, "Conkling thereupon made up his mind that the game was lost, and took the earliest train to Baltimore . . . where he spent the day." And Hoadley, who was in a position to know, rejected as fiction the romantic story of a woman influencing Conkling. So do the facts.

Conkling had broken with the Republican machine at the St. Louis convention, and for months had been secretly advising Tilden's friends. Twelve days after the November election, J. Thomas Spriggs, sometime mayor of Utica and Conkling's neighbor, after spending an hour with him, wrote Tilden he could rely on Conkling's hearty coöperation. Conkling told Spriggs the Democrats should stand firm and take the position "that Tilden has been elected, and by the Eternal, he shall be inaugurated." Others had given like advice; but Tilden preferred to pussyfoot. In an ex post facto observation, Blaine said the Republicans would have backed down if the Democrats had stood firm.

After the Senate sustained the Louisiana decision by a strict party vote, the House vote disclosed what could have been done had there been aggressive Democratic leadership. Two Republican representatives voted to reverse the commission's decision. Their careers and background explain their bolt. Both were of Puritan heritage. One was Henry Lillie Pierce, a Free Soiler and a founder of the Republican party. A rich manufacturer, he was constantly trying to conceal many of his acts—his beneficences. A Protestant, he fought Know Nothingism, and gave of his bounty to Catholics and Protestants alike. Four years earlier, when Pierce first graced Boston's city hall, Wendell Phillips said that if Diogenes came to Boston he would find his honest man in the mayor's chair. The other was the philosopher, Julius Henry Seelye, president of Amherst College, who taught his students that the highest aspiration of which they were capable was to become Christian philosophers, Christian scholars, Christian ministers, Christian men. His life exemplified his teachings.

After the House vote, Congress met in joint session and again Ferry spoke the required formula and directed the tellers to announce the result. Whatever Ferry's knowledge of the Florida returns may have been is not known, but he did know the Louisiana certificate was fraudulent. The law provided that electors' votes be certified in triplicate, one for deposit with a United States district judge and two for delivery to the President of the Senate, one by mail and one by hand. When Thomas C. Anderson, United States deputy collector of the Port of New Orleans, handed a certifiicate to Ferry in Washington, Ferry pointed to the unlawful indorsement on the envelop. Anderson illegally opened the envelop, saw that the certificate had also been improperly indorsed, and hastily returned to New Orleans, where the electors were secretly summoned to sign a substitute certificate. Two of them could not be found and their names were forged, and Anderson arrived in Washington just within the prescribed time and gave the forged certificate to Ferry. Outside of the Louisiana conspirators, Ferry alone knew it was a forgery. Tilden's counsel took it for granted that all the certificates were in due form. None examined them; without the slightest scrutiny by any one save Ferry, the two Hayes certificates, one forged and both fraudulent, were entered as exhibits. This was only a small part of the corruption. Hewitt said later of the Louisiana electoral vote:

"The vote of that state was offered to me for money, and I declined to buy it. But the vote of that state was sold for money."

After the Louisiana vote had been counted for Hayes, no objections were raised until Oregon was called, with its two sets of certificates. One gave all three electoral votes to Hayes; the other gave two to Hayes and one to Tilden. The second was the result of fraud, and was designed to give the election to Tilden. The Hayes electors had won fairly, but one was ineligible, being a postmaster. The governor, La Fayette Grover, a Democrat, certified the election of two Hayes electors and the defeated Tilden candidate for elector with the highest vote. To complete the burlesque, the defeated Tilden candidate constituted himself an electoral college and declared two vacancies existed, which he filled by appointment. His "appointees" voted for Hayes while he voted for Tilden. This was no worse than the Republican chicane, and Tilden managers stoutly defended this attempted theft of an electoral vote—which was all Tilden needed. Tilden himself was party to this fraud; but it availed him nothing, as the two Hayes electors also met as an electoral college, declared a vacancy, and appointed the disqualified postmaster. Their votes were adjudged the true votes of Oregon. Democratic objections raised to the Vermont and Wisconsin returns fared in like fashion.

The counting ended in the early morning of March 2, two days before Inauguration Day. As Ferry rose to announce the result to a joint session of Congress, a Democratic member exclaimed:

"Come, Democrats, let us not remain to witness the consummation of this infamy!"

The order, uttered on the spur of the moment, reflected the sentiments of the majority, and presently "all but a baker's dozen of the Democrats withdrew."

Ferry's face paled, but he proceeded with the prescribed formula in a grim voice. As he declared Hayes had been elected president, an oath roared from the lobby followed by:

"You lie!"

Ferry's voice trembled as he continued. After he had declared Wheeler elected Vice-President, the New York *Sun* correspondent noted that "the same voice broke in with another oath, whereat Mr. Ferry glanced ominously over his shoulder and incontinently brought his prepared speech to a conclusion, and . . . hurried from the speaker's chair as though his guilty conscience had conjured up countless shotguns leveled at his heart."

It was now 4:10 A.M.

The masterpiece of machine politics was finished.

Democratic Congressmen issued an address to the American people charging that Hayes was made President by "manifest fraud"; and the House, by a vote of 137 to 88, adopted a resolution proclaiming Tilden the true holder of the title. On that same morning the New York *Sun* appeared as it had on the day it told of the assassination of Lincoln—in mourning format.

Hayes kept his end of the deal with the southern Democrats; and the last of the carpetbagger-Negro governments vanished on April 24 when he withdrew Federal troops from Louisiana. Two weeks earlier, South Carolina's government had been turned over to the Democratic claimants. Friends of Packard, governor of Louisiana through the same shifting of votes that gave the state to Hayes, said Hayes would impeach his title as President if he recognized the Democratic government. Nevertheless, he did.

Supporters of Tilden never referred to Hayes as President. Democratic and independent journals, when polite, called him Mr. Hayes. Others, like the New York *Sun,* usually spoke of him as His Fraudulency; and this journal observed Hayes's visit to New York by printing his portrait with "Fraud" written across the forehead. Democratic state conventions in 1877 denounced all Republican politicians as bribers and election thieves; and party newspapers and spokesmen carried on the good work. Legislatures under Democratic control joined the chorus.

Acting on a petition from the general assembly of Maryland, the lower House of Congress started investigating the Florida and Louisiana frauds in the spring of 1878. Crooked election officials, including the contrite chairman of Florida's board of canvassers, confessed that offices and money had been used as bribes to rob Tilden of the presidency. The attempted theft of an electoral vote in Oregon was forgotten, and Tilden again was the unsullied symbol of reform.

Despite these disclosures, Democratic Congressmen who had opposed the investigation still clung to their belief that the old rule of politics—let sleeping dogs lie—should have been observed. Representative Alexander H. Stephens, later governor of Georgia, foresaw the inquiry ending "in a contemptible farce or a horrible tragedy." It ended in both. The tragedy was Tilden's.

When the investigation was some four months old, White-

"Gambling on the Returning Board. Chandler—'Now you see it, and now you don't!'" Drawn by J. A. Wales. *Leslie's Weekly,* December 9, 1876.

law Reid's *Tribune* began its famed series of articles showing that immediately after the 1876 election, some of Tilden's intimates embarked on a conspiracy of bribery and corruption to prevent him from being defrauded of the presidency. The revelations were based on cipher telegrams that passed between Tilden's nephew in Tilden's home and vote-buying agents in Florida, Louisiana, South Carolina, and Oregon, and between Tilden's secretary in his law office and these same agents.

The plot was carried out chiefly in cipher correspondence over a period of four weeks, and failed only because of haggling over the price of votes, indecision, hesitation, tardiness, and timidity. The cipher despatches had been purloined from a mass of some thirty thousand campaign telegrams which had been subpœnaed by a Senate committee soon after the 1876 election. Some twenty-nine thousand were returned to the telegraph company and burned. Not an incriminating Republican despatch remained.

Smith M. Weed, one of Tilden's four preconvention campaign managers, was a major principal in the plot. Weed was a veteran in the art of ballot-box corruption, and warmly defended his attempted purchase of the South Carolina returning board for $80,000 to give the presidency to Tilden. He said:

"I looked upon it as paying money for the recovery of stolen property, or as a ransom to a robber, and that it was justifiable to pay these thieves who had it in their power for doing what every man knew to be right."

Weed was a railroad lawyer and promoter, and an old pal of Tweed. He had bargained to buy three of South Carolina's seven votes for $80,000, the money to be held in escrow until the votes had been cast for Tilden. By mutual agreement, Colonel Pelton, Tilden's nephew, journeyed from New York and Weed from South Carolina. They met in Baltimore. But Pelton had an explanation instead of the $80,000 Weed expected.

"The old man is against it," said Pelton, referring to Tilden. The story runs that when Edward Cooper, treasurer of the Democratic National Committee, and a brother-in-law of Hewitt, learned of the venture, he informed Tilden, who ordered the negotiations dropped.

"Cipher Mumm(er)y. Exhumed by the New York *Tribune*." The New York *Sun* had published a portrait of Hayes with "Fraud" branded on his forehead. Nast did the same for Tilden after the *Tribune* decoded the cipher telegrams. *Harper's Weekly*, November 2, 1878.

A fortnight later, however, Pelton raised money for a vote in Oregon. But haggling over the price, which Pelton whittled down from $10,000 to $8,000 to "purchase Republican elector to recognize and act with Democrat," resulted in the money arriving too late to complete the deal before the Electoral College met.

Another vote-buying agent was Manton Marble, Tilden's friend and adviser, who wired from Florida: "Have just received proposition to hand over a Tilden decision of board and a certificate of governor for $200,000." Marble's efforts failed only because of days spent in haggling over the amount of the bribe. Marble lacked Weed's refreshing frankness before the congressional investigators, and said his telegrams were only "danger signals."

Tilden disclaimed all knowledge of the cipher telegrams "except what has been derived from or since the publications of the *Tribune*," and after this self-serving declaration, emphasized these truths:

> The pregnant fact always remains that none of the corrupt boards gave their certificates to the Democratic electors, but they all gave them to the Republican electors. . . .
> These false and fraudulent certificates, now confessed and proved to have been obtained by corrupt inducements, were afterwards made the pretexts for taking from the people their rightful choice for the Presidency and Vice-Presidency.

Pelton assumed all blame for the plot, and like all his associates, testified Tilden knew nothing of their plans. To accept their testimony is to deny the soundness of mind of all involved. Even stout Democratic journals rejected their denials, while Republican journals, recalling Tilden's tacit acquiescence to Tweed's theft of the New York governorship for Hoffman, snatched the brand with which the *Sun* had stamped "Fraud" on Hayes to sear Tilden's brow.

45

THE MOBS ARISE—THE COMMUNISTS EMERGE

IN THE EARLY SUMMER OF 1877, AS THE SOUTH BASKED IN the peace that came with the passing of the carpet-bagger, mobs rose in the North, battled police and state militia, seized strategic railroad centers, closed shops, factories, and mills, pillaged, burned, and killed, and paralyzed the nation's industry. Scores were slain and wounded in this fortnight of terror. It had an innocent beginning. On Saturday, July 14, forty firemen and brakemen on the Baltimore and Ohio Railroad quit their jobs, at Camden Station, a Baltimore suburb, in protest against a third 10 per cent wage cut in three years, and the fourth in seven. Two days later the walk-out was an uprising. By the week-end it was an insurrection with the menacing proportions of a rebellion. This 10 per cent cut was fairly general on all the roads. Upwards of fifty thousand railroad employees struck, chiefly on northern lines operating between the Atlantic and the Mississippi. The strike invaded the South to a mild degree, and employees of the Texas Pacific Railroad walked out in protest against the cut. Several western roads were either immune from the strike or any prolonged walk-out because they quickly acceded to the demands of the strikers to restore the wage cut, compromised with them, or did not impose a cut. Another fifty thousand men, in nearly every field of employment, quit work in sympathy or through fear of the mobs. But the bulk of this second fifty thousand struck voluntarily, for their wages were lower than those of the underpaid railroad workers, and they had been striking periodically throughout the decade in an effort to better their lot.

Disciples of Karl Marx fanned the flames with the centuries-old class hatreds they brought with them from Europe; they urged all employees to join one big union, and advocated a class-conscious labor republic. Their English language organ hailed the strike as "the great labor war ... the beginning of a revolution," and besought the strikers not to surrender. Nothing short of revolution would satisfy the Reds.

The outbreaks attracted world-wide attention. Brief accounts of the riots were cabled to European newspapers, and a London despatch to the Chicago *Inter-Ocean* on July 26 said, "The strikes have made a deeper and more painful impression in England than any event since the war of secession in 1861. . . . The newspapers have generally expressed the hope that the United States Government would succeed in suppressing the insurrection."

Marx himself gloatingly commented on the despatches from the United States, for he confused the workers with the rabble; in a letter to his collaborator, Friedrich Engels, as the riots were drawing to a close, Marx envisaged the strikers as the nucleus of "an earnest workers' party."

The Marxists had a fertile field. Besides the 100,000 strikers, they played with the emotions of the unemployed, who numbered nearly 4,000,000 in a population of approximately 46,000,000. Why should any one live in a slum? There would be palaces for all in the new order.

Class hatred as the dominant issue, the all-in-all, of a political movement was a new note in American life where all men were equal before the law. Marxists had hitherto sought to divide the nation in classes through their organs and their well-drilled propagandists. During the strike they shouted

Death, garbed as a Communist, seeks to lure an American workman. In the background is a building denominated "Foreign." In the
middle-distance, a Communist front organization, masked as a Committee of Safety, attacks a policeman, the symbol of law. This is the
first anti-Communist cartoon we have encountered. *Harper's Weekly*,
February 7, 1874.

their alien pleas and their blood-lust cries from the street corners and the hustings.

The Communists had emerged into the open.

Some were veterans of the Paris Commune, but most of them were Germans who had their own press, the *Arbeiterstimme,* of New York, and the *Verbote,* of Chicago. They celebrated the Centennial by introducing the Trojan horse to the United States. American workers shied at the words Socialist and Internationalist. The Marxists remedied this. They first changed and name of the Internationalist Workingmen's party to Social-Democratic Workingmen's party, and when it made no headway under the new label, it became the Workingmen's party. This was in July, 1876. The following month, their English-language weekly, the *Socialist,* became the *Labor Standard.* These verbal masks made the journal and the party distinctly American.

The Communists' hopes for a revolution were high, in the first few days of the strike, as the governors of Pennsylvania, Illinois, Maryland, and West Virginia called upon President Hayes for aid. Hayes thereupon issued proclamations, one for each of the four states, warning "all persons engaged in or connected with said domestic violence and obstruction of the laws to disperse, and retire peaceably to their respective abodes. . . ." This was a necessary prelude to despatching Federal troops to quell the outbreaks. For a time it looked as if Federal assistance would be invoked by the authorities in New York, Indiana, Missouri, and California. A gunboat stood by in San Francisco Bay, ready to send a landing party to the city's aid, and army garrisons near New York City were reinforced on the eve of a Communist meeting in the metropolis. There were riotous outbreaks in other states, including Ohio, the President's home, where one mob terrorized Cleveland for a day, and another burned the Ohio and Mississippi Bridge at Mill Creek.

The gravity of the situation was emphasized by a special Cabinet meeting on Sunday, July 22, at which it was proposed to declare Pennsylvania, Maryland, and West Virginia in a state of siege, and issue a call for seventy-five thousand volunteers, treble the size of the regular forces. Illinois, at this time, had no need of Federal troops.

But the call for volunteers proved unnecessary, for in all affected communities, committees of safety were organized. These vigilantes consisted of Union and Confederate veterans, and others familiar with firearms; they were equipped with muskets, rifles, and revolvers. In some cities, these volunteer forces passed the ten thousand mark, outnumbering the police twenty-five to one.

Marx's misconception of the strikers was dramatically emphasized by the striking railroad men, who maintained law and order in several localities by force of arms; where red tape prevented local authorities from supplying the troops with food, these strikers provided the rations.

Throughout this period of violence and bloodshed, the sympathies of the press and public remained with the striking railroad men. This was largely because of the refusal of many railroads to arbitrate, the justice of the strikers' demands, and the character of the mobs. Save for the few extremists among them, railroad men everywhere were conspicuous by their absence from the mobs after the first fatal riot. An Associated Press despatch noted this in describing the gory scenes in Pittsburgh, and on July 28, three days after Marx confided to Engels his hopes of an American proletariat, a Chicago despatch thus described the local rabble—a description fairly applicable to all urban mobs: "The working classes proper have not been identified with the howling organization of Communists, thieves, thugs, and riffraff forming the mob." A subhead of an article in

Leslie's Weekly summed up the truth in this wise: "Communism rampant in the northern states."

The first violence occurred the Monday following the Saturday walk-out when the firemen and brakemen at the B. & O. junction in Martinsburg, West Virginia, struck after a formal protest against the latest wage cut and other grievances. Prior to the fourth cut, B. & O. brakemen received $1.50 and $1.75 a day, and firemen $1.35 and $1.53, there being two classes of each. But more rankling than the wage cuts were the injustices involved in promotion; for, regardless of seniority or merit, a worker would frequently find himself passed over for a backscratcher or one with political influence. Moreover, the prevailing custom was to dismiss members of grievance committees. Conductors, engineers, and shop workers were not much better off than firemen and brakemen. The B. & O. strikers demanded a minimum of $2.00 and a maximum of $3.50 a day for all workers. Most roads paid slightly higher wages than the B. & O., and the men on these lines also worked full time. But throughout the depression the B. & O. had kept its entire organization intact in the hope of better days. This meant less work for all, but it saved many from joining the army of the unemployed. All railroads felt the hard times. In 1873 their aggregate profits were $46,000,000; these fell to $22,000,000 in 1876. Several roads were in the hands of receivers. But railroad workers, like the public, thought of the lines as symbols of the dead Jim Fisk and the living Jay Gould, the corrupt Credit Mobilier and ruinous rate-cutting wars by the four big trunk lines in their struggle for control. The freight rates were often selfishly used. Railroad directors used them to enrich themselves by granting favorable rates to enterprises in which they were interested. Fisk, aided and abetted by Gould, did the same with the Stokes oil refinery. They were used to punish enemies. Fisk did this, again with

Gould's sanction, to impoverish Stokes for stealing his favorite concubine. They were used against the public, and led to the enactment of intrastate laws in the West regulating passenger and freight rates alike; in 1873, two years after the first of these measures was made law in Illinois, the oath-bound Patrons of Husbandry moved on Congress, awakening the nation to the need of Federal regulation of interstate commerce. This solidarity was composed of farmers whose lodges were called Granges, and the measures they sponsored were designated granger legislation. The roads used the discriminatory rates against themselves in their internecine strife, being as blind as the mobs that now beset them.

The first mob arose in Martinsburg when the strikers drove off men sent to replace them. This mob, its ranks recruited from the slums and the saloons, defied the local authorities. Governor Henry N. Matthews then ordered out the militia. West Virginia had only four companies of militia, which meant a maximum strength of 160 muskets. But Americans reasoned a military force was a needless luxury to a self-governing people. They had not considered mob rule in a land where every wrong could be settled peacefully if the will were there. There was no penalty for a militiaman deliberately failing to respond to a call, for, again, Americans did not anticipate such a situation. And half the meager military force of the state refused to obey the governor's order because of sympathy with the strikers. On Tuesday morning a mob of eight hundred jeered the two loyal companies on their arrival at Martinsburg; a few seconds after the first freight started, under military protection, it came to a dead stop as a striker ran to a switch to sidetrack the train. A guardsman ran toward the switch-throwing striker, who fired at him, inflicting a scalp wound. The guardsman fatally wounded his assailant. The mob now fired a volley, which was answered by some of the soldiers, while others took to their heels, followed by the train crew. Presently all the militia were in flight.

To the flight of these guardsmen, and the refusal of the other two companies of the West Virginia militia to serve, may be traced the terror that started before the week was out.

The triumphant mob remained at the junction, determined to prevent the moving of any freight. The following day, Wednesday, five companies of the United States Artillery, acting as infantry, were ordered to Martinsburg, the state having been proclaimed in insurrection. The regulars arrived on Thursday, and their very presence, as in the South during the comparatively tame days of reconstruction, restored order. But only two trains were started westward, for lack of train crews.

The following day the strike was general. The strikers adopted resolutions reciting their grievances and emphasizing their willingness to take out passenger and mail trains. They relied on forcing the roads to comply with their just demands by halting all freight. Let us quote from the resolutions adopted at Baltimore: "... we have soberly and calmly considered the step we have taken, and declare that at the present rate of wages ... we cannot provide our wives and children with the necessaries of life, and that we only ask for wages that will enable us to provide such necessaries." In these resolutions, which held to the truth, is seen the directing hand of the oldest and most powerful, richest and most conservative of American national labor organizations —the Brotherhood of Locomotive Engineers. Its membership included all organized railroad employees, there being no Big Four then. The brotherhood at no time sanctioned the strike, although its officers, as individuals, assisted in drafting the various resolutions adopted on the various roads.

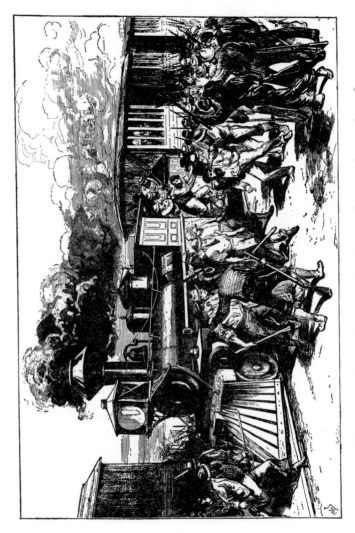

The start of the rioting—armed strikers and sympathizers drag the fireman and engineer from a B. & O. freight train at Martinsburg, West Virginia, July 17, 1877. *Leslie's Weekly, August 4, 1877.*

The union had planned to call a strike on all lines that failed to rescind the wage cuts, but had not decided on a date; some brotherhood officials had suggested August 10, and others had urged postponement to October. The walk-out on July 14 had upset their program, and the brotherhood did the best it could with an outlaw strike that had been thrust upon it. The last thing desired by the brotherhood was violence, as most of the railroads were avowedly out to destroy the union. Violence would only play into the hands of the brotherhood's foes.

But the strike passed completely from the control of the brotherhood on Friday. The mobs had taken over. On that day Governor Hartranft authorized the use of the Pennsylvania militia as he hurried east from Cheyenne, Wyoming; Governor John Lee Carroll, of Maryland, ordered out the militia to disperse the mob besieging the railroad junction at Cumberland.

On Friday evening a mob gathered around the armory of the Sixth Maryland Regiment, Front and Fayette streets, Baltimore, as the militia responded to the call. At 5:30 P.M. the mob was small, not more than three hundred. Two unarmed soldiers, in uniform, were seized near the armory and hurled over a railing into Jones's Falls. Police dragged them from the stream. Another unarmed soldier bound for the armory was forced into a tobacco shop and compelled to remove his uniform. The tobacconist lent him a pair of trousers. Soon the mob was hurling stones and bricks through the windows of the armory. At 7:30, John Murray, of the Baltimore *Sun*, visited the armory. Five minutes later, the mob had increased both in numbers and temper, and occasional stone-throwing became general. At 8:15 the mob had grown to between five and six thousand, with its due share of women and boys. At this hour Colonel Clarence Peters ordered his three companies, forty men

The Sixth Maryland Regiment Battling a Baltimore Mob
Harper's Weekly, August 11, 1877.

each, to proceed to Camden Station. The armory occupied
the second and third stories of a warehouse. The narrow
doorway permitted the passage of two men abreast. Companies I and F first moved out of the armory, in a perfect

hail of stones. Four guardsmen fell senseless to the ground. As Company B filed out, the stones were accompanied by pistol and revolver shots. As the soldiers beat a quick retreat into the armory, the Baltimore *Sun* reporter asked if their muskets were loaded.

"No, they will not let us load," came the answer.

But when Company B again moved out of the armory, the muskets were loaded. The troops fired in the air, but this warning was answered with stones and pistol shots. Now the soldiers shot into the mob, killing one and wounding several.

All three companies remained the targets of countless brickbats and occasional pistol shots, on their march to the station. Before reaching Frederick and Baltimore streets, one guardsman was shot in the hand and fifteen injured by stones without an answering shot from the troops. At this point some soldiers took it upon themselves to return the fire. For the next five blocks the battle raged, and eleven civilians were killed and many wounded. Private W. H. Young was the most seriously injured among the guardsmen. He was shot in the head, and his face was crushed by a brick.

At the station the mob made its final rally of the night, one of the shots wounding a brakeman in the chin. Here the police fired into the rioters, injuring several fatally.

An hour before the Sixth moved out of its armory, the Fifth Maryland Regiment, numbering 150 muskets, was stoned en route from its armory over the Richmond Street Market to Camden Station. The mob dispersed as the troops charged with fixed bayonets. Captain W. P. Herbert, Lieutenant W. H. Rogers, a sergeant, a corporal, and four privates were severely injured. All were struck by brickbats save Rogers, who received a saber slash.

The attack on the Sixth was carefully planned. It was a

dark night, and street lamps along the line of march were extinguished shortly before the soldiers moved out of the armory.

An hour after peace had seemingly been restored, the train despatcher's house at Camden Station was destroyed by an incendiary.

The following morning Brigadier-General Henry L. Abbot detrained at the President Street depot with three companies of the United States Engineer Corps as five hundred hoodlums groaned and hissed. The mob followed the troops up President Street on their way to the Sixth Maryland Regiment armory. Suddenly the troops were showered with stones, one injuring Private Michael Corcoran on the head. General Abbott had ignored the mob. But he noticed the stones. He gave the command, "Halt!" The mob disappeared. General Winfield Scott Hancock, commander of the Department of the East, arrived a little later, and in the evening, a detachment of 100 marines reached the city. But the Baltimore authorities were not relying entirely on the military, for Mayor Ferdinand C. Latrobe had sworn in 3,000 citizens as special policemen. The police made 200 arrests during the day, and at night about fifty of a mob of 2,500 were made prisoners. Not one of these 250 prisoners was a railroad striker.

Few slept in Baltimore Saturday night, and before daylight Sunday the streets swarmed with people. Alarms of fire and riot had been ringing throughout the night. Early Sunday morning the mob tried to destroy the B. & O. shops, which covered several acres in West Baltimore, by setting fire to a train of thirty-seven oil cars. The mob sought to prevent the firemen from extinguishing the flames, and exchanged shots with the police before taking flight. While the police and firemen were at work on the oil cars, the mob put the torch to the lumber-yard and planing mill of Turner and Cate, completely destroying this extensive plant.

Sunday's known casualties were eight dead and seventeen wounded civilians, and eight wounded policemen.

Midnight brought peace to Baltimore, and on Monday the authorities were so confident of its continuance that the marines were despatched to Pennsylvania where a mob in Pittsburgh had wrought havoc over the week-end.

46

THE SIEGE OF THE ROUNDHOUSE

FOR TWO SUCCESSIVE DAYS SEVERAL HUNDRED MEN SUCCESSfully resisted every effort to move freight trains out of Pittsburgh. Day and night they held the Twenty-eighth Street Crossing, in the heart of the vast freight yards of the Pennsylvania Railroad, and while they controlled this narrow strip, they were masters of the Gateway of the West. If a crew was found to take out a train, the engineer was invited to leave his cab, and dragged out if he hesitated.

At this point the railroad ran through verdant rolling country-side, and on the hillsides close to the tracks was an attentive and cheering audience of small boys, tramps, and hoodlums, numbering not more than a thousand, while mothers with their youngsters, and other cautious ones, watched the drama from the farther hills. Up to the early afternoon of Saturday, July 21, the handful of railroadmen on the Crossing had hardly any other reinforcements than the discontented unemployed and volunteers from the saloons—thugs, thieves, and other undesirables. Up to the noon hour, a squad of police could have cleared the Crossing without trouble and averted the week-end of carnage, arson, pillage, and terror. Also, they could have arrested the ringleaders in the early rioting, mostly hoodlums, for whom warrants had been issued. So could the sheriff. But both dodged making the arrests. Their shallow pretenses at law enforcement prepared the ground for the grim harvest. The reasons for the inactivity of the county and city authorities were known to the whole town, although it took a legislative investigating committee to spread them on the record. There were two major reasons, one political, the other economic. One overlapped the other. The railroad had long been unpopular with the entire business element because of the discriminatory freight rates which operated as a tariff in favor of western manufacturers against Pittsburgh manufacturers. Since the strike, Pittsburgh business men were as wholeheartedly with the railroad employees as the sympathizing workers. These two groups being of one mind, and as they represented almost the entire electorate, no vote-seeking politician dared offend them. If the elective officials of the community would not move against the strikers, what chance was there of any mass movement of policemen who valued their jobs—they were all appointed on a strictly party basis—against the rioters without an order from the mayor? He gave no such order. This injection of sordid politics into a situation in which lives were the principal stakes was directly responsible for Pittsburgh's week-end of pillage, arson, and carnage.

Shortly after Pittsburgh had its Saturday midday meal, its last peaceful repast for some time, several hundred men from the mills, factories, shops, and foundries, shut down until Monday, joined the spectators on the hills and grassy slopes. Also on the hills at this time were several companies of militiamen, all drawn from Pittsburgh and its suburbs. With the exception of Hutchinson's Battery and a cavalry troop, they were an undisciplined lot; they mingled with the spectators, swapping compliments with the women, and taking nips from neighbors' flasks. Soon they heard a train coming from the East—the train with the Philadelphia militia. As the train pulled into the Union Depot, out poured six hundred sleepy and hungry soldiers who had been hurriedly summoned to their armories the night before. They had been nine hours on the train, a journey filled with excitement, for several attempts had been made to wreck it, and no one had snatched more than a few winks of sleep. They freshened up while munching sandwiches and washing them down with coffee from tin cups. Major General Alfred L. Pearson, of Pittsburgh, the divisional commander, outlined conditions to Brigadier-General Robert M. Brinton, commander of the Philadelphia troops, and ordered him to clear the Crossing. One brigade, with two commissary wagons bringing up the rear, marched up Liberty Street, which skirted the railroad on the north; Brinton led the other up the tracks, Keystone Battery wearily dragging its two Gatling guns over the ties. The crowd fell back quietly as Brinton neared the Crossing; he deployed his command in skirmish lines among the network of tracks, posting Keystone Battery and its Gatling guns on a hillside ten feet above the road-bed. From the more distant hills, near the confluence of the Allegheny and Monongahela rivers, spectators beheld a colorful panorama as the troops rested on their arms, seemingly as immobile as the roundhouse that dominated the scene. But for the turret-like vents and the gracefully arched windows which broke the expanse of its massive walls of brick and stone, the roundhouse would have passed for a fort. The picturesque structure abutted on the Crossing and extended westward almost to Twenty-seventh Street, if that thoroughfare had been carried across the tracks. Only the plaintive lowing of cattle broke the silence that followed the disposition of the troops. These live stock were dying of hunger and thirst in the railroad stock-yards, inarticulate victims of the strike.

The more desperate among the crowd quickly returned to the Crossing. This was a public thoroughfare and they felt they had the right to remain there. Brinton ordered a company to clear the Crossing, arms aport, to avoid injuring any one. The hoodlums yelled defiance as their sheer massed weight resisted the attempt to dislodge them. The mob—it was no longer a crowd—hissed and groaned. Brinton now ordered another company to charge, this time with fixed bayonets. This cleared the Crossing. One of the mob received a bayonet thrust. A drink-emboldened hoodlum waved his hat and shouted: "Give them hell!" Instantly stones and other handy missiles were hurled at the troops from all sides.

Brinton met the brickbat bombardment by ordering the troops to form a hollow square. The Gatling guns and the commissary wagons were placed in the approximate center of the rapidly forming quadrangle of bayonets. A few infuriated ones rushed the troops and tried to wrench the muskets from their hands. One man thrust himself in front of Private Baker of Company E, First Philadelphia Regiment, and demanded: "You wouldn't shoot fellow workingmen, would you?" Baker was a fellow worker, but he then symbolized justice militant, the might of the state. He ignored his interrogator who drew a navy revolver, thrust it in Baker's face, and commanded him to halt. The soldier knew but one command—to form a hollow square—and started to follow this order, but only for a second longer, for a bullet tore through his forehead and out the back of his head.

This was the first Pittsburgh fatality.

As Baker dropped lifeless between the tracks, one of his comrades fired. Another followed suit. There ensued a general fusillade, so rapid as to sound like one volley. Three sides of the square had been formed. Two of these lines faced the hills. A third faced Liberty Street, looking down Twenty-sixth Street. The musket balls had swept in all three directions.

The hour now lacked twenty minutes of five. There were nine lifeless bodies besides Private Baker's. Eight were civilians, and one a Pittsburgh militiaman. A second Pittsburgh soldier was wounded. There was no telling the exact civilian casualties, as the mob dragged away many dead and wounded. Quite a few of the dead and injured were in no wise involved in the dispute.

The Pittsburgh militiamen who had been fraternizing with the spectators now deserted. Some threw down their arms. The mob fled with them, hundreds shouting their intention to storm the United States Arsenal and be avenged on the Philadelphia troops.

Brinton wanted to pursue the compact mass headed for the United States Arsenal to prevent their seizing the store of arms and ammunition. But he could not act without word from General Pearson, to whom he despatched an aide. Pearson rejected the proposal and ordered Brinton to remove his troops to the roundhouse, and to hold it.

The commandant of the arsenal, Major Adelbert R. Buffington, dissuaded the mob from molesting army property. The mob knew of other stores of arms, and they broke up into sections, their ranks constantly swelling. Some returned to the Crossing, and a small band of hoodlums marched past the roundhouse and fired their revolvers in the air, defying the troops to come out. Another section of the mob stole the commissary wagons, leaving the troops supperless.

By nightfall a mob of about two thousand was at the Crossing, yelling and hooting. Now and then some one shouted, "The police are coming!" and the mob fled in all directions, only to return on learning it was a false alarm.

Mobs now roamed the city, their ranks recruited mainly from the underworld of thugs, thieves, and hoodlums.

A mob of fifteen hundred burglarized Johnson's gun factory.

A mob of five hundred raided the armory of Company F. Here were weapons. The mob fixed bayonets to the muskets. Here were drums. Amateur drummer boys appropriated these. Being patriotic thieves, they broke open the flag case. With the Star-Spangled Banner at their head, this thieving five hundred, some shouldering muskets, others brandishing revolvers and swords, marched to the beat of the stolen drums to James Bown's gun shop, stripping it of muskets, rifles, pistols, revolvers, ammunition, and hunting knives—the entire stock—worth fifty thousand dollars. Most of these brand new arms and munitions being readily salable, were taken home by the thieves.

A smaller mob roused an old gunsmith sleeping behind his shop on Penn Street. He had hidden his wares. The leader of the mob silenced his protests with: "Give us arms or we'll cut your throat!" The gunsmith recognized cut-throats when he saw them, and parleyed no further.

Soon the mob returned to the Crossing and began their attack on the roundhouse as they shouted: "Butcher all the Philadelphia troops!" The Philadelphians held their fire.

Suddenly the mob ceased firing, and the short silence was followed by a boisterous cheer as a large gang of roughs hove in sight, trundling three brass field-pieces, loot from the armory of Knapp's Battery. Two cannon were wheeled into position on a hill commanding the roundhouse, and a third planted some five hundred feet below the Crossing. The cannoneers had only a few iron shot, and it was decided to fire them from the third cannon; the two pieces on the hill were to use cobblestones.

These primitive projectiles have been used by armies in the field. Two Turkish cannon-balls of stone adorned the marble gateway to New York's original City Hall Park. These stone-shot were the gift of the Turkish Government to Commodore Oliver Hazard Perry, who presented them to the metropolis.

The hour was about ten o'clock. The Union Depot had been evacuated a short time before. Hotels and lodging-houses on Liberty Street and on the side streets close to the tracks had been practically emptied of their guests, and the few remaining ones departed to safer quarters when the mob swung past with the three cannon. But the mob had no powder, and so these field-pieces remained silent, despite some contemporary accounts of their assault on the round-house.

After the excitement over the cannon subsided, several hundred well-armed men advanced on the roundhouse, which was silent as the tomb, as it had been since the troops sought its shelter some five hours earlier. Shortly before the advance on the roundhouse, one Philadelphia company threw down its arms because Brinton would not let the troops answer the fire of the mob. Two of their comrades had just been shot, one in the arm, another in the leg. Brinton restored discipline by recalling that each man had had only twenty rounds of ammunition when they left the Union Depot, and that it was folly to waste their fire in sheer revenge. Moreover, their orders were to hold the roundhouse, nothing more. When guards at the windows reported the advance, this erstwhile mutinous company received their chance, and their thirty-five muskets fired into the attacking force when it was within pistol shot. Then the roundhouse returned to its sepulchral silence, as the first shrieks and groans of the wounded heralded the panic retreat of those who had escaped the deadly volley.

Before the attack, several well-disposed citizens surreptitiously visited the roundhouse with supplies of civilian clothes and urged the troops to don them and escape. Flight would be easy. They could leave as their well-wishers entered, by the lumber shed. They would be regarded as part of the mob, and they could mingle with the thieves pillaging the two thousand freight cars that cluttered the tracks and sidings for nearly four miles, and thereafter each man could decide for himself. The troops were also told that the two Pittsburgh regiments had refused to come to their rescue. Did they fear the mob? The rebellious militiamen feared nothing. The Philadelphia troops killed one of their men and wounded another, so why help them? The truth is the Pittsburgh militia was in a downright funk. No one was more justly censorious of their cowardice than Captain E. Y. Breck, of the Hutchinson Battery, who had several friends join the mob as spies. Upon receiving intelligence of the mob's plan to take the roundhouse by storm, Breck took two of his three field-pieces, shotted with canister, to the roundhouse. The mob had stolen the battery's third cannon from the armory, but what became of it remained a mystery for hours. Breck also pleaded with the beleaguered soldiers to escape in citizens' garb, for the mob was bent on annihilating them. But not a man quit his post. They could hold the roundhouse until the help promised by Pearson arrived. And what with the cannon Breck provided, and their own two Gatling guns, they were in excellent shape, although without food since detraining in the afternoon.

Half an hour before midnight the mob began a steady fusillade, shooting through the windows of the roundhouse. Under the cover of this curtain, an oil car was switched to a track leading to the roundhouse. The tracks to the roundhouse were downgrade. The oil car was set afire and pushed down the track while the mob shouted over and over: "Roast 'em alive!" The flaming oil car exploded, as it passed some stalled box-cars, setting them afire. Other cars were set afire and sent after the burning oil car. Quite a distance away from the roundhouse stood a train of coke on the Allegheny Valley Railway tracks. The end car was uncoupled, pushed to a siding connecting with the Pennsylvania tracks, and coke and car drenched with petroleum. The car was then switched to a track leading to the roundhouse, set afire and shoved on its

The burning of the roundhouse at Pittsburgh, with other havoc wrought by the mob. Drawn from sketches on the scene by J. W. Alexander and Jacob Beeson. *Harper's Weekly,* August 11, 1877.

mission of destruction toward the doomed building. This was the first burning car to touch the wall of the roundhouse, the others having fallen short of it by many feet. Flames soon spread to the near-by machine-shop and other railroad buildings, but the roundhouse remained uninjured. Fire-engines clattered to the scene, but the mob would not let any railroad property be saved. The firemen were permitted to play the hose on private property. The mob, which never numbered more than five thousand, a mere fraction of the city's population, was supreme.

The roundhouse, although literally walled in flames, remained unharmed, and the maddened mob sent more flaming cars toward it.

From midnight on, the roundhouse was of secondary concern to most of the mob who were looting the freight cars, decamping with the booty, and returning for more. Barrels of whiskey were tapped and free drinks were to be had for the taking. The contents of crates and boxes were emptied on the tracks, and men, women, and children, black and white, scrambled in friendly spirit for the loot. No one fought over anything, for there was more than enough for all. Women walked of with bolts of textiles under one arm and a ham or groceries under the other. One woman, with an infant in her arms, rolled home a barrel of flour with her feet. Tramps and others discarded their old clothes and shoes for new ones. A thin man put on a dozen shirts, one over another. Small boys walked home wearing derbies and silk hats, one on top of another, like old clothes men. Men staggered under bolts of leathers and packages of shovels and axes. Rolls of carpet, hardware, and other loot were sold to persons too timid to steal themselves. They drove in all sorts of wagons to the loot market alongside the tracks on Liberty Street. Sewing-machines were sold for ten cents to a dollar. Prices of everything else were proportionate, the supply exceeding the demand. Drugs, corned beef, silk umbrellas, bologna sausages, lace parasols, stationery, boots, shoes, picture frames, yarns, thread, kegs of wine and spirits —almost everything conceivable in merchandise went to the highest bidders on the Liberty Street auction block.

One of the most active looters was a Pittsburgh policeman in full uniform. He may be described as typical of a large part of the police of Pittsburgh and other large cities, for they were political appointees all, and were the run of the roughs of their respective communities.

But let us leave the pillaging policeman—there were no doubt others, but the legislative record tells of only one— and the rest of the busy thieves and return to the roundhouse where scores of freight cars are blazing, some almost wholly consumed.

The intense heat from the burning cars and buildings on all sides of the roundhouse had penetrated every particle of its thick brick wall, and at two o'clock the fixed guards had to be withdrawn from the windows, it being impossible to stand close to the wall. Officers and men now clustered together in the center of the smoke-choked building; and from this mass, one after another would dash constantly to the windows to keep momentary watch. There was no real relaxation of this necessary vigilance. Through the flames came the mob's occasional chant, "Roast 'em alive!" As a further grim reminder of the fury of their foe, bullets spattered against the wall on the Twenty-eighth Street side of the building.

At 4:15 A. M., about half an hour before dawn, the flames had spent their force, save in the immediate vicinity of the roundhouse. The hour may be given with exactitude because of the presence of fact-hungry journalists. But like the officials, the newspapermen were ignorant of the actual number of dead and wounded. There was no complete record of those who died at their homes from gunshot wounds. Moreover, officials were deliberately vague respecting casualities and arrests. This was not peculiar to Pittsburgh. It was common wherever violence, tumult, and riot reigned. Such vagueness is understandable; for a community, like an individual, does not voluntarily bare its shame. Saturday's casualties, from the first encounter at the Twenty-eighth Street Crossing to midnight—as reported—were nineteen dead and nine wounded, a manifestly erroneous report, as the number of wounded in armed clashes is ordinarily about double that of the slain.

While the last remaining minutes of the night of terror still hung over the city, and the flames illumined the sky for miles, the fourth cannon stolen by the mob, the field-piece from Hutchinson's Battery, was wheeled into Liberty Street by a silent horde until it was within a few yards of the roundhouse. One of the mob shouldered a keg of powder. They had advanced under cover of a blanket of smoke so dense that they could barely see the wall on which they had trained the gun. The cannon was loaded with spikes and jagged fragments of coupling pins.

Since the fixed guards had been removed from the windows, officers had taken turns with men in keeping the unbroken vigil. It was their way of relieving the monotony of breathing smoke and drinking water, with which the roundhouse was fortunately supplied. An officer saw what seemed like the dim outline of the cannon in the heavy cloud of smoke. Brinton quietly ordered fifty muskets to the windows facing the field-piece. As he looked out, the cloud of smoke lifted, revealing the cannoneer about to pull the lanyard. At Brinton's command, fifty muskets roared as one. The mob retreated, leaving eight dead and many wounded around the cannon. The troops permitted the removal of the wounded. Shortly after dawn, a lone member of the mob

"Pittsburgh in the hands of the mob." Drawn from sketches by J. W. Alexander and Jacob Beeson. *Harper's Weekly*, August 7, 1877.

attempted to fire the cannon. Several musket balls dropped him lifeless before he reached the gun. Not long after, another volunteer was killed while essaying the same rôle. Thirteen dead lay beside the cannon before it was abandoned.

But the mob felt its turn would soon arrive. Save on the Liberty Street side of the roundhouse, the flames had grown more intense with each minute. The troops could not hold out much longer. Brinton, too, was counting the minutes until six o'clock arrived, when Pearson promised to send troops to his aid. But six o'clock came, and six-thirty, and still no help. At ten minutes of seven the mob howled its delight as burning embers fired the roof of the roundhouse. There was no way of extinguishing the flames, and Brinton and his officers now decided to seek refuge in flight. "It is better to be shot to death than burned to death," one of them grimly observed. Their ranks had been thinned out in the early morning hours by family men, and militiamen on the point of collapse, who escaped in civilian clothes. There had been about one hundred and fifty of these technical desertions. Fortunately, the mob had also diminished in numbers, and when early church-goers left their homes, little more than one thousand remained at the Crossing. Another fortunate circumstance was the absence of rioters armed with telltale muskets and rifles. Their arms now were pistols and revolvers. Need of rest, and the knowledge that reinforcements were encamped at Shady Lawn, three miles from Pittsburgh, accounted for the withdrawal of most of the mob. Drink took a toll of hundreds; some of these managed to make their homes, but others, like the tramps, lay on the streets when drink overcame them.

At 7:30 A. M., having first spiked the two cannon Breck had provided, Brinton and his command set out for the United States Arsenal. Hoodlums shot at them from street corners, from windows of top floors, from behind chimneys, from street-cars. And as the troops passed a police station, its steps crowded with policemen, a policeman fired at them. The first sign of humanity came from worshipers who rushed from a Catholic church to rescue a seriously wounded soldier who had been shot from a roof top. They carried him to the priest's house. An elderly woman ran to the street as a militiaman fell from a sniper's bullet in front of her dwelling, and carried him into her home with the aid of neighbors. As the troops approached the arsenal, the mob attacked them in a body. Brinton brought the Gatling guns into play with deadly effect. The mob fled. When the troops reached the arsenal, six of them were wounded, three fatally, including Lieutenant J. Dorsey Ash of the Keystone Battery.

Brinton expected food and shelter at the arsenal. He was denied both. The yard of the arsenal was shady, and surrounded by high stone walls. Might his troops stay there a spell? Buffington also denied this request. He had an excuse for his conduct. Let it be said that Buffington had a record for bravery in the Civil War. He had a three-sided defense. First, he had a force of only ten men. Second, he feared the mob might put the torch to the powder magazines across the street and create destruction for blocks. Third, it was not in his line of duty. We may dismiss the first and the last excuses as absurd—officers of the Philadelphia troops called all of them scurvy. But there was a ghostly suggestion of merit in the second, for in 1862 an accidental explosion in the old arsenal killed seventy-four outright. But we can dismiss this also because Buffington's force of ten regulars, with the aid of Keystone Battery alone, could have held off any mob. One thing more may be recorded to Buffington's credit on this Sunday morning. He took in the six wounded soldiers and set up a temporary hospital.

Brinton and his tired troops, without sleep for two nights,

and foodless since the sandwiches and coffee of the previous afternoon, left the inhospitable Buffington and marched across the Etna Bridge over the Allegheny River. The mob followed at a safe distance, abandoning the pursuit upon reaching the open country. The militia kept to the highroad until they reached a ravine at Claremont, eight miles from Pittsburgh. They trudged the ravine slowly, for all were weak, and at the end of a half-mile climb they pitched camp on a wooded eminence overlooking the Allegheny County Poorhouse. The inmates and their keepers served them with food, and many officers and men fell asleep before finishing the meal. There was no attempt at discipline now. They commanded the whole terrain from their encampment, and even the most drink-crazed, vengeful mob would not venture near.

The sentries, and others still awake, watched the smoke still rising from the burning cars and buildings in distant Pittsburgh where the major part of the mob had resumed activities by noon. They sacked and wrecked private homes and stores as well as railroad property, rounding out their mischief and pillage with more arson. The mob required liquor to keep itself going, and saloon keepers who had neglected to hide their stocks lost even their last bottle.

A citizens' committee appealed to the mob leaders, hoodlums all, in various stages of intoxication, only to be ordered off. The committee then visited officers of the striking railroad men who truthfully replied they had no influence with the motley horde of tramps, thugs, Communists, and riffraff.

The depredating incendiaries carried on unchecked, firing the Union Depot and the grain-elevator, one of the largest in the world; by four o'clock, Liberty Street was a wall of lurid flame for three solid miles. Only a providential breeze saved the city from being reduced to ashes. By sunset every railroad building, railroad car, and all other property of

both the Pennsylvania and Panhandle roads were smoldering
ruins. The locomotives, numbering more than 160, alone remained standing, fit only for the junk heap. The dead for

Pittsburgh police recovering property stolen by the mob during the
riots. *Leslie's Weekly,* August 18, 1877.

the day were reported at 34 and the wounded at 100, a
reported total of 53 dead and 109 wounded for Saturday
and Sunday. These scaled-down figures did not tell the whole
story; Lieutenant Ash and three other wounded Phila-

delphians were dying, but there was no word of the number of dying civilians.

It was not until Sunday that Pennsylvania asked the President for "a military force sufficient to suppress disorder and protect persons and property against domestic violence." The next day, business was completely suspended in Pittsburgh. Its most distinguished citizen, James Scott Negley, a major-general of the Civil War and a veteran of the Mexican War, organized a committee of safety. He paraded the streets in the afternoon at the head of a company of Civil War veterans, and by nightfall had several thousand vigilantes under his command.

When the Philadelphia troops returned home Monday, they learned how a little preparedness had crushed the mob spirit at the very outset. Their mayor, William S. Stokley, had sworn in eighteen hundred auxiliary policemen, mostly Civil War veterans, and four hundred additional firefighters. During the night the police, with drawn clubs, routed a mob from the West Philadelphia depot. No one was injured. When the mob fired a train of eighteen oil tanks and box-cars laden with barrels of oil, firemen saved nine cars. Four were burned by an exploding oil tank. Philadelphia remained comparatively quiet until Thursday, when the police killed a non-Communist at a Workingmen's party riot. Two days later a Marxist group of propagandists left resolutions at the city hall urging all men "receiving stipulated wages to unite themselves into one amalgamated union who [sic!] will elect a national labor congress with power to regulate wages until such time as the wage system shall be abolished." None of the delegates, the press noted, was an American.

On the preceding Monday a mob in Harrisburg, the state capital, disarmed a dozen militiamen near their armory, plundered a gun shop, and subsequently returned the loot after a plea from the mayor. At night the mob seized the

Western Union offices, only to surrender them peacefully
to a sheriff's posse of one thousand.

There were other riots throughout the state during the
week. The most sanguinary was at Reading on Monday
where a mob of 3,000 showered the contents of six cars of
stone upon 253 militiamen as they filed through a narrow
railroad cut. Some of the mob used pistols and revolvers.
One soldier was shot through the neck. As the detachment
emerged into the open, "only about fifty were unhurt." When
the troops were shot at as they left the cut, they fired a
volley. Seven were killed, and fifty wounded, at least six
of them mortally. Of the wounded, twenty were soldiers and
five were policemen. At night the mob burned the new
$150,000 bridge spanning the Schuylkill River.

Federal troops reached Pennsylvania on Monday. There
was but one serious encounter between the state troops and
a mob after the Reading riot. This was in and near Shamokin
on Wednesday where the customary plundering was accompanied by the tearing up of tracks. The casualties included four known dead and five wounded. One of the
slain was a civilian who was seen leaving the railroad depot.
This was his sole offense. The mob stoned him to death.

47

ACROSS COUNTRY WITH THE MOBS

THE SMALLEST COMMUNITY DIRECTLY AFFECTED BY THE railroad strike was the New York village of Hornellsville where the Erie had extensive car shops. It was a typical American village—no tenements, no slums. On the day that Pittsburgh's mob took over the Gateway of the West, Hornellsville was apprehensive, for all Erie employees working or living in the village were on strike against the 10 per cent wage cut, and three regiments of militia were momentarily expected. But when the troop train pulled into the depot and the strikers greeted the militia with smiles and friendly waves of the hand, all apprehension vanished. The Erie was in receivership because Gould and Fisk had looted the road, and an injunction had been granted restraining all and sundry from interfering with the operation of the road. This made the strikers law-breakers, which was hard for the men to understand. After their leader had been arrested for contempt of court, neighbors persuaded them to accept the wage cut pending the advent of better days, and work was resumed on Thursday morning; and the troops left the peaceful village for turbulent Buffalo where three rioters had been slain in a struggle for the Lake Shore roundhouse, and two officers and six privates knifed and bludgeoned. The arrival of the troops from Hornellsville was signalized by a riot in the stock-yards in which a militiaman was wounded.

Further west, in Cincinnati, a mob burned the Ohio and

Mississippi Bridge across Mill Creek; and in two other Ohio cities, Zanesville and Columbus, where Workingmen's party agents were active, the rabble closed factories, mills, and shops.

Several Indiana towns and cities were beset by rioters. Fort Wayne, the most important western railroad junction outside of Chicago, was completely controlled by striking railroad men for several days. But it was a beneficent control, for they took over when the mobs grew more powerful than the police. The strikers published a broadside warning against violence. They enforced law and order. They guarded rolling-stock, shops, stock-yards, and other railroad property. They had guards on foot and mobile forces on hand-cars, armed with rifles and revolvers. They provided business and industry, both big and little, with as many armed guards as were required, on a moment's notice. They frowned on sympathetic strikes and walk-outs. They took over the passenger and mail service of the Pittsburgh, Fort Wayne, and Chicago Railroad, and operated the road on schedule under their own superintendent. On the Tuesday following the Pittsburgh riots they successively routed two gangs of tramps. When scores of drunken hoodlums and strikers came from near-by Columbia City on hand-cars to pillage the city, the Fort Wayne men drove them off. This maintenance of peace by railroad strikers was not peculiar to Fort Wayne.

Wisconsin and other midwestern states had their days of turbulence and fears. On the Monday night the bridge was burned at Cincinnati, a drunken orator in St. Louis thus addressed a Missouri crowd: "They talk of bringing troops to quell us. By God, let them come, and when they do, get out your little knives and pistols and shoot hell out of them. Kill a few, and the balance will run like sheep." Railroad strikers persuaded the St. Louis police to close the saloons the next day. In nearly all large communities where mobs were on the rampage, saloons were shut throughout the second week of the strike. No one took the drunk seriously. And no one took the sober Communists lightly, or their Trojan horse, the Workingmen's party. For days the Communists had been inciting mobs to force men to quit their jobs.

On the night of the drunk's harangue, "most incendiary speeches were made" at a Red rally in St. Louis. Policemen guarded newspaper plants, all having been marked for destruction. The Communists visited the *Westliche Post* to force a walk-out of the printers. They were being driven out when its noted editor, Dr. Emil Preetorius, exclaimed: "A moment!" Every one halted. "You're villains and cowards!" continued Preetorius, who then gave them his back. On Thursday, nine executives of the Workingmen's party were arrested for inciting to riot. The same day they met in Lucas' Market, and led a mob of two thousand into the manufacturing district. They routed four hundred employees from Belcher's sugar refinery, extinguished the furnaces and dismantled the machinery. Next they invaded forty other industrial establishments and hustled the workers to the sidewalk. The mob then burned an abandoned chair factory and the adjoining lumber-yard. As the Mississippi River steamboat *Centennial* was about to paddle down stream to New Orleans, the mob took possession of the vessel and forced the captain to sign an agreement raising the wages of the crew, who had made no demand for an increase. By this time the St. Louis mob subsided, the mayor having recruited eleven thousand auxiliary policemen, most of them armed with muskets and rifles.

A strike was called Thursday noon in Kansas City. But this Missouri community met the challenge by closing all saloons, and business was suspended at the mayor's request. The city had no alternative, for like other American communities at the time, its police force was intended only to handle habitual criminals and occasional law-breakers.

The strike was a week in reaching Chicago, the national headquarters of the Communists. On Sunday the Marxists held meetings throughout the city and issued two proclamations, one to party members everywhere to sustain the country-wide strike, and another, of like tenor, to all workers. These appeals were signed "The Executive Committee of the Workingmen's party of the United States," and carried the signatures of the corresponding secretary, Philip Van Patten, and his aide, A. B. Parsons, who subsequently turned anarchist and was hanged for his part in the fatal Haymarket riot. Violence was preached at these meetings, and all comrades were told to assemble at a mass-meeting in Market Street on the morrow.

As the telegraph told of the uprisings in Pittsburgh and elsewhere, the Chicago authorities, with only four hundred policemen in a city of neary half a million population, gladly accepted the offer of the Grand Army of the Republic to serve as vigilantes. On Monday "a howling mob, ten thousand strong," assembled around six platforms in Market Street where revolution was preached in English and German. The Reds derided the veterans by dubbing themselves the Grand Army of Starvation. One Red declaimed to the howling ten thousand: "Better one thousand of us to be shot down in the streets than ten thousand of us die starving." These meetings had been planned weeks before the strike as a prelude to a march on the city hall. They were part of the Communist program of promoting unrest. But the city hall demonstration was abandoned as the strike presented the Reds with all the ingredients for an uprising— years of paralysis of the nation's industry with its attendant unemployment, privation, poverty, and discontent.

To lessen the extent of the anticipated rioting, Monroe

Heath, Chicago's mayor, issued two orders. One shut all saloons. The other closed all gun shops. This second order directed the removal to safe quarters of all private stocks of arms and ammunition, with the result that the mob seized only 150 revolvers, 50 rifles, and a gross of brass knuckles from the shop of a neglectful gunsmith at 522 South Halstead Street.

The Chicago mob swung into action on Tuesday, mildly at first, merely forcing men to quit their jobs, and closing shops and factories. At 2 p. m. they had taken possession of all the railroad yards. The Chicago *Inter-Ocean* said of the mob: "Many of them were in an intoxicated condition." But on Wednesday morning the mob grew bolder and derailed a passenger train, and only the alertness of the suspicious engineer, who slowed down, saved scores of passengers from death and injury. From then on, until late at night, clashes between the rabble and the police were frequent and savage. In the evening, the police dispersed a Communist rally of twenty thousand on Market Street. Shots were exchanged and four policemen wounded, one fatally. Part of the mob then took the Chicago, Burlington & Quincy roundhouse, extinguished the fires in the engines, and were engaged in other sabotage when routed with a loss of five dead.

Thursday's rioting started early in the morning after the Second Illinois Regiment dispersed a crowd in the open space near Turner Hall, Halstead and West Twelfth streets. This gathering was the overflow of a Communist meeting in the hall. This was a bloodless affair, but before the noon hour was over, six policemen were shot in two encounters, one on the near-by Halstead Street viaduct, now no more, and another on the railroad tracks below. The mob suffered heavily, but the precise extent remains unknown. In describing twelve dead and fifteen wounded in the Halstead Street riots, a newspaper noted that "it is probable the number is much larger because many were carted away" by the rioters.

That afternoon several hundred Bohemian women from the cottages and tenements on the prairie near the lumber-yard district found themselves standing outside the high wooden fence of the Goss & Phillips Manufacturing Company plant which extended along Fisk—now Carpenter—Street from Twentieth to Twenty-second streets. They might have gone on deeper into the city, or returned home, if a small crowd of men on Fisk Street had not stared at them. Some of the women had babes in arms. The calico dresses of many were patched and ragged. Only a few wore shoes. The bare feet of the rest were deeply tanned like their faces. The stout sticks carried by a number belied the meekness common to Bohemians. Quite a few of these women had only just emerged from girlhood. Others were grandmothers. As the crowd of men increased, the women began talking among themselves. Was it because the men stared at them? Or were they asking themselves why were they in the city standing against a high wooden fence? Perhaps it was the latter, for suddenly several hundred women threw their combined weight against the fence, and presently there was no fence.

It is necessary to go back to the roundhouse battle of the night before, where five were slain. Two of the dead were boys of fourteen. Both lads were Bohemians. A few of the men killed and wounded during the rioting on the viaduct and elsewhere were Bohemians. The Marxists had carried on their proselytizing chiefly among the Bohemians, Germans, and other immigrants from the continent of Europe.

As the fence crashed, a squad of police appeared. The women hissed and yelled, and picked up stones and threw them. One of three policemen stoned in the near-by viaduct riots had a fractured skull. The police fired several shots to frighten the stone-throwers. One bullet plowed through the body of a girl of fourteen. The women returned to their prairie dwellings, and the police went back to their precinct house on Hinman Street, now West Twenty-first Place. The police station vanished with the prairie.

This was the last stand of any Chicago mob, for while the police were active throughout Friday and Saturday routing mobs, chiefly from the lumber-yards, the belligerence of the rioters ended with the arrival of United States regulars, bronzed Indian fighters all, during the forenoon and afternoon of Thursday.

An unofficial casualty list placed the total known dead at twenty-one, and the wounded at ninety. One of the slain was Frank Norbeck, "who headed the Communist movement for several years." Among the wounded was Nicholas Schilling, another Communist chief. Another of the dead was a policeman. Most of the casualties occurred on Wednesday and Thursday. There was the usual attendant looting. Roving gangs of thieves, principally youths, armed with revolvers, worked unhampered in the city and its suburbs. A farmer driving to town with a wagon of vegetables was held up at Adams and Throop streets, and the highwaymen divided his little silver before seeking another victim.

At the beginning of the week, when the Chicago Communists were getting into their stride, the disorders started in San Francisco without the pretext of a railroad strike. They began Monday night after an orderly meeting of ten thousand adjourned at ten o'clock. Between fifteen hundred and two thousand of the audience were tramps, thieves, and hoodlums who merged into a "shouting, swearing, and yelling mob" with Chinatown their goal. They halted at Leavenworth and Geary streets before a two-story frame house, with a fruit store and wash house, or laundry, on the street floor, and dwelling quarters overhead. The stores were brilliantly lighted with kerosene lamps. The proprietor was a peaceful, hard-working Chinese. The mob methodically unhinged the doors and threw them into the street. A hoodlum grabbed the Chinese by the queue while others mauled him. The few pieces of furniture were broken and the clothes scattered around. The wrecking finished, the mob fired the house by hurling the lighted kerosene lamps against the walls.

The incendiarism was designed to lure the police guard from Chinatown. There was a strong agitation against coolie labor among the Pacific Coast workers, a circumstance frequently capitalized by the criminal element. On their march to Chinatown, the mob wrecked five more wash houses and manhandled the owners, stoned the Gibson Chinese Mission on Washington Street, and drank the contents of a liquor store on Turk Street before starting on their final drive of the night—the sack and loot of the Chinese quarter. But they never entered its precincts, for the police beat them off with their clubs.

Another meeting of workingmen was held on Tuesday, and was composed "largely of property owners," for American workers were not the poverty-stricken lot the Marxists painted them. These San Franciscans formed the nucleus of a true Workingmen's party organized a few weeks later by Denis Kearney, a member of the Draymen and Teamsters' Union. This political group—it ceased to function as a party after three years—was known from its inception as the Kearney movement. It fought unjust taxes, railroad domination, bankers, coolie labor, and sought a solution of the unemployment problem. Kearney's organizing genius, his persistence and native eloquence, placed the Chinese Exclusion Act on the Federal statutes three years after his Workingmen's party disbanded. Washington first knew him in 1876 when he represented organized labor before a Senate committee. In this alone is seen the basic Americanism of Kearney and his movement. He was not an ordinary workingman, but the head of a prosperous trucking business which he purchased in 1872 upon his retirement from the sea—he had been first mate of a coastal vessel. Kearney and his adherents did not attempt to divide Americans into an employing and an employer class, each hating the other. They derided the workers of other states who permitted the Communists and other Marxists to monopolize the label, Workingmen's party. The Kearneyites did not regard the professional agitators of alien doctrines as workers. Although an outspoken foe of violence in all forms, and a firm believer in the Republic and its institutions, this did not deter Kearney's political enemies from falsely denouncing him as a Marxist. Railroad-controlled newspapers published garbled versions of his utterances to support this charge, and to justify his frequent arrests.

There was a third meeting on Tuesday, at which a committee of safety was organized. The rabble took the day off. The following evening two meetings were held. One was an anti-coolie demonstration in front of the city hall; a speaker was subsequently arrested for inciting to riot. The other was an assembly of the committee of safety in Horticultural Hall. A little after eight o'clock a courier rushed into the hall with word that the torch had been put to the lumber yards near the Pacific Mail dock, and that the police could not handle the mob. W. T. Coleman, president of the committee, despatched 150 vigilantes, armed with clubs, to the water-front.

Within the next hour five were slain and scores wounded by revolver shots. Of the dead, one was a vigilante, and one the driver of a hose cart. A rioter was shot dead while slashing a fire hose, a pedestrian was killed by a fire truck en route to the water-front. The mob shot two policemen, one in the head and another in the leg, and seriously injured three with stones.

The fire was extinguished on Thursday, along with the hoodlumism that started it. Mayor A. J. Bryant issued a proclamation warning all citizens "for the last time" not to congregate on streets so that the "thoroughfares may be unobstructed for the operation of the police, military, and committee of safety." This proclamation was heeded, because it was backed by four companies of Confederate and Union veterans, armed with rifles and navy revolvers, and three thousand vigilantes equipped with stout clubs and small arms. The latter patrolled the streets with the police. Two more wash houses were burned by small gangs before peace was completely restored, one in the city, and the other across the bay in San Pablo.

On Friday night, by way of proving that hoodlumism draws no color line, some yellow rowdies decided to mix it up in Chinatown, and were having a free-for-all until police batons put them to flight.

The white rioters were composed wholly of "hoodlums, thieves, and internationalists," to borrow the phrase of William Irwin, governor of California.

48

THE CITY THAT SLEEPS OVER A VOLCANO

WHILE THE MOBS WERE RAMPANT FROM COAST TO COAST an apprehensive nation looked to New York City for answer to the question: Will the insurrection end in rebellion? The metropolis was calm. But the country regarded this calm as ominous. The authorities shared the view, and Washington reinforced the Federal troops in the metropolitan area as the rioting entered the second week. On Monday, July 23, every hotel in the city was linked by telegraph with police headquarters. Four national-guard armories were also wired to headquarters and to Tompkins Square, their parade ground, where the Communists were to meet on Wednesday night. Officers and men of the four regiments slept beside their arms. A Washington despatch described a Marxist plot to foment disorders in the three cities fronting on the mouth of the Hudson—New York, Jersey City, and Brooklyn; it was feared these outbreaks might culminate in the dreaded rebellion. In the considered opinion of Washington, the Tompkins Square meeting would determine whether "this strike is a spasmodic affair or a rebellion from underneath." Typical of the country-wide feeling toward the gathering was this note in a Baltimore despatch to a metropolitan journal: "Public attention in this city is concentrated on the meeting in New York to-night and the deepest interest is felt in the result."

These fears were born long before the strike. Nor were they idle fears. When Oliver Charlick was police commis-

This anti-Communist cartoon in *Harper's Weekly*, February 1, 1879, bore the punning caption, "Very Social"—Communists also called themselves Socialists, and Socialists called themselves Communists. The pun also covered the grisly dialogue: First Conspirator: 'After we have killed all Kings and Rulers, *we shall be the Sovereigns.*' Second Conspirator: 'And then we can kill each other. What sport!' "

sioner under Mayor Havemeyer, an investigation disclosed "a communistic conspiracy, extensive and formidable," and he and other police officials were convinced that "New York City slept over a volcano." Charlick, who died in 1875, regarded those who plotted to overthrow the government by revolution as unworthy of the freedom of speech. In recalling his utterances on the Marxist menace, the press frowned down all suggestions to ban Communist meetings although aware of Communism's clandestine methods. In its issue of July 25 the *Herald* said: "The gospel of Communism has been preached in secret for a long time."

The gory gospel was spread systematically through the Workingmen's party, by a means hitherto unknown to political groups in America—a propaganda machine, openly described as such. The constitution of the party provided: "Every section shall choose one organizer.... The organizer conducts the local propaganda and is responsible to the section. The organizers of the various sections of one locality shall be in constant communication with each other in order to secure concerted action." There was no secret made of this propaganda machine, for the Communist organ, the *Labor Standard,* from which we quote, published the constitution in toto. New York City had a section in each of the ten wards where the party was organized, as well as a section for each foreign-language group.

The *Labor Standard* preached a weekly sermon on subversive propaganda which reached its peak during the rioting. It urged the strikers to carry on the "revolution" under the caption: "Appeal to Arms." The article left nothing to the imagination, as witness: "The struggle may last a number of years; but the war is declared, the parties engaged can no more leave the field without a final decision, and all compromises are henceforth impossible." The "Appeal to Arms" extolled the Commune of 1871 as the "Parisian

Troops of New York's Seventh Regiment awaiting a possible riot call. *Leslie's Weekly*, August 11, 1877.

workingmen's government" and pronounced this fiat for American workers: "Let workingmen everywhere stand forth with men and money for those who are so heroically fighting the battle of labor."

On the night before the Tompkins Square meeting, besides the Seventh and three other national guard regiments which slept in their armories, all units of the local commands held themselves in readiness. The city's entire police force was either on patrol or on reserve. A police commissioner was so confident of suppressing any riots or series of riots at their inception, that he told the press:

"We fear nothing but the torch."

This was a real fear, for the police reasoned that if the French Communists could destroy one-quarter of Paris by fire in 1871 they might carry out their threat to destroy all New York. Moreover, threats to burn the city were heard frequently from Communist lips. As late as the eve of the Tompkins Square meeting, a police spy overheard the threat in Justus Schwab's saloon and restaurant, 50 East First Street, the rendezvous of German Marxists. Schwab was an intellectual, a militant one. On a shelf behind his bar was a green-painted plaster bust of Shakespeare flanked by prints of dramatic scenes of the bloody days of the Paris Commune of six years earlier. One showed the burning of the Hotel de Ville, the other depicted the mob at the razing of the Vendôme Column. New York had no monument to a conqueror, but it had a city hall more beautiful than the one fired by Parisian Communists, and it was guarded from a like fate. Remembering the wanton shooting of Archbishop Darboy and other Parisian clergy by the Communists, and the sack of the churches, the police unobtrusively protected New York's places of worship and the homes of its clerics with plain-clothes men.

Dark had fallen when the Marxists assembled in Tompkins Square. Estimates of the crowd varied from five to ten thousand. There were three rostrums. French Communists spoke from one, Germans from another, and a third was for those who understood English. Over the English-language stand floated a banner inscribed: "Let the workingmen of the world unite." One speaker told the English-language section: "Stick together and we can proclaim the social republic in five years."

The speakers were silent on the gains labor had made

in the Republic they were seeking to overthrow. None ad-
verted to the eight-hour day instituted in the government
printing plant by Hayes on March 19, but several dwelt
on the proposals to arrest advocates of a Marxist proletariat,
and emphasized that no one had moved against Jay Gould
for suggesting a monarchy for the United States. The infamous Gould, who had done more to corrupt and besmirch

Justus Schwab
Leslie's Weekly, February 21, 1874.

the country's institutions than any other man, did not quite
say this. He said the riots could be quickly suppressed in
a monarchy, implying that monarchs did not have to consider the effect of their actions on voters.

The meeting was disappointingly tame. Its presiding
deity, Schwab, and his attendants in the Marxist heaven,
now talked of reform through the ballot, not revolution.

There was not even the faintest suggestion of incitement to riot. They were cautious lads that night, for their speeches were being noted verbatim by shorthand writers from the city's courts. Schwab had visited police headquarters before the meeting. Usually talkative, he kept silent on what was said to him after he left the marble pile on Mulberry Street by a detective who walked with him to the corner. This detective assured the Marxist chief that if a shot were fired at the meeting, Schwab and his lieutenants would not leave the scene alive.

As the meeting adjourned, three hundred hoodlums marched in military formation up Avenue A, on the west side of Tompkins Square. They were probably animated by nothing more than the exhibitionism which is part of the hoodlum cosmos. Instead of obeying the order to disperse, they threw stones, injuring several policemen so that they required surgical treatment. The police charged the rowdies with swinging batons. Many hoodlums fell with injured skulls. No record was kept of the injured, and the police permitted them to be dragged away. At midnight, the ten stage-coaches of the Broadway and Twenty-third Street line, which had been held at police headquarters in anticipation of a telegraphed appeal for the reserves, left Mulberry Street with tired policemen, and dropped them at their homes. As the stage-coaches departed, headquarters telegraphed to the armories that all was quiet. And the next day the country read with relief that the Tompkins Square meeting had been almost as innocuous as a soirée of parlor pinks.

49

THE WORST MAN ON EARTH

THE FOLLOWING DAY NEGOTIATIONS FOR A SETTLEMENT OF the railroad strike were under way on most of the affected roads, and by August 3 the strike was a thing of the past. But this did not end the troubles of the roads, for on the eve of the Tompkins Square meeting, coal-miners at the Meadow Brook mines, near Scranton, struck for a living wage, and forty-five thousand men in the Pennsylvania anthracite mines were out by the end of July, with several thousand additional on strike in the bituminous fields of Maryland, West Virginia, and Illinois. The mines were largely owned or controlled by the railroads. The wage slashes that attended the depression, coupled with the reduced output of the mines, brought the income of thousands of miners down to $2.50 to $4.00 a week. The plight of the miners and their families moved the country as the leading newspapers recorded conditions, and material aid was not lacking. A Scranton miner who put in a solid month's work had $19 left after paying for his mining supplies. Out of this he paid $4.30 for rent, leaving him $14.70 for food, clothes, fuel, and other necessities. The diet of this miner and his family was Indian corn-meal mush varied with potatoes and a little pork on pay-days—there were two pay-days monthly. The most skilled miner could not make more than $25 monthly. In the home of a Welsh miner, the wife, like the Bohemian women on the Chicago prairie, went shoeless that there might be a few more crumbs for the children. The miners were chiefly immigrants, the Welsh and Irish predominating, with a slight admixture of German stock. Those who came from farms fared better than the rest, for they raised corn, tomatoes, beans, and other vegetables, and a few boasted chicken runs.

At dawn on the first of August, three thousand miners assembled in a patch of woods on the bank of the Lackawanna River just north of Scranton proper. Who called the meeting was never determined. The miners, to the last man, denied having issued the summons. One of their number assumed the chairmanship, and immediately several strangers rose and denounced the operators as slave-drivers, and all who had returned to work in the shops and mines as blacklegs. One of these unknowns drew from his pocket a letter which he attributed to W. W. Scranton. It was an obvious fiction. In it—so ran the fabrication—Scranton berated the miners as no better than slaves and said he would have them yet working for 35 cents a day. The miners, mostly illiterate, howled down the chairman and all who sided with him as he denounced the letter as a rank forgery. The meeting incontinently ended amid shouts of "Go for the blacklegs!" and "Go for the shops!"

Five hundred miners, many of them armed with pick handles and pistols, immediately descended upon the Delaware, Lackawanna, and Western Railroad shops, clubbed the workers, indulged in wild gun play, and emptied the place. A mechanic who had roused the ire of the mob fled with most of the miners at his heels. A Catholic priest, the Reverend Dr. J. W. Dunn, was walking up the road as the mob raced toward him in pursuit of the fleeing workman. The priest halted the mob in the name of the Lord, and was pleading with the miners when another mob came tearing toward them shouting: "Kill him!" Several yards

Fatal clash between mob and vigilantes in Scranton, Pennsylvania, August 1, 1877.
Leslie's Weekly, August 18, 1877.

ahead of the second mob ran the breathless object of its vengeance, R. H. McKune, mayor of the city. McKune rushed to the cleric's side, grasped his arm and panted, "Save me!" The first mob, which had been moved by the clergyman's fervent appeal not to take human life, cried out to the rival mob: "Don't kill him!" While Father Dunn was addressing McKune's pursuers, one of them stepped forward and struck the mayor across the face with a cudgel, breaking his jaw. With blood streaming from his mouth, the mayor fell unconscious in the dust of the road.

Instantly the cry was raised that the mayor and Father Dunn had been murdered. The bell in the First Presbyterian Church tolled the riot call agreed upon by the vigilantes—a violent clangor—and thirty-eight men, armed with Remington rifles, rushed from their homes, and were marching in twos when they reached Washington Street and Lackawanna Avenue. Here the mob, including the inevitable curious ones, were assembled to the number of three thousand to five thousand. The vigilantes passed through the mob unmolested; but immediately thereafter stones and pickhandles were hurled at them amid yells of "kill the sons-of-bitches!" Several vigilantes were hit. They fired, killing three and wounding twenty-five, several of them fatally. Some of the mob returned the fire, injuring two more vigilantes.

Some two thousand troops were rushed to the Scranton fields the next day. Disorders of a minor sort occurred in other sections, but the presence of the soldiers, including both regulars and militia, soon made for peace.

In the last week of August the coal strike ended. It received its death blow on August 13 from F. C. Dinning, president of the Pittston Coal Company and the Butler Coal Company, when he announced a 10 per cent wage increase for all employees. Other operators followed suit.

"Workingmen are human, reasonable, and not grasping," said Dinning.

None of Dinning's men had struck.

The day following the fatal Scranton clash, strikes and all else gave way in popular interest to an event in the Wall Street district, "the dreadful assault on Jay Gould!"—to borrow the hawking cry of newsboys that afternoon. Just before noon Gould turned from Broad Street into Exchange Place. Immediately behind strode a man who towered head and shoulders above him, which did not bespeak extraordinary build, for the dwarfish Gould weighed only 110 pounds. The stalker, A. A. Selover, a vestryman in Christ Church and a member of the brokerage house of Shirley and Dunham, overtook Gould at 65 Exchange Place, reached down, grabbed him by the coat lapels, and shook him vigorously, as he exclaimed:

"I'll teach you what it is to tell lies!"

Gould seized Selover's coat, but let go when Selover slapped his face and followed this with a blow on the chest that sent Gould's jeweled scarf pin and gold pencil sliding along the sidewalk. Selover slipped and fell, but clung to Gould, whose head he pounded against a steel-mesh lattice as they rolled over on the sidewalk. The lattice fenced off an areaway eight feet deep, two feet wide, and five feet long. The bottom of the pit was of stone. The pit gave Selover an idea which he proceeded to carry out. A crowd watched him rise to his feet, holding Gould by the vest. Selover stood Gould erect for a moment. Then he seized him by the collar, raised him aloft so the crowd could see him, and exclaimed:

"Gould, you're a damn liar!"

Gould's brownish-yellow face turned pallid, and from his bloodless lips came the cry:

"Won't somebody take this man away? He will murder me!"

A man unacquainted with Gould started to his assistance. Selover momentarily held Gould in the air with his right hand, as he brushed aside the well-meaning rescuer with his left. Putting Gould back on terra firma, Selover struck him several resounding blows, called him ugly names, and then once more raised him above his head only to drop him into the pit, where he lay apparently lifeless. Selover then went to his office, followed by the approving grins of the crowd. A policeman rushed after him but halted when told what had happened.

Selover laughingly assured reporters at his office that he had no thought of murdering Gould, but merely sought to thrash him publicly, and was happy at having succeeded.

"For weeks and months Gould lied to me in the most varied and most persistent manner with the sole thought of swindling and robbing me as he had swindled and robbed others," said Selover. "He told me to sell Western Union short."

The assault was greeted joyously by press and public. Men who knew Gould gloated over it, and gave vent to their feelings. Russell Sage and his partner, James Keene, Wall Street's famed plunger, were summering at Long Branch. "Jay Gould is the worst man set on earth since the beginning of the Christian era," said Keene. "He is treacherous, cowardly, false, and a despicable worm incapable of a generous motive. He is destitute of every principle of honor and common humanity."

This extravagant speech was essentially true. Beginning with the friends of his youth, Gould had defrauded all who trusted and befriended him. After driving one benefactor to suicide by his treachery, he swindled the dead man's daughters, a circumstance recalled as a mob milled through

Wall Street chanting, "Who killed Leupp?" and responding with the name of Gould as they hunted him during the Black Friday panic he and Fisk created. Charles M. Leupp was one of the most beloved men of his day. Newspapers of the early fifties referred to him as New York's richest merchant. His purse was always open to the worthy, and during his closing years, he was a leader in raising funds for the needy. One of his last acts was as chairman of the committee that gave the concert for the relief of the poor at the Academy of Music on January 11, 1855, which was the beginning of organized work of relief. Selover probably recalled the tragic fate of the noble Leupp as he manhandled Gould. Selover was only one of several who assaulted Gould publicly. In 1874 a lawyer he had victimized mauled him in Delmonico's. After Selover's attack, Gould ceased being the town's punching-bag. He accomplished this through two hired gunmen. They were his constant shadows. One had a reputation as a killer, and besides a navy revolver, packed a stiletto, his favorite weapon.

50

FRIENDS OF THE WORKERS

WHEN PEACE WAS RESTORED THROUGH THE COUNTRY, some politicians heeded the counsels of the nation's foremost labor leader, whose far-seeing utterances played a large part in holding public sentiment with the striking railroadmen throughout the terror—T. M. Arthur, head of the Brotherhood of Locomotive Engineers. He had inveighed against the futility of walk-outs, strikes, and lockouts, and advocated the establishment of boards of arbitration, their decisions to be final and binding. This reform was started on its long uphill climb when the Republicans of the home state of President Hayes wrote into their state platform "that provision be made for statutory arbitration between employers and employees, to adjust controversies, reconcile interests, and establish justice and equity between them."

It did not go as far as Arthur had proposed, but it was a big step forward. The Ohio Republicans acted in August, and after the fall elections their admirable plank was forgotten save by the few who felt that an entire nation should not suffer because participants in an industrial dispute refused to arbitrate. The prevailing opinion was that there would never be another strike like it, and that everything connected with it might as well be forgotten.

This was the attitude of a Pittsburgh grand jury which heard testimony on the rioting, incendiarism, thieving, maiming, and killing, and then filed a presentment where-

in they sought to laugh off the city's shame, using Governor
Hartranft and the state militia as the targets of their jesters'
bladders, saying: "Their martial achievements under the
lead of the governor, their commander-in-chief, have their
parallel only in that tremendous feat of the French king who
marched his army up the hill, and then marched it down
again."

Yet this presentment, stripped of its ghastly and unseemly
humor, mirrored the attitude of all law-enforcement agencies called upon to deal with the crimes of the summer.
Hundreds of rioters, and a few thieves, had been arrested
by the police and the military. Their trials, like the Pittsburgh presentment, were held back until after the election to
avoid repercussions at the polls. Most of the accused were
freed, and in the few convictions obtained, nominal penalties
of a few days' imprisonment, or a few dollars' fine, were imposed.

As the year drew to a close, Congressmen and other officials discussed the summer's events and their causes, a few
sincerely and understandingly, and others after the manner
of vote-seeking demagogues. Hendrick B. Wright, a Pennsylvania Representative, advocated a Federal appropriation of
$10,000,000 to be distributed among the 4,000,000 unem-
ployed—about $2.50 per man. Wright knew this would solve
nothing, and the only charitable explanation for this trans-
parent vote-catching device is that he was in his cups; for
he had an unusual background including forty-six years
of active practice in law and politics, holding his first office,
that of district attorney, in 1834.

Most of the discussions were carried on by Marxists, who
coupled their attacks on the American system with assaults
on Christianity. They held meetings in every populous center of the country; the largest in the East was convened
by Schwab in Newark, New Jersey, on December 29, 1877,

under the high-sounding name of the Workingmen's National Congress.

It was not until early in 1878 that Schwab, blatantly blasphemous, described the mission of the Marxists. He probably thought it was time to heed his master's dictum that religion is the opiate of civilization. And he mocked Christianity and applauded Marxism, saying:

"Christ told us, especially the capitalists, how to be charitable, to feed the hungry and clothe the naked, but He had not told us how to do it; the Socialist Labor party is going to do what He failed to do."

Schwab did not use the choicest English, but it was excellent for one who had been in the country only a few years. He fled his native Frankfort-on-the-Main to escape military service. He could not speak French, which did not deter him from attending a celebration of the anniversary of the French Revolution of 1848, observed by one thousand five hundred members of New York's French colony who understood no German and spoke little English. The walls of Germania Hall were decorated for the occasion with red flags and Communist slogans—all in French. One read: *Du pain ou du plomb*—"Bread or lead," or "Bread or bullets."

Throughout the winter of 1877-78 Communist leaders expressed a willingness to unite with other political groups. On May 9, 1878, the New York *Tribune*, noting the new departure, said:

Communism is organizing itself into leagues and holding conventions and asking for an alliance with political factions. We do not believe it can ever be the ruling power in the United States, but it can easily become the tyrant of certain localities ... ; and whenever the flame of insurrection breaks out, New York can hardly escape attack. It is well to look to the situation and consider how we shall meet it; above all, how we shall awake in our children the conservative religious sentiment which animated our fathers.

Old-line politicians hurried to the Communist bargain counter. A vote is a vote, and if the Communists were willing to trade, why not trade? So the top-hatted Kingman Page dropped into Schwab's cellar saloon and restaurant and had a lager beer with the Communist chief, and invited him to visit Herr Dorsheimer, the lieutenant-governor of New York. The bartender, a simple soul, whose only ambition was to own his own saloon, was astonished to hear Schwab tell Dorsheimer's emissary that if the Herr lieutenant-governor wished to see him, let him call at his saloon.

A few days later, on June 10, the lieutenant-governor paid his respects to Schwab, and they talked in German over their steins, first standing at the bar, and then seated at a table. And the word spread of the confab, and Dorsheimer would say no more than that Schwab was not as black as he was painted and was not the type to advocate bloodshed, and so on. He protested it was just a friendly visit, nothing more.

Schwab was absent when reporters called at his saloon, but the bartender told of the visits of Page and Dorsheimer, and when asked why the lieutenant-governor called, he grinningly replied: "Votes, I suppose."

It was votes. For Dorsheimer was ambitious to succeed Conkling in the United States Senate. Conkling's term would end the following March, and the complexion of the state legislature chosen in November would decide whether Conkling or Dorsheimer would go to Washington. Dorsheimer was apprehensive, for the four Democratic factions opposed to Tammany, or rather to its leader, Honest John Kelly, were talking of fusion with Republicans on local and legislative candidates in the metropolis. Dorsheimer, a lieutenant of Tilden, was also a friend of Honest John; and while the Tammany chief and Tilden were making the preliminary moves in their struggle for control of the forthcoming Democratic State Convention, and Dorsheimer was dreaming of Washington, let us visit the national capital where the colored Cohenites are becoming a problem to the police.

It is mid-September, and for days Washington despatches told of Isaac Cohen who "marches around the capital with a long tail of black strikers behind him," and who "for months had been getting his living out of the poorest and most ignorant class of colored people here, and at the same time doing his utmost to breed riot and discontent."

Cohen emerged from the turbulence of the preceding year the self-styled leader of the unemployed and downtrodden colored people. The job paid him well, for while the colored Cohenites marched, Cohen rode at their head in a buggy. His followers excused this capitalistic touch because he told them he was flat-footed. He called his black adherents members of the Workingmen's Relief Association, of which he was president, treasurer, and chairman of the board. He never appeared in the street without a mob of Negroes at his heels. At first he confined his harangues to the Negro quarter, and when he could count on a minimum of a hundred colored men being at a given place at a given time, he fared forth into other sections of the capital, his buggy his rostrum. He was always sure of a sprinkling of whites being attracted by the fervent "Hallelujahs!" of the Negroes as he mouthed, "We, the people," or some other favorite phrase. At first mild, Cohen became violent in his spoutings as time went on. His dusky lieutenant, who answered to the name of George Washington, reflected his master's mood. Washington passed the hat as Cohen reached his peroration, and kicked the shins of colored spectators who hesitated about dropping a coin in his hat, their howls of pain lost in a Hallelujah chorus. After the collection, the coins were emptied into Cohen's cupped hands. On Wednesday, September 18, Cohen called a meeting of his followers on the east front of the Capitol; and that morning the New York *Tribune* said: "Isaac Cohen, who passes the hat around in Washington and advises the unemployed to plunder and burn if they cannot get work, has been going around the departments with a pack of curbstone loafers at his back and muttering, 'We, the people.'"

Barred from the Capitol, Cohen called a general strike for the following day, ordering his followers to assemble at the association's headquarters at 2 P. M. and march with him to every point in the city where colored laborers received less than $1.50 a day and force them to strike.

As a consequence, the capital police were armed with rifles, and the War Department ordered two companies of the Second Artillery, armed as infantry, from Fort Mc-Henry, to be quartered at the arsenal, and supplemented the handful of troops in the barracks with one hundred marines, and another one hundred marines were despatched to Fort Whipple, opposite Georgetown.

During the afternoon it was reported that the Cohenites would raid the Treasury. All Treasury clerks who had seen service were provided with revolvers and rifles, and the twelve crippled soldiers on night duty were replaced by fifty able-bodied veterans, all well-armed.

At 5:30 P. M., Cohen climbed into his buggy, and presently 450 blacks were trotting behind, ignorant of where he was leading them, but blindly following. Cohen defiantly halted at the gate of the arsenal, tossed the reins to the nearest black, and immediately began bellowing that all colored workers in the national capital would be on strike in a few hours, and repeated his threat to use force if persuasion failed.

The following forenoon the Cohenites set forth to make good their leader's promise. With Cohen perched in his inseparable buggy, they marched to a brick-yard where scores of Negroes were employed. It was noon, and the black workers were eating their food in the open when the Cohenites halted at the plant. They looked for a speech from Cohen, but instead, George Washington himself took up his position near the buggy and commanded the workers to quit, and quit at once, for if they didn't force would be used.

The brick-yard laborers had been enjoying their meal and George Washington's talk until he threatened them. Then they dropped their dinner pails, seized pickaxes and anything else that would serve as weapons, and defiantly shouted, "Come on!" Any type of fighting, other than mouth-fighting, was not in Cohen's thoughts, and he ordered a hasty retreat.

On Saturday afternoon he led one hundred Negroes in another parade, halting at three places where pavement was being laid by colored workers, and his harangues beguiled about one hundred to quit work. Now two hundred marched behind his buggy, and soon this number was swelled to four hundred by black sidewalk loafers. The general strike was on—so thought the hallelujah-shouting Cohenites as they marched. But the parade and the general strike both suddenly ended at Seventh and E Streets where George Washington made the mistake of hitting a white policeman. In the mild mêlée that followed, Cohen lashed his horse and drove off, leaving his followers to look after themselves. In court the next morning, the judge asked George Washington to give his real name.

"William Simms," said Cohen's lieutenant, who was sent to jail to work out a ten-dollar fine.

We will now visit the metropolis where our old acquaintance, the corrupt Cardozo, is back in the political arena, this time as a reformer, along with another infamous crook,

Theodore Allen. Both are working to save the good people
of the city from Tammany's predatory braves. Like Cardozo, The Allen—seldom was he called anything else—was
in politics for what it would bring him. The was a gambler,
and a crooked one. His den was at 615 Broadway, once the
site of St. Thomas' Protestant Episcopal Church, and more
recently the scene of a foul murder, according to the authorities, with The himself the admitted slayer. The dead man
was Edward Malloy, a detective, once accused by The of
intimacy with his wife. This was the suspected motive.
But the slayer said his revolver went off accidentally, and as
there was only The and his victim in the room, The's word
prevailed. Although indicted for murder in the first degree,
the influential killer was out on bail, pending trial. Malloy
was slain on Primary Day, September 17, and a metropolitan
journal began its story of the slaying thus: "The notorious
gambler and Jack-of-all-evil, The Allen, killed Edward Malloy..." Police found Malloy lying on the fourth floor of
The's gambling den, a bullet through his forehead, just
above the right eye.

The was one of six brothers, and all save one were criminals. The started out as a hoodlum, ballot-box stuffer, and
thief. In 1859 he was sent to the penitentiary for theft. When
he came out, he turned to policy, and was on the road
to riches as a policy dealer until Shang Draper and Al Adams
took the business away from him. The always maintained
a saloon, which served as a front for his criminal enterprises,
and as a feeder for his mercenary political machine, essentially personal, although it sometimes bore the name of a
national party. Six years earlier, in 1872, he took a leaf
from the Communists' book and called it the United Workingmen's Reform Club, with headquarters over his bar at
Prince and Mercer streets. The occupied the entire building,
misnamed the St. Bernard House. Its patrons were reckless

criminals like those who frequented the saloon he had owned a block to the north, at Mercer and Houston, when he was first convicted of theft. Like Cohen, Schwab, and the rest of them, The Allen was a devoted friend of the workers. He was a leader in the Labor Reform party, and a top man locally in the National Greenback Labor party, the new name of the National, or Greenback, party.

The killing did not interfere with The's political leadership, for he called a meeting of his political machine at 123 Houston Street a few days after Malloy's death, and resolutions were adopted praising Malloy's killer for his frank and manly character, and denouncing the newspapers for the "imputations cast upon a noble man and a true patriot." The true patriot and noble man was The himself. Consequently, it was only fitting that a fortnight after the shooting of Malloy, one thousand five hundred of The's followers should make merry at a barbecue in Hamilton Park, where an ox was roasted whole, and beer booths flourished under every other tree. The gambler-killer was host, and a lavish one. Everything was free and plentiful; there were sandwiches of all kinds for the fastidious, and chunks of roast ox and sea biscuit for the others, and beer galore for all. Many of The's guests drank themselves into unconsciousness. But at the end of the day they were carted home by The's henchmen who had hired trucks and drays for the occasion.

The barbecue was on October 2. The election was only a month and three days away. And respectable newspapers supporting the Republican-fusion municipal ticket, headed by Edward Cooper, son of the philanthropist, covered the affair, and quoted The's political opinions. He had no doubt of the election of young Cooper over Augustus Schell, the Tammany candidate. Here it should be noted that the barbecue cost The nothing: Cooper footed the bill.

This fight on Tammany was aimed at Honest John Kelly. It was a repetition of the fight on Tweed, and again the silent back-stage director of the struggle was Tilden. Like Tweed, Honest John was marked for destruction because he had seized control of the Democratic State Committee and had become avowedly anti-Tilden. But unlike Tweed, nothing could be pinned on him that came within the statute of limitations. He was comptroller of the metropolis, and his management of the city's finances was above reproach, for he had made his pile long before Tilden made him boss of Tammany, and no longer looted public funds. As in his fight on Tweed, Tilden let his friends do his work. They accused Honest John of being an absolute boss, knowing that a political machine calls for this type of leadership. But the average voter did not know this, so the specious charge made an excellent issue. This same charge could have been made any day since Tilden made him Tweed's successor. It was the only accusation they could fairly bring against him, unless they dipped into the distant past.

At the Democratic State Convention in the last week of September, the Tildenites nominated George H. Bradley for associate judge of the Court of Appeals over William H. Sawyer, Honest John's candidate, with only eleven votes to spare, and also prevented the adoption of a pro-Greenback plank which, the Tammany leader argued wisely, might spell the difference between victory and defeat for the legislative ticket as well as the party's only state-wide candidate. The Tilden delegates forced through a plank praising the resumption of specie payments, which were to start on January 1, and this poor sop to the Greenbackers: "We congratulate the state and country upon the practical relative value of the greenback currency of the government with gold and silver." The greenback, worth only 81.1 cents in 1870, was now worth 97.5 cents, and was to reach par on December 17.

The entire currency question—greenbacks, silver coinage, and specie resumption—cut through party lines, but its chief support came from Democrats. During a debate in the House, William H. Felton, a Democrat from Georgia and a Baptist minister, characterized the resumption act "as unjust and wicked as the labor strikes which . . . startled and alarmed all good citizens," and added: "The only difference was that the last was illegal and violent; the other sought to cover the outrage they perpetrated by the forms and sanctions of law. The only difference was, one was speedily and justly suppressed; the other, panoplied in gold and protected by political influence, smiles in its bloated security upon the wrecks of fortune—the blasted hopes and the suffering poverty it has created." And in this same debate, the famed William Darrah Kelley, Republican from Pennsylvania, spoke of "the forty or fifty men who hold the money-bags of our eastern cities" visiting Washington to influence the Hayes administration on the currency question.

Despite the party platform, New York Democratic candidates praised Greenbacks and all they betokened. Typical of their appeal for Greenback support was that of Fernando Wood, chairman of the House Ways and Means Committee, although his career as a swindler and thief had been public property for more than a quarter of a century. Wood told a noisy audience of fifteen hundred in National Hall, Forty-fourth Street between Eighth and Ninth avenues: "I'm the biggest Greenback man in the crowd. We are all for Greenbacks, and for the honest, and freest circulation of money." Wood announced in his opening sentence that he had hired the hall for himself, by way of disclaiming alliance with any faction. There were no other speakers, unless we include the hecklers. One interrupted Wood with: "Tammany Hall and all of you can go to hell! Give us work!"

Angrily Wood shouted back: "I came here to explain myself. It is my meeting. I don't ask for any man's vote. But I won't be put down by tramps!"

"Who made the tramps?" came from the audience.

"I'll tell you I've been the friend of the workingmen, and then see if there is any man who is fit to stand by my side as the friend of the workingmen," continued Wood. "Who, in 1855, when the workingmen marched the streets shouting, 'Work or bread!' gave three thousand hungry men ruined brick walls to pull down, and when they had piled the bricks in one place, had them carried and piled in another place?"

Wood provided work for idle men, but not three thousand. The precise number was 125, and they were put to work for a few days only, at a dollar a day, on the ruins of the old city hall. The work stopped shortly after Wood had been mayor less than three weeks. It was all within the law, as we learned from Wood's own lips, on January 22, 1855, when he told a committee of complaining workmen that he had hired as many "as the charter would allow without any violation on my part." Yet no newspaper bothered to cite the record which Wood had falsified. They published his obvious untruths, and let it go at that. Wood also misstated the record elsewhere in his demagogic spouting, especially when he described himself as a friend of the workingmen. He should have been, for he owed them much, having obtained his financial start by fleecing longshoremen in his water-front groggeries. These workers were forced by crooked stevedores to buy vile home-made rotgut on credit from Wood, who not only charged them for what they drank, but for liquor never served them.

And Wood, an old hand at every form of election thievery, was reëlected by a narrow margin of 797 votes. He was one of the few Tammany candidates to escape the Republican-fusion sweep, which carried into office all city-wide candidates from mayor down; in the state, the Republicans elected their nominee for the Court of Appeals and ninety-eight assemblymen, thereby assuring Conkling's return to the Senate. The Democrats elected twenty-eight assemblymen, and the Greenbacks, two. Honest John's candidate for mayor was defeated by a majority of 19,361; and Tilden's choice for Appeals Court judge lost by 34,661 votes. The Greenback vote for Gideon J. Tucker, its Court of Appeals nominee, was 75,133. Two years before, the Greenbacks polled but 1,987 in the state, and in the nation, 81,737. This year, its national vote exceeded a million.

Tilden's friends, to save his face before the nation, for he was still angling for another chance at the presidency, held up Cooper's election to the mayoralty as a Tilden triumph. They were silent on the rout of his state-wide candidate.

Cooper's election recalled his rôle in the cipher despatches. As treasurer of the executive committee of the Democratic National Committee, he paid $15,000 for traveling expenses to several engaged in the abortive plot to buy electoral votes for Tilden. This was innocent in itself. He also gave a cipher to one of the emissaries sent south to see what could be done for Tilden. This code was never used, so again Cooper played an innocent part. Tilden's nephew, a principal in the plot, said he intended to get the bribes for the returning boards from Cooper. But this was not binding on Cooper, so his rôle, so far as the record disclosed, was still innocent. Cooper himself testified that he first knew of the corruption when Pelton showed him a cipher telegram asking for $80,000 to buy South Carolina's votes, and that he immediately informed Tilden who, he said, put a stop to his nephew's activities. But he never told these things until after translations of the incriminating ciphers were published, and he was haled before a congressional investigating committee.

Many Democratic leaders, including William Purcell, chairman of the New York Democratic State Committee, and editor of the Rochester *Union-Advertiser*, blamed the cipher despatches for the loss of New York, New Jersey, and Connecticut, the three eastern states carried by Tilden in 1876, as well as other Democratic defeats.

"They," said Purcell, referring to the cipher despatches, "lost to the Democratic party the great advantage of the cry of fraud accomplished in the actual counting in of Hayes by presenting a prima facie case of fraud in the unsuccessful efforts of men in the closest family, personal and political relations to the Democratic candidate to do the same for him."

But the nation heard no explanation of the Democratic defeats from Tilden and Honest John, whose struggle for mastery of Tammany and the state organization might determine the results of the next presidential canvass. They felt toward one another like the average Democrat in the South toward a white neighbor who voted Republican. In South Carolina, where the Republicans held a state convention but did not nominate a ticket, Wade Hampton was reëlected governor with 169,550 votes. Republicans, to the number of 213, wrote in the names of others as their choice for governor. Some suspected the Reverend Dr. E. Cooke, the venerable president of Claflin University, of Orangeburg, of being one of the 213, and when they met him on a train, the *Zion Herald* related, "he was called a damned son of a b----, and all the vulgar and insulting epithets that can be raked from the slang phrases of those low, grog-shop politicians." The language used toward the eminent divine, other than the ancestral taunt, was left to the imagination, for the church journal said, "The insults and the abuse cannot be described."

51

RULE OR RUIN

WITH THE DAWN OF 1879, THE NATION'S FOUR outstanding political figures held the center of the stage as they battled for control of their respective parties in New York. Besides the contest between Tilden and Honest John, the President was out to crush New York's senior Senator. The battle between Conkling and Hayes began in 1877 when Conkling publicly slurred his title as President and derided his civil-service reform at the state convention of the New York Republicans. In his inaugural address, Hayes said that Federal officials should owe their whole service to the government and to the people; that appointments to office were not to be made nor expected merely as rewards for partizan service; that members of Congress should not expect their traditional control over appointments; and that all appointees were to serve so long as their personal characters remained untarnished, and the performance of their duties satisfactory. He demanded a reform that would be thorough, radical, and complete, a return to the principles and practices of the founders of the government, who "neither expected nor desired from public officers any partizan service." He observed that he had been elected by the zealous labors of a political party. But he also noted that he would strive "to be always mindful of the fact that he serves his party best who serves his country best." His references to civil service ended with: "In furtherance of the reform we seek, and in other important respects a change of great importance, I recommend an amendment to the Constitution prescribing a term of six years for the presidential office and forbidding a reëlection." Hayes thereafter issued an order divorcing Federal officials from political activities, an order that was violated whenever it suited his administration. Conkling went further than mere derision of the President's civil-service stand, for he had the convention adopt a plank emphasizing that national office-holders in the state, including clerks and subordinates of every degree, numbered 7,465, or one to every 152 voters, as a foundation for this sophism: "We can conceive of no condition of affairs, short of the extinction of manhood and patriotism, in which a postmaster or clerk could subdue to his partizan will 152 other electors, or exert any other influence beyond such as his character might give him."

The convention refused to indorse the Hayes administration or to voice its belief that he, and not Tilden, had been elected President. The pro-Hayes plank began: "The lawful title of Rutherford B. Hayes to the presidency is as clear and perfect as that of George Washington." Conkling and his delegates defeated the proposed plank 295 to 105. And by way of heaping contumely on his foes—most of them called themselves reformers—Conkling told the convention: "When Doctor Johnson said that patriotism was the last refuge of a scoundrel, he ignored the enormous possibilities of the word reform."

Within five weeks of this sneer at the reformers and this fresh taint on Hayes's title, the President retaliated by sending to the Senate the nominations of Theodore Roosevelt, merchant, banker, and philanthropist, for collector of the Port of New York, and L. Bradford Prince for naval officer. Roosevelt, whose son and namesake was to be President, was to displace Chet Arthur, also destined to fill the same

exalted office, the way being paved for each by an assassin's
bullet. Prince was to succeed Alonzo B. Cornell. The only
offense of Cornell and Arthur was their loyalty to Conkling.
No charges had been lodged against either man. The move
against them was an abuse of presidential authority, and the

Theodore Roosevelt, father of President Theodore Roosevelt
Leslie's Weekly, March 2, 1878.

Republican-controlled Senate so decided in not confirming
Roosevelt and Prince.

On July 11, 1878, Hayes removed Arthur and Cornell.
Roosevelt had died the previous February, and Hayes appointed, *ad interim,* Edwin A. Merritt for collector, and Silas
W. Burt for naval officer. When the names were before
the Senate the following February, Conkling would again

have blocked Hayes had he not riled several Republican Senators by reading job-begging letters to Arthur from the President's secretary, a Cabinet officer, and others near to Hayes, to show that public advocates of civil-service reform were secret champions of spoilsmanship. Merritt was confirmed by a vote of thirty-three to twenty-four, and Burt, thirty-one to nineteen.

Conkling bided his time to even the score, and made no secret of his intention to name Cornell for governor of New York.

Tilden's fight on Honest John abetted Conkling's plan. Honest John was displaying the same deep-rooted open contempt for him that Tweed did. He despised Tilden for his cowardice, and said so, publicly and privately, and unburdened himself to one of Dana's reporters in this wise: "Tilden was elected by the votes of the people, and he had not sufficient courage after he was elected to go forward, as a brave man should have done, and say to the people of the country, 'I have been elected by the votes of the people, and you see to it that I am inaugurated.' Nothing of the like did Mr. Tilden."

In his drive on Honest John, Tilden had deprived him of nearly everything worth-while in patronage. Only a few jobs remained to Tammany, such as sheriff, register, and county clerk. These were fee jobs, and for years Tilden knew, in common with all in the inner circle of politics, of the custom to increase official fees for the benefit of the party campaign chest. While these traditional transgressions were committed by subordinates, their principals were responsible, and could be removed from office.

Early in 1878, the Cooper faction, Tilden's own, had drafted charges against all three officials. But it was decided to wait until after the election to file the charges with the governor. Yet no action was taken until after Cooper was

inaugurated mayor in January, 1879, and then only against
Henry A. Gumbleton, county clerk. Governor Robinson
removed him on the night of March 17, and appointed
Hubert O. Thompson, Cooper's political aide, to the va-

Alonzo B. Cornell
Harper's Weekly, September 27, 1879.

cancy. Another removal was that of our old friend, Hank
Smith, from the police commission. This ouster was designed
to give the Tilden faction control of the appointment of
election inspectors in the metropolis in the forthcoming
election, when an entire state ticket would be chosen. A

crooked election is impossible without crooked election inspectors.

Tilden was also bent on removing Honest John as city
comptroller, and his compliant mayor sent the commissioner
of accounts to examine the Tammany chief's books. While
this was going on, Kelly told the press that his proposed
removal was part of a general scheme to remove all Tammany men from office, and added: "Tilden, Robinson, and
Cooper would be more delighted to remove me than any
one else." But Honest John escaped the ax, for there was
neither a penny missing nor misspent in his handling of the
city's finances.

Tilden did not show his hand until he had named a slate
of Sachems, with himself at their head, in opposition to
Honest John's ticket. As a Tilden supporter observed, Honest John and his faction could not be ousted from Tammany
Hall while he controlled the Sachems, or a majority of them.
As trustees of the Society of Tammany, which owned the
Hall, the Sachems held the key and could lock the door
at their pleasure, and the faction admitted alone could wear
the label of Tammany, which is always good for at least
half of the Democratic vote on Election Day. The election
of the Sachems was held on the night of April 21, and Honest John and his associates overwhelmed Tilden and his
men. One of them was Isaiah Rynders, an all-around black-
guard, a veteran organizer of repeaters and other types of
election thieves, generically known as ward bummers. Adherents of the Rynders type provoked the *Tribune* to note:
"Mr. Tilden, who made a good record once as a Reformer,
has since committed his fortunes to as rascally a gang of
corruptionists as New York has ever known."

A little later it thus defined him: "Mr. Tilden is a railroad
wrecker, a speculator in elevated railroad stock, a manipu-
lator of cipher despatches, and a man with a grievance who

Honest John Kelly kicks over Tilden's money barrel for the ensuing
year's Presidential campaign as he prepares to attack Governor Robinson. Nast's caption, borrowed from the *Washington Post*, a Democratic
journal, "New York Must Be Carried," is followed by the observation:
"A slight difference of opinion between the two noble generalissimos
as to *how*, and by *whom*, it is to be done." *Harper's Weekly*, November 8, 1879.

means to be the candidate of the Democratic party for the presidency, or to destroy the party."

Tilden planned to renominate Robinson for governor. Two weeks before the state convention Tammany announced it would not support Robinson, and it was generally understood that the Tammany chief would back a third ticket if the governor ran again. Tilden had put Cooper in the field against the Tammany mayoralty candidate in the preceding fall, thereby placing his approval on party bolting.

The Republicans held their convention first, meeting in Saratoga on September 3. The Federal administration faction, or more properly, four anti-Conkling groups, had as many candidates for the gubernatorial nomination. Conkling backed Cornell, the rejected of Hayes, and won on the first ballot, Cornell receiving 234 votes to the 216 cast for his five rivals, there being an added starter. The rest of the ticket, save one, were Conkling's personal selections. The exception was James W. Wadsworth, candidate for comptroller.

A week later the forces of Tilden and Honest John assembled in Syracuse. The Tammany men buttonholed every delegate they knew, friend or foe, and said: "Tilden won't figure in this convention." "Why not?" was the usual astonished retort. "Because he ciphers," came the punning response.

But there was no time for humor once the gavel fell. Honest John, an able speaker himself, left the presentation of his case on the floor to Augustus Schell and others, notably Lieutenant-Governor Dorsheimer, who had deserted Tilden after the cipher disclosures. When Robinson and several others had been nominated for governor, Tammany took over the show. While Peter Mitchell was assailing Robinson, some one roared from the gallery: "Put those Tammany roughs out!" Mitchell called the interrupter an impudent pup. Jeremiah McGuire, sometime speaker of the assembly, denounced Tilden as "the greatest fraud of the age." Dorsheimer sought to turn the tide with an eloquent plea for harmony, and after reciting Robinson's acts against Tammany, strode up and down the middle aisle as he asked delegates from other counties if they would not have followed Tammany's example under similar circumstances. While Honest John was silent, he was not idle. Seated near him was his friend, Patrick H. Cowen, a delegate from Saratoga, who was next recognized. Cowen extolled State Senator John C. Jacobs, the chairman of the convention, and popular with all, and moved his nomination for governor by acclamation. The anti-Tildenites cheered and clapped, and as Jacobs shook his head in disapproval, the Tildenites joined in the applause. As the demonstration was subsiding, Major W. H. Quincy, secretary of the convention, a member of Tammany, put the motion, which was carried by a thundering aye, with only one or two feeble noes, and he then declared Jacobs the unanimous nominee of the convention.

With few exceptions, the spectators joined in the fresh applause, started by Tammany, its supporters, and its claque. The entire proceedings, from the moment Quincy put the motion, violated every principle of parliamentary procedure. When delegates and spectators quieted down, Jacobs said he regretted the secretary had assumed the duties of the chair without authority, and that had his own wishes been consulted, he would not have permitted his name to go before the convention.

Having failed to stampede the convention, Tammany moved a recess of two hours, confident of persuading a sufficient number of wavering ones in that time of the folly of naming Robinson. But the Tilden leaders successfully opposed the motion, which was lost, 217 to 166. A shift of twenty-six votes would have spelled defeat for Tilden.

Schell then warned the convention that "under no circumstances will the Democracy of the City of New York support the nomination of Lucius Robinson." He repeated Tammany's offer to support any man but Robinson. He paused in the vain hope that the olive-branch would be extended. Resuming, he said it was evident the convention had determined to name Robinson, and then concluded: "I desire now to announce to the convention that the delegation from New York will now retire from the hall."

To a deafening din of cheers, groans, catcalls, and hisses, the Tammany delegates marched out, followed by quite a few upstate delegates. For ten minutes after the bolt, the convention was unable to proceed because of the uproar. The bolters went to the Vanderbilt House, but its largest parlor could not accommodate even the delegates, and Honest John declared an adjournment for four hours to enable a committee to hire the largest available auditorium. Shakespeare Hall was selected, and when the rump convention was called to order, David Dudley Field was elected chairman. The delegates and the thronged galleries gave back a stentorian "No!" after Field said Robinson had been crammed down their throats, and inquired if they liked the dose. Then Dorsheimer nominated Honest John for governor, and as the Tammany chief arose, he was greeted with cries of "Three cheers for Governor Kelly!"

There was one trait for which the Tammany boss was noted: he would not deceive a friend. These men were his friends, and when the cheers ended, his first utterance was: "Of course, I don't expect to be elected governor." To the shouts of "You will! You will!" he shook his head and continued: "I have no such anticipation. I expect, however, to defeat a man who has committed great outrages against the people of New York. I expect to convince Governor

Robinson after he has retired to private life that he has committed a grievous wrong, a great wrong, against the Democratic party not only in the county of New York but

Nast shows Honest John Kelly falling into the barrel on top of Governor Robinson. The quotation on the wall refers to the attempt to make Colonel Pelton, Tilden's nephew, the scapegoat in the cipher disclosures. *Harper's Weekly,* November 22, 1879.

in every county of the state." He likened the nocturnal removal of Gumbleton to "the plans of the midnight assassin and the burglar."

The bolt was a boon to Conkling, and Honest John's decision to tour the state made certain a Republican victory. He could count on a sizable audience wherever he went, but in upstate Republican strongholds the Conkling machine provided him with welcoming throngs, headed by one or more brass bands. The Tammany chief captured the blackest of black Republicans with his picturesque characterizations of his foes, especially Tilden, "that old humbug of Cipher Alley," and "his puppet governor and puppet mayor." He cited Robinson's part in the coalition with the New York City Republicans in the preceding municipal election as demonstrating his unworthiness of Democratic support. As for himself, he was the true Democratic candidate for governor. At this point Honest John would read the twenty-eight word resolution adopted unanimously by Tammany on September 6: "Resolved, That in case the Democratic State Convention insists upon the renomination of Lucius Robinson as the candidate for governor, the Tammany delegation will leave in a body."

This was his letter of marque.

To each of his audiences he repeated that he had no hope of election, and was ambitious only to defeat the puppet governor of the old humbug of Cipher Alley.

The election amply realized Honest John's hopes. He defeated Robinson and elected Cornell, who ran 19,686 votes behind Wadsworth, the high man on his ticket. Cornell polled 42,777 more votes than Robinson. The tally for governor stood: Cornell, 418,567; Robinson, 375,790; Kelly, 77,566. Tilden had deprived Tammany of the mayoralty and a few other city and county offices; but Honest John more than retaliated, for besides the governorship, his bolt cost the Tilden machine five other state offices. The only Tildenite elected was the nephew and namesake of Horatio Seymour, nominee for state engineer and surveyor. While Honest John and his supporters did not oppose the Tilden ticket from lieutenant-governor down, they were not overzealous

After the New York State election of 1879. *Harper's Weekly*, November 22, 1879.

in their behalf. Wadsworth won the comptrollership by the scant majority of 5,926, and George G. Hoskins, low man on the Republican ticket, nosed in as lieutenant-governor by 290 votes.

The rule-or-ruin struggle between Tilden and Honest John extended into the metropolis, with the Tilden nominees winning handily in the three-cornered local contests. These victories were made possible by the knifing of the Republican ticket by the anti-Conklingites. They numbered about ten thousand in the metropolis, and one of their victims was Elihu Root, candidate for judge of Common Pleas, who lost by about three thousand votes. But for the defection of the anti-Conklingites, Root and the Republican nominees for sheriff, county clerk, and coroner—there were three coroners chosen— would have won.

After the election, Honest John's foes repeated the campaign charge that he had sold out to Conkling. There was a deal, but not a sale, and the deal was incidental. Money was passed, but not to Honest John, beyond his campaign expenses. Largesse went to some of his entourage, but he did not need any. All he exacted of Conkling and Cornell was a promise that if they could not prevent the New York City Republicans from uniting with the anti-Tammany Democrats in the next municipal election, they could see that he had a fair hand in naming election inspectors.

Honest John's immediate concern after the election involved Richard Flanagan, Tammany leader of the Thirteenth Assembly District, and one of the defeated candidates for coroner. The other nominees for coroner had paid the $3,500 levy on their nominations. Demands upon Flanagan to pay went unheeded, and it was rumored he had traded votes with the Tilden faction. Tammany's first post-election meeting was on December 26. Honest John was in the chair. Fixing his eyes on Flanagan, he told the district leaders that one of the candidates for coroner "had not only been unfaithful, but had not paid his assessment." Although not named, Flanagan jumped up and said he did not see why he should pay $3,500 for a nomination for coroner. Did the boss think he had given him the nomination for sheriff? Honest John had had his say, and made no response.

This incident of the night after Christmas in the closing year of our decade is novel because it is the first public admission by a party leader of the sale of nominations, a time-honored custom observed by all machines. It remained for Honest John to put on the record what a few knew and many suspected. Occasionally men of distinction, 'and party workers of merit, who are unable to pay the assessments, to use the euphemism of Honest John, find places on the tickets of dominant machines. But these are exceptions, for elections cannot be won without money.

But we must be getting on, for the people are preparing to welcome another decade. The end of ours found the nation better off materially. Hard times were giving way to prosperity. This was attributed by some to the resumption of specie payments, by others to the fact that we were again selling more abroad than we purchased, and by many to the confidence of the people in the government. This last was reflected in the little paper currency turned in for gold. And people talked of the prosperity the year had brought, as if it were permanent and had solved everything. This note was sounded by editorial writers who ignored the still unsolved problems bared in all their stark horror in 1877: the crowning achievement of the spoilsmen—their theft of the presidency; the subsequent insurrection precipitated by the attempts of railroad-merging Jay Goulds to divide their little world into a subject working class and a ruling employing class, and the endeavors of the equally class-conscious Marxists to out-Gould the Goulds by merging employees and employers in the sacrosanct state. A few realized, including the journalistic interpreters of the year's events, that neither the Resumption Act nor the favorable turn in the tide of trade solved anything of consequence. It is also fair to assume that some of these understanding ones attended watch-night services on this New Year's Eve, and prayed for deliverance from the Marxists, the Jay Goulds, the professional reformers, the spoilsmen, the demagogues, and other enemies of the Republic.

INDEX

Abbott, Henry L., Brigadier-General, command stoned by Baltimore mob, 453

Adams, Charles Francis, Alabama claims settled by, 208; Greeley nomination, opposed by, 210; loftiness of, 192; presidency, proposed for, 189; vote for at Liberal Republican Convention in, 193

Adams, John, on nepotism, 200

Aiken, Richard Francis, 178

Alabama claims, 205-6

Albany Regency, 126

Alcorn, James Lusk, Senator, 412

Allaire, Anthony J., police captain, 264

Allen, Theodore, gambler, killer, and political reformer, 505-6

Allen, William, presidential nomination aspirant, 367

American Protestant Association, 101-3

Americus Club, 50-51

Ames, Adelbert, governor of Mississippi, 397; resigns to escape impeachment trial, 414

Ames, Oakes, bribes congressional colleagues, 221-4; censured by Congress, 224; death of, 224

Anderson, Thomas C., 433-4

Andrews, Rufus F., assails Andrew D. White, 120

Anthony, Susan B., arrested and fined, 237; friends of, 236; Greeley disliked by, 232

Anti-Masonic party, 52

Arbeiterstimme (New York), 444

Arbitration boards, proposed by T. M. Arthur, 498

Armstrong, James, Conkling lieutenant, 117

Arthur, Chester A., Collector of the Port of New York, 166; Conkling's agent, 257-8; Conkling aid at Saratoga convention, 379; counsel to tax commission, 166; Murphy's advocate, 66; removed by Hayes, 515

Arthur, T. M., Brotherhood of Locomotive Engineers' head, 498

Ash, J. Dorsey, Lieutenant, of Keystone Battery, slain in Pittsburgh riot, 469

Askin, John D., Orangemen's parade leader, 102

Association of the Bar of the City of New York: see Ring judges.

Astor, John Jacob, Tweed Ring, white washed by, 83-4

Babcock, Orville C., and Baez, 181; Grant dismisses, 350; and Santo Domingo annexation scheme, 172 *et seq.*; Sumner threatened by, 177; in Whiskey Ring frauds, jury acquits, 350; Whiskey Ring, gifts from, 348

Baez, Buenaventura, usurper President of Dominican Republic, 173; graft charges against, 181; Sumner denounces, 176

(1)